Correctly Handling the Word of Truth

CORRECTLY HANDLING THE WORD OF TRUTH

Reformed Hermeneutics Today

edited by
Mees te Velde
and
Gerhard H. Visscher

WIPF & STOCK · Eugene, Oregon

CORRECTLY HANDLING THE WORD OF TRUTH
Reformed Hermeneutics Today

Copyright © 2014 Wipf and Stock Publishers. All rights reserved. Except for brief quotations in critical publications or reviews, no part of this book may be reproduced in any manner without prior written permission from the publisher. Write: Permissions. Wipf and Stock Publishers, 199 W. 8th Ave., Suite 3, Eugene, OR 97401.

Wipf and Stock
An Imprint of Wipf and Stock Publishers
199 W. 8th Ave., Suite 3
Eugene, OR 97401

www.wipfandstock.com

ISBN 13: 978-1-62564-911-9

Manufactured in the U.S.A.   10/09/2014

Scripture quotations marked (NIV) are taken from the Holy Bible, New International Version®, NIV®. Copyright © 1973, 1978, 1984, 2011 by Biblica, Inc.® Used by permission. All rights reserved worldwide.

Scripture quotations marked (ESV) are from The Holy Bible, English Standard Version® (ESV®), copyright © 2001 by Crossway, a publishing ministry of Good News Publishers. Used by permission. All rights reserved.

Scripture quotations marked (RSV) are from the Revised Standard Version of the Bible, copyright © 1946, 1952, and 1971 National Council of the Churches of Christ in the United States of America. Used by permission. All rights reserved.

Contents

Contributors | vii
Acknowledgments | ix
Abbreviations | xi
Introduction | xiii

1 The Two Books Debate: What if Scripture and Science Seem to Say Different Things? | 1
—*Jason Van Vliet*

The Two Books Debate: A Response | 17
—*Barend Kamphuis*

The Two Books Debate: A Rejoinder | 21
—*Jason Van Vliet*

2 Interpreting the Bible in and with the Church: An Evaluation of 'Post-Liberal' or 'Post-Critical' Hermeneutics | 24
—*Cornelis P. Venema*

Interpreting the Bible in and with the Church: A Response | 56
—*R. Dean Anderson*

Interpreting the Bible in and with the Church: A Rejoinder | 60
—*Cornelis P. Venema*

3 The Hermeneutics of Dogma | 62
—*Barend Kamphuis*

The Hermeneutics of Dogma: A Response | 75
—*Arjan de Visser*

The Hermeneutics of Dogma: A Rejoinder | 80
—*Barend Kamphuis*

4 Interpreting Historical Narrative: Truth Claim, Truth Value, and Historicity | 83
—*Cornelis Van Dam*

5 "For the Word of YHWH will certainly come true" (1 Kgs 13:32): Some remarks on the Reformed Hermeneutics of Biblical Historical Narrative | 116
—*Koert van Bekkum*

6 The Structure of Jeremiah: Confessional Integrity and Quality Control | 127
—*Jannes Smith*

7 1 Timothy 2:12–15: Is Paul's Injunction about Women still Valid? | 142
—*Gerhard H. Visscher*

Paul's Injunction about Women: A Response | 155
—*Rob van Houwelingen*

Paul's Injunction about Women: A Rejoinder | 168
—*Gerhard H. Visscher*

8 Christian Ethics and God's Use of the Bible | 171
—*Ad L. Th. de Bruijne*

Christian Ethics and God's Use of the Bible: A Response | 187
—*Theodore G. Van Raalte*

9 A Soteriological Perspective on Our Understanding | 195
—*Hans Burger*

A Soteriological Perspective on Our Understanding: A Response | 208
—*Alan D. Strange*

10 The Reader as Focal Point of Biblical Exegesis | 215
—*Gert Kwakkel*

11 Another Wax Nose?: Accommodation in Divine Revelation | 226
—*Theodore G. Van Raalte*

Subject Index | 253
Scripture Index | 257

Contributors

R. Dean Anderson is Minister of the Word, Free Reformed Churches of Australia, Rockingham, Western Australia.

Hans Burger is Postdoctoral Research Fellow of Systematic Theology, Theological University of the Reformed Churches in the Netherlands, Kampen, the Netherlands.

Ad L. Th. de Bruijne is Professor of Ethics and Spirituality, Theological University of the Reformed Churches in the Netherlands, Kampen, the Netherlands.

Arjan de Visser is Professor of Diaconiology, Canadian Reformed Theological Seminary, Hamilton, Ontario, Canada.

Barend Kamphuis is Professor of Systematic Theology, Theological University of the Reformed Churches in the Netherlands, Kampen, the Netherlands.

Gert Kwakkel is Professor of Old Testament, Theological University of the Reformed Churches in the Netherlands, Kampen, the Netherlands and Faculté Jean Calvin, Aix-en-Provence, France.

Jannes Smith is Professor of Old Testament, Canadian Reformed Theological Seminary, Hamilton, Ontario, Canada.

Alan D. Strange is Professor of Church History, Mid-America Reformed Seminary, Dyer, Indiana, USA.

Mees te Velde is Professor of Church History and Church Polity, Theological University of the Reformed Churches in the Netherlands, Kampen, the Netherlands.

Koert van Bekkum is Assistant Professor of Old Testament, Theological University of the Reformed Churches in the Netherlands, Kampen, the Netherlands.

Rob van Houwelingen is Professor of New Testament, Theological University of the Reformed Churches in the Netherlands, Kampen, the Netherlands.

Cornelis Van Dam is Professor Emeritus of Old Testament, Canadian Reformed Theological Seminary, Hamilton, Ontario, Canada.

Theodore G. Van Raalte is Professor of Ecclesiology, Canadian Reformed Theological Seminary, Hamilton, Ontario, Canada.

Jason Van Vliet is Professor of Dogmatics, Canadian Reformed Theological Seminary, Hamilton, Ontario, Canada.

Cornelis P. Venema is Professor of Doctrinal Studies, Mid-America Reformed Seminary, Dyer, Indiana, USA.

Gerhard H. Visscher is Professor of New Testament, Canadian Reformed Theological Seminary, Hamilton, Ontario, Canada.

Acknowledgments

This book owes its original impetus to a request from the academic faculty of the Theological University of Kampen, the Netherlands, to the academic faculty of the Canadian Reformed Theological Seminary to hold a joint conference. The latter agreed to do so and suggested that it be held on a topic as relevant as possible to the question of where our faculties and federations are at present. Hence, Reformed hermeneutics became the theme for the conference. A location was chosen, as were speakers. A wider spectrum of speakers was actually invited—also brothers from the Westminster Theological Seminaries, both in Philadelphia and in California. But perhaps because of the brevity in notice and closer proximity, it was unfortunate that only our brothers at the Mid-America Reformed Seminary were able to join us for the actual conference. We thank them and all those who presented papers, who responded to the papers, contributed to the discussion, and all those who attended the conference. It was, in every way, a success as mentioned also in the Introduction.

With respect to the publication of this book, we thank the Stichting Afbouw Kampen, the Netherlands, and the Publication Fund of the Canadian Reformed Theological Seminary. Both made funds available for editing the book. This is also the first volume to appear under the name of a new series connected to the CRTS Publication Fund, namely, *Lucerna: CRTS Publications*. Hopefully there will be many more.

While both editors were actually quite unavailable—the one for medical reasons and the other for sabbatical and travelling reasons—the real editors actually became Dr. Jason Van Vliet and Dr. Koert van Bekkum, who did much of the work in our absence. We thank them wholeheartedly for their labors and their determination to see this volume in print. We also thank those who graciously assisted them. Dr. William Helder was found willing to give a careful reading of all the papers from our Dutch colleagues to ensure the quality of the English. And Dr. Deanna Smid took a very careful look at the English of all the papers. We thank also Leanne Kuizenga, our Faculty Administrative Assistant at CRTS, for coordinating much of the work.

We also thank those at Wipf and Stock Publishers for their kind cooperation with us to see this volume come into print.

It is our wish that this volume would contribute to a better understanding of the work of our respective seminaries and the challenges of remaining Reformed today.

M. te Velde
G. H. Visscher

Abbreviations

CGK	Christelijke Gereformeerde Kerken in Nederland
EABS	European Association of Biblical Studies
ET	English Translation
GKN(v)	Gereformeerde Kerken in Nederland vrijgemaakt
HALOT	Koehler, L., W. Baumgartener, and J.J. Stamm, *The Hebrew and Aramaic Lexicon of the Old Testament*. Leiden: Brill, 1994–1999
LXX	Septuagint
MT	Masoretic Text
PKN	Protestantse Kerk in Nederland
SBL	Society of Biblical Literature

Introduction

From January 14-16, 2014 the Fourth Annual Conference of the Canadian Reformed Theological Seminary, Hamilton, Ontario, Canada, gathered in Ancaster, with speakers from three Reformed theological institutions—in Canada, the United States, and the Netherlands— and with more than one hundred and seventy participants from six continents. The theme of the conference, which also became the title of this book containing its proceedings, was "Correctly Handling the Word of Truth: Reformed Hermeneutics Today."

The first part of this theme refers to a passage from Scripture itself, that is, the encouragement of Timothy by Paul in one of his pastoral letters (2 Tim 2:11-19). What is happening in this verse (15)? The dying apostle is seeking to instruct the younger Timothy about how he ought to give leadership to the people of God, also after he, Paul, has gone on to glory. And he suggests, as he does throughout these epistles, that above everything else, Timothy needs to handle the word of truth ever so carefully. "Correctly handle" the word of truth. The verb here seems to refer to highway building, to the life of a construction engineer. It's talking about "cutting a path in a straight direction," "cutting it straight . . ." (cf. Prov 3:6, 11:5, Septuagint). The idea is that just as the Roman roads back then—many of which are still used today—are marvelous examples of careful and skillful work, so Timothy must use skill and care as he teaches, preaches, and handles the Word of God.

This is, in a sense, the task of the big word "hermeneutics." It is not a science and it is certainly not a form of engineering. There are no absolute rules, no essential computer algorithms, despite the fact that digital analysis has become part of the exegetical process. At the same time, however, it is more than an art. Most people teaching hermeneutics in theological seminaries, both at the introductory as well as the advanced level, would like to think of it as a discipline wherein we learn to read God's Word better and in a more aware fashion—aware of the gaps in our world and theirs, aware of what we ourselves bring to the text in the reading process, aware also of the weakness of our own hearts and minds. "Correctly handling the word of truth" calls for precision, accuracy, and even, for preparing your own heart. In the first century sloppiness in building a road from Rome to Jerusalem would be disastrous. So too, sloppiness today in building a road from our places to the New Jerusalem will be disastrous.

This naturally leads to the second part of the theme of the conference. What does it mean to read the Scriptures in the tradition of the Reformers in the (post)modern, globalized world of the twenty-first century? If correctly handling the word of truth implies reading the Scriptures in a more aware fashion, then it is important that we actually meet the challenges of building these roads in this century. Accordingly, this book addresses nine important issues relating to these challenges.

The first topic is *The Two Books Debate: Scripture and Science* and the relation between special and general revelation. In his contribution (Chapter 1) Dr. Jason Van Vliet argues that the key to grasping this issue is in properly understanding general revelation. Creation reveals how great and truly divine God is, but mankind receives God's invisible qualities in such a rebellious way that general revelation is "sufficient to convict men and leave them without excuse" (Belgic Confession, Article 2). Human knowledge about creation cannot be used to overrule the special revelation in Scripture, and special revelation, not general revelation, sets the pace and the parameters for understanding God's revelation. This also applies to the "how" of creation and the interpretation of the word "day" in Genesis 1.

In his response Dr. Barend Kamphuis agrees that the knowledge of nature as such is not the same as God's general revelation. General revelation is about the knowledge of God, and that is something different. It should be added, however, that also special revelation is about the knowledge of God and the work of God. That is why it is not possible to draw scientific conclusions from, for instance, Genesis 1. Only by acknowledging the limits of scientific knowledge on the one side, and by reading the Holy Scriptures as the book that teaches us about God and our salvation on the other side, can Christians accept the differences between Scripture and science without losing their faith.

Finally, Van Vliet explains in a rejoinder why he thinks that Kamphuis' response has the wrong emphasis in his approach to Genesis 1, and why he maintains that the chapter is about the "how" of creation.

The second issue is the relation between the *(Post-)Critical and Confessional Reading of the Scriptures*, which is addressed by Dr. Cornelis P.

Venema (Chapter 2). Venema offers an overview of the history of pre-critical, historical-critical, and post-critical approaches to biblical interpretation and an evaluation of the emergence in contemporary (evangelical) theology of an interest in the "theological interpretation" of Scripture from the perspective of a confessional hermeneutic. Venema's main point is not that a classic, orthodox view of the divine inspiration and authority of the Bible provides an easy solution to all the challenges of biblical interpretation. His point is that only an ecclesiastical reading of the Bible will overcome the historical distance between the ancient text and the modern reader. Liberal approaches that do not privilege the final authority of the biblical canon inevitably lead to methods of interpretation that deconstruct the biblical texts and look for their meaning behind or outside of their canonical context.

The response to this contribution by Dr. R. Dean Anderson highlights that a belief in the inspiration and authority of the Bible also encourages a real attempt to think through God revealing himself in history, even where that is not explicated in Scripture.

In a rejoinder to this response, Dr. Venema argues that this is indeed the case, although it is more important to observe that the present situation of the church is not radically different from that of the church throughout its history.

The third topic is the *Hermeneutics of Dogma*. In his contribution addressing this issue (Chapter 3) Dr. Barend Kamphuis discusses the historicity of dogma and of the confessions. In his view, dogmas always call for an interpretation against the background of their time of development. Historicity can even be called the power of dogma. The gospel could be confessed not only in the discussions with Pharisees and Sadducees, but also in later times against Gnostics and Neoplatonic philosophers. In a similar way, the confessions of the church are not timeless summaries of the Bible, but the confession of the truth of the Bible in a specific historical situation, so that they are able to oppose their times and to preach the gospel. In this way, the Christian commitment to dogmas and confessions is a clear expression of openness and catholicity, for they are of great help in listening to believers from other cultures and times and in continuing to search for images which are apt for the mystery of the gospel and for language which we can understand today.

In his response Dr. Arjan de Visser observes a change in emphasis in Kamphuis' treatment of revelation and Scripture. Twenty-five years ago, in his inaugural address, he highlighted the clear language and perspicuity of Scripture. Now he stresses the fact that revelation is pure, but not adequate. Accordingly, the emphasis is now on the metaphorical nature of dogmas. This seems to imply that the clarity of revelation is undermined. How is the perspicuity of Scripture to be defended and what are the controls in his quest for a new language?

In a rejoinder to these critical questions Kamphuis states that his understanding of the perspicuity of Scripture has indeed been enriched, in particular with regard to the openness and catholicity of this doctrine: if you believe in the clarity of Holy Scripture, you always have to listen to other people who listen to the same Word.

A fourth topic is the use of *Methods in Biblical Exegesis*. In his contribution (Chapter 4) Dr. Cornelis Van Dam offers a thorough discussion of a distinction that is often used in evangelical, Presbyterian, and Reformed circles in analyzing historical narratives, that is, the distinction between "truth claim" and "truth value." In his view, both the origin of this distinction and the outcome of its use show that it does not do justice to the nature of Scripture as God's Word which is perspicuous and sufficient. In addition, it ultimately makes certainty about the historicity of an event dependent on human reasoning. In a concluding section Van Dam proposes what he thinks to be a more biblical approach to historical narrative.

With help of the elements "text," "past," and "intended audience," and based on the principle of *sola Scriptura* the contribution of Dr. Koert van Bekkum (Chapter 5) sketches a more general outline of the Reformed hermeneutics of historical narrative. In addition, he considers how literary devices in ancient Hebrew narrative can be used to understand the literary, (redemptive-)historical, and theological meaning of a biblical narrative. He uses the story about King Jeroboam, two prophets, two donkeys, and a lion in 1 Kings 13 as an example.

The value of rhetorical criticism for Reformed exegesis is the focus of the contribution of Dr. Jannes Smith (Chapter 6). The author presents a hypothetical structure for the Book of Jeremiah. Since it is one thing to have a hypothesis, and quite another to determine whether it will hold up to critical scrutiny, a second part introduces and applies some critical methods to test the validity of the hypothesis. Finally, Smith assesses the profits and perils of the critical methods themselves and suggests what a Reformed Old Testament scholar can and cannot say. In this way the structure of the book of Jeremiah functions inductively as a test case for the interplay of confessional integrity and quality control.

A fifth important hermeneutical issue is the *Understanding of Biblical Texts Against their Social-Historical Background*, for instance with regard to the commands of the apostle Paul concerning the role of women in the church. The contribution of Dr. Gerhard H. Visscher on Paul's injunction about women in 1 Timothy 2 (Chapter 7) takes its point of departure from a 2013 Report for the Synod of the Reformed Churches (Liberated) in the Netherlands in favor of women in office in the church. Visscher notes how in the history of interpretation scholars have used contextual and background issues to explain 1 Timothy 2:11, places the arguments of the verses 13–15 in the broader context of Paul's teaching, and asks whether the regular hermeneutical principles have been followed or ignored. In this way Visscher presents his exegetical and theological objections to the outcome of the Report.

In his response one of the authors of the Report, Dr. Rob van Houwelingen, offers additional exegetical observations, further explains the hermeneutical model and stresses that the church can still learn from 1 Timothy 2. In his view, Paul's reference to the history of Adam and Eve in Paradise is only one of the arguments besides those referring to the social background of Ephesus during the first century. In his proscriptions Paul was still able to make links with a non-Christian environment. In the twenty-first century, however, a direct application of these proscriptions creates or strengthens an isolation from society that might unnecessarily hinder the proclamation of the Gospel. After all, the church of today also offers a different application of many other elements in the apostles' instructions.

In his rejoinder to this response Visscher argues that while he agrees with the general hermeneutical method of the report, he opposes an application of a biblical teaching that is in his view completely different from what a biblical author says to the people in his own historical context. In addition, when an inspired author such as Paul backs up his argument with a reference to creation, he is making a reference to what God demanded of mankind from the very beginning and what he still demands today of our culture and all cultures.

A sixth hermeneutical subject is the *Use of the Bible in Christian Ethics*. In his contribution (Chapter 8) Dr. Ad de Bruijne uses the example of the Bible and homosexual practice to show that the traditional use of the Bible is experiencing a crisis affecting many orthodox and evangelical churches in the Western world. In answer to this crisis he sketches a third way between modernist orthodox certainty and postmodern relativism. In his view, this third way should choose as its starting point the Bible's grand salvation-historical narrative. In addition, a modern epistemological foundation should be exchanged for trust that God spreads enough light through the Bible to find out what is pleasing to God and what attitude and practice best suits God's purposes and coming kingdom in the given situation. According to De Bruijne, the key question with regard to homosexuality should be: how can we deal with it in a manner that does justice to God's salvation-historical course in Christ with men and women, and with sexuality, from creation to the coming kingdom? Only in this way will Christians learn to use the practical gift of discernment and to experience that not they, but God himself uses the Bible in order to show a way forward.

In his response Dr. Theodore G. Van Raalte argues that the traditional use of the Bible has always been going through a crisis and has survived so many other trials that it most certainly can also survive the most recent postmodern challenges. Furthermore, the common practice of using the Ten Commandments and systemizing scriptural data cannot be qualified as "foundationalist." According to Van Raalte, the work of someone like the French Reformer Antoine de Chandieu (1534–1591) shows that it is precisely by conforming to the canons of reason that we can be certain that our theological definitions reflect the truth of Scripture. Christians should still be able to say, "Thus says the Lord," because he himself has pronounced distinct and clear commands on the issue.

A seventh topic is a hermeneutical question concerning the extent to which faith in Christ leads to a *Christian Understanding*. In his contribution (Chapter 9) Dr. Hans Burger reflects on the New Testament notion that in Christ, Christians find all treasures of wisdom, knowledge, and the renewal of their understanding. He starts by describing the negative influences of modern foundationalism on Dutch Neo-Calvinism and proposes to take our "participation in Christ" as a hermeneutical starting point in order to overcome these problems. In his view it is important to pay attention to the dynamics of sin and salvation and to emphasize what is given in Christ. We need to reflect on the moral, spiritual, and hermeneutical formation of individual Christians and vital Christian communities where faith, love, and hope are nourished. In this way, reading the Scriptures will lead to a new Christian understanding of God, of the world, and of ourselves and our neighbors—in the light of Scripture.

In his response Dr. Alan Strange agrees with Burger's criticism of the Western obsession with epistemology. He is more critical, however, of the "critical realism" that is underlying Burger's view. With help from the work of Cornelis Van Til and his disciples he offers an alternative "biblical epistemology" based on 1 Corinthians 2.

The eighth subject is the postmodern attention on the *Reader as a Focal Point in Biblical Exegesis*. The contribution of Dr. Gert Kwakkel (Chapter 10) evaluates in general terms the claim that texts get their meaning from readers and then relates the results of this evaluation to reading the Scriptures. In his view, there is much reason to be critical of the idea that the meaning of a text depends entirely on the individual reader. But confronting this view can help interpreters to develop a more accurate understanding of the process of interpretation. Moreover, it reminds Christians that the Bible should be read in the context of God's communication with his people and in connection with the congregation of Jesus Christ. Using some examples from the Book of Hosea, Kwakkel shows that focusing on the reader may be a helpful interpretive tool, in particular when it makes sense to go beyond what was meant or intended by the human authors of the biblical books.

The last hermeneutical topic is the question of the extent to which the Reformed notion of *Accommodation of Divine Revelation* needs further qualification, since the principle that God accommodated his message to its recipients has been contested in recent theological reflections. In his contribution (Chapter 11) Dr. Theodore G. Van Raalte shows that the notion is used by a variety of scholars. He opts for a strong defense of the traditional notion of accommodation. Without guidelines and boundaries, however, the principle can undermine scriptural authority and become destructive to the very revelation and to the very God Reformed theologians purport to explain. In his view, it is important both to realize that accommodation is not an accommodation of the truth as such, but of the means or modes of revealing this truth, and also to distinguish between ontological and soteriological forms of accommodation. Finally, Van Raalte offers an evaluation of the varying uses of the principle throughout history and offers some guidelines for the employment of accommodation in the Reformed confessional context.

The contributions about these nine concrete issues, as well as the responses and rejoinders, offer an excellent overview of the way Reformed theologians deal with contemporary hermeneutical challenges. In this discussion confessional scholars speak for themselves and have a fair and brotherly debate about Reformed hermeneutics today. The conference was not meant as a meeting between the Canadian Reformed federation and the federation of the Reformed Churches (liberated) in the Netherlands. Accordingly, the debates in this book cannot be read as a discussion between these churches or between two or three seminaries. Nevertheless, generally we see a clear difference in emphasis between the theological approach in the contributions, responses, and rejoinders from the Netherlands and those from Canada and the United States. The latter scholars primarily stress the importance of Scripture as the ultimate foundation of faith and theological reflection, accentuate obedience to God, highlight principles, and offer clear-cut theological outcomes; while the former underline spiritual formation and the limited nature of human knowledge, and underscore that Christians only worship God as God if they acknowledge the open, catholic character of Reformed principles like *sola Scriptura* and the perspicuity of Scripture. Obviously all of us as Reformed scholars agree on the importance of all of these aspects, but the differing views might just be due to a trend to rank some of these aspects higher than others. This difference in emphasis appears in the reflections on the notions of metaphor and accommodation in divine revelation (Chapter 2–3; Chapter 11); in the approach of questions regarding the historicity of Old Testament narratives (Chapter 4 and 5); in the views of the use of the Bible in Christian ethics (Chapter 8); and in the underlying philosophical positions in rethinking the Christian understanding of reality (Chapter 10).

These differences even lead to diverse concrete results in the reflections on general and special revelation (Chapter 1) and on Paul's injunctions about women (Chapter 7). During the conference, the Dutch theologians wondered why it is necessary to declare that the understanding of the word "day" in Genesis 1 as ordinary day is more biblical than other views of Genesis 1. This might be justified from an exegetical perspective, but, in their view, this does not say very much about the nature of creation. Moreover, an exegetical error is not the same as a confessional error.

The North American theologians, in turn, were surprised to observe that their Dutch colleagues did not agree with one another on the issue of women in office, but also stated that these differences in opinion did not affect the confessional character of their theology. From the North American point of view it was clear from the outset that it is not a valid option to suggest that in a Reformed church it is just as acceptable for women to be in office as not to be in office, and so to give equal plausibility to both positions.

During the conference, several terms were used to characterize the differences in emphasis and position: a common-sense view versus a continental approach to theological problems; a scholastic versus a monastic tradition in theology; a modern, foundationalist Reformed theology versus a postmodern version of it; Reformed versus non-Reformed theology, or an approach narrowing Reformed tradition versus an open Reformed theology.

For us, as Principal and Rector of the institutions involved and as editors of this book, this is not the place to choose one of these classifications or to judge which approach is more biblical. We are happy to testify that during the conference, the participants were open and frank with each other, enjoying Christian fellowship and also vigorous discussions at times as we called each other to account. Undoubtedly, the diverse theological positions are influenced by our cultural and philosophical contexts. But all Reformed theologians agree that the Gospel is not only colored by its environment, but also deeply counter-cultural, for God's Word is not chained.

We hope and pray that this book will contribute in a similar way to the conversation among Reformed and evangelical people all over the world. As Paul says, we seek our "approval" from God, and that ultimately it is not just before people that we don't need to be ashamed, but before God. This then is God's Word to everyone who speaks or responds in these days: "Do your best to present yourself to God as one approved, a workman who does not need to be ashamed and who correctly handles the word of truth" (2 Tim 2:15).

Dr. Gerhard H. Visscher
Principal, Canadian Reformed Theological Seminary, Hamilton, Canada

Dr. Mees te Velde
Rector, Theological University, Kampen, The Netherlands

1

The Two Books Debate

What if Scripture and Science Seem to Say Different Things?

Jason Van Vliet

Joe had a lingering, niggling problem. Let me explain.[1]

Joe grew up in a solid, Reformed home. And whether it was at home, or in church, or at school, the message concerning the beginning of this world was always the same. God miraculously created all things in six days. In fact, to this day Joe can still remember the big chart that Miss Jansen, his kindergarten teacher, put up on the wall with beautiful pictures of what God created on each day. A bright patch of light on the first day. Sun, moon, and stars on the fourth day. An elephant, a horse, and of course Adam and Eve, on the sixth day. He never forgot Miss Jansen's large, colorful creation chart.

So far, so good. Now, after high school, Joe studied engineering and eventually got a job in a robotics firm. He also loved to read up on the latest scientific developments: astronomy, geology, chemistry, biology . . . he loved them all. He was also impressed by all the new discoveries: from the stunning hi-res photography sent by the Mars Rover to the exploration of

---

1. This speech was originally given to a diverse audience at a more popular level. Thus, it is also presented here in a similar style. All Scripture quotations in this article are from the New International Version (NIV84).

microbial life at the bottom of the Mariana Trench—some ten kilometers below the surface of the ocean. It was all very fascinating stuff!

But for Joe it also caused a problem. The same scientists who were making all these great discoveries also said that the universe is about thirteen billion years old, and that life forms developed, by a process of evolution, over millions of years. What's more, these scientists held that death was commonplace in the world long before human beings ever walked the face of the earth. And all of these discoveries did not seem to fit with what the Bible says. It was all so very different compared to what Miss Jansen taught him with that big, colorful chart in kindergarten.

One day Joe finally shared his problem with a Christian brother at church, Bob. Like Joe, Bob was into scientific things. Much to his relief, Joe learned that Bob had also experienced the same tension. However, Bob said to Joe, "You just have to work through it using the two books doctrine." "What's that?" asked Joe. "Well, basically, it's like this," Bob explained. "What God wants us to know about salvation he teaches us in the Bible, and what God wants us to know about creation he teaches us through science. The Bible is one book, creation is another book. They don't contradict each other. They're just teaching us about different topics. It's even in one of our confessions, right at the beginning of the Belgic Confession somewhere." Joe thought that Bob made an interesting point about the two books. But was Bob correct? That's another—and a very important—question.

* * * *

It's not uncommon for people to refer to the two books of God.[2] The first one is the book of "God's word in Scripture," and the second one is the book of "God's works in creation."[3] These two books are also sometimes called *special revelation* and *general revelation*, respectively. Moreover, it is often said that the first book, Holy Scripture, teaches us about salvation, while the second book, creation, teaches us about science.[4] So, at first glance, it would seem that as long as we go to the Bible for answers about salvation and to creation for answers about science, all should be well. For instance, this is precisely what Roland Frye has argued:

---

2. For a brief, recent, and popular discussion of the two books doctrine see Lisle, "The Two-Book Fallacy," 23. This article was followed by letters to the editors as well as an editorial response in *Reformed Perspective* 32.9/10 (Jul/Aug 2013) 8–9.

3. Frye, "The Two Books of God," 260.

4. Ibid.

> Science and faith will conflict irreconcilably *only if* we insist upon confusing and conflating the two books of God. And if we do that, the result will be either bad for science or bad for religion, or bad for both. Our purpose should be to avoid such confused readings, and to concentrate upon getting the most we can out of each of these books.[5]

In theory that might sound reasonable. Yet, as Joe discovered, in practice it's just not that easy. For example, the first book, the Bible, does speak about *how* God created the heavens and the earth. It may not contain every detail that our curious minds would like to know about how he did it. Yet certainly God does speak about it in his Word. He even says how long it took him to do it. Genesis 1 speaks of six days.[6] However, after carefully and thoroughly studying creation, a rather substantial number of scientists have come to different conclusions. They have concluded that the development of life forms on earth took millions of years and involved some sort of evolutionary process.

So it looks like we've reached an impasse. God's Word in Scripture seems to say one thing, and God's work in creation seems to say another. The two books appear to contradict each other. And yet we firmly believe that God does not speak out of two sides of his mouth: "God is not man, that he should lie" (Num 23:19). In fact, he *is* the truth (Isa 65:16; John 14:6). So, from the very start we can establish that God does *not* deceive us!

Yet what do we do with Joe's lingering problem? The answer to that question has everything to do with hermeneutics, which is the study of how we correctly interpret the Word of God. To be more specific, should the book of creation cause us to interpret the book of Scripture differently? In other words, should general revelation guide us as we interpret special revelation? Or is it the other way around? Should special revelation teach us how to use general revelation?

In answer to these questions, here is the main point that I'll aim to put forward in this article: If we elevate the role of general revelation beyond what God intended it to accomplish, then we may very well begin to feel tension between what Scripture says and what science says. However, precisely because general revelation is *God's* revelation we must keep it within its God-ordained boundaries. And if we do that properly, then we are well on our way to reducing the tension.

---

5. Ibid., 266; emphasis mine.
6. Scholars interpret the six days in different ways; however, this topic will be dealt with in more detail later on in this article.

Let's explore this matter in three steps. First, we'll analyze a proposal written by David Diehl about how to understand the relationship between the two books. Second, we'll go to the Belgic Confession and see what it actually says about these two books. Third, we'll apply this concretely to hermeneutics. And along the way, we'll always endeavor to give the final authority to Holy Scripture, the Word of God.

David Diehl's proposal

David Diehl is concerned that North American Christians do not have a very solid understanding of general revelation, the book of creation.[7] Although interestingly, in a footnote he remarks that Calvinists with Dutch heritage are an exception.[8] However, before any Calvinists, even those of Dutch extraction, start resting on their laurels, Diehl has a challenge for them. He wants their doctrine of general revelation to be even more robust than it presently is. First, though, he sums up the status quo. According to Diehl people who take the Bible seriously can all agree on the following:

1. General revelation is an ongoing revelation of God through his works of creation and providence.
2. General revelation gives a knowledge of God's general character and will.
3. This knowledge of God from general revelation has been darkened and distorted by sin.
4. In spite of sin, general revelation itself is clear, and therefore God is not unjust when he punishes people who reject or suppress his revelation.
5. Scripture and the grace of the Holy Spirit are needed to enable us to understand the message of general revelation properly.[9]

So far, so good. Indeed, most, if not all, Reformed theologians could agree on these five points. After all, it sounds very much like what God himself says in passages such as Romans 1:18–23 and 1 Corinthians 1:6–16. However, next comes Diehl's challenge. He wants to put four items on the agenda for enhancing the doctrine of general revelation. After summarizing his agenda, we'll evaluate it.

---

7. Diehl, "Evangelicalism and General Revelation," 441. The rest of the references to Diehl are all from the same article.

8. Ibid., 443, see note 7.

9. This is a summary, and to some degree a simplification, of Diehl, 443–45.

First, Diehl wants us to be more serious about the *objective authority of general revelation*.[10] For him, it comes down to the following: When the first book, the book of God's Word, says something, we are very prompt to say, "That's it. Thus says the Lord. End of the argument." Scripture has divine authority, and when God speaks, then we do not argue back and say, "Yes, but . . ." Instead we submit. This is fine, but then Diehl wonders why we don't ascribe the same kind of authority to general revelation, which is also divine revelation. For him, if God reveals, through the book of creation, that the universe is millions, or even billions, of years old, then why don't we simply submit and say, "That's it. Thus the Lord has revealed, so thus we must believe"? The same God wrote both books, so they should have equal authority. According to Diehl, then, we are failing to work out the full implications of the fact that we have a "twofold authority for theology,"[11] both special and general revelation.

Second, Diehl counsels us to take what he calls the *creational specificity* of general revelation more seriously.[12] As explained above, everyone can agree that the magnificent creation speaks volumes about its Maker, the Lord our God. Look at a newborn baby. After considering all the intricate biological systems that are packed inside such a beautiful, little bundle, who can deny that there is a God, and that he is a master Designer, far surpassing all human engineers and inventors? However, now Diehl adds that general revelation not only teaches us about God and his attributes, but it also reveals something about creation, including its "specific nature and laws."[13] Consequently, he asserts, "any knowledge of creation is a knowledge of general revelation to the extent that it is indeed true knowledge."[14] To make this concrete, according to Diehl if a scientist discovers that the nearest star, Proximi Centauri, is 4.2 light years away from the earth, then assuming his calculation is correct, that fact is not only a scientific discovery, it is also a divine revelation, which has divine authority. He even goes so far as to call this authority "infallible."[15] He bases his position on Psalm 19:1 where the Holy Spirit says, "The heavens declare the glory of God; the skies proclaim the work of his hands." For him the first part of that verse speaks about the traditional understanding of general revelation, namely, that it teaches us

---

10. Summary of ibid., 445–48.
11. Ibid., 446.
12. Summary of ibid., 448–50.
13. Ibid., 449.
14. Ibid., 449.
15. Ibid., 448.

something about who God is. However, he maintains that the second part of the verse expands general revelation to include creation and how it works.[16]

Third, Diehl promotes the *epistemological priority of general revelation*.[17] For him general revelation includes the "laws of logic" and the "natural setting of God's ... world."[18] So, following Diehl's argument, if you want to understand how the apostle Paul is debating with the Judaizers in Galatians you need to understand the basic rules of logic and argumentation. In other words, you need general revelation in order to understand special revelation. Similarly, if you want to understand Psalm 23, you need to know something about sheep, and you gain that knowledge by studying the book of creation. Once again, general revelation is needed in order to properly interpret special revelation. And for Diehl it would be "unfair to general revelation"[19] if theologians, on the basis of special revelation, would reject well-substantiated scientific views such as "the Copernican view of the solar system, the great antiquity of man according to modern anthropology, and the big-bang view of the age of the universe."[20] For him that would contradict the epistemological priority of general revelation.

Fourth and finally, Diehl urges us to take the *christological progressiveness* of general revelation more seriously.[21] We all recognize that there is progress toward Christ within special revelation. Did not Christ himself say to the Emmaus walkers that all Scripture was fulfilled in him (Luke 24:27)? Well, if there is progress in the first book, Scripture, then we should also be able to affirm that there is progress in the second book, general revelation. Consequently, if general revelation becomes clearer and fuller as time goes on, and more scientific discoveries are made, then we should also use that progress in general revelation to understand special revelation better.

That, in sum, is what Diehl puts forward in order to enhance the doctrine of general revelation. Let's now proceed to evaluate his position.[22] In many ways, the crux of the matter revolves around this question: precisely *what* is God revealing to us in general revelation? On the basis of Romans

---

16. Ibid., 448. Diehl does not provide a detailed exegesis of Psalm 19:1. He simply brings it in as a scriptural justification and immediately moves forward with the rest of his argumentation.

17. Summary of ibid., 450–53.

18. Ibid., 450.

19. Ibid., 453.

20. Ibid., 453.

21. Summary of ibid., 453–55.

22. This evaluation was formed independently. However, later I became aware of a review article which confirms the same basic points of criticism. See Byl, Review of "General Revelation and Evangelicalism," 1–13.

1:20 we can all agree that God is revealing that he exists, and that he is powerful and wise. But, as Diehl argues on the basis of Psalm 19:1, is God also revealing how and when this world first came into existence? Furthermore, are the laws of logic and our observations about sheep or stars included in general revelation? In short, the answer is no. Psalm 19:1 is Hebrew poetry. In fact, this particular verse is a Hebrew chiasm; that is to say, it has a beautiful criss-cross structure to it. Following this pattern it is apparent that "the glory of God" and "the work of his hands" are parallel. In other words, the one matches up with, and further explains, the other. Stated more plainly, the Holy Spirit is not speaking about one thing, God's attributes, in the first half of the verse, and then another thing, God's creation, in the second half of the verse. As Dr. J. Ridderbos, an OT scholar, writes, "Lines *a* and *b* are substantially synonymous."[23]

So what is the book of creation teaching us? Job 12:7–9 (emphasis mine) sends us in the right direction:

> But ask the animals, and they will teach you,
> or the birds of the air, and they will tell you;
> or speak to the earth, and it will teach you,
> or let the fish of the sea inform you.
> Which of all these does not know
> that *the hand of the Lord* has done this?

The point is that the book of creation is teaching us something about its Creator. It's revealing *him*. Now it's true that creation has laws (e.g., gravity, and the speed of light) and logic has its laws as well (e.g., the law of non-contradiction, and the law of the excluded middle). However, as you study those laws, or other aspects of creation, God is not revealing to you—authoritatively and infallibly, to use Diehl's terms—how and when the universe first began. Instead, he is revealing to you how great and truly divine he is. To be sure, anyone may study creation or the laws of logic to discover how it all ticks. And they may come to solid, well-substantiated conclusions. However, and this is the key point, the Word of God does not allow us to elevate those findings to the same level as the Word of God. In this regard, while we may not agree with everything that G. C. Berkouwer wrote, he was certainly on the mark when he said:

---

23. Ridderbos, *Commentaar*, 164; translation mine. A quick scan of commentaries on the Psalms in the early church confirms that the same exegesis was prevalent at that time. See Blasing and Hardin, *Psalms 1–50*, 146–49. For example, Theodoret of Cyrus writes, ". . . At the sight of a painting the painter comes to mind. Much more, to be sure, does the sight of creation lead the viewers to the Creator" (147). Also see Calvin, *The Book of the Psalms*: "The repetition which he [David] makes in the second clause is merely an explanation of the first" (309).

It will not do simply to equate the knowledge of nature with the knowledge of God's general revelation, for this revelation deals with the knowledge of God himself. In our opinion, therefore, it is wrong to say, as is sometimes done, that natural sciences "investigate" God's general revelation.[24]

So, scripturally speaking, we cannot agree with Diehl's expansion of the content of general revelation in his second point about creational specificity. Once that is established, our evaluation of his other three points falls into place rather quickly. Concerning his first point, about the authority of general revelation, it is true that general revelation, as *divine* revelation, also has full, divine authority. But then we need to add: concerning what? When God reveals, through his creation, that he is the Maker of everything, he does so with authority. When God reveals, through his creation, that he is powerful and wise and consistent, he does so with full authority. However, we may not stretch that same divine authority onto "well-substantiated scientific views," as Diehl calls them.[25] Even if they are well-substantiated, they are not part of God's authoritative general revelation. This distinction is crucial: God's works of creation are the *instrument* through which God reveals *himself* to us; they are not the *end goal* of what God is revealing.[26] And since general revelation is God's own revelation, it is he—and not we—who decides how he wants to use it, and how he wants it to be used.

Likewise, for Diehl's third point, it is true that we need the basic laws of logic and some observations about creation to understand the Word of God properly. However, if the laws of logic and observations about creation are not part of the final content which God is revealing to us in general revelation, then we ought not to speak about the "epistemological priority" of general revelation. Rather we should simply say that God created us

---

24. Berkouwer, *General Revelation*, 288–89. Also see Diehl, who is well aware of Berkouwer's position and rejects it saying, "if my point about the creational specificity of general revelation is valid, then any knowledge of creation is knowledge of general revelation to the extent that it is indeed true knowledge" (449). However, as seen above, Diehl's exegesis of Psalm 19:1 is shaky at best; therefore, his criticism of Berkouwer is also suspect.

25. Diehl, 452.

26. In Romans 1:20 τοῖς ποιήμασιν is a dative of instrument or means. See, for example, Schreiner, *Romans*, 86: "People perceive his eternal 'power and deity' (δύναμις καὶ θειότης, v. 20) *through* observing the created world" (emphasis mine). The content of general revelation is "knowledge of God's existence and of some of his attributes such as goodness and justice," see Bavinck, *Reformed Dogmatics*, 1:313. Also see Gootjes, "What Does God Reveal in the Grand Canyon?" 21: "Scripture limits *the content* of general revelation to knowledge about God and in one instance, knowledge of God's will (Rom 2:14–15). It nowhere indicates that (scientific) discoveries should be considered revelations."

with logical and linguistic abilities which we need to use, properly, as we interpret his Word.

And finally, Diehl is correct, of course, that science progresses and every day it is making many new, wonderful, and very useful discoveries. Through all these discoveries (and again, the key concept here is *instrument*) it becomes all the clearer just how powerful, how wise, and how consistent God the Creator is. At the same time, we must never lose sight of the truth that whatever God says in his Word is always fuller and clearer than whatever he reveals in his works. In this sense, the book of his Word is vastly superior to the book of his works, if we may even call the latter a book. However, this takes us to the second stage of our investigation.

What does Article 2 of the Belgic Confession really say?

This well-known article of our confession begins with the following words:

> We know him [that is, God] by two means: First, by the creation, preservation, and government of the universe; which is before our eyes as a most beautiful book, wherein all creatures, great and small, are as so many letters leading us to perceive clearly God's invisible qualities—his eternal power and divine nature, as the apostle Paul says in Rom 1:20. All these are sufficient to convict men and leave them without excuse. Second, he makes himself more clearly and fully known to us by his holy and divine Word as far as is necessary in this life, to his glory and our salvation.[27]

Let's begin with a number of preliminary observations:

1. Obviously, "the creation, preservation, and government of the universe" is not literally a book, and just as obviously, Holy Scripture is literally a book. Whether you look at them with the naked eye, or with telescopes, or with microscopes, created things such as stars, stones, and cells have no letters or words written on them. They have neither pages nor bindings. Scripture is different. It is a book. It has words and sentences, pages and a binding.

2. For this reason, the Belgic Confession is eager to point out, even twice, that when it speaks of creation as "a most beautiful book," it is using a metaphor, or to be more precise, a simile. Please note: the universe before our eyes is not a book, but it is "*as* a beautiful book." The word

---

27. All quotations of the Belgic Confession are from the *Book of Praise: Anglo Genevan Psalter*.

"as" indicates a simile. Likewise, all the creatures, great and small, are "*as* so many letters leading us to perceive clearly." Again, "as" indicates simile. Actually, the original French puts it nicely when it says, "all creatures, small and great, *serving as* letters . . . [or] *used as* letters."[28]

3. The Belgic Confession clearly teaches a superiority of special revelation over and above general revelation. The universe is compared to "a most beautiful book"[29] with letters leading people "to perceive clearly." Surely, this is not some kind of low-grade, inferior divine communication. Yet, if you compare what God reveals through his universe to what he reveals in his Word, the Word comes out on top—hands down. Not only is it "clearer," but it is also "fuller." Perhaps we could say it this way: in Scripture the resolution is so much higher and the picture is so much bigger and broader.

So, even if we continue to speak of two books, let's have it straight in our minds from the start: these are not two equal books. They are not, so to speak, a two-volume set, standing side-by-side on the shelf of God's revelatory activity. They are two *different and distinct* means: one is *compared* to a book, one *is* a book; one is strikingly beautiful, the other is even clearer and fuller than the first; the one reveals to us God's invisible qualities, the other reveals everything we need to know about God for this life, unto his glory and our salvation.

Let's probe this a bit further. If you look more broadly at Reformed confessions, it is not a given that general revelation is described by comparing it to a book. For example, the Belgic Confession is based, in large part, upon an earlier confession, the French or Gallican Confession of 1559. Article 2 of the Gallican Confession is almost identical to Article 2 of the Belgic Confession in the way that it is worded.[30] One difference is noteworthy: the word "book" is not used at all in connection with creation, and there is no mention of the creatures, great and small, being compared to letters or words. Likewise, the Westminster Confession of Faith, another major Reformed confession, speaks about general revelation in the very first

---

28. All references to the original text of the Belgic Confession are taken from Bakhuizen van den Brink, *De Nederlandse Belijdenisgeschriften*. In the original French, the first simile uses the common conjunction *comme*: "devant nos yeux *comme* un beau livre." However, the second reads as follows: "toutes creatures petites et grandes *servent de* lettres, pour nous faire contempler les choses invisible de Dieu." The expression *servir de* is an idiom meaning "to serve as, be used as." See Mansion, "servir de," entry d.

29. The Latin of BC 2 has a superlative, *libri pulcherrimi*, while the French (*un beau livre*) and Dutch (*een schoon boec*) do not.

30. Also for the text of the Gallican Confession see Bakhuizen van den Brink, *De Nederlandse Belijdenisgeschriften*, 72.

sentence of the first article of the first chapter,[31] but there is no mention of this revelation being some kind of book. So, indeed, it is legitimate to compare general revelation to a book. Obviously, the Belgic Confession makes that comparison. However, this book simile is not the be-all-and-end-all of the doctrine. We ought to keep things in perspective. Other solid Reformed believers have confessed general revelation in a way that is faithful to Scripture without making use of the two books analogy in any way, shape, or form. As long as proper distinctions are made, speaking of *two* books is a legitimate option, but it's not a dire necessity.

Furthermore, when we follow through with the book analogy of Article 2 in the Belgic Confession, we should also follow it all the way through. Yes, creation is like a most beautiful book, with spectacularly sculpted letters, yet the *reception* of God's general revelation is dismal and downright rebellious, unless the Holy Spirit intervenes. The Belgic Confession does not say that general revelation takes people 30 percent of the way to knowing God properly at which point special revelation takes over for the remaining 70 percent. That would be similar to the nature-grace paradigm of the Roman Catholic Church. Rather, our confession says that all this strikingly beautiful revelation of God's invisible qualities is received in such a rebellious way, that it is "sufficient to convict men and leave them without excuse." John Calvin helps us understand this sad and miserable truth when he writes in his *Institutes*:

> Just as old or bleary-eyed men and those with weak vision, if you thrust before them a most beautiful volume, even if they recognize it to be some sort of writing, yet can scarcely construe two words, but with the aid of spectacles will begin to read distinctly; so Scripture, gathering up the otherwise confused knowledge of God in our minds, having dispersed our dullness, clearly shows us the true God.[32]

Evidently, there is a lot of similarity between what Calvin writes here and what Guido de Brès writes in the Belgic Confession. It may even be that de Brès took his cue from what he read in Calvin's *Institutes*.[33] Be that as it may, the key point is this: the undeniable beauty of the creation book

---

31. Pelikan and Hotchkiss, *Creeds and Confessions*, 2:604.

32. Calvin, *Institutes*, 1.6.1.

33. The French translation of the 1559 *Institutes* 1.6.1 includes in its analogy both a beautiful book and well-formed letters (*un beau livre et de caractères bien formés*), while the original Latin text only refers to a beautiful book (*pulcherrimum volume*). Therefore, it may be that Guido de Brès, reading the French translation, took over Calvin's double-simile of both a book and letters in his Belgic Confession.

should not lead us to conclude that it is pregnant with all kinds of revelatory potential through which God gives us precise knowledge on all kinds of interesting topics such as the age of the earth or the mechanics of how the original creation process worked. That's not what *God* designed general revelation to do. That's not what he says about general revelation in the context of Psalm 19, or Job 12, or Romans 1. And that's not the context in which the Belgic Confession places it either.

The Two Books and Responsible Hermeneutics

Once God's general revelation is defined and applied along the lines that he has revealed in Scripture, then it also becomes clear how the two books function in hermeneutics, the proper interpretation of God's holy Word.

To begin with, special revelation, not general revelation, sets the pace and the parameters for understanding God's revelation. One of the fundamental rules of responsible exegesis is that clearer passages are used to help interpret less clear passages. You don't start on the doctrine of baptism with a difficult passage like 1 Peter 3:21–22. Rather you start with Matthew 3:5–6, and Matthew 28:18–20, and Romans 6:1–4, and then you work your way toward 1 Peter 3. Similarly, since Scripture is both clearer and fuller than general revelation, you start with God's holy Book, the Scriptures, and from there you work your way out into the universe, which is like a most beautiful, but comparatively less clear, book.

Now it can certainly happen that, after carefully studying creation, people discover something that appears to call for a revised understanding of Scripture. However, when that discovery begins to push the interpretation of Scripture, more and more, in an unnatural, exegetically unsustainable direction, then it's time to pause and review that basic rule of responsible hermeneutics: God's special revelation, not human discoveries within creation, sets the pace and the parameters.

Let's be concrete. After extensive and careful research, there are many scientists who have come to the conclusion that life forms evolved over a very long period of time, indeed, millions of years. Convinced by this research, some Christians have felt the need to re-interpret the word "day" in Genesis 1. For them "day" either becomes a long era, or a poetic device, or an analogy.[34] However, whatever particular interpretation they follow, "day" is no longer a day in the normal, literal sense of the word.

---

34. For a list of the spectrum of interpretations of Genesis 1 and particularly the word "day" see Poythress, *Redeeming Science*, 81–85. Poythress himself adopts the "analogical day theory."

However, when your hermeneutics take you in that direction, then you also start to rub up against other passages in the Bible. Let me give you three examples. The first, and most well-known, of course, is the fourth commandment. In Exodus 20:9 the Holy Spirit speaks about six days of labor, and by that we all understand six normal, literal, historical days. Just two verses later, in Exodus 20:11 the Holy Spirit speaks about the six days in which the Lord made "the heavens and the earth, the sea, and all that is in them." There is no indication that the Holy Spirit is changing the way in which he uses the word "day" from verse 9 to verse 11. So, changing the "days" of Genesis 1 into non-literal days rubs up against the fourth commandment.

Still, there is a second and more immediate exegetical problem. In Genesis 1 the word "day" is used repeatedly in that familiar phrase, "and there was evening and there was morning, the [first, second, third, etc] day." Interestingly, though, it is also used in Genesis 1:14 about the God-ordained function of the sun, moon, and stars. The Holy Spirit says, "let them serve as signs to marks seasons and *days* and years." Now we all understand that the changing phases of the moon and the shifting constellations of the stars have helped people, for centuries, to mark off months, seasons, and years—normal, literal, historical months, seasons, and years. So, when the word "days" is used, right between literal "seasons" on the one side and literal "years" on the other side, it breaks the normal rules of exegesis to interpret the word "days" in the middle of Genesis 1:14 as a non-literal day. Furthermore, there is no indication that the Holy Spirit is using the word "day" in a different way in verse 19 ("the fourth day") than he did five verses earlier in verse 14 ("seasons and days and years"), or for matter, verses 16 and 18, too. So, interpreting "day" in Genesis 1 in a non-literal way rubs up against what the Holy Spirit says right within that same chapter.

Thirdly and finally, throughout the Old Testament, when the word "day" is used with ordinal numbers, such as first, second, or third, it consistently refers to a normal, literal day. This happens over one hundred times in the OT, and the meaning is always the same: a normal, literal day.[35] So, when we interpret the word of God, using the normal rules of exegesis, the conclusion is really quite clear: Genesis 1 is speaking about normal, literal, historical days. Even theologically liberal, yet highly trained, Hebrew scholars are willing to admit this.[36]

---

35. Van Dam, "What did the days of 'creation week' consist of?" 94.

36. It is striking that the two most modern, and widely-used, Hebrew dictionaries list the meaning of יוֹם in Genesis 1:5 as a normal, 24-hour day (see *HALOT*, 399 and the *Dictionary of Classical Hebrew*, 4:166). James Barr, who is certainly *not* an advocate of the six-day creation view, nevertheless admits that this is what the Hebrew text literally

So, since a non-literal interpretation of "day" in Genesis 1 rubs up against the fourth commandment, and Genesis 1:14–18, and the use of "day" with ordinal numbers throughout the OT, responsible hermeneutics require us to take another look at the scientific data and ask, "Is there another defensible way in which we can understand what we have discovered?" And thankfully, there is. There are many Christians who adhere to the plain meaning of "days" in Genesis 1 while at the same time doing very careful, thorough, and productive scientific work.[37]

Now, all of this does not mean that there will not be hard questions to answer. Responsible hermeneutics involves really hard work sometimes. When it comes to what God reveals concerning the creation of his world, there are challenging things to deal with, just like there are for every other doctrine—from atonement to eschatology. For example, how do you fit together all the details of God's revelation in Genesis 1 and Genesis 2? That is a challenge! However, following the solid principles of Reformed hermeneutics we can make good headway. And when we get bogged down, we continue with that sage advice: *ora et labora*. Pray and work. We patiently seek further insight.

Conclusion

So, what about Joe? Can we help him with his lingering, niggling problem? And what about Bob? Was he right? Well, to begin with Bob, he was correct, but only partially so. The Belgic Confession does speak, in a certain way, about two books. However, our confession certainly does not put the book of God's Word and the book of God's works side-by-side on the shelf as two equal volumes in one revelatory set. What God reveals through his creation is less clear than what he reveals in his Scripture. Responsible hermeneutics demands that we use the clearer to interpret the less clear.

Furthermore, God ordained an important, but limited, role to general revelation. It reveals the great glory of the powerful and wise Creator. And it does that spectacularly well! But we have no indication from God himself that he intended to authoritatively reveal all kinds of other knowledge on other topics through general revelation. Since it is *his* revelation, he—not

---

means. He also asserts that virtually all Hebrew and OT scholars believe that the writer of Genesis intended to convey to their original readers that "creation took place in a series of six days which were the same as the days of 24 hours we now experience" (see http://creation.com/oxford-hebraist-james-barr-genesis-means-what-it-says). I wish to thank my colleague, Cornelis Van Dam, for pointing out these references to me.

37. To receive a small sample of this kind of work one might turn to Ashton, ed. *In Six Days*.

we—is the one who chooses how it will be used. To say it in another way, it's not called *general* revelation because of its content. It doesn't reveal all kinds of general knowledge to us about this, that, and the next thing. It's called general revelation because of its recipients. Through creation, God reveals his great glory to everyone on the face of the earth, not just a few.[38]

So, as long as Joe properly understands the relationship between special and general revelation, and as long as he applies that consistently in how he interprets Scripture, he can go ahead and explore all kinds of fascinating details in creation. Maybe he'll even invent a new kind of robot that is greatly beneficial to society. Yet in all he does, and all he explores, God's holy Word always has the final say. Added to that, "thus says the Lord" not only rings with sovereign authority, but it also provides rest to troubled souls. And that, after all, is what Joe was looking for.

Bibliography

Ashton, John, ed. *In Six Days. Why Fifty Scientists Chose to Believe in Creation*. Green Forest, AR: Master, 2001.

Bakhuizen van den Brink, J. N. *De Nederlandse Belijdenisgeschriften*. Amsterdam: Ton Bolland, 1976.

Barr, James. "On the meaning of Genesis." No pages. Online: http://creation.com/oxford-hebraist-james-barr-genesis-means-what-it-says.

Bavinck, H. *Reformed Dogmatics*. Edited by John Bolt. Translated by John Vriend. Grand Rapids, MI: BakerAcademic, 2003.

Berkhof, L. *Introductory Volume to Systematic Theology*. Grand Rapids, MI: Eerdmans, 1932.

Berkouwer, G. C. *General Revelation*. Grand Rapids, MI: Eerdmans, 1955.

Blasing, Craig A. and Carmen S. Hardin. *Psalms 1–50*. Ancient Christian Commentary on Scripture. Edited by Thomas C. Oden. Downers Grove, IL: InterVarsity Press, 2008.

Book of Praise: Anglo-Genevan Psalter. Winnipeg, MB. Premier Printing, 2010.

Byl, John. "General Revelation and Evangelicalism." *Mid-America Journal of Theology* 5.1 (1989) 1–13.

Calvin, John. *The Book of the Psalms*. Translated by James Anderson. Reprint. Grand Rapids, MI: Baker, 1984.

Diehl, David. "Evangelicalism and General Revelation: An Unfinished Agenda." *Journal of the Evangelical Theological Society* 30.4 (1987) 441–55.

Frye, Roland Mushat. "The Two Books of God." *Theology Today* 39.3 (1982) 260–66.

Gootjes, N. H. "What Does God Reveal in the Grand Canyon?" in *Teaching and Preaching the Word: Studies in Dogmatics and Homiletics*. Edited by Cornelis Van Dam. Winnipeg, AB: Premier Publishing, 2010.

Lisle, Jason. "The Two-Book Fallacy." *Reformed Perspective* 32.7 (May 2013) 23.

---

38. Berkhof, *Introductory Volume to Systematic Theology*, 128.

Mansion, J. E., ed. "Servir de." *Harrap's Standard French and English Dictionary.* London: Harrap & Co., 1961.

Pelikan, J. and V. Hotchkiss. *Creeds and Confessions of Faith in the Christian Tradition.* New Haven: Yale, 2003.

Poythress, Vern Sheridan. *Redeeming Science: A God-centered approach.* Wheaton, IL: Crossway, 2006.

Ridderbos, J. *Commentaar op het Oude Testament.* Kampen: Kok, 1955.

Van Dam, Cornelis. "What did the days of 'creation week' consist of?" *Clarion* 38.5 (Mar 3, 1989).

The Two Books Debate

A Response

Barend Kamphuis

Long ago, before I started to study theology, I studied physics for two years at the University of Groningen. The first lecture I heard there was about classical mechanics. And the first statement of our lecturer, Professor Smith, an American scientist, was: "You can never become a good physicist if you don't believe that everything that happens can be explained by natural causes." Well, there I sat as a Reformed boy who believed in creation, in miracles, in the resurrection of Jesus Christ: I could never become a good physicist unless I changed all my beliefs. Physics appeared to be a dangerous science, just as dangerous as maybe biology or geology. I had to make up my mind.

As you know, I did not become a good physicist. I also did not change my beliefs. But I do not think that Professor Smith was right. It is possible to become a good physicist and yet to believe that not everything can be explained by natural causes. But this professor's statement was nevertheless very helpful to me. It made me think about the relation between science and Scripture, exactly the theme of this evening.

For in a certain sense Professor Smith was right. In physics there is no room for anything other than natural causes. Physics is an experimental science, and you can only do experiments with data from our world that you can isolate and manipulate and so use to control your hypotheses. It is not only impossible; it would even be blasphemous to do experiments with God's interventions in our world. This is not only true for physics, I think, but also for other sciences—for example, experiments about the effects of prayer, in which Christians pray for one group of patients and do not pray for a control group, are unacceptable: "You shall not tempt the Lord your God" (Matt 4:7).[1] So Professor Smith was right in excluding from physics any causes other than natural ones. His mistake was that he made this exclusion absolute. Even when we can reckon only with natural causes in physics, we can believe in creation, in miracles, in the resurrection. We cannot do physical research into these events, we cannot do experiments with them, but this is just a confirmation of our faith that our God is transcendent, above this world.

This has, as far as I can see, important consequences for the field of physics and other natural or social sciences. You cannot do anything else than exclude God from your research. But then you know in advance that you will never find him—not because God or God's work is absent from this world, but because of the character of your research, the instruments you use for your scientific work. Yuri Gagarin did not meet God when he traveled in space for the first time, in a small revolution around the earth. Of course he didn't. Even if he had traveled for years in space, he would not have met God otherwise than in faith and in prayer or when God would reveal himself to him. Regardless of how far our telescopes can see, they will never see God or heaven. However far our research in history and in biology or geology may go back in time, it will never find God's action in creation and salvation. The scientific method is insufficient for this.

That is why we always have to put the results of science in perspective. Scientific results can give us many beautiful and useful insights, be it into the origin of the universe and the earth, be it into the origin of species, be it into the deepest structures of matter, be it into our expectations for the future. But they can never give us the ultimate truth in all these things. Scientific research is restricted in method, and therefore also restricted in results. It is only one way of looking at our reality. As believers we know that our reality is much greater, much deeper, than any scientist can discover.

So from another side I come to the same conclusion as my colleague Jason Van Vliet. You cannot use the results of scientific research as another book of God's revelation with the same authority as Holy Scripture. God's revelation in Scripture is clear, not hypothetical, not restricted in advance by its method. In comparison, scientific results have only a relative meaning. I also agree with Professor Van Vliet that Scripture and the Reformed confessions do not teach us something like the "two books doctrine." Indeed, the knowledge of nature as such is not the same as God's general revelation.

---

1. All Scripture quotations in this article are from the Revised Standard Version (RSV).

General revelation is about the knowledge of God, and that is something different.

But I have something to add to this. Also special revelation is about the knowledge of God and the work of God, or, as the Belgic Confession says in Article 2: "[God] makes *himself* more clearly and fully known to us by his holy and divine Word as far as is necessary for us in this life, *to his glory and our salvation*" (emphasis mine). This means that we have to read the Bible with this point of view: we want to know our God and his work, we want to learn how to glorify him and how to receive our salvation. We do not read the Bible for information about anything else as such, be it about the history of Israel or the beginnings of the Christian church, be it about biology and the origin of species, be it about astrology and the expansion of the universe, and so on. If we read the Bible with these interests, we read it wrongly; we ask questions of the Bible that it does not answer, and the answers we will find may be wrong, because the questions were wrong.

That is why I think it is not possible to draw scientific conclusions from Genesis 1. This chapter teaches us clearly that our God, the Lord, created everything and that all he created was very good. It belongs to the books of Moses, which means it was written after the fall, in a world full of sin and evil. It tells us that God the Lord is not the origin of that sin and evil. Everything he created was good, very good. In this respect Genesis 1 is a theodicy, that is, an attempt to answer the question how we can have a good and almighty God and evil in the same world. Genesis 1 is also directed in the first place to Israel, the people who were delivered by God from Egypt, the house of bondage. It tells his people that, however weak they may be, their God is the God of heaven and earth, creator of all things, for whom nothing is impossible. They can fully trust in him. In this respect Genesis 1 is a comfort for the people of the Lord. A theodicy and a comfort is what Genesis 1 has been not only for Israel but always for the people of God. So we also may read its clear message in our days and glorify God and be comforted.

But, of course, we are also interested in other questions, not only the questions of God and the origin of evil and of the power of God, but also in scientific questions about the origin of species and man, the origin of the earth and the universe. There is nothing wrong with these questions, but let us be cautious about drawing answers to them from Genesis 1. Is it really written to answer these questions? If not, we put the wrong questions to Genesis.

When I read that on the second day God made the firmament, the *raqia'*, I look to the sky and praise God: everything is in his hands. No blizzard can separate me from the love of God. But when I try to understand it as scientific information, these verses are dark to me. What physical reality corresponds to this *raqia*'? God's revelation in Genesis 1:6–8 is still clear. But maybe I put the wrong questions to it.

That is also important for the question regarding the meaning of the word "day" in Genesis 1. I agree with Professor Van Vliet that there are strong indications that we have to read this word in the sense of a normal day. Especially the relation with the fourth commandment indicates this. But there are also indications pointing to another interpretation. In any case, the lights that are signs for days and years are made only on the fourth day, but what were the signs for days before that? Also the fact that Genesis 2 tells us the creation story in another way has to make us cautious. Maybe the question about the exact length of the creation days is not a good question. For us, confronted with scientific theories about millions of years before man came on earth, it is a very important question. But is it good to ask this question of Genesis 1? The fact that from Augustine via Bavinck to your and our late Professor Harry Ohmann many orthodox theologians left room for a less literal interpretation may also be an indication that Holy Scripture does not give us a clear answer to this question.

In Reformed theology, creationism has never been a dominant conviction. As far as I can see, creationism tries to combine knowledge from Holy Scripture with scientific knowledge. The respect creationism has for Holy Scripture is very appealing. But this combination of different sorts of knowledge is dangerous. Maybe we have to say to Joe, in the example given by Professor Van Vliet, that we have no definitive solution for his lingering problem. But if he learns to see the limits of scientific knowledge on the one side, and reads the Holy Scriptures as the book that teaches us about God and our salvation on the other side, he can accept the differences between Scripture and science without losing his faith.

The Two Books Debate

A Rejoinder

Jason Van Vliet

I want to thank Br. Kamphuis for his thoughtful response to my speech. And he had to do it in English, which is a terribly complicated and horribly inconsistent language. It would have been a lot nicer for him to do it in Dutch. So I say, "*Bedankt meneer. Je bent een moediger mens dan ik.* [Thank-you, sir. You are a braver man than I.]"

I am also encouraged to hear that concerning the relationship of special and general revelation, he comes to the same conclusion that I did. Also, he agrees that concerning the word "day" in Genesis 1 there are strong indications that "we have to read this word in the sense of a normal day."

At the same time, if I sense it correctly, he wants to give some breathing room for "another interpretation" or "a less than literal interpretation." Of course, time prevents me from getting into everything he said, but let me pick three items which focus on three key words: Bavinck, theodicy, and questions.

1. *Bavinck*. Did Bavinck give more room for different interpretations of Genesis 1–2 than Van Vliet is presently doing? Well, Bavinck wrestled with the issue of how to interpret these chapters, just like we all do. There *are* some challenging questions here. Perhaps Br. Kamphuis is referring to Bavinck's conviction that the first three days of creation were, and I quote, "extraordinary cosmic days."[1] At the same time, Bavinck also said, and I quote, "to reckon with millions of years, in the

---

1. Bavinck, *Reformed Dogmatics*, 2:499.

past or in the present, is child's play and *unworthy of mature minds*, and is at best of no greater value than the gigantic numbers of Indian mythology."[2] Bavinck also said, "The theory of the animal ancestry of humans violates the image of God in man and *degrades the human into an image of the orangutan and chimpanzee*. From the standpoint of evolution, humanity as the image of God cannot be maintained."[3] So which quotable quote of Bavinck shall we pick? In the end, we are still left with the challenging, yet exciting, task of interpreting the first chapters of Genesis using a hermeneutic that is both Reformed and responsible.

2. *Theodicy.* Twice Br. Kamphuis said, "Genesis 1 is a theodicy," or "a theodicy and a comfort is Genesis 1." I say this respectfully, but also plainly: I do not think that this is the correct emphasis. Are there aspects or verses in Genesis 1 which have implications for the topic of theodicy? Yes, of course. However, you can say that about many, perhaps even most, verses in the Bible. However, it's a different thing to characterize Genesis 1 as "a theodicy" because this suggests that the main topic about which God is speaking in Genesis 1 is: "How can a good God have sovereign control over such a sin-filled world?" I respectfully submit that that is not the main topic of Genesis 1. Genesis 1, like the rest of Genesis, is *history*—special, inspired, divinely-selected and divinely-selective history, but history nonetheless. It's the revealed history of how God created the world. After all, he's the uniquely qualified One to reveal this history because he was the only One present when it happened. So, the key question God is answering in Genesis 1–2 is: "How did I, the Lord God, create everything?" not "How do I, the good God, still rule over such a sin-filled world?"

3. *Questions.* Br. Kamphuis speaks about "scientific questions about the origin of species and man, the origin of the earth and the universe" and then adds that we should be cautious about "drawing answers [to those questions] from Genesis 1." Let me mention two things: First, these are not uniquely scientific questions. They are, at root, *human* questions. Whether scientifically trained or not, whether living in the twenty-first century AD or the twenty-first century BC, people—as humans beings—are curious: where do we come from? And where does everything we see come from? I agree that we should not unnaturally force God's Word in Genesis to answer questions that God is not speaking about there. *But . . .* if the human question is: "Where

---

2. Bavinck, "Creation or Development," 849–74; emphasis mine.
3. Bavinck, *Reformed Dogmatics*, 2:520; emphasis mine.

do the different species of animals come from?" then Genesis 1 *is* the go-to place for an answer because that is what God is talking about in that chapter. It's not the only thing he reveals in that chapter, but it is certainly one of the things he reveals. If the human question is: "Where do human beings come from?" then Genesis 1–2 *is* the go-to place for an answer because that is what God is talking about in those chapters. And in those chapters God gives answers to those particular questions in a way that science is simply not able to do. As Br. Kamphuis rightly said at the beginning of his response we cannot do physical research into the event of creation; we cannot do experiments with the event of creation. That's right, because the creation event cannot be duplicated in a lab or a computer model. So, yes, it is true that we should not push God's Word to answer questions that it is not addressing. Yet, by the same token, we should not expect science to answer questions that it is not able to answer either.

Bibliography

Bavinck, H. "Creation or Development." *Methodist Review* 83 (1901): 849–74.
———. *Reformed Dogmatics*. Edited by John Bolt. Translated by John Vriend. Grand Rapids, MI: BakerAcademic, 2003.

2

Interpreting the Bible in and with the Church

An Evaluation of 'Post-Liberal' or 'Post-Critical' Hermeneutics[1]

Cornelis P. Venema

Introduction

In modern treatments of the doctrine of Scripture, two topics have dominated the attention of theologians. On the one hand, the classic Christian doctrine of the divine inspiration and authority of the canonical Scriptures has been challenged by the assumptions of modern thought since the time of the Enlightenment. From the perspective of the Enlightenment, traditional Christian convictions regarding the Scriptures are no longer tenable in the modern period. The older doctrine, which proceeded from the conviction that the Scriptures were in their entirety the inspired Word of God, and therefore the authoritative standard for Christian faith and practice, has undergone withering critical examination by the measure of human reason and the dictates of modern science. In response to the repudiation of the

---

1. My title derives in part from Henry Vander Goot's *Interpreting the Bible in Theology and the Church*. All Scripture quotations in this article are from the English Standard Version (ESV).

inspiration and authority of the Scriptures in modern thought, many orthodox and evangelical theologians have endeavored to defend the older doctrine of Scripture that prevailed in the Christian church in the pre-modern period. Throughout the modern period, many treatments of the doctrine of Scripture have focused upon the continued viability of the Christian church's convictions about the inspiration and authority of the Scriptures of the Old and New Testaments.

On the other hand, the topic of hermeneutics or the interpretation of Scripture has become a special focus in more recent discussions of Scripture. While the inspiration, authority, and veracity of the Scriptures remain important topics on the docket of contemporary theologians, in some respects they have been superseded by increasing attention to the question of biblical interpretation. Whatever the nature of Scripture's inspiration and authority, the problems attendant upon the determination of the *meaning* of the biblical texts have become a preoccupation. Moreover, in contemporary discussions of hermeneutics, the question is no longer simply how the text of Scripture is to be interpreted—the traditional interest of hermeneutics as a method for understanding biblical texts.[2] Now the question of scriptural hermeneutics has become wedded to the broader theoretical and philosophical problem of *the general way in which any text is interpreted,* whether it is a biblical or a non-biblical text.

Rather than simply describing a particular way of reading biblical texts, whether in the older, medieval understanding of the "fourfold sense" of Scripture or the Reformational understanding of grammatical-historical exegesis, a theory of general hermeneutics raises the question of the way in which historical texts of any kind are to be interpreted. Within the setting of what has become popularly known as "post-modernism," the interpretation of Scripture is regarded as a specific instance of the general problem of interpreting historical documents. Since the interpreter or the interpretive community inescapably filters the meaning of texts through the interpretive grid of their social world and experience—broadly understood to include such factors as social environment, historical situation, ethnic and cultural identity, gender, worldview assumptions, and the like—the meaning of the text is determined largely by the biases of the reader. In its most radical form, modern hermeneutics leads to a "reader-response" or radically "deconstructionist" approach in which the text has as many meanings as there are interpreters or interpretive communities. For this reason, one notable evangelical theologian, D. A. Carson, has spoken of the "hermeneutical

---

2. See, e.g., Berkhof, *Principles of Biblical Interpretation.*

morass" of the newer approach to the interpretation of Scripture.[3] Within the framework of so-called "post-modernism," it is no longer permissible to speak of *the* meaning of biblical texts, which is accessible and capable of being ascertained by its interpreter. All that remains is an irreducible plurality of *meanings* that diverse interpreters or communities of interpretation discover in their particular reading of the biblical texts.

While the focus of this essay will be upon the second of these topics, the interpretation of Scripture, I am convinced that this topic is closely related to the first. The problems posed by some contemporary approaches to hermeneutics represent, in part, the consequence of a loss of conviction regarding the uniqueness of Scripture as a divinely-inspired authority, and of its consequent usefulness for the church's instruction in the gospel of Jesus Christ (cf. 2 Tim 3:16–17). It is no accident that the church at the time of the Reformation approached the interpretation of the Scriptures with confidence in their sufficiency and clarity, rightly interpreted according to their proper sense and meaning, to confirm and regulate the church's faith and practice. Because many in the modern period have lost the conviction that the Scriptures are divinely-authored, sufficient and clear in their teaching, there has been a corresponding loss of confidence in the church's ability to ascertain their meaning. The confession of the nature of Scripture has far-reaching implications for a proper approach to the interpretation of Scripture. In this area of Christian theology, as in all others, there is an intimate interplay between theory and praxis, between the doctrine of Scripture and its consequent usefulness for the church's determination of God's will and purpose.

The subject of my essay is the recent emphasis upon the role of the church and its creedal "rule of faith" (*regula fidei*) in the interpretation of the Bible, particularly as this has been articulated in what has become known as a "post-liberal" or "post-critical" approach to biblical hermeneutics. Throughout much of the history of the Christian church, the interpretation of Scripture was not the special prerogative of the academy or the individual exegete. Rather, the interpretation of Scripture found its locus within the church as an interpretive community. The creedal and confessional consensus of the church served as a guide or hermeneutical key to the reading of Scripture. In the modern period of biblical criticism, however,

---

3. Carson, *Gagging of God*, 93–137. Cf. Thiselton, *Two Horizons*, 11: "Traditionally hermeneutics entailed the formulation of rules for the understanding of an ancient text, especially in linguistic and historical terms. . . . However, hermeneutics in the more recent sense of the term begins with the recognition that historical conditioning is two-sided: *the modern interpreter, no less than the text, stands in a given historical context and tradition;*" emphasis Thiselton's.

the interpretation of Scripture has become the province of biblical scholars and individuals who do not read the Bible in and with the church. The interpretation of Scripture has largely been untethered from the church's interpretive tradition, especially as this is codified in the ecumenical creeds and confessions. The scholarly study and exegesis of biblical texts in the modern period, especially in the tradition of historical criticism, has largely taken place without regard for the church's consensual reading of Scripture. In more recent discussions of the interpretation of Scripture, however, a number of attempts have been made to recover a more "theological" and ecclesiastically-sensitive approach to the interpretation of Scripture. As an alternative to the methodology of historical criticism and the non-creedal approach of evangelical hermeneutics, recent discussions of hermeneutics have sought to retrieve aspects of the older, pre-critical tradition of biblical interpretation, which emphasized the role of the church in the reading of biblical texts.

1. Pre-Critical Biblical Interpretation and the Church

In order to orient our reflection on the attempt to articulate a post-critical approach to hermeneutics, we need to begin with a brief review of the principal features of what today is often termed the "pre-critical" tradition of biblical interpretation. At the risk of oversimplification, the pre-critical tradition of biblical interpretation displays several common features.[4]

First, throughout the history of the church in the patristic, medieval, and Reformation periods, the interpretation of the Bible proceeded from the conviction that it should be read as a single book. In the course of settling the boundaries of the canon, the church recognized the Old and New Testaments as a unified work. Even the language of "old" and "new" testaments expressed a fundamental conviction that all of the canonical books formed a single whole, and that every part of the testimony of Scripture was ultimately related to all the other parts. The canonical form of Scripture demanded that the Bible be read in a self-referential manner and that the teaching of any part be interpreted within the context of the whole. The Scriptures were understood to be self-interpreting, and the hermeneutical rule of comparing Scripture with Scripture was a commonplace.

---

4. For helpful descriptions of pre-critical approaches to biblical interpretation, see Steinmetz, "Superiority of Pre-Critical Exegesis," 27–38; Steinmetz, "Theology and Exegesis," 27; Frei, *Eclipse of Biblical Narrative*, 17–50; Lindbeck, "Postcritical Canonical Interpretation," 28–31; and Muller and Thompson, eds., *Biblical Interpretation*, 335–45.

Second, to use the language of Hans Frei in his book, *The Eclipse of Biblical Narrative*, the pre-critical tradition of biblical interpretation read the Bible as a "realistic narrative" that recounts the story of the Triune God's work to accomplish his purposes in creation, redemption and the consummation of his kingdom at the end of the age.[5] Despite the differences between the medieval practice of distinguishing the "fourfold sense" of the biblical text and the Reformation's emphasis upon the one, "literal sense" (*sensus literalis*) of the biblical text, a basic consensus prevailed that the biblical history is recounted *in* the text and not under or *behind* the text.[6] The interpreter's task is not to look for the real history behind the story recounted in the biblical text, but to view all of history in terms of the literal sense and truth of the biblical story. Even in the medieval tradition's distinction between the four senses of Scripture, the literal sense was foundational to the others. For this reason, the first phrase of a classic couplet regarding the fourfold sense of Scripture, declared that "[t]he letter teaches what happened."[7] The other senses or meanings of the biblical text—the allegorical, the tropological, and the anagogical—were tied to the literal sense, which limited the freedom of the interpreter in the application of the text to the church.

Third, in the interpretation of the Bible, the pre-critical tradition was directed by its adherence to the "rule of faith" set forth in the ecumenical creeds. The biblical history was understood as a story that could only be read in a trinitarian manner. The God of Israel was understood to be the God and Father of Jesus Christ, and the story of Christ's coming in the fullness of time was understood to be the center and focal point of the entire biblical history. The christological and trinitarian rule of faith served the interpretation of Scripture, not only by identifying the center of the biblical story but also by emphasizing the way all of Scripture witnesses to the identity and character of the Triune God.

Fourth, in the pre-critical tradition, a variety of hermeneutical strategies were performed to exhibit the unity of the teaching of the Bible. Perhaps the most important means to exhibit the unity of the scriptural story was typological interpretation. The story of the Old Testament was shown to be fulfilled in the New Testament story of Christ by means of a broadly typological hermeneutic, which exhibited the similarities between the Old

---

5. Frei, *Eclipse of Biblical Narrative*, 17–50.

6. Steinmetz, "Superiority of Pre-Critical Exegesis," 29: "The allegorical sense taught about the Church and what it should believe, and it corresponded to the virtue of faith. The tropological sense taught about individuals and what they should do, and so it corresponded to the virtue of love. The anagogical sense pointed to the future and wakened expectation, and so it corresponded to the virtue of hope."

7. As quoted in Muller and Thompson, *Biblical Interpretation*, 340.

Testament types and their New Testament fulfillments.[8] The Old Testament history was read as a preparation for the story of Christ, as promissory of its New Testament reality and fulfillment. The meaning of the Old Testament texts could not be finally determined apart from the way in which they were interpreted in the light of the New Testament.

And fifth, the interpretation of Scripture in the pre-critical tradition was a task performed by and within the church as the primary interpretive community. The interpretation of biblical texts, accordingly, was ordinarily carried out in conversation with a long history of engagement with these same texts. Rather than the task of isolated individuals who read the text as though they were the first to uncover its meaning, the interpretation of Scripture required familiarity with the church's history of exegesis. The biblical interpreter was engaged in the task of exegesis as a member of the church, and therefore as one who recognized the direct significance of the biblical texts for the present life of the church. As a member of the church, the interpreter of the Bible did not approach the text as though there were a great historical "distance" between the contemporary church and the historical community that gave birth to the biblical text. The biblical text was received in the conviction that it spoke directly and freshly to the church as a single community throughout the course of its history.

In my summary of the pre-critical approach to the interpretation of the Bible, I have deliberately sought to identify broad areas of consensus. However, at the time of the Reformation, one significant difference emerged between the Roman Catholic Church and the Reformation on the relative authority and relation between the church's interpretive tradition and the Bible. Whereas the Roman Catholic Church ascribed a kind of priority to the church's magisterium to determine infallibly the meaning of the Bible, the Reformation countered by distinguishing carefully between the supreme authority of the Scriptures as the final and exclusive norm for the church's faith and practice and the subordinate authority of the church's interpretation of the Scriptures (*sola Scriptura*). The difference in the relative authority of the church's interpretive tradition and the Word of God in Scripture was expressed in terms of the familiar distinction between the Bible as the *norma normans* ("the norm that norms") and the church's confessional tradition as the *norma normata* ("the norm that is normed").

---

8. Lindbeck, "Postcritical Canonical Interpretation," 29–30.

2. Historical-Critical Biblical Interpretation and the Church

Although the main features of the pre-critical approach to the interpretation of the Bible have persisted throughout the history of the church to the present day, a significantly new approach emerged in the period after the Reformation within the context of the eighteenth-century Enlightenment. In the modern era, the historical-critical approach to the interpretation of the Bible became predominant in the academy. In this approach, several of the principal features of the church's tradition of interpreting the Bible were challenged in a thorough-going fashion. Whereas in the pre-critical period the Bible was read as sacred Scripture, as a divinely-authored canon that normed the church's faith and practice, it was now to be interpreted within the academy in an objective, scientific manner. The same scientific and historical standards that were used in the interpretation of texts within the humanities (*wissenschaften*) were now to be employed in the interpretation of Scriptural texts.[9]

The emergence of the modern, historical-critical approach to the interpretation of the Bible is often illustrated by reference to the programmatic lecture in 1787 of the German scholar, J. P. Gabler, "An Oration on the Proper Distinction Between Biblical and Dogmatic Theology and the Specific Objectives of Each."[10] Gabler's lecture sharply distinguished the respective tasks of biblical and dogmatic theology. Whereas biblical theology aims to discover what the biblical authors believed at the time of the writing of the biblical texts, dogmatic theology aims to articulate the universal truths of religion that hold for all times and places. Biblical theology describes what the biblical texts *meant* when they were first written; dogmatic theology seeks to discern which aspects of the Bible's teaching express the universal truths of reason. According to Gabler, "[t]here is truly a biblical theology, of historical origin, conveying what the holy writers felt about divine matters; on the other hand there is a dogmatic theology of didactic origin."[11] While Gabler's intention in drawing a sharp distinction between biblical and dogmatic theology was to open the way for a thoroughly rational and universal understanding of religion, he clearly articulated one of the most striking features of the historical-critical approach. Rather than interpreting

---

9. For helpful summaries of historical-critical approaches to the interpretation of the Bible, see Frei, *Eclipse of Biblical Narrative*, 51–65; Thiselton, *The Two Horizons*, 51–84; and Klink and Lockett, *Understanding Biblical Theology*, 29–58.

10. Gabler's lecture is printed as an appendix in Ollenburger, *Old Testament Theology*, 499–506.

11. Ollenburger, *Old Testament Theology*, 495.

the Bible as Holy Scripture, the canonical norm for the church's teaching and practice, Gabler anticipated a new approach that would treat the biblical writings in a strictly scientific and historical manner.

Though the language of a "historical-critical method" tends to oversimplify the complex history of modern approaches to the interpretation of the Bible, there are several identifiable characteristics of this dominant method in the modern period.

First, in the historical-critical approach to the interpretation of the Bible, the biblical texts are treated primarily like any other texts that function as *historical sources*. Viewed as historical sources, the biblical texts have no canonical status or presumed unity as a body of texts that were given to the church by God and therefore properly belong to the church that receives and interprets them. The study of the biblical texts as historical sources belongs to the academy and follows the same procedures that apply to any body of texts in authenticating their reliability and truthfulness.

Second, contrary to the assumptions of pre-critical interpretation, the historical-critical method does not proceed from the conviction that the canonical Scriptures are a unified whole or that they can best be understood by reading them in their canonical context. The tendency of the historical-critical approach is to treat biblical texts in isolation from each other, and to endeavor to ascertain how the text assumed its present form. The end result of this approach is to relativize the authority of the canonical text, and to substitute a historically-reconstructed text at an earlier stage in its historical formation. Before the biblical texts can be interpreted, the historical-critical approach assumes the responsibility of determining what in the text (and at what stage of its development) is authentic.

Third, because the historical-critical method of biblical interpretation focuses upon the original *Sitz im Leben* of the text, as this is historically reconstructed and authenticated by the best scholarly methodology, it aims to establish what the text *originally meant* and not what it might now *mean* for its contemporary reader.[12] The tools of historical-critical exegesis are all forged in the furnace of a pursuit after an "objective" knowledge of the meaning of the biblical texts in their original historical setting. However, because the determination of what the text meant is the sole outcome of historical-critical study, the results of such study can, in the nature of the

---

12. Cf. Allison, *The Historical Christ*, 38–39: "Determining what that text [Mark 13:26] meant in the first century is one thing; determining what it means for us today is quite another.... [A] text is never the sole determinant of its interpretation or application. Readings are rather joint productions; they require not only judgment as to what a text meant to those in the past but also judgment as to what it should or can mean in the present, and the latter involves convictions extrinsic to the texts themselves."

case, be only of academic interest. The interpretation of biblical texts becomes a strictly descriptive exercise whose findings do not have normative or probative significance for the present faith and practice of the church.

Fourth, the historical-critical method of treating the biblical texts inevitably drives a wedge between the story recounted in the biblical narratives (*geschichte*) and the actual history (*historie*) that is able to be ascertained by the methods of a scientific historiography. Since the science of history precludes the possibility of the kind of history recounted in the Bible— where the Triune God is the principal subject and history finds its center in the incarnation of the Son of God in the fullness of time—historical criticism is unable to grasp the actual content or subject matter of the biblical witness. Rather than reading the Bible as a grand and unified account of the works of the Triune God in creation and redemption, as was the case in the pre-critical period of biblical interpretation, historical-critical methods reduced the content of Scripture to the barest minimum of what could be verified by the canons of historical science (employing the criteria of analogy and probability). In its more consistent expression, historical criticism left the interpreter of Scripture with a description of what the biblical authors may have believed or taught at the time they wrote the biblical texts.

And fourth, as these characteristics of the historical-critical method suggest, the great (insuperable) challenge confronting the modern interpretation of Scripture is the problem of the "historical distance" between the ancient biblical text and the contemporary interpreter. The problem of historical distance that emerges in the historical-critical approach is well expressed by Robert Jenson:

> But at the same time, historical-critical consciousness and practice make a crisis of all interpretation, a crisis intrinsic to Western modernity and increasingly disastrous for it, and so far unresolved in the church. In modernity, scholarly reading of texts becomes labor to build bridges across the historical distance between readers and the time and place from which the texts come, to overcome a 'hermeneutical gap' between ourselves and Jesus or St. Francis or Socrates. The question had eventually to arise: Can this ever really succeed?[13]

Although Jenson goes on to argue that this problem can be mitigated by the recognition that the same community that produced the Bible, namely, the church, continues to be its primary interpreter, he properly diagnoses one of the principal features of the historical-critical approach. If the

---

13. Jenson, *The Works of God*, 278. For a discussion of the problem of historical distance in biblical hermeneutics, see Thiselton, *The Two Horizons*, 53–68.

interpretation of biblical texts primarily aims to determine what they meant in their original historical situation, such interpretation does not have the competence to determine what the ancient text must mean for the modern reader. Because the modern reader lives in a different world than the one occupied by the biblical writers, there does not seem to be any way to traverse the distance between them. The historicism that undergirds the interpretive method of historical criticism precludes any direct link between the biblical text and the modern interpreter.

3. Post-Critical Biblical Interpretation and the Church

A significant development in the recent history of theology is the attempt to retrieve some of the features of the pre-critical approach to the interpretation of Scripture. Some describe the attempt to retrieve aspects of the classic approach to biblical interpretation as the return to a more "theological interpretation" of Scripture.[14] Others describe it as a "post-critical" or "post-liberal" approach.[15] While this approach does not deny the legitimacy of some aspects of the historical-critical interpretation of the Bible, it aims to restore the interpretation of Scripture to its proper place within the church as an interpretive community. It also aims to treat the canonical form in which the Bible has been acknowledged and received by the church as the authoritative standard for its faith and practice. The story of recent attempts to retrieve aspects of the church's pre-critical interpretation of the Bible is a complicated one, which includes a number of important theologians and a bewildering diversity of hermeneutical approaches. For my purpose, it will have to suffice to consider three figures who have played an important role in articulating a theological approach to the interpretation of Scripture that honors the church's role as an interpretive community: Karl Barth, Brevard Childs, and George Lindbeck. Each of these theologians has contributed significantly to the development of a post-critical approach to biblical interpretation that aims to overcome problems in the historical-critical tradition of biblical interpretation.

---

14. Cf. Treier, *Introducing Theological Interpretation of Scripture*.

15. Cf. Phillips and Okholm, eds., *The Nature of Confession*. Since a number of influential proponents of a post-critical or post-liberal approach to biblical interpretation taught at Yale University and Yale Divinity School (e.g., Hans Frei, Brevard Childs, and George Lindbeck), this approach is sometimes associated with what is termed the "Yale School."

3.1. Karl Barth: Theological Interpretation

Perhaps the most influential and important figure in the post-liberal retrieval of a theological approach to the interpretation of the Bible is Karl Barth. Against the background of nineteenth-century liberal theology and its adherence to the historical-critical method of interpretation, Barth launched his theological work in the early twentieth century with an appeal to what he called "the strange new world within the Bible."[16] The first illustration of what Barth meant by this language was the publication in 1919 of the first edition of his commentary on the book of Romans, *Der Römerbrief*. In the preface to the first edition of his commentary, Barth conceded the legitimacy of the historical-critical approach to the interpretation of the Bible. However, he also informed his readers that "were I to choose between it [historical criticism] and the venerable doctrine of Inspiration, I should without hesitation adopt the latter, which has a broader, deeper, more important justification."[17] Barth's qualified appreciation for the classic Christian doctrine of inspiration signaled his desire to recover aspects of the older tradition of a theological interpretation of the Bible. However, Barth's recovery would be self-consciously post-critical, that is, it would not represent a simple repristination of the classic Christian doctrine of inspiration.

The starting point for Barth's doctrine of Scripture is his insistence that it is a *form of and witness to the Word of God*.[18] Whereas the classic doctrine of inspiration located the Word of God in the objective, God-breathed text of Scripture, Barth insists that God's revelation of himself always occurs through God's own action and may not be directly identified with the biblical texts themselves. Rather than directly identifying the Word of God with the revealed truth that is inherent in the inspired text, Barth identifies the Word of God with God himself as he freely, graciously, and actively employs the witness of Scripture to make himself known. For Barth, "[t]he Word of God is God himself in Scripture."[19] Since God is always the acting subject in his revelation of himself, and since only God can make himself known to us,

---

16. See Barth, *The Word of God*, 28–50.

17. Barth, *The Epistle to the Romans*, 1.

18. My sketch of Barth's doctrine of Scripture and approach to its interpretation is based upon the following: Barth, *Church Dogmatics*, vols. 1/1 and 1/2; Barth, "The Authority and Significance of the Bible"; Barth, *Evangelical Theology*, 26–36; Barth, *The Göttingen Dogmatics*, vol. 1. For studies of Barth's doctrine of Scripture, see Bromiley, "The Authority of Scripture in Karl Barth," 271–94; Bromiley, *Introduction to the Theology of Karl Barth*, 3–44; Runia, *Karl Barth's Doctrine of Holy Scripture*; Vanhoozer, "A Person of the Book?" 26–59; and McCormack, "The Being of Holy Scripture," 55–75.

19. Barth, *Church Dogmatics*, 1/2: 457.

the Scriptures are not the Word of God for us unless and until God elects to use them to witness to Jesus Christ.

The primary emphasis in Barth's doctrine of Scripture as a form of the Word of God is upon its function as a *witness* to Jesus Christ. Because the Scriptures witness to the Word of God in Jesus Christ, they point the reader away from themselves. The biblical authors serve as witnesses, not to themselves and their fallible words but to Jesus Christ, and in this way they become God's Word to us: "The participation of human words in God's Word is the principal element in the Scripture principle."[20] By virtue of God's decision to employ the human witness of the biblical authors, they participate in God's act of revelation through Jesus Christ. Thus, the relation between the biblical texts and the act of God in revealing himself through their witness is not direct, but dialectical and indirect. There is a kind of "distance" (*diastasis*) that always remains between the Bible and revelation: "The Bible is one thing and revelation another."[21] But since God elects to employ the unique witness of the Scriptures to Jesus Christ, the Bible functions as a form of the Word of God. The perfection, power, and truth of Scripture reside, not in Scripture itself as a thoroughly human witness, but in its subject or christological content. According to Barth, "[t]he presence and Lordship of Jesus Christ . . . has its visible form, in the time between His resurrection and His return, in the witness of His chosen and appointed prophets and apostles."[22]

Because Barth emphasizes the nature of the Bible as a form of the Word of God in its witness to Jesus Christ, he defines the inspiration and infallibility of the Scriptures in terms of God's action in making them serviceable to a knowledge of Jesus Christ. Unlike the traditional doctrine of inspiration, which emphasizes that the biblical texts are the Word of God in human language, Barth's doctrine of inspiration, consistent with his view of God's action in the event of revelation, emphasizes God's freedom to speak through the human author's witness. In Barth's understanding of the inspiration of Scripture, the accent falls upon God's present speaking through the biblical texts. The witness of Scripture takes place through the power of the Holy Spirit. Rather than defining inspiration as a past action with an abiding result, Barth's view tends to collapse the difference between inspiration as a past act and illumination as a present action. The present action of the Holy Spirit in and by means of the fallible testimony of the biblical texts enables the Bible to become the Word of God for the contemporary reader.

---

20. Barth, *The Göttingen Dogmatics*, 1:212.
21. Ibid., 1:216.
22. Barth, "The Authority and Significance of the Bible," 57.

According to Barth, we should not identify the Word and infallible truth of God with the fallible human words of the biblical authors. These qualities are not inherent "once for all in this book," since that would circumscribe the freedom of God to speak as and when he wills through their thoroughly human and fallible testimony.[23] To ascribe infallibility to the biblical witness, apart from the Holy Spirit's use of this witness to reveal the Word concerning Jesus Christ, would diminish the necessity of the Spirit's miraculous use of the Bible in making it become for us the living Word of God. From Barth's perspective, the older doctrine of inspiration imperils the freedom of God to speak through the Scriptures. Rather than placing the Word of God at our disposal, a proper doctrine of inspiration maintains the priority of God's sovereign action in the revelation of himself in Jesus Christ.

Consistent with his emphasis upon the priority of God's sovereign action in using the biblical witness as an instrument of revelation, Barth strongly affirms the function of the Bible as a canonical authority in the church. In this respect, Barth's view of Scripture has a distinctly Protestant accent. Though the canon of Scripture may have been recognized in the course of the church's history, this recognition occurred in response to God's prior decision to constitute the canon and exercise his authority over the church by means of its witness: "The establishment of the canon [by the church] is the confession of God's election and calling of His witness."[24] Because of God's election to grant canonical status to the biblical writings in their witness to Christ, these writings are the authoritative measure for the church's confessions and theologians. The authority of the confessions derives from the degree to which they conform to the Scripture's witness. Similarly, the task of theology is to test the church's confessions against the biblical witness, and to express the Christian faith in conformity to the standard of Scripture.[25]

Though Barth's doctrine of Scripture does not represent a simple return to the older Christian doctrine of Scripture in the pre-critical period, it does provide a basis for the retrieval of a distinctively theological interpretation of Scripture. In Barth's interpretation of the biblical witness to Jesus Christ, a number of features of the pre-critical method of interpreting biblical texts are present in modified form. Though Barth concedes that the

---

23. Barth, *Church Dogmatics*, 1/2:530. For illustrations of Barth's acknowledgment of the fallibility of the Scripture's witness, see Beale, *The Erosion of Inerrancy*, 281–83.

24. Barth, "The Authority and Significance of the Bible," 60.

25. Barth, *Church Dogmatics*, 1/2:620. Cf. Barth, *Evangelical Authority*, 31–32: "Even the smallest, strangest, simplest, or obscurest among the biblical witnesses has an incomparable advantage over even the most pious, scholarly, and sagacious latter-day theologian."

modern historical-critical method has closed the door to a return to the pre-critical doctrine of the inspiration of Scripture, he does exhibit in his theological writings a renewed respect for and adherence to the church's historic approach to the interpretation of Scripture. The five features of the pre-critical approach that we identified earlier are all present in Barth's theological interpretation and exegesis of biblical texts. Although Barth's actual exegetical practice is complex and at times difficult to understand, he interprets the Bible as a unified whole, a canonical witness that must be read as self-referential and self-interpreting. Barth also treats the Bible as a coherent witness to the Triune God who is revealed in Jesus Christ. The story or narrative that is recounted in Scripture is viewed by Barth as the story of God's self-revelation in Jesus Christ, whether in creation or redemption. Furthermore, while Barth subordinates the church to the canon of Scripture, he regularly interprets the canonical Scriptures in conformity with the church's "rule of faith" as this is expressed in the historic creeds and confessions of the church.

In addition to these similarities between Barth's approach to the interpretation of the Bible and the pre-critical approach, there are some respects in which Barth's approach especially aims to overcome the problems inherent in the modern historical-critical method. Barth's well-known expression, "the strange new world within the Bible," captures well his insistence that the canonical Scriptures must be read from the standpoint of faith and, therefore, may not be filtered through the grid of extra-scriptural criteria such as the criteria of historical science or contemporary human experience. According to Barth, the problem of much modern interpretation of the Bible is that the biblical texts are read by the standard of extra-scriptural considerations. Rather than beginning with modern experience or the presumed standards of scientific history, the interpreter of Scripture has to be willing to enter the world of the Bible and honor its particularity as a comprehensive narrative or story of God's revelation in Jesus Christ. The interpreter of the Bible does not aim to distill general truths from the biblical text, or to take the measure of the biblical narrative by the standards of what modern historical science is willing to regard as authentic history. The aim of biblical interpretation is ultimately to hear the Word that God speaks through the biblical witnesses who recount the history of God's acts in creation and redemption, all of which witness to his self-revelation in Jesus Christ.

For Barth, the critical deficiency of much historical-critical interpretation of the biblical texts is the failure to read the Bible as a "realistic narrative" of God's self-revelation in the history of Jesus Christ. In the nature of the case, historical criticism cannot interpret the biblical texts and their witness to God's revelation in Jesus Christ. In the historical-critical understanding of history, God and his acts are excluded entirely as real acts in history. From the standpoint of historical science, God is not an actor within the causal network of events in space and time. The biblical history or narrative of God's self-revelation in Jesus Christ, accordingly, remains inaccessible to historical science which rules out the possibility of God acting in history. For this reason, Barth rules out as theologically impermissible any reading of the biblical texts that appeals to extra-textual categories or conceptual schemes in their interpretation. The meaning of the biblical witness cannot be located in the extra-textual constructions of the "real history" that lies behind the biblical texts. Nor can this meaning be discovered by a conservative apologetics that endeavors to prove the historical reliability of the biblical history. The meaning and truth of the Bible is inseparable from the biblical narratives of God's self-revelation in history. In Barth's estimation, the interpretation of Scripture requires that the interpreter enter the world of the Bible, and in order to do so the interpreter has to abandon the historical-critical attempt to find the real story behind the story to which the Bible bears witness, namely, the identity of the Triune God as he is revealed in the Person and work of Jesus Christ.

3.2. Brevard Childs: Canonical Interpretation

A second figure who has played an important role in recent discussions of a theological approach to the interpretation of Scripture is Brevard Childs.[26] Influenced by Karl Barth's renewed interest in a theological interpretation of Scripture as an instrument of divine revelation, Child's contribution focuses upon what he terms a "canonical" approach or method of biblical interpretation. Like Barth, Childs' canonical approach does not repudiate the historical-critical method altogether. Rather, Childs aims to move beyond the limitations and problems of this method to an approach that recognizes the priority and finality of the canonical shaping of the Scriptures.

While Childs does not dismiss or reject outright the historical-critical investigation of the pre-history and origins of the biblical text (e.g., source criticism, form-criticism, tradition criticism), he emphasizes the objective reality or givenness of the canonical form of the Christian Scriptures. The task of biblical interpretation is not to seek the meaning of the text in the

---

26. See Childs, *Old Testament Theology* and *The New Testament as Canon*. For treatments of Childs' view, see Driver, *Brevard Childs, Biblical Theologian*; Klink and Lockett, *Understanding Biblical Theology*, 141–56; and Seitz and Greene-McCreight, eds, *Theological Exegesis*, 3–51.

alleged source or form of the text at some (earlier) stage in the history of its production. Nor is it enough to interpret the biblical text in terms of its original audience, so far as this can be determined by historical-critical methods. While historical-critical study of the formation of the biblical and canonical text may shed light on the meaning of the text in its final form, the canonical form of the text must be granted a privileged status. The interpretation of Scripture, therefore, must not seek to find the history that lies behind or underneath the text, and then ascribe priority to some aspect of this history insofar as it is authenticated by historical science. Nor does the interpretation of Scripture aim to identify a normative form of the text at some earlier stage in its development, rather than the final form it takes as part of the canonical Scriptures. The task of biblical interpretation is to determine the meaning of the biblical texts in their canonical context, not in some historically-reconstructed context that is posited by the historical-critical interpreter.

Because the canonical approach grants privileged status to the final, canonical form and setting of the biblical texts, Childs maintains that it restores the proper ecclesiastical context for the interpretation of the Bible. Unlike the historical-critical approach, which rejects the pre-critical tradition of biblical interpretation as historically untenable, the canonical method is able to enter fruitfully into conversation with the history of the Christian church's interaction with Scripture. This is possible because pre-critical and post-critical canonical interpretation share the same attachment to the canonical form of the text as the basis for their interpretive efforts. Furthermore, because the canonical approach recognizes that the Bible consists of a single, coherent and inter-related witness, it is able to read the Bible in harmony with the pre-critical tradition of interpretation. The interpreter of the canonical Scriptures is obliged to read the Bible as a single book, and to view the Old and New Testaments as a unified witness to the one story of God's dealings with his people throughout history, culminating in the coming of his Son as the fulfillment of Israel's history. Like the pre-critical tradition of interpretation, the canonical method is able to embrace and accommodate the hermeneutical strategies of typology and spiritual-allegorical exegesis in the reading of Scripture.

From the standpoint of a canonical approach, the problem with the historical-critical approach to the interpretation of biblical texts is that it enters into an adversarial relation with the church's interpretive tradition. For example, the historical-critical approach interprets biblical texts in terms of the original historical context (so far as this can be reconstructed) that produced them. The inevitable consequence of this method is that the biblical texts are interpreted outside of the canonical context in which they are found, and their meaning is restricted to what the author may have intended at the time they were initially written. Within the framework of this approach, the text means what it "originally" meant, not what it now means within the broader horizon of the entirety of the biblical canon. The canonical approach, however, properly recognizes that the meaning of the text can ultimately only be determined in continuity with the church's determination of its final, canonical form. Another way of making this point is to say that the canonical form of the biblical texts is a form that expresses the church's own interpretation of their meaning. If the enterprise of biblical interpretation is to be conducted in continuity with the church throughout history, then it must occur within a canonical context.[27]

3.3. George Lindbeck: Ecclesial Interpretation

The last figure whom I wish to consider in this sketch of the emergence of a theological and post-liberal approach to the interpretation of the Bible is George Lindbeck.[28] While Lindbeck shares a number of the emphases that we have seen in Karl Barth and Brevard Childs—the Bible needs to be read theologically as a canonical testimony to the story of the Triune God's work in creation and redemption—his contribution to the formulation of a post-modern approach to the interpretation of the Bible focuses especially upon the church and its role as an interpretive community. In recent discussions of a post-liberal approach to the interpretation of the Bible, Lindbeck's formulations have played an especially influential role.

In his important study, *The Nature of Doctrine: Religion and Theology in a Postliberal Age*, Lindbeck sets forth a comprehensive understanding of the formulation and understanding of doctrine in different religious communities. According to Lindbeck, three broad approaches to the subject of doctrine may be distinguished. The first approach, which he terms "cognitive-propositional," is found among conservative theologians who view

---

27. Childs, *The New Testament as Canon*, 40: "Decisive for this process of interpretation is the context in which it is carried on. The function of canon is to assure it's involving a received tradition which has been shaped toward the end of engendering faith in the Risen Lord of the scriptures. However, a canonical context includes not only the scope of the sacred literature, but the means by which the reader engages the scriptures, namely, an expectation of understanding through the promise of the Spirit to the believer."

28. See Lindbeck, *The Nature of Doctrine*; Lindbeck, "Barth and Textuality," 361–76; Lindbeck, "Scripture, Consensus, and Community," 74–101; and Lindbeck, "Postcritical Canonical Interpretation," 26–51. For critical assessments of Lindbeck's view, see McGrath, "An Evangelical Evaluation of Postmodernism," 23–44; and Volf, "Theology, Meaning & Power," 45–66.

doctrines as propositions that make direct truth claims about reality. The second approach, which he terms "experiential-expressive," is represented among liberal theologians (e.g., Schleiermacher) who view doctrines as descriptions of human religious experiences. The third approach, which he terms "cultural-linguistic," is the one Lindbeck finds most satisfying. In the cultural-linguistic approach, doctrines express the view of reality embodied in a religious community's authoritative texts. Borrowing from the insights of modern linguistics and the philosophy of language (e.g. Ludwig Wittgenstein), Lindbeck maintains that the doctrines of a religious community are set forth in the privileged texts of the community. These religious texts, which in the case of the Christian church are found in the canonical Scriptures, describe and create the world that the religious community and its members occupy. The doctrines of a particular religious community find their cultural-linguistic expression in the peculiar "language game" whose grammar and rules govern the faith and practice of its adherents. According to Lindbeck, a religion is "similar to an idiom that makes possible the description of realities, the formulation of beliefs, and the experiencing of inner attitudes, feelings and sentiments. Like a culture or language, it is a communal phenomenon that shapes the subjectivities of individuals rather than being primarily a manifestation of those subjectivities. It comprises a vocabulary of discursive and nondiscursive symbols together with a distinctive logic or grammar in terms of which this vocabulary can be meaningfully deployed."[29]

Although Lindbeck's theory of the cultural-linguistic nature of religious doctrine is highly abstract and philosophical in nature, he articulates it to provide a conceptual basis for his endorsement of the kind of postliberal approach to the interpretation of the Bible that we have seen in figures like Karl Barth and Brevard Childs. Like Barth and Childs, Lindbeck emphasizes that the canon of the Old and New Testaments is the privileged text of the Christian community. The task of biblical interpretation is not to look for the meaning of the text under or behind the canonical form which represents the normative standard for the church's teaching or cultural-linguistic norms. Since the canonical text creates an all-embracing framework for the interpretation of reality, there is no extra-canonical or extra-textual world available to a member of the church who engages the biblical texts. The world of the church is precisely the world as it is formed and expressed in the church's canonical texts. Therefore, Lindbeck endorses Barth's insistence that the interpreter needs to enter "the strange new world within the

---

29. Lindbeck, *The Nature of Doctrine*, 33.

Bible" and employ a canonical hermeneutic much like that found in the pre-critical period of church history:

> Stated compactly and technically, the issue which concerns us is the extent to which the Bible can be profitably read in our day as canonically and narrationally unified and internally glossed (that is, self-referential and self-interpreting), whole centered on Jesus Christ, and telling the story of the dealings of the Triune God with his people and his world in ways which are typologically (though not, so at least the Reformers would say, allegorically) applicable to the present.[30]

For Lindbeck, the problem with historical-critical approaches to biblical interpretation is that they subordinate the meaning of the biblical texts to extra-biblical criteria of truthfulness. Historical criticism goes outside of the world described in the biblical narrative, and in doing so fails to see that the interpreter of Scripture has to live within and describe the world as it is defined by the biblical texts themselves. Because the Bible constitutes the "interpretive framework for all reality,"[31] the interpreter of the Bible must not apply extra-textual standards of interpretation in order to discover its true meaning. In the historical-critical approach to the biblical narratives, the narrative meaning of the biblical texts within their canonical framework is lost. Rather than interpreting the biblical narratives in a self-referential manner, the interpreter focuses upon "whether they are accurate reports of the events which they tell. The narrative meaning of the stories was confused with their factual (scientific and historical) meaning, and was thereby lost."[32]

Because Lindbeck views the Bible as a canonical description of the cultural-linguistic world in which the ecclesial community lives and interprets reality, his primary contribution to a post-liberal hermeneutic is his special emphasis upon the ecclesial community as the only proper interpreter of Scripture. The Bible must be read in terms of the *sensus fidelium*, the sense of the faithful, and not in terms of the sense of individual theologians, certainly not of theologians who interpret the text outside of a framework constituted by the Scriptures themselves. In a comprehensive sense, the church's interpretation of Scripture is not only the task of academic theologians and

---

30. Lindbeck, "Scripture, Consensus, and Community," 73.

31. Ibid., 77.

32. Ibid., 83. With this statement, Lindbeck, like his fellow post-liberal theologians, contests the usual historical-critical distinction between *Geschichte*, the biblical history written from the standpoint of faith, and *historie*, the real history as it is authenticated by historical science. This distinction inevitably posits a historical referent outside of the world of the biblical narrative that becomes a critical standard for interpreting it. Cf. Childs, *Old Testament Theology in a Canonical Context*, 16.

clerics but also of the church community in its various manifestations. Such interpretation may take a variety of forms, and comes to expression not only in academic studies but also in the church's liturgical and sacramental practices. There is an inseparable conjunction between the Bible and the church, and between the church and the Bible. Rather than ascribing priority to the Bible in relation to the church (the historic Protestant view) or ascribing priority to the church in relation to the Bible (the historic Roman Catholic view), Lindbeck speaks of their "coinherence." The Bible forms the church even as it was formed by the church.[33] Just as the church community lives within the world of the Bible, so the Bible is only to be interpreted by the church. The social, cultural, and linguistic conventions of the church community are all formed by the canonical Scriptures. Consequently, the church would cease to be the cultural-linguistic community that it is, if it were to relinquish the task of biblical interpretation to interpreters who approach the biblical texts outside of the framework of the church's self-understanding.[34]

4. Biblical Interpretation in and with the Church: An Evaluation of a "Post-Critical" Approach to Biblical Interpretation

Undoubtedly, my overview of the history of pre-critical, historical-critical, and post-critical approaches to biblical interpretation is at best a sketch of a very complex subject. In spite of my attempt to present these approaches in terms of their common features, there remains a great deal of diversity within each of these periods of the history of the church's interpretation

---

33. In this way, Lindbeck tries to overcome the historic dispute between Roman Catholic and Protestant churches on the relative priority of the church and the Bible. Rather than ascribing priority to one or the other, Lindbeck maintains that we should speak of the "coinherence of Bible and church, of their mutually constitutive reciprocity" (Ibid., 78).

34. It must be observed that Lindbeck's cultural-linguistic view of the Bible assumes one of the most significant features of post-modernism: the only criteria by which to measure the church's communal interpretation of Scripture are criteria such as consistency, coherence, churchly consensus, and pragmatic usefulness. None of these criteria authorize the church to say that its doctrines are a true reflection of reality. They may be true "for the church," but we have no basis for asserting that they are true for all humans. Lindbeck's position shares one of the fundamental tenets of post-modernism, namely, an anti-foundationalism that rejects any appeal to objective criteria for adjudicating competing truth claims among different religious communities. Since each of these communities occupies its own cultural-linguistic world, the truthfulness of its doctrines is limited to the circle of those who share this common world. In this respect, Lindbeck's post-critical approach to the interpretation of Scripture is more non-theological and post-modernist than the positions of Barth and Childs.

of the Bible. For my purpose, however, the most pressing question raised by the overview of this history is the role of the church in the interpretation of Scripture. In the period of biblical criticism, the interpretation of the Bible was significantly detached from its location within the church. The hermeneutical problem of interpreting biblical texts that were written in an earlier and different historical situation became a preoccupation in the period of historical criticism. The more recent efforts to articulate a post-liberal or post-critical approach share a common concern to retrieve aspects of the pre-critical approach, especially in terms of a renewed emphasis upon the church's role in the interpretation of the canonical Scriptures. In my judgment, this emphasis represents a necessary corrective to the historical-critical divorce of biblical interpretation from the ecclesiastical community. Nonetheless, there are aspects of the post-critical approach that are problematic and militate against a genuine re-appropriation of important aspects of pre-critical interpretation.

4.1. The Church's Doctrine of Scripture: A sine qua non

In order to retrieve essential elements of the pre-critical tradition of biblical interpretation, it is necessary to return to the classic doctrine of Scripture that was a commonplace in the pre-critical period. Although a significant difference emerged at the time of the Reformation regarding the relative authority of the Bible and the church in the determination of the church's faith and practice, the Roman Catholic and Reformation doctrines of Scripture shared important, common convictions regarding the inspiration and authority of the canonical Scriptures. Because the Scriptures were the Word of God given through the instrumentality of human authors, the interpretation of Scripture was necessarily a theological task. The biblical texts were not read to ascertain simply what they might have meant to the human authors at the time of their initial writing. Rather, these texts were read as Holy Scripture, a normative and authoritative Word that must be read in a spirit of humble submission to their teaching. Because the whole Bible was a God-authored standard for the church's faith and practice, the church was obliged to read them as a unified testimony to the truth of the gospel of Jesus Christ. The nature of the Scriptures required that they be read as a self-referential and self-interpreting book. The common hermeneutical strategies of the pre-critical approach—interpreting biblical texts within their broader canonical context, reading the Old Testament in the light of the New and the Old Testament as preparatory to the New, looking for typological and analogical connections throughout the story recounted in the Scriptures, granting priority to the literal sense of biblical texts—were undergirded by foundational convictions about the divine authorship and inspiration of the Bible.

My point is not that a classic, orthodox view of the divine inspiration and authority of the Bible provides an easy solution to all the challenges of biblical interpretation. Nor does it provide an obvious answer to all the questions raised within the historical-critical tradition of biblical interpretation. The point is that an approach to biblical interpretation that does not privilege the final authority of the biblical canon will inevitably lead to a method of interpretation that deconstructs the biblical texts and looks for their meaning behind or outside of their canonical context. A basic problem in the post-liberal retrieval of aspects of the pre-critical approach is its unwillingness to challenge the basic assumptions of the critical approach with respect to the inspiration and truthfulness of Scripture. However, unless the assumptions of the historical-critical method are challenged at their root, the determination of the meaning of biblical texts will necessarily require an approach that grants the interpreter an inappropriate priority in the interpretive process. Unless the Word of God is *given* or *available directly* in the biblical texts themselves, the interpreter of these texts will always be tempted to isolate the text from its biblical context and to determine its meaning upon the basis of a critically-reconstructed understanding of the history that lies behind and outside of the text. To the extent that the post-liberal retrieval of aspects of the church's historic interpretation of Scripture is not correlated with a retrieval of the historic doctrine of inspiration, the interpretation of Scripture will not be based upon the necessary foundation of a coherent, unified and self-interpreting body of canonical writings.

Only within the framework of the classic orthodox doctrine of Scripture is it possible to justify a hermeneutical approach to interpretation that aims to identify *the* meaning of biblical texts. To state the matter rather boldly: if God is the primary author of the Bible, then the meaning of biblical texts coincides with their divinely-intended meaning and this meaning is capable of being apprehended by the believing community. However challenging may be the task of ascertaining the meaning of a biblical text in its canonical context, this task must be governed by the undergirding assumption that it *has a discernible meaning, and this is the meaning that coincides with God's intention as this is expressed in the biblical texts themselves.* Because God has condescended to reveal himself through the instrumentality of the scriptural writings, and because these Scriptures are a sufficient, perspicuous, and supremely normative standard for the Christian faith—the church is obliged and competent to determine adequately their divinely-intended meaning.

Without this basic presupposition regarding the self-attesting, divine authority of the Scriptures, it will not be possible to retrieve the essential features of the church's pre-critical tradition of Scriptural interpretation. When contemporary architects of a post-critical approach to interpretation fail to challenge some of the basic assumptions of historical-criticism—e.g., that the biblical writings include irreducibly different theologies, that the biblical writings are not infallible in the proper sense of the term, that the biblical history is rife with inaccuracies and mythological forms, etc.— extra-canonical criteria of truthfulness will inevitably become a measure for sifting through the biblical texts and authenticating their truthfulness. Without a truly theological doctrine of Scripture, it is scarcely possible to have a sure foundation for a theological interpretation of Scripture.

4.2. The Canonical Form of Scripture

One of the contributions of the post-liberal endeavor to recover a theological reading of the Bible is its emphasis upon the canonical form of Scripture. As we have noted, the historical-critical method encouraged the interpreter to reconstruct the pre-history of the biblical texts by identifying the different authors (redactors) and historical circumstances that preceded the final form of the text within the biblical canon. Although advocates of an interpretation of the biblical text within their canonical context (Childs) acknowledge that such an historical reconstruction of the text's pre-history may help to illumine the meaning of the text in its final canonical form, they reject any method of interpretation that does not grant a basic interpretive priority to the text's canonical form.

There are several important implications of the canonical form of Scripture for its interpretation. In the first place, when the interpretation of biblical texts occurs in a canonical context, the meaning of these texts is intra-canonical and not extra-canonical. The ultimate horizon for the interpretation of any particular text is determined by its location within the boundaries of the canon as a whole. Accordingly, there is a surplus of meaning that can be ascertained through comparing Scripture with Scripture.[35] While few post-critical interpreters explicitly affirm the older idea of a *sensus plenior*, at least in the theological sense of a meaning in texts that ultimately

---

35. An obvious example of this is the so-called "mother promise" (*protevangelium*) in Genesis 3:15. When this promise is interpreted in terms of its canonical setting, its Scriptural meaning and significance cannot be limited to *what it meant* at the time of its first pronouncement or textual recounting. The story of the fulfillment of this promise, as it unfolds within the biblical narratives, constitutes the larger canonical framework within which it must be understood.

derives from the Bible's divine author and surpasses what was known to the original human author, post-critical interpreters are able to recognize the more fulsome meaning of biblical texts within the broader framework of the Bible as a whole. Furthermore, the shape of the biblical canon, comprised as it is of two testaments, the old and the new, has profound and far-reaching significance for the way the Bible is to be interpreted. When the Bible is read within a canonical context, the Old Testament must be interpreted in the light of its New Testament fulfillment. The God of Israel, who is identified in the narratives of the Old Testament Scriptures, is the God and Father of Jesus Christ, and the history of God's covenantal dealings with his Old Testament people is part of a larger and continuing story that finds its culmination and definitive expression in the incarnation of Jesus Christ in the fullness of time and the outpouring of the Holy Spirit at Pentecost.

Contrary to the atomism and historicism that characterized the historical-critical approach to Scripture, post-critical interpreters of Scripture propose a reading of the Bible that attends primarily to its realistic narrative of God's self-revelation in his acts of creation and redemption. The Bible is not a loosely connected collection of stories, wisdom writings, and prophetic books, but the self-revelation of the Triune God in the history of creation and redemption. Consistent with the church's "rule of faith," especially as this is set forth in the great ecumenical creeds of the early history of the church, a post-critical reading of Scripture attends firstly to the unifying story of the works of God, the Father, the Son, and the Holy Spirit. The grand narrative of Scripture constitutes a unifying structure within which the particular biblical texts have their meaning as part of the larger story. In this approach, the Christ-centeredness of the entire biblical canon is emphasized, and the Bible is interpreted holistically as a single narrative with a common focus throughout. In each of these respects, the post-liberal approach represents an important step in the recovery of a significant feature of pre-critical biblical interpretation.

4.3. The Problem of Historical Distance

In addition to their emphasis upon an approach to the interpretation of the Bible that grants priority to its final canonical form, advocates of a post-critical approach are eager to find a solution to one of the vexing legacies of historical criticism, namely, the problem of "historical distance" between the ancient texts of Scripture and the contemporary interpreter. Due to its methodological focus upon the determination of what the biblical texts originally *meant* in the historical situation from which they stemmed, historical criticism was bound to leave the biblical interpreter with an insuperable difficulty, namely, bridging the gap between what the ancient text meant and what it might possibly mean to a modern interpreter whose historical situation is radically different. The solution to this difficulty was often found in relegating the meaning of the text to its historical value as a description of what the biblical authors believed within their own historical circumstance and worldview.

In order to derive any lasting value from the biblical texts, the contemporary interpreter was then compelled to distinguish sharply between the historical meaning of the text (what it meant) and conceptual constructions that express its present religious meaning (e.g., an "existentialist" reading, a "social-gospel" reading). For example, in Rudolph Bultmann's discernment of the contemporary meaning of biblical texts, the historical form of the text needs to be demythologized in order to uncover its true significance for an authentic kind of human existence. In one way or another, the historical-critical approach obliged the interpreter of the biblical text to move from what the text originally meant to what it might now mean in a different time and place. In order to bridge the gap between a historically-reconstructed past and the present, the biblical interpreter was obliged to superimpose contemporary worldviews and pre-commitments upon the biblical texts in order to exhibit their relevance for the church today. In more recent times, the historical-critical emphasis upon the historical distance between the ancient and the modern world, between the biblical texts and the contemporary reader, has led inexorably to hermeneutical strategies that deconstruct the biblical texts or grant priority to the contemporary reader in the discernment of their present meaning.

In post-liberal approaches to the interpretation of the Bible, the solution to this problem of historical distance lies in a recognition of the church as a continuing body throughout history. The same church that produced and subsequently recognized the canonical Scriptures, continues to be the community that receives and interprets the Scriptures. In the words of Robert Jenson, a contemporary proponent of a post-critical approach to biblical interpretation,

> [T]he error of almost all modern biblical exegesis is a subliminal assumption that the church in and for which Matthew and Paul wrote, or in which Irenaeus shaped the canon, and the church in which we now read what they produced are historically distant from each other. That is, the error is the subliminal assumption that there is no one diachronically identical universal church: nearly all modern biblical exegesis in fact presumes a sectarian ecclesiology. But while Athens may perhaps have disappeared

into the past and been replaced by Paris or New York, Paul's church still lives as the very one to which believing exegetes now belong. Moreover, this church remains in the same relation to canonical Israel as on the day of Pentecost.[36]

The interpretation of the Bible is a communal task that belongs to the whole church throughout history. For this reason, the contemporary reading of the Scriptures is in direct continuity, indeed is an act of the same community through time, with the reading of the Scriptures in the past. The church's present interpretation of the Bible represents a "further appropriation of a continuing communal tradition within which we antecedently live."[37]

While this feature of a post-critical approach to biblical interpretation is a welcome development—especially when contrasted with the isolation of the interpretation of Scripture in the academy that occurs in the historical-critical tradition—it needs to be strengthened by an even more important consideration: the church today shares the identical location in redemptive history with the church since Pentecost, and will continue to share that historical location until the revelation of Christ at the end of the age. It is ultimately a species of historicism, a conceit of contemporary thought, to regard contemporary history as fundamentally distant from a past that no longer exists and a future that cannot be known. Within the framework of a biblical understanding of history, the coming of Christ in the fullness of time is an event of decisive importance for the whole of history. Jesus Christ is, to use the words of the author of Hebrews, "the same, yesterday, today, and forever" (Heb 13:8). Christ, who first came in "the fullness of time" (Gal 4:4) will conclude God's redemptive purposes when he comes a second time. In the meantime, in "these last days" (Heb 1:2), the canonical witness to Jesus Christ will serve as the single foundation upon which the church will continue to be built in every generation (Eph 2:20). The Scriptures' witness, sufficient to the need of the church in every period of its history, remains a perpetual standard for the church's faith and practice. The canonical Scriptures were provided by God for the instruction and edification of the church throughout its entire history from Pentecost until Christ's second advent. Therefore, the Bible has an integral role in the history of redemption and can never be treated as a relic from the past, as is the case in the historical-critical assumption of an unbridgeable historical distance between the church's past and present.

---

36. Jenson, *The Works of God*, 279–80.
37. Ibid., 280.

4.4. The Church as an Interpretive Community

Though an emphasis upon the church as the primary interpreter of the canonical Scriptures helps to address the problem of historical distance posed by historical-criticism, the nature and boundaries of the church's role need to be carefully defined. In the formulations of some post-liberal theologians, the role of the church in the process of interpretation tends to diminish the privileged place of the canonical Scriptures as the exclusive source and norm for the church's faith and practice. Furthermore, the church's interpretation of the Bible is reductionistically viewed as little more than the social-cultural-linguistic conventions of one religious community, and not an apprehension of the truth of the Word of God that lays claim upon all human beings who bear God's image.

Although the church is the appropriate community within which to interpret the Scriptures, it is necessary to distinguish between the authority of the inspired Scriptures and the subordinate authority of the church's interpretation of Scripture. One of the inevitable consequences of a failure to affirm the uniqueness of Scripture as the inspired Word of God is the subordination of Scripture to the tradition of the church. In the writings of some post-liberals, the church's role as an interpretive community is associated with a broad understanding of Christian tradition. The Scriptures are themselves viewed as having been produced by the church, and therefore the ongoing task of Scriptural interpretation is qualitatively indistinguishable from what took place when the church first produced the Scriptures and determined their canonical boundaries. While historic Protestantism has always recognized the role of the church in the "recognition" of Holy Scripture, the Reformers were careful to insist that they do not "become" the Word of God for the church because of the church's action. The action of the church in relation to the canonical Scriptures was a reflexive, and not a constitutive, one. The Scriptures are, in the final analysis, self-authenticating (*autopistos*). What the church recognized is that these canonical books were authored and granted to the church by the Triune God himself. The Scriptures were to be interpreted theologically precisely because they were the canonical standard for the faith and practice of the church throughout its entire history until Christ's second coming.

In Karl Barth's treatment of the interpretation of Scripture, unlike many of his post-critical followers, there is a clear recognition that God has "elected" the Scriptures as a divinely-authored norm for the church's faith and practice. The Word of God in Scripture expresses God's own act in bearing witness to himself through the witness of the human authors of Scripture. Although Barth fails to identify the Word of God with the words of

Scripture in a direct sense, he does retain a clear view of the primacy of the Scriptures in their authority over the church. The Scriptures are the church's book, but they are not simply the expression of the church's faith in the past and not, as they are interpreted afresh, of the church in the present. The subjectivism that characterized the historical-critical tradition was exhibited in its reduction of the biblical text to an expression of what the biblical authors once believed and taught about God in times past. For Barth, such subjectivism can only be answered by way of a recognition of the uniqueness of the Scripture's witness to Jesus Christ. In the formulations of many post-critical interpreters of Scripture, however, the biblical texts are only granted a kind of priority in the understanding of the "cultural-linguistic" conventions of the Christian church. But this is a priority whose only warrant is the church's tradition and practice. As is true of many expressions of post-modernism, the post-liberal approach to biblical interpretation finds itself unable to break with the historical-critical assumption that the Bible is finally a book that expresses the religious sensibilities and convictions of the Christian church. The Bible's teaching is true for the church. But what is true for the church may not be true for other communities that have their own privileged texts or cultural-linguistic conventions.

Though the post-liberal approach fails to distinguish adequately between the *final* authority of the canonical Scriptures and the *relative* authority of the church's interpretive tradition, its emphasis upon the church's role in the interpretation of Scripture is proper and necessary. In this respect, the general consensus among post-liberal theologians that the canonical Scriptures should be read in conformity to the church's "rule of faith" (*regula fidei*) is a welcome one. The role of the church as an interpretive community does oblige the contemporary interpreter of the canonical Scriptures to read them in sympathy with the creedal consensus of the church. The Reformation doctrine of *sola Scriptura* may not be confused with an individualistic and anti-ecclesiastical reading of the Bible.[38] Admittedly, inasmuch as the Scriptures alone are an inspired and infallible rule for faith and practice, the creeds and confessions of the church are always legitimately subject to critical testing by the standard of the Bible. The subordination of the creed and confession to the standard of Scripture also requires a fresh study of the biblical texts, which may occasionally warrant a revision of the church's confessional standards. For Reformed theology, there is no escape from this requirement in the supposed infallible teaching authority of the church's

---

38. See Mathison, *The Shape of Sola Scriptura*, 237–53. Mathison rightly argues that the Reformer's doctrine of *sola Scriptura* may not be confused with modern evangelical individualism, which denies the appropriate use of the confessions in the interpretation of Scripture.

magisterium. Nevertheless, the presumption of the church in its interpretation of the Bible is that the creeds and confessions are themselves the fruit of the church's engagement with Scripture, and are therefore regulative of the church's exegesis. Within the context of the history of the Reformed churches, the role of the church as an interpretive community requires that the interpretation of Scripture take place in a way that shows respectful submission not only to the ecumenical creeds but also to the Reformed confessions.[39]

In this respect, there is a kind of inevitable circularity in the reading of Scripture in the church. On the one hand, the biblical texts must be read in sympathy with the church's rule of faith, on the assumption that this rule of faith is itself a faithful summary of scriptural teaching. Because the confessions codify the consensus of the church's exegetical labor in the interpretation of Scripture, they may not be set aside in the hermeneutical enterprise of biblical interpretation. On the other hand, since the Scriptures alone are inspired and infallible, the confessions may never be immunized against the prospect of reformulation upon the basis of a new and better reading of the biblical texts.[40] The interpretation of Scripture is an ongoing task, which will never be concluded or achieve perfect understanding prior to the return of Christ.[41]

The recognition of the church's role in the interpretation of Scripture, however, must not be viewed reductionistically as a matter of sociology or ecclesiology, as it appears to be for some post-liberal theologians. A proper recognition of the church's role (and of the subordinate authority of the church's creeds and confessions in biblical interpretation) stems from a theological conviction regarding the abiding presence of the Spirit of Christ within the church. The same Spirit who superintended the writing of the

---

39. For a discussion of the role of the church's confessional tradition in the interpretation of the Bible and theology, see also Trueman, *The Creedal Imperative*; Holmes, *Listening to the Past*; and Pelikan, *The Vindication of Tradition*.

40. Cf. Carson, *Jesus, The Son of God*, 79: "Rightly deployed, confessional standards ought to guide, shape, and enrich our exegesis; wrongly deployed, they become cut off from the biblical texts that nurtured and developed them."

41. In the period of Reformed orthodoxy, a distinction was drawn between the church's knowledge of the truth as a pilgrim community (*theologia viatorum*) and as a perfected community (*theologia beata*). By means of this distinction, it was acknowledged that the church's interpretation of the revelation of the Triune God in Scripture will always be marked by incompleteness and imperfection in this life. While the distinction, to speak anachronistically, was not drawn in order to concede a postmodernism that denies the possibility of any real apprehension of God's Word of truth in Scripture, it does remind us that the interpretation of Scripture is an unfinished task. Even the best creeds and confessions are fallible summaries of the Bible, and must be tested by the standard of the infallible Scriptures.

Scriptures is present with the church throughout the history of its engagement with Scripture. At this juncture, Karl Barth's doctrine of Scripture as an instrument of divine revelation expresses an important theological truth regarding the action of the Holy Spirit in and with the Scriptures. For Barth, the doctrine of revelation does not merely entail the objective availability of the Word of God in the canonical Scriptures. Though Barth improperly denies the availability of the infallible Word of God in the inspired (past tense) texts of Scripture, he makes an important point when he argues that God's revelation in Scripture demands that the Spirit speak in and through the biblical texts. Unless the interpreter hears the Word of God in Scripture, which can only actually occur by virtue of the Spirit's use of the biblical text, the Word of God is not made known to its recipients. A truly theological reading of Scripture must acknowledge that the Spirit of Christ, who has been poured out upon the church and abides with the church forever (John 14:15–31), enables the church to receive and understand the Scriptures. Reading the Bible in and with the church as an interpretive community is born of the recognition that the church's historical reading of Scripture, codified and summarized in the historic creeds and confessions, represents in part the fulfillment of Christ's promise to send the "Spirit of truth" to enable the church to know him and his Word of truth.

Bibliography

Adam, A. K. M. *Faithful Interpretation: Reading the Bible in a Postmodern World.* Minneapolis, MN: Fortress Press, 2006.

———. *What is Postmodern Biblical Criticism?* Minneapolis, MN: Fortress Press, 1995.

Allison, Dale C., Jr. *The Historical Christ and the Theological Jesus.* Grand Rapids, MI: Eerdmans, 2009.

Barth, Karl. "The Authority and Significance of the Bible: Twelve Theses." In *God Here and Now*, 55–74. London: Routledge, 2003.

———. *Church Dogmatics.* Vol. 1/1: *The Doctrine of the Word of God.* Translated by Geoffrey W. Bromiley. Edinburgh: T. & T. Clark, 1956.

———. *Church Dogmatics.* Vol. 1/2: *The Doctrine of the Word of God.* Translated by G.T. Thomson and Harold Knight. Edinburgh: T. & T. Clark, 1956.

———. *The Epistle to the Romans.* 6th ed. Translated by Edwyn C. Hoskyns. London: Oxford University Press, 1933.

———. *Evangelical Theology: An Introduction.* Grand Rapids, MI: Eerdmans, 1963.

———. *The Göttingen Dogmatics: Instruction in the Christian Religion.* Vol. 1. Translated by Geoffrey Bromiley. Grand Rapids, MI: Eerdmans, 1991.

———. *The Word of God and the Word of Man.* Translated by Douglas Horton. Gloucester, MA: Pete Smith, 1978.

Beale, G. K. *The Erosion of Inerrancy in Evangelicalism: Responding to New Challenges to Biblical Authority.* Wheaton, IL: Crossway Books, 2008.

Berkhof, Louis. *Principles of Biblical Interpretation*. Grand Rapids, MI: Baker, 1950.
Bromiley, Geoffrey W. "The Authority of Scripture in Karl Barth." In *Hermeneutics, Authority, and Canon*, edited by D. A. Carson and John D. Woodbridge, 271–94. Grand Rapids, MI: Baker Academic, 1995.
———. *Introduction to the Theology of Karl Barth*. Grand Rapids, MI: Eerdmans, 1979.
Carson, D.A. *Collected Writings on Scripture*. Wheaton, IL: Crossway, 2010.
———. *The Gagging of God: Christianity Confronts Pluralism*. Grand Rapids, MI: Zondervan, 1996.
———. *Jesus, the Son of God: A Christological Title Often Overlooked, Sometimes Misunderstood, and Currently Disputed*. Wheaton, IL: Crossway, 2012.
Childs, Brevard S. *Old Testament Theology in a Canonical Context*. Philadelphia: Fortress Press, 1985.
———. *The New Testament as Canon: An Introduction*. Valley Forge, PA: Trinity Press International, 1994.
Driver, Daniel R. *Brevard Childs, Biblical Theologian: For the Church's One Bible*. Grand Rapids, MI: Baker Academic, 2010.
Frei, Hans W. *The Eclipse of Biblical Narrative: A Study in Eighteenth and Nineteenth Century Hermeneutics*. New Haven: Yale University Press, 1974.
Holmes, Stephen R. *Listening to the Past: The Place of Tradition in Theology*. Grand Rapids, MI: Baker Academic, 2002.
Humphrey, Edith M. *Scripture and Tradition: What the Bible Really Says*. Grand Rapids. MI: Baker Academic, 2013.
Jenson, Robert W. *Canon and Creed*. Louisville, KY: Westminster John Knox Press, 2010.
———. *The Works of God. Systematic Theology* 2: New York: Oxford University Press, 1999.
Klink, Edward W. III, and Darian R. Lockett. *Understanding Biblical Theology: A Comparison of Theory and Practice*. Grand Rapids, MI: Zondervan, 2012.
Lindbeck, George A. "Barth and Texuality." *Theology Today* 43 (1986) 361–76.
———. *The Nature of Doctrine: Religion and Theology in a Postliberal Age*. Philadelphia: The Westminster Press, 1984.
———. "Postcritical Canonical Interpretation: Three Modes of Retrieval." In *Theological Exegesis: Essays in Honor of Brevard S. Childs*, edited by Christopher Seitz and Kathryn Greene-McCreight, 26–51. Grand Rapids, MI: Eerdmans, 1999.
———. "Scripture, Consensus, and Community." In *Biblical Interpretation in Crisis: The Ratzinger Conference on Bible and Church*, edited by Richard John Neuhaus, 74–101. Grand Rapids, MI: Eerdmans, 2009.
Mathison, Keith A. *The Shape of Sola Scriptura*. Moscow, ID: Canon Press, 2001.
McCormack, Bruce L. "The Being of Holy Scripture is in Becoming: Karl Barth in Conversation with American Evangelical Criticism." In *Evangelicals and Scripture: Tradition, Authority and Hermeneutics*, edited by Vincent Bacote et al., 55–75. Downers Grove, IL: InterVarsity Press, 2004.
McGrath, Alister E. "An Evangelical Evaluation of Postmodernism." In *The Nature of Confession: Evangelicals & Postliberals in Conversation*, edited by Timothy R. Phillips and Dennis L. Okholm, 23–44. Downers Grove, IL: InterVarsity Press, 1996.
Muller, Richard A., and John L. Thompson, eds. *Biblical Interpretation in the Era of the Reformation*. Grand Rapids, MI: Eerdmans, 1996.

Neuhaus, Richard John, ed. *Biblical Interpretation in Crisis: The Ratzinger Conference on Bible and Church.* Grand Rapids, MI: Eerdmans, 2009.

Ollenburger, Ben C., ed. *Old Testament Theology: Flowering and Future.* Rev. ed. Winona Lake, IN: Eisenbrauns, 2004.

Pelikan, Jaroslav. *The Vindication of Tradition.* New Haven: Yale University Press, 1984.

Phillips, Timothy R. and Dennis L. Okholm, eds. *The Nature of Confession: Evangelicals & Postliberals in Conversation.* Downers Grove, IL: InterVarsity Press, 1996.

Runia, Klaas. *Karl Barth's Doctrine of Holy Scripture.* Grand Rapids, MI: Eerdmans, 1962.

Seitz, Christopher, and Kathryn Greene-McCreight, eds. *Theological Exegesis: Essays in Honor of Brevard S. Childs.* Grand Rapids, MI: Eerdmans, 1999.

Smith, James K. A. *The Fall of Interpretation: Philosophical Foundations for a Creational Hermeneutic.* 2nd ed. Grand Rapids, MI: Baker Academic, 2012.

Steinmetz, David C. "The Superiority of Pre-Critical Exegesis." *Theology Today* 37 (1980) 27–38.

———. "Theology and Exegesis: Ten Theses." In *A Guide to Contemporary Hermeneutics: Major Trends in Biblical Interpretation,* edited by Donald K. McKim, 27. Grand Rapids, MI: Eerdmans, 1986.

Thiselton, Anthony C. *The Two Horizons: New Testament Interpretation and Philosophical Description.* Grand Rapids, MI: Eerdmans, 1980.

Treier, Daniel J. *Introducing Theological Interpretation of Scripture: Recovering a Christian Practice.* Grand Rapids, MI: Baker Academic, 2008.

Trueman, Carl R. *The Creedal Imperative.* Wheaton, IL: Crossway, 2012.

Vander Goot, Henry. *Interpreting the Bible in Theology and the Church.* New York and Toronto: Edwin Mellon Press, 1984.

Vanhoozer, Kevin J., ed. *Dictionary for Theological Interpretation of the Bible.* Grand Rapids, MI: Baker Academic, 2005.

———. *The Drama of Doctrine: A Canonical-Linguistic Approach to Christian Theology.* Louisville, KY: Westminster John Knox Press, 2005.

———. *First Theology: God, Scripture & Hermeneutics.* Downers Grove, IL: InterVarsity Press, 2002..

———. "A Person of the Book? Barth on Biblical Authority." In *Karl Barth and Evangelical Theology: Convergences and Divergences,* edited by Sung Wook Chung, 26–59. Grand Rapids, MI: Baker Academic, 2006.

Volf, Miroslav. "Theology, Meaning & Power: A Conversation with George Lindbeck on Theology & the Nature of Christian Difference." In *The Nature of Confession: Evangelicals & Postliberals in Conversation,* edited by Timothy R. Phillips and Dennis L. Okholm, 45–66. Downers Grove, IL: InterVarsity Press, 1996.

Young, Frances. *The Making of the Creeds.* Philadelphia: Trinity Press International, 1991.

Interpreting the Bible in and with the Church

A Response

R. Dean Anderson

I have been asked to provide a ten minute response to the paper of Dr. Venema. It is always a little difficult to decide what and what not to squeeze into a ten minute response. I am thankful that on many fundamental points I can express my whole-hearted agreement with the thrust of what Dr. Venema wishes to communicate to us. There is, of course, little historical distance between his paper and my response, but—if I interpret him rightly—the question of historical distance should not be a factor anyway, given that our mutual context is thoroughly ecclesiastical. Nevertheless, as I understand it, a response is supposed to engender discussion. Let me have a go at that.

Having briefly reviewed the history of the interpretation of the Bible, Dr. Venema, as I read him, in reaction to "post-critical approaches to biblical interpretation" pleads for four principles that should be axiomatic to proper and appropriate biblical interpretation. First, we should have a high view of the inspiration and authority of Scripture, and second, third, and fourth, we need an approach which is canonical, ecclesiastical and confessional. The canonical approach is seen to sweep away "historical-critical" attempts at finding an original meaning in pre-canonical forms of biblical texts. The ecclesiastical approach is posited as the answer to the historical gap between the Bible books and ourselves—the bridge is the universal church. And the confessional approach is its corollary. If the church has always been involved in interpreting the canon of Scripture and such interpretation is rightfully done in the church, then any further engagement in this process must take account of the findings of the church through the centuries.

I am particularly pleased that Dr. Venema has earmarked the question of the inspiration and authority of Scripture as the first pre-supposition. Indeed, it is the self-attestation of Scripture to its own inspiration and authority that is fundamental to any believing approach to the interpretation of Scripture. In fact, this is so fundamental that I wonder whether justice is done to it by juxtaposing it to the other three principles. Could one not argue, for example, that the "post-liberal endeavor to recover a theological reading of the Bible" by its emphasis on the canonical form of Scripture is not so much a "contribution" as a subterfuge, hiding the real issue, namely, a faith commitment to the self-attesting inspiration and authority of Scripture? What good is a canonical reading of Scripture, if the reason for one's acceptance of the canon is an incidental accident of history brought about by some faith community, with little or no real historical or factual basis?

One reason that may lead Dr. Venema to value—with appropriate disclaimers—the post-critical canonical approach is his apparent disdain for any critical historical investigation into the pre-canonical state of the books of the Bible. It is certainly possible that I have misunderstood him at this point, but in a paper on the history of biblical interpretation I found it rather surprising that no reference is made to the concept of the history of revelation. A canonical approach to interpretation (Scripture interpreting Scripture) is starkly pitted against the historical-critical method. Looming in my mind is a rather monstrous caricature that Dr. Venema would surely also oppose: that of a method of interpretation where the full weight of developed dogmatics is read into every Bible book regardless of its position in the history of revelation *versus* an approach which attempts to think through the way each Bible book came into being and took its place in the developing history of this world.

It is true that, traditionally, historical-critical interpretation stemmed from a non-believing approach to the Bible, suspicious of miracles and of divine revelation, and leaving virtually nothing unique to the books of the Bible compared with other literature. This has led to many theories making canonical books little less than fraudulent man-made attempts at persuasion of contemporaries. But does this fact negate the entire enterprise? Does historical-critical interpretation *have* to enter "into an adversarial relation with the church's interpretive tradition"? Could one not argue that belief in the inspiration and authority of the Bible as a divinely given canon *encourages* a real attempt to think through God's revelation of Himself in history, even where that is not explicated in Scripture? After all, if we indeed accept the biblical worldview, may we not think through world history as the gradual unfolding of God's revelation of Himself and his plan of salvation to mankind? Of course "historical-critical" investigation would then be conducted from a *believing* standpoint, one which accepts a biblical worldview, the canon, the divine authority of the biblical books and attempts to think through their origin on their own terms, taking into account what we can learn of ancient civilisations. Any theory proposing that the canonical form is in some way fraudulent would be *ipso facto* rejected.

Take, for example, the early chapters of Genesis. The book of Genesis does not tell us anything of its origin or date of composition. Internal evidence suggests the time of the kings (e.g., Gen 36:31). Of course the book may have been dictated by divine inspiration to an unnamed prophet at that time. But is it not perhaps more probable that there is some connection between God's revelation of antediluvian events at the time of the kings (i.e., a "Genesis") and what his people may have known from the time of Noah and beyond? May we postulate a series of proto-literate cuneiform tablets in the Sumerian language? Such tablets may have eventually been copied into the later literate Sumerian and from there translated into Akkadian and finally into Hebrew. They may therefore have formed a documentary basis for what became the first part of the book of Genesis in the time of the kings. I forego here a discussion of any number of connections and differences to ancient Sumerian literature and the possibility that such a hypothesis could explain certain stylistic features. To my mind, such a hypothesis seems more probable than a prophetic dictation of new revelation in the time of the kings, let alone the idea that Yahwistic prophets got together to compose a theological critique of Babylonian ideas on origins. Answers to these questions give rise to others. What did Noah, for example, know about God, creation, the fall? If Genesis was composed by Moses or by prophets in the time of the kings, what can we assume that Noah or Abraham actually knew? And if they knew of these things, how?

Let me return to the importance of the concept of the history of revelation by way of an illustrative question: If we have a canonical approach, does this mean that we must, for example, interpret the divine plural of Genesis 1 as a reference to the Trinity? Or may we, mindful of God's gradual unfolding of knowledge of himself, posit that while Genesis 1 certainly does not deny the Trinity, it does not reveal it either?

Finally, a few words on the problem of historical distance. I fail to see how the idea of the church interpreting Scripture in a long line of tradition since Pentecost in any way helps to solve this problem. Historical cultural change happens by definition mostly slowly and imperceptibly. Unless I understand Dr. Venema incorrectly, it is an undeniable fact that the cultures in which the churches of Christ in the modern world now find themselves are quite different to the cultures (plural) in the first-century Roman world. If this is not what is meant by "historical distance," I have missed something.

How does the idea of a continuing church absolve this fact? How does the idea of a continuing church absolve present-day interpreters from first establishing the meaning of the biblical text to its first audiences (i.e., original audience(s) and perhaps later intra-canonical interpretation) before proceeding to deduce its meaning for today? Have I wrongly interpreted the third point under section 2 as a criticism (namely, that the historical-critical method focuses on *Sitz im Leben* and what the text originally meant)? How can one not focus on this if one is to do responsible exegesis and provide a firm foundation for interpreting the biblical text for today?

Hopefully my comments and questions will engender some measure of discussion.

Interpreting the Bible in and with the Church
A Rejoinder

Cornelis P. Venema

I am grateful for Dr. Anderson's thoughtful engagement with my paper. I am especially gratified that he approves my basic argument that an approach to the interpretation of Scripture must begin with, and be based upon, the pre-supposition that it is the inspired and authoritative Word of God.

Dr. Anderson does raise several critical observations regarding my paper, and I will take these up in the order in which he presents them:

First, Dr. Anderson expresses the concern that, in my endeavor to maintain the unity and coherence of the Scriptures, I may have left myself open to an approach in which the "full weight of developed dogmatics is read into every Bible book regardless of its position in the history of revelation." I concur wholeheartedly with Dr. Anderson that such an approach to the interpretation of Scripture would be a-historical, and would neglect to acknowledge that the scriptural canon presents the history of revelation in a manner that requires careful attention to the historical location of the canonical books. We may not read back into the earlier record of the history of revelation what is made known to us at a later point in this history. My principal point was not to deny the historical nature of biblical revelation, but to insist that the interpretation of any biblical text must ultimately take into account the totality of the canonical Scriptures. The Bible may not be read atomistically or historicistically. It must be read as a unified and coherent book, and all texts must be interpreted intra-canonically.

Second, Dr. Anderson expresses the worry that my essay does not appreciate the tradition of historical-critical interpretation, particularly the benefits that have come to the church by this method of interpretation. I would observe that my essay offers only the most generic version of the historical-critical method, and does so to illustrate certain typical, and objectionable, features that mark this approach. I am quite willing, however, to concede that the emphasis upon the historicity and particularity of the biblical writings in their specific time and place, is an essential feature of any responsible hermeneutic. I am also appreciative of many of the contributions of historical-critical studies to biblical interpretation. For example, study of the New Testament Gospels has been greatly enriched by historical-critical methods that seek to identify the unique "voice" of each of the Gospel writers in their testimony to Jesus Christ and the coming of God's kingdom in him.

And third, perhaps Dr. Anderson's major criticism of my paper lies in his contention that an approach to biblical interpretation that privileges the church as the primary interpretive community does not solve the problem of "historical distance." He asks: "How does the idea of a continuing church absolve this fact?" I would respond by, firstly, acknowledging that the role of the church as interpretive community does not eradicate entirely the problem of historical distance. However, it does mitigate the problem rather considerably. If the Scriptures remain in their entirety a divinely-authored and truthful norm for the faith and practice of the church, now as in times past, the interpretation of Scripture is always an on-going task of the church. And it is a task that is enriched and rendered fruitful by entering into a long history of interpretation, especially as this is summarized in the church's confessions. But even more importantly, the continued presence of Christ's Spirit, who furnishes the church for its interpretive task, provides a basis for confidence that the church will not fall away fundamentally from the truth of the Word of God. I also would reiterate a point that I make in my essay: the present situation of the church is not radically different from that of the church throughout its history. The church remains in this "time between the times" of Christ's first and second advents, and she continues to read the abiding Word of God in Scripture that speaks with clarity and sufficiency to her faith and practice until Christ comes again.

3

The Hermeneutics of Dogma

Barend Kamphuis

Introduction

April 30, 1944. Dietrich Bonhoeffer wrote his first great theological letter to his friend Eberhard Bethge. At that moment Bonhoeffer had already been in prison for more than a year. That year was filled mostly with preparations for the legal process he was expecting. But this process did not happen, and for many months this was a source of annoyance to him. Once he could accept this, he could devote himself to theology again.

Surprisingly, after this time his letters are about hermeneutics. Bonhoeffer says in this letter of April 30 that the time of religion is over. For Bonhoeffer, religion is a historically determined phenomenon, characterized by metaphysics (God belongs to a world beyond this world), by concentration of the inner self (God is important only for the soul of man), by individualism (the individual man is central) and by infancy (we need God if we are faced with problems we cannot solve).[1] Now it is time for a world without religion. But for this world we need a different style of proclamation: "How do we speak about God—without religion . . . how do we speak in a 'worldly' manner about God?"[2] This calls for a different interpretation

---

1. Bethge, *Dietrich Bonhoeffer*, 979–82.
2. "Wie sprechen wir von Gott—ohne Religion . . . wie sprechen wir 'weltlich' von

of theological concepts. A few days later, on May 5, Bonhoeffer writes about this subject as follows: "At this moment I am thinking about how concepts such as atonement, faith, justification, regeneration, sanctification can be interpreted in a 'worldly' manner."[3] In fact, after this point in time everything Bonhoeffer writes is about this question of the "worldly," not religious, interpretation of biblical and theological concepts.

At present, however, it is not my goal to evaluate Bonhoeffer's diagnosis of a world come of age or its results. I want to point to the importance of hermeneutics. Bonhoeffer is in prison in Berlin, the prime target of the Allied and Russian armies, as he knows. He is in the heart of darkness of the Second World War. Increasingly he realizes that his detention will end in martyrdom. Especially after July 20, 1944, the failure of the attempt on the life of Hitler by Von Stauffenberg, his martyrdom is almost a certainty for him, for he was involved in the preparations for that attempt. But in the midst of all that violence and in the shadow of the gallows he thinks about hermeneutical questions: how can we interpret theological concepts so that they make sense again? How can we learn to speak the Word of God so that the world is changed and renewed by it? Bonhoeffer searches for a new language, "maybe wholly without religion, but liberating and saving, like the language of Jesus, by which men were frightened and yet were conquered by its power, the language of a new justice and truth, language which proclaims the peace of God with man and the nearness of his Kingdom."[4]

Evidently a man can be preoccupied with hermeneutics even more than with his own fate. Thinking about hermeneutics cannot be done without engagement. Hermeneutics is not a technique you can use to be relevant or to say something novel and surprising. On the contrary, it is a searching for a language that fits the gospel in this present time—language that does justice to the power of Jesus' words. Hermeneutics is about the question "to be or not to be" for the church in our times. The meaning of theology as a whole is at stake.

This also means that hermeneutics is a matter of grace, not in the first instance a matter of competence. Of course, you need some technical competence: you must have the ability to read and to interpret, to place texts in their context, to do justice to the historical perspective. But these are

---

'Gott.'" Bonhoeffer, *Widerstand und Ergebung*, 405.

3. "Ich denke augenblicklich darüber nach wie die Begriffe Busse, Glaube, Rechtfertigung, Wiedergeburt, Heiligung 'weltlich' . . . umzuinterpretieren sind." Ibid., 416.

4. ". . . vielleicht ganz unreligiös, aber befreiend und erlösend, wie die Sprache Jesu, dass sich die Menschen über sie entsetzen und doch von ihrer Gewalt überwunden werden, die Sprache einer neuen Gerechtigkeit und Wahrheit, die Sprache die den Frieden Gottes mit den Menschen und das Nahen seines Reiches verkündigt." Ibid., 436.

only marginal considerations. Bonhoeffer was rightly convinced that a new language has to be provided. It is not for us to predict when the sound of this new language will be heard; that is something for which you have to be called. Using non-religious interpretations is not a theological program. Rather, it calls for a total change of the church and for conversion, a *metanoia* of the Christian.[5]

In Reformed theology we speak mostly about biblical hermeneutics: how should we read Holy Scripture? This question is rightly central for us, for the Scriptures are central. Moreover, systematic theology is also concerned with questions about biblical hermeneutics—for instance, about the perspicuity of the Bible. But another question is also important for systematic theology: that of the hermeneutics of dogma. How should we read the doctrinal statements of the church? That is my concern in this paper.

First, I will discuss the historical character of dogma and its consequences for the explanation of dogma. Second, I will examine the consequences of this for commitment to the confession. Then I will discuss the interpretative room, or freedom, that the dogmas of the church offer. Finally I will make some remarks about the metaphorical character of dogma.

1. The historicity of dogma

"Dogma is in its concept and in its development a work of the Greek spirit on the base of the gospel." This is the thesis about Hellenization stated by Adolf von Harnack.[6] With this statement he focuses on the two great and old dogmas of the Trinity and of Christology. In both he sees that the Greek desire for physical immortality has been expressed. According to him, this desire seems to have taken possession of the simple gospel of Jesus Christ. In the doctrine of the Trinity the essential divinity of Jesus Christ is fastened down, for only if he is God by nature can he communicate divine immortality to us. In Christology the unity between Christ's divine and human nature is expressed, for only in this way can man participate in divine immortality. Central is the Person of the Son of God, Jesus Christ, our Saviour, God and man. According to Harnack, this is all Hellenization of the simple message of Jesus. In the Gospel that Jesus proclaimed there was no place for the Son, only for the Father.[7]

---

5. Ibid., 535.

6. "Das Dogma ist in seiner Conception und in seinen Ausbau ein Werk des griechischen Geistes auf dem Boden des Evangeliums." Harnack, *Lehrbuch der Dogmengeschichte*, 20.

7. Harnack, *Das Wesen des Christentums*, 154–55.

With this analysis Harnack placed a heavy emphasis on the hermeneutics of dogma. The context in which dogma has its origin receives a decisive meaning—so decisive, in fact, that dogma itself is at stake. For Harnack the hermeneutical decision of the interpretation of dogma as Hellenization means that today we can abolish dogma. For him the Reformation is the definitive de-Hellenization of Christianity and therefore the principal de-dogmatization. Indeed, Luther did not take this decision, but Harnack does it in Luther's name: away with the dogma!

How should we evaluate this approach? Maybe Reformed people are inclined to start with what Harnack got wrong. But I will start with what he got right. Harnack has convincingly proved the historicity of dogma. Since Harnack, the idea that there is a straight line from biblical texts to dogmatic statements is impossible. The terminology of dogma is historically determined. Terms like *ousia*, *hypostasis*, *prosōpon*, *phusis* do not have their origin in the Bible but in Greek philosophical terminology, and even if they are used in the Bible, they have a different meaning than in dogma (e.g., *hypostasis* in Heb 1:3). But that is not all. Also the problems that are answered in dogmas are given within their historical context: the characteristic Greek ontological questions have had a significant influence on the development of dogma. For example, they are questions about the relation of divine and human being, the relations of mutability and immutability, of death and life. And the very moment when you enter a different climate, the questions change. You can see this already in Augustine. In his work, moral and anthropological points of view are far more important and influence the development of doctrine. In summary, dogmas always call for an interpretation against the background of their time of development.

So far Harnack is right. But he is also wrong. As much attention as Harnack paid to the historicity of dogma, he paid very little attention to his own historical determination. The Jesus Harnack espouses has exactly the same ideas as liberal professors of theology in the late nineteenth century. That should have been a warning! But Harnack would not have been warned. Everything that did not fit in his framework was depreciated. According to him, dogma was in all its aspects a deterioration of the original gospel. But this so-called original gospel itself had its origins more in Harnack's mind than in the Person, words, and deeds of Jesus. So you see how complicated hermeneutical sensitivity is. Your interpretation of dogma itself has to be interpreted.

I realize this myself when I interpret old dogmas differently than Harnack. I do this from a Reformed confessional point of view and I want to maintain this position. But from this point of view I think it is possible to do more justice to dogma than Harnack did.

Indeed, the dogmas of the Trinity and of Christology are influenced by their context, in their terminology and in the way the questions are put. But was there any other realistic possibility? The Church Fathers could not place themselves outside of their times. They were called to proclaim the gospel in their own times. Should Athanasius have formulated Luther's doctrine of justification? Then maybe he would not have been sent into exile so often. But then he would also have had little importance for his own times and for our times. He became a Church Father by asking the questions of his times. So this is an important conclusion: historicity is not a stain on dogma that should be removed. On the contrary, historicity is the power of dogma. The gospel could be confessed not only in the first century in Jerusalem but also in the fourth century in Alexandria; not only in the discussions with Pharisees and Sadducees, but also against Gnostics and Neoplatonic philosophers. For a great part, the value of dogma lies precisely in its historical determination.

But there is more. If you see the historicity of dogma, you also can see that often it stands exactly in opposition to its time. By accepting the questions and terminology of its context, dogma appears to have a transforming power. We can see this in the dogma of the Trinity. You could speak about divine hypostases in a Neoplatonic way. Then *Logos* and *Pneuma* are realizations of the divine being on a lower level than that of the one God—all part of a gradual condescension from the divine being to us. Via spiritual beings and our own soul you eventually arrive at the lower material being. This whole scheme, in which salvation consists in gradual condescension from God to us and in gradual ascension by us to God, was broken through when the church confessed the essential similarity of the divine Persons. Father, *Logos*, and *Pneuma* are not the steps of descending stairs; they are three Persons who participate in the one divine essence. They have the same glory and receive the same adoration. This is how the Nicene-Constantinopolitan confession of AD 381 speaks: the Spirit is, together with the Father and the Son, worshipped and glorified. Salvation is not a gradual process, in which we eventually participate in the divine being. It is the incomprehensible mercy of God, in the descending of his Son for us men and our salvation. We cannot boast in a kinship between our soul and the divine Spirit: "Let him who boasts, boast of the Lord" (1 Cor 1:31).[8] So, at precisely the point at which the dogma is influenced by its Hellenistic context, it appears to contain a radical de-Hellenization of the Christian confession.[9]

---

8. All Scripture quotations in this article are from the Revised Standard Version (RSV).

9. Lohse, *Epochen der Dogmengeschichte*, 71–72.

Thus, the hermeneutics of dogma has two sides. On the one hand, hermeneutic sensitivity puts dogma in perspective: you realize how much dogma is determined historically. But on the other hand, it also has a concentrating effect. You discover how the core of the gospel is maintained and passed on in totally different contexts. For example, you realize the depths of the doctrine of the Trinity. It is not a technical solution for the complicated problem of how the one can also be three. On the contrary, it is the clear confession that God alone is our Savior in Christ through the Spirit. Not only does this confession go very deep into its own time, it also changes that time radically. This combination of concentration and putting in perspective is the core of hermeneutic sensitivity for the history of dogma.

2. The relative commitment to the confessions

Of course, this has consequences for your view of the confessions. In Kampen, as in Hamilton, we not only want to offer a theological education that is faithful to Holy Scripture, but also one that is confessionally Reformed. What does this commitment to the confessions involve when you have a hermeneutical sensitivity and responsibility?

We have to admit, also in this respect, that it means putting things in perspective. Our confession is not a summary of the Bible in the first place. When you have a good summary of a textbook, you can close the book and study the summary. Such is not the relationship between the Bible and the confessions. You are not allowed to close the Bible because you have a confession. The confessions are not summaries of the Bible, but just the *confession* of the truth of the Bible in a specific historical situation. And only as such it becomes also a summary: a human summary of the divine Word with the specific goal to confess in its own time the name of Jesus Christ.

For example, when our spiritual forefathers at Dordrecht had to confess the doctrine of election, they did not find themselves in a sort of vacuum in which they—without any conditions—could make a confession straight from the texts of the Bible. Neither did they find themselves in the position of Augustine, who had to defend the irresistible power of the grace of God in our heart against the moralism of Pelagius. On the contrary, they took their specific position against that of the Remonstrants, who were Protestant representatives of the humanism of that time and who taught that man makes his own contribution to God. They even had to refute, chapter by chapter, the "Remonstrance." So they had to engage themselves in discussions about the relation between time and eternity, between divine and human causality, first and second causes, free will and bound will. Centuries later it was easy for Kohlbrugge to say that the doctrine of justification should have been set as the central point at Dordrecht. *Then* they would have dealt with Arminius decisively![10] But then, in fact, you require from the synod of Dordt that it had to step outside of its own time. Then I would also have liked to see other elements in the Canons. For example, Calvin speaks fittingly in the line of Augustine about the relation between Christ and election: we are elected in Christ; Christ is the mirror of our election.[11] The Canons do not say much about this important subject. That is a pity. Maybe we would have done things differently; however, we do not find ourselves in the same situation. Why do the Canons not accentuate much more the doctrine of grace: that it is grace to receive grace? Does taking the starting-point in God's sovereignty and eternity not have something paralysing in it? Maybe, but in Dordrecht they did not have the liberty to choose a starting point of their own. The Remonstrance dictated the movement from election in eternity, via the history of the work of Christ and via God's work today in the believer, to the expectation for the future. You also see this order in the Canons: eternal election (1), limited atonement through the work of Christ (2), regeneration (3/4), and perseverance of the saints (5). I think you can question this sequence. Looking back from the vantage point of knowing Christ, you can speak about eternal election. But if you turn those two around, you can easily run into problems. You can lose Christ as the mirror of election. The reception of the Canons in Reformed Protestantism shows this danger. Fortunately, each chapter of the Canon starts in the history of salvation. That provides a possibility to escape from thinking with eternity as the starting point. But anyhow, we need this possibility in view of the structure of the Canons as a whole.

In short, the Canons are not the definite summary of the Bible about election. Their historically determined character cannot be overlooked. That is a matter of the contingency of the confession. Hermeneutical sensitivity teaches you that between the Bible and the confession lies history, which is always contingent from a human point of view.

Does this mean that there cannot be a commitment to the confession? I do not think so. You commit yourself to the confessional documents as they are: not the last word about any point of doctrine, but the historically determined confession of it. You realize that your own view on, and explanation of, doctrine is also determined by your own context and can never be the last word. You are glad to be corrected by the confessions in your own

---

10. For these words of Kohlbrugge, see Berkouwer, *Geloof en Rechtvaardiging*, 44n46.

11. Calvin, *Institutes*, 3.22.1 and 3.24.5.

one-sidedness when you forget elements of the gospel or are even in danger of going against it. You love the confession, even and precisely when you see the scars of history on it. You generate the opportunity in the church that we can address each other regarding our commitment to the confession: this is the doctrine we want to defend. This is more than "communion in confessing;" it is a definite commitment to the confession. But it is a commitment to the confession as what it is: a human, historical expression of the gospel. It is not the eternal Word of God, but the contingent human answer to it.

This means that there is always relativity in the commitment to the confession. The best form of subscription cannot change this. Even if you have a commitment to all the articles and points of the doctrine, you do not have a commitment to all letters and commas and periods and constructions. There will always be discussion about the limit of the subscription. The commitment and the subscription are without reservations. But they are not absolute.

So the commitment to the confession appears to have two sides. That is why Guillaume Groen van Prinsterer *cum suis* spoke about being "broadminded and unambiguous,"[12] and Klaas Schilder about being "sympathetic-critical."[13] Groen van Prinsterer spoke specifically about subscription in a legal sense, while Schilder spoke about the relation of Holy Scripture as *norma normans* and confession as *norma normata*. But in both cases two sides of the commitment are expressed. Hermeneutical sensitivity to the character of the confession underlines this. It is a confession of the same gospel that we want to confess today. But it was a confession of this gospel in a different time. The words of our ancestors become our words. But we realize that we would have done things in a different way. The commitment to the confession has to be maintained. But it is a critical commitment. It can be abused from two sides: confessionalism and theological liberalism. But we have to take that risk. Fortunately, the confession has its own strength. Precisely when we place it in the context of its own time, the importance and beauty of the confession will become apparent.

3. The catholic room offered by dogma

We have to add another point of view. Part of the hermeneutics of dogma is that dogma not only indicates a boundary but also offers interpretative room. It is clear that dogma indicates a boundary: "This is the catholic faith,

---

12. Rasker, *De Nederlandse Hervormde Kerk*, 164; Janssen, *By This Our Subscription*, 69.

13. Schilder, *Kompendium Dogmatiek* 1, 16.

which except a man believe truly and firmly, he cannot be saved." So the Athanasian Creed speaks after giving expression to trinitarian and christological dogma.[14] The boundary is clear.

But inside this boundary there is room. For we confess in dogma the doctrine of Holy Scripture. That is the doctrine which is revealed to us. But although it is revealed, this doctrine remains a mystery to us: "O the depths of the riches and wisdom and knowledge of God! How unsearchable are his judgments and how inscrutable his ways!" (Rom 11:33). We need each other to understand more of it. Only with all the saints do we learn to comprehend the love of Christ in all its dimensions (Eph 3:18–19). But even then we cannot come further than a stammering, a speaking in fragments and points of view. It is not given to us to have an overview of the whole. And just because of this we have to leave room for each other.

Think about the doctrine of the Holy Trinity. The formula is simple enough: one in essence, three in persons. But who understands wholly what he is saying with these words? Who is able to comprehend the fullness of the divine essence? Nobody is. That is why there is interpretative room in the church when we speak about Father, Son, and Holy Spirit—room also for different ways of experiencing their work.

Maybe one Christian directs himself to God the Father, the Creator of all things, and gravitates toward his providence. The other has a deep experience of sin and guilt and takes shelter at the cross of Jesus Christ. The third one lives from the power and the gifts of the Holy Spirit. We have no reason to reproach each other for this or to look down upon each other because of this. We have room for diversity in the church. You might call it a "trinitarian spread." We cannot make one framework that fits the experience of faith for all Christians. The doctrine of Trinity itself excludes this.

There is a center: Jesus Christ the crucified. A faith in divine providence that forgets this center becomes a general religiosity which is less than Christian. Living with the Spirit without Christ becomes a theology of glory, in which the reality of sin and the necessity of atonement is forgotten. But also, the one who takes refuge at the cross of Christ may not forget that he who was crucified is now the Lord of glory. Where Jesus Christ the crucified is forgotten, there the boundaries of catholicity are transgressed. But inside these boundaries we have much room. It is room in which you can draw breath and in which you let other Christians draw breath as well. We do not fix one framework for the experience of faith. "Dogmatic" is often a term

---

14. "Haec est fides catholica, quam nisi quisque fideliter firmiterque crediderit, salvus esse non poterit." Denzinger, *Enchiridion symbolorum definitionum et declarationum*, 52.

for one-sidedness and narrowness. But it can also be a term for openness and catholicity.

In the doctrine of Christology you can see the same catholic room. "Great indeed, we confess, is the mystery of our religion: He was manifested in the flesh, vindicated in the Spirit, seen by angels, preached among the nations, believed on in the world, taken up in glory" (1 Tim 3:16). Who is able to penetrate this mystery? Who really understands what it means that God became man?

The message about Christ is brought to us in a story. It starts with the incarnation, the birth of our Savior. It continues about his life on earth. It comes to a high point at the transfiguration on the mountain and to its lowest point at his suffering and death on the cross. Then the story goes upward again: resurrection, ascension, Pentecost. And we expect that in the future the story will end at the Second Coming of Christ, the point in time when every tongue will confess that Jesus Christ is Lord, to the glory of God the Father.

It is not possible to do justice to this whole story, to all of its moments, in your theology or in your experience of faith. Maybe for one Christian the incarnation is a miracle that is enough for all his life. The other lives from the power of the resurrection. Maybe one almost forgets the ascension, the other the transfiguration. Eastern Orthodoxy has a specific feast-day for the transfiguration; for us in the West it is almost a passing incident, without deeper meaning. If we leave room for each other, we can learn from each other. Christian doctrine not only has a "trinitarian spread," it has also a "christological spread."

Again, the center is Jesus Christ the crucified. A theology of incarnation that forgets this center can become pagan pantheism, in which divine and human reality merge without tension. A theology of resurrection can become superficial optimism, in which the necessity of atonement is forgotten. Here again there are boundaries. But just because we have boundaries we should not assume that we do not have interpretative room. Inside these boundaries we can draw breath and learn from each other, worldwide and over the ages. Do we have to criticize Eastern Orthodoxy because in its theology divinization, *theopoiesis*, is so central? Maybe it is more important to accept with joy that there are elements of the gospel maintained there that we have almost forgotten. Do we have to struggle with each other as Reformed and Charismatic people because each is trying hard to understand the mystery, be it with a concentration on the cross, or be it with a concentration on Pentecost? We can save each other from sectarianism by pointing always to Jesus Christ the crucified. But let us enjoy the room of the gospel, the fullness of revelation, the catholicity of the church.

4. Metaphor

"What no eye has seen, nor ear heard, nor the heart of man conceived, what God has prepared for those who love him . . ." (1 Cor 2:9). According to Paul, the doctrine of the gospel lies outside of our experience and our understanding. It is a mystery. We can speak about it, but only because the mystery is revealed to us. That is what Paul says immediately thereafter in 1 Corinthians 2:10, "God has revealed to us through the Spirit." But the question remains: how could God reveal anything to us that lies outside the reality of our experience? Would it not pass over our heads? Would it not remain cryptic?

The answer to this question can be found in God's grace. God's grace is so great that he decided to reach us with his inexhaustible mysteries. He enters our reality with his revelation. He accommodates himself to our experience and our capacity for understanding. From God's side revelation is always a form of condescension and accommodation. Calvin says that God does the same as women who take care of little children and use childish language.[15] God stoops to our level in order to reach us with his revelation. So we receive knowledge about what we cannot understand, the secrets of the gospel.

How does this accommodation work? God accommodates himself to our experience and our understanding by revealing the gospel in images that are borrowed from our reality. That means that everything we know from the gospel has the form of metaphors. In a metaphor a word that belongs to one context is used for another context.

God uses words, images, and descriptions from contexts that we know, to reveal to us the unsearchable mystery of the gospel. We from our side cannot do anything else than stick to these metaphors. We may find our comfort in the salvation through the cross of Jesus Christ, we may sing about it, fortunately we may also dogmatize about it, trying to speak and think systematically about it, but we can never escape this metaphorical language. We cannot speak about God's revelation using a scholarly language in which we have left behind us all figurative language.[16] We always use images from our context to speak about what goes far beyond our experience and understanding.

---

15. "Quis enim vel parum ingeniosus non intelligit Deum ita nobiscum, ceu nutrices solent cum infantibus, quodammodo balbutire?" Calvin, *Institutes*, 1.13.1; cf. Huijgen, *Divine Accommodation*, 157.

16. Contrary to Schilder, *Heidelbergsche Catechismus* 4, 99; cf. De Jong, *Accommodatio Dei*, 215.

This means that each dogmatic statement points beyond itself. *Deus semper maior*, God is always greater. God reveals himself and his acts to us. We may confess him as our Triune God who came to us in Jesus Christ. But we always do so in metaphors. God's revelation is always pure, but never adequate, because metaphors "always contain the whisper 'it is *and it is not*.'"[17] Our confession is not pure, because it is human, and it is not at all adequate. That is why we continue to search for images which are apt for the mystery of the gospel. We continue to search for language which we can understand today. We do so in the expectation that one day we will finally see God in Christ as he is (1 John 3: 2). However, until that time we hope that as an anticipation of the eschatological revelation we will receive the words by which the world will be changed.

That brings me back to the start: Bonhoeffer's urgent questions addressed to church and theology. The hermeneutical question for the interpretation of the gospel in our time is the great question of systematic theology. With this question a tide of further questions comes over us. We have hardly learned to pose these questions, let alone to answer them. How can we express the relation between God's transcendence and immanence in a world that seems to lack all experience of God? What is the meaning of the doctrine of the Trinity for our view of social structures in a time when all structures have lost their stability? How can we express the doctrine of the person of Christ so that it has meaning again in a time that does not think ontologically, but functionally and relationally? What is the meaning of our being in Christ for the believer who wrestles with his identity? How can we express the doctrine of the covenant so that not only the exclusivity, the closed circle of the covenant, but also the open, inviting character of the covenant can be expressed in a society that consists more and more of communities that exclude each other? What do sacraments mean for our time, a time that longs for visibility, tangibility, and actuality? We can continue with these questions. Only posing them is already a life-long task.

But I believe with Bonhoeffer that there is the great possibility of finding a new language by which the world is changed and renewed. I believe that we are asked to search for this new language. I believe that finding it requires the dedication of all our scholarly and spiritual energy. But I also believe that we can rely on God in this. He will us give the words that we need. Hermeneutics in systematic theology is at its core a matter of desire, of prayer, of expectation, of faith. This faith will not be put to shame.

---

17. Sallie McFague, quoted in Brümmer, *Liefde van God en mens*, 16.

Bibliography

Berkouwer, Gerrit C. *Geloof en Rechtvaardiging*. Dogmatische Studiën. Kampen: Kok, 1949.

Bethge, Eberhard. *Dietrich Bonhoeffer. Theologe—Christ—Zeitgenosse*. München: Kaiser, 1986.

Bonhoeffer, Dietrich. *Widerstand und Ergebung. Briefe und Aufzeichnungen aus der Haft*. Edited by Christian Gremmels et al. Dietrich Bonhoeffer Werke 8. Gütersloh: Kaiser, 1998.

Brümmer, Vincent. *Liefde van God en mens*. Kampen / Kapellen: Kok Agora / Pelckmans, 1993.

Calvin, John. *Institutes*. In *Opera Selecta* 3–5, edited by Petrus Barth et al. Monachii: Kaiser, 1928–1936.

De Jong, Jacobus. *Accommodatio Dei: A Theme in K. Schilder's Theology of Revelation*. Kampen: Mondiss, 1990.

Denzinger, Heinrich. *Enchiridion symbolorum definitionum et declarationum de rebus fidei et morum*. Lateinisch-Deutsch ed. Edited by Peter Hünermann. Freiburg: Herder, 2005.

Harnack, Adolf von. *Lehrbuch der Dogmengeschichte* 1. *Die Entstehung des kirchlichen Dogmas*. Tübingen: Mohr, 1909.

———. *Das Wesen des Christentums*. Edited by T. Rendtorff. Gütersloh: Kaiser, 1999.

Huijgen, Arnold. *Divine Accomodation in John Calvin's Theology: Analysis and Assessment*. Reformed Historical Theology 16. Göttingen: Vandehoeck & Ruprecht, 2011.

Janssen, Roelof C. *By This Our Subscription: Confessional Subscription in the Dutch Reformed Tradition Since 1816*. Kampen: Theologische Universiteit van de Gereformeerde Kerken (Vrijgemaakt), 2009.

Lohse, Bernhard. *Epochen der Dogmengeschichte*. Stuttgart / Berlin: Kreuz, 1978.

Rasker, Albert J. *De Nederlandse Hervormde Kerk vanaf 1795. Haar geschiedenis en theologie in de negentiende en twintigste eeuw*. Kampen: Kok, 1974.

Schilder, Klaas. *Heidelbergsche Catechismus* 4. Goes: Oosterbaan & Le Cointre, 1951.

———. *Kompendium Dogmatiek* 1. Kampen: Van de Berg, n.d.

The Hermeneutics of Dogma
A Response

Arjan de Visser

The presentation by Barend Kamphuis brings back good memories. I was a student at the Theological University in Kampen in the 1980s, the time that Prof. Jaap Kamphuis (father of Barend) was professor of Dogmatics. Those were the last years of his professorial career and it was our privilege as students to sit at the feet of a man who was a mature theologian and an inspiring teacher. I was also privileged to be the assistant of Prof. Kamphuis for two years and I cherish the memories.

Soon after I finished my studies at the seminary in Kampen, Barend Kamphuis was appointed to succeed his father as professor of Dogmatology. I remember reading his inaugural speech *Klare taal* (1988) with much appreciation. I was impressed for two reasons: First, because the speech was a sophisticated defense of the perspicuity of Scripture. Second, because the young professor demonstrated that he had the ability to express himself in *klare taal* (clear language).

That was twenty-five years ago. Fast forward to today's presentation on the hermeneutics of dogma. Some first impressions: Our speaker demonstrates that he still has the gift of clarity of language. In addition, we see that he has developed into a mature theologian who has an excellent grasp of theological issues. Another striking aspect is the existential quality of his presentation. This is not theoretical stuff. This is an effort to make the study of doctrine real and contemporary!

At the same time, if we compare today's presentation with the speech of twenty-five years ago there seems to be change in direction (or shall we say emphasis). Reading this presentation caused me to dust off my old copy of *Klare taal* and reread that speech. There is indeed a marked difference. In his inaugural speech Kamphuis defended the clarity of Scripture over against theologians such as Karl Barth, G. C. Berkouwer, and H. M. Vroom. The fact that God speaks to us in human language, our speaker said, does not take anything away from the perspicuity of revelation. God's Word is clear. That is why the church has been able to develop the so-called 'analogy of faith' (*analogia fidei*).

In today's presentation on the hermeneutics of dogma we hear a different emphasis: God's revelation is always pure, our speaker says, but never adequate. God speaks to us by using metaphors and there is something elusive about metaphors. Metaphors always "contain the whisper 'it is and it is not.'"

The 1988 inaugural speech ended with the statement: "The Scriptures are *clear* as the Word of the Triune God."[1] The speech we heard today says: God's Word is never adequate because it comes to us in the form of metaphorical language. The speech ends with the call to search for a new language to express the truth of the gospel.

In order to have into a fruitful discussion about these things, it may be helpful to distinguish between the hermeneutics of dogma and the hermeneutics of Scripture. I will start with the second issue.

My question to Dr. Kamphuis is if he could explain more fully what he means by his statement that God's revelation comes to us in the form of metaphorical language? We all know that the Bible contains metaphors (e.g., God is the *Rock* of our salvation, Jesus Christ is our Chief *Shepherd*, we are *temples* of the Holy Spirit, etc.). But it sounds as if our speaker is saying that pretty much everything that is revealed to us in the Scriptures comes to us in the form of metaphorical language. Much will depend on how you define "metaphor," but if you define a metaphor as something that contains the whisper "it is and it is not," the implication must be that God's Word loses some of its clarity.

I'm wondering how this can be harmonized with our Reformed confessions. In article 5 of the Belgic Confession we confess that "we receive all these books, and these only, as holy and canonical, for the regulation, foundation, and confirmation of our faith." In article 7 we confess that "this Holy Scripture fully contains the will of God and that all that man must believe in order to be saved is sufficiently taught therein."[2] These confessional

---

1. Kamphuis, *Klare taal*, 48; translation and emphasis mine.
2. All quotations of the Belgic Confession are from the *Book of Praise: Anglo Genevan Psalter*.

statements are based on the assumption that, despite historical distance, God still speaks to us today as powerfully and clearly as he spoke to those who received his word first. The ancient word is still adequate and clear.

In his inaugural speech of 1988 Dr. Kamphuis defended the perspicuity of Scripture by referring, inter alia, to the way the New Testament acknowledges the authority of the Old Testament.[3] He pointed to Hebrews 3 where Psalm 95:7 is quoted in such a way that the ancient word has lost nothing of its authority and relevance: "So, as the Holy Spirit says: 'Today, if you hear his voice, do not harden your hearts.' . . . See to it, brothers, that none of you has a sinful, unbelieving heart that turns away from the living God" (Heb 3:7–13).[4]

Today we hear Dr. Kamphuis saying that "everything we know from the gospel has the form of metaphors." What does this mean? How is the confession that God has created everything a metaphor? How is the confession that Jesus Christ came to save his people from their sins a metaphorical statement? What is metaphorical about the confession that those who have died in Christ will be raised from the dead?

In the past, Reformed theologians have argued that even though God accommodates himself to the human capacity to understand, this does not take anything away from the reliability and relevance of the Scriptures for today.[5]

My question to Dr. Kamphuis is: If you say that God's revelation is metaphorical, how are you going to protect the perspicuity and reliability of the Scriptures?

My second question focuses on the hermeneutics of dogma. I appreciate the speaker's explanation about the historical background of our confessions and how that needs to be taken into account as we work with our confessions today. Indeed, the gospel must be proclaimed in such a way that it will speak powerfully to people who live in the current world. I have been a missionary for fifteen years so I know something about the need for contextualization.

At the same time, I'm convinced that the gospel has its own built-in contemporary relevance. If I may share with you an anecdote from my experience as a missionary: In 1989 I went to the mission field in South Africa

---

3. Kamphuis, *Klare taal*, 30–31.

4. All Scripture quotations in this articles are from the New International Version (NIV84).

5. See, for example, De Jong, *Accommodatio Dei*, Second statement (*stelling*): "The value of K. Schilder's contribution to the doctrinal idea of accommodation is especially that in his approach God's adaptation to the human capacity to understand does not take anything away from the full reliability of God's speaking in the Scriptures."

with the assumption in my mind that not everything in our Reformed confessions would be applicable to the African situation. I thought that the Heidelberg Catechism might 'work' in Africa but I was not planning on doing much with the Canons of Dort because I assumed that the Canons of Dort deal with issues that are irrelevant to African Christians. As a result, for the first number of years I never used the Canons of Dort in my teaching. But one day our theological students asked: "What is this other confession that we have in the Reformed tradition, the Canons of Dort?" So I gave them a copy of the Canons of Dort. How amazed I was when the next day they came back to me and said: "This is fantastic stuff! Why haven't you given this to us before?" It was an embarrassing lesson. Not only had I underestimated the capacity of my African students to understand a sixteenth-century confession, I had also underestimated the relevance of the Canons of Dort for people of a different cultural and historical background.

Coming back to the speech of Dr. Kamphuis: I appreciate his concern that the cross and the resurrection should remain central, and I hear what he says about the need for finding ways to rephrase the gospel in contemporary ways. But I trust he would agree that the truth of the gospel remains the same, whatever the culture, whatever the time. Man is a sinner in need of salvation, whether that is in the sixteenth century or the twenty-first century, whether in the Netherlands or in Africa, whether in a post-modern, pre-modern, or modern society. Man is saved by grace. We are sanctified by the work of the Holy Spirit. Christ gathers together his church from among all nations. These truths are always relevant.

When our speaker says that we need to work hard to make sure that the gospel will reach the people of the current society around us, and that we need to give answers to current questions (not the questions of five hundred years ago), I can agree with him. At the same time, we need to remember that every time and culture asks the wrong questions because it is in darkness. Preachers of the gospel need to challenge the questions that are being asked! The problem is often not that Christian preachers are giving irrelevant answers but that the world is preoccupied with the wrong questions.

Dr. Kamphuis ends his speech by calling the church to develop "a new language." I'm wondering what this means, especially if it involves searching for new images and metaphors. Our speaker quotes a phrase from Sallie McFague, a feminist theologian who once suggested we should use the models of "God as mother, lover and friend."[6] This may not be what Dr. Kamphuis has in mind when he suggests we should develop a new language,

---

6. McFague, *Models of God*, 78.

but it raises the question: Where are the controls in your quest for a new language? To what extent are you going to allow yourself to be guided by Biblical and confessional language (whether metaphorical or not)?

Bibliography

De Jong, Jacobus. *Accommodatio Dei: A theme in K. Schilder's Theology of Revelation*. Kampen: Mondiss, 1990.

Kamphuis, Barend. *Klare taal: De Duidelijkheid van de Schrift*. Barneveld: De Vuurbaak, 1988.

McFague, Sallie. *Models of God: Theology for an Ecological, Nuclear Age*. Minneapolis, MN: Fortress Press, 1987.

The Hermeneutics of Dogma
A Rejoinder

Barend Kamphuis

First I want to thank Dr. de Visser for his response. Within the limitations of a short response he engages in a profound discussion of my presentation. His memories of my father as his teacher are moving for me.

In the discussion at the conference in Hamilton we dealt with many aspects of my presentation and of the response by Dr. de Visser. Here I want to answer only one question: did I change my view on the clarity of Scripture since my inaugural address in 1988?

Of course I did! Only God is immutable. Moreover, I would have done a bad job teaching and studying systematic theology during more than a quarter of a century if I had done so without changing my view at any point. In those years I read new publications about the subject and I had discussions with my students and others theologians that helped me to see some aspects more clearly than I did in 1988. I want to mention especially the great study in two volumes, *Die Klarheit der Schrift*, by Bernhard Rothen. Rothen gives a profound analysis of Luther and Barth at this point, much more profound than what I could give in my prior address. I learned much from this text.

Let me mention two points that I now would add to what I said in 1988. First, the clarity or perspicuity of Holy Scripture is a matter of faith. And faith is being certain of what we do not see (Heb 11:1).[1] So we have to accept the clarity of the Bible by faith, even if we do not see it, even if we

---

1. All Scripture quotations in this article are from the Revised Standard Version (RSV).

cannot prove it. Many words of the Bible may be dark for us, and however long we study them, they will remain dark. But we believe that the Word of God is "a light shining in a dark place" (2 Pet 1:19), for we believe that God is light and that in him is no darkness at all (1 John 1:5) and that the Bible is his Word. More than I did in 1988, I would now stress this character of the doctrine of the perspicuity of Holy Scripture as a confession of faith. This is important to me: only by faith can we see the light shining.

Second, this light does not shine only for me, but for everyone who reads the Bible in faith. This means that the perspicuity of Holy Scripture can never be an argument establishing that I read the Bible in a proper way. Maybe another reader understood God's Word better than I. If you believe in the clarity of Holy Scripture, you always have to listen to other people who listen to the same Word. The light of this Word is so powerful that it shines in many dark places. I have learned to be more respectful of other opinions and theologies because I believe that God's Word is clear. If I were to rewrite my inaugural address, I would have to give this aspect its proper place.

Nevertheless, I stick to the confession of the clarity of the Bible. That it is a matter of faith does not diminish it. The confession of the Trinity or of the Incarnation is also a matter of faith. That makes these confessions not uncertain, but more certain. And again, the fact that the Bible is clear not only for me but also for you does not diminish its clarity. It makes this clarity even greater: the light is clear for all.

Indeed, I also maintain the confession that God's Word is pure but not adequate. But this statement does not contradict the confession of the clarity of Holy Scripture. The Bible itself teaches us the incomprehensibility of the mysteries of God: to him be the glory forever (Rom 11:33–36). Our Confession states this; see the Belgic Confession, Article 13. In Reformed theology this incomprehensibility of God is maintained always. Herman Bavinck starts his discussion of the doctrine of God in the second volume of his *Reformed Dogmatics* with the confession of the mysteries of this doctrine. Even Klaas Schilder, who so strongly taught the perspicuity of the Bible over against Karl Barth, acknowledged that God is always greater than his revelation. The Bible is clear precisely in its revelation of the hiddenness of God. So I do not accept the reproach that my speaking about the metaphorical character of our language about God is an aberration of the confession of the clarity of the Holy Scripture. It is precisely because I accept this clarity that I have to confess that God is always too great for me to understand.

Bibliography

Bavinck, Herman. *Reformed Dogmatics*. Vol.2, *God and Creation*. Grand Rapids, MI: Baker, 2004.

Rothen, Bernhard. *Die Klarheit der Schrift*. Göttingen: Vandenhoeck & Ruprecht, 1990.

4

Interpreting Historical Narrative

Truth Claim, Truth Value, and Historicity

Cornelis Van Dam

In discussions on understanding portions of Scripture that clearly and unambiguously narrate historical events the distinction is being made in conservative circles between Scripture's historical truth claim and truth value with a view to validating the truth of the narrative. After the truth claim of a passage has been determined, the question is asked whether the passage does indeed have the truth value it claims to possess. I find this methodology questionable and so I would like to use this opportunity to ask whether such an approach to historical narrative is warranted as a model for biblical exegesis. I will also propose another way. For the purpose of this presentation, the historical narrative in view is for the most part that recorded in Joshua, Judges, 1 and 2 Samuel, and 1 and 2 Kings.[1]

The Main Issue

By distinguishing between the truth claim and truth value of a biblical narrative recounting a historical event, one is separating what is not separated in Scripture. After all, what the Bible states to be true is true (cf. John 17:17).

---

1. I have benefited from feedback from Al Wolters and Carl Van Dam. Needless to say, the views expressed are my own.

When God through his Word informs us of the history of his people we can accept this account as accurate and consistent with what transpired. By importing the categories of truth claim and truth value with respect to what is clearly historical narrative, one is casting doubt on the veracity of the biblical account (cf. Gen 3:1). Furthermore this methodology suggests that we, millennia after the events have taken place, will need to make a judgment on its historicity and be able to separate error from truth with the academic resources at our disposal.

Such a manner of approaching the historical narratives in Scripture does injustice to the nature of God's Word, which is trustworthy, perspicuous, and sufficient. It inevitably leads to questioning Scripture's narratives even if they are obviously meant to be taken as historical accounts. This approach can therefore lead to an outright denial of its obvious statements of fact. The history of this methodology, be it under different names, bears this out.

To be clear, I do not question the good intentions of Bible-believing scholars who employ this methodology. Some make it abundantly clear that for them Scripture's truth claim coincides with its truth value.[2] However, ultimately this strategy of seeking to validate the truth of what is clearly historical narrative is self-defeating, as we hope to see.

I realize full well that there are some difficult historical questions that can arise in studying the Old Testament. And I am not suggesting that we abandon the field to critics. Evangelical scholars should be fully engaged in the investigation and defense of Scripture, also with respect to any thorny issues concerning its historical narrative. But, we must do so on our own terms, assuming the veracity of what is recounted as historical, and not on the terms of critical scholarship. When and if we use their paradigms we should make it clear that we do not share the presuppositions that inform the understanding and framework within which they approach the text.

Before getting further into this topic, let us first briefly consider how this methodology works:

A Summary of this Methodology

Some of the steps to follow in determining whether the truth claim of a text is valid or not[3] are identical to any good exegetical procedure.

---

2. As explicitly acknowledged, e.g., by Long, *The Art of Biblical History*, 29 and Kaiser, *A History of Israel*, 15.

3. I am making use of the study by Long, *The Art of Biblical History*. Long employs this methodology as a believer and clearly acknowledges his faith presuppositions

First, find out what the text actually intends to say. This is of course a vital and basic step. It requires careful listening to the text and deciding on its genre, content, and context. Every serious exegete will do this in order to determine the meaning of the passage, but conservative scholars have generally not done this to establish the truth claim with a view to determining its truth value.

Second, in order to ascertain the truth value of a text, the text should be subjected to two checks.[4] First, one must decide whether the internal testimony of the passage is consistent with the truth claim made. Part of this determination is making sure that standards of coherence and consistency are applied which are appropriate for the genre of the passage. For that reason, "a literary reading of the biblical text must precede any historical reconstruction."[5] Extra-biblical literature can be used in this process because an awareness of ancient narrative conventions and literary strategies can cause us to reassess earlier judgments regarding a text's sense and coherence.[6]

The second check for determining the truth value of a text is to see whether the truth value of its claims jives with other passages of Scripture and with extra-biblical evidence in whatever form.[7]

On the basis of these two checks, the exegete attempts a historical reconstruction that is convincing in view of the evidence adduced.[8]

(e.g., 29). Long's distinction is basic to the methodology employed in Kaiser, *A History of Israel*, 16, and, e.g., Van Bekkum, *From Conquest to Coexistence*, 36-40. There is, however, a significant difference between these two examples. Kaiser starts off with the priority and trustworthiness of Scripture as his basic premise (Kaiser, *A History of Israel*, 14-15), while Van Bekkum's study posits the biblical text and archaeological resources as two sources of information that stand on an equal footing with each other. His study is "a dialogue between the monologues of 'text' and 'artefact'" (Van Bekkum, *From Conquest to Coexistence*, 2). The approaches of Long and Kaiser are very similar. Long, *The Art of Biblical History*, e.g., 219-21 (and also 194-98). Long gives priority to the biblical text over the archaeological evidence. See his chapters 7 and 8 in Provan et al., *A Biblical History of Israel*.

4. See Long, *The Art of Biblical History*, 184-94 and, e.g., Kaiser, *A History of Israel*, 13-16.

5. Lawson Younger as quoted by Long, *The Art of Biblical History*, 187; also see 186. Elsewhere, Long writes: "*Literary understanding is a necessary condition of historical understanding, and both literary and historical understanding are necessary conditions of competent biblical interpretation.*" A little further he notes: "much of the Bible makes *historical truth claims*, and these claims will never be rightly understood unless the *literary* mode of their representation is itself understood." Provan et al., *A Biblical History of Israel*, 81, emphasis Long's, who wrote the chapter in which this quote is found.

6. Long, *The Art of Biblical History*, 187.

7. Ibid., 189-93.

8. Ibid., 193-94.

Let us now consider the background and main features of this approach, how it functions in practice, and the concerns this methodology raises.

The Main Features of this Approach and Resulting Concerns

The Influence of Enlightenment Thinking

Seeking to validate the truth claims of what is obviously Old Testament historical narrative is doing scholarship in the spirit of the Enlightenment. After all, a key principle of the Enlightenment is that autonomous human reason is the final authority of what is true or not.[9] Not surprisingly, a consistent historical-critical approach to the Bible as determined by Enlightenment thinking has denied Scripture's claim to divine inspiration and so cast doubt on all aspects of the Old Testament, including the historicity of its accounts of Israel's past.[10] The net result of much critical scholarship has been that very little of the Old Testament narrative meets the criteria of historicity and so its reliability is either questioned or denied.

The methodology of approaching the text of the biblical narrative with a view to determining whether its truth claim matches its truth value is part of the historical-critical method as influenced by the Enlightenment.[11] That

9. See, e.g., Plantinga, "Two (or More) Kinds of Scripture Scholarship," in *"Behind" the Text*, 27–31. This chapter first appeared in *Modern Theology* 14 (1998): 243–78 and subsequently in fuller form as chapter 12 in Plantinga, *Warranted Christian Belief*. The historical-critical method as referred to in this paper is the method as influenced by the Enlightenment. It can be argued that the historical-critical method also has roots in the desire of the Reformation to get to the literal historical meaning of the text. Johnson, "The Historical-Critical Method," 91–108.

10. This development has been documented by Frei, *The Eclipse of Biblical Narrative*. See also the survey in Osborne, "Historical Narrative and Truth in the Bible," 674–75. For Calvin accepting the factuality of biblical narrative (including his idea of accommodation), see Parker, *Calvin's Old Testament Commentaries*, 96–108. The rise of science and scientific reason as the sole standard of truth was an important element in doubting the historicity of biblical narrative. See, e.g., Van Leeuwen, "The Quest for the Historical Leviathan," 145–49.

11. E.g., "Spinoza was at pains to demonstrate that the literal meaning of the text was to be sharply distinguished from the question of truth, and that the subject matter of the Old Testament was not events but the lessons which they convey." Childs, "The Sensus Literalis of Scripture," 88–89. In contrast, for Calvin there could be no question about the factuality of an account. Parker, *Calvin's Old Testament Commentaries*, 96. For a brief and incisive contrast between scholarship faithful to Scripture and that birthed by the Enlightenment, see Gaffin Jr., "The Redemptive-Historical Response," 179–81. It is of interest to note that Long suggests that the historical-critical method, applied in

method is ultimately hostile to Scripture as the Word of God. You know a tree by its fruit, our Savior said (Matt 7:15–20), and the fruit of seeking to validate Scripture's historical truth claims before accepting them is clear. As the years go by, less and less of the Old Testament is deemed historically trustworthy because autonomous human reason cannot justify believing what Scripture states as historical fact. History also shows that when conservatives adopted the hermeneutical methodology of critics, they could easily sacrifice their dogmatic presuppositions of an infallible Bible. It was then only a matter of time and conservatives reached the same conclusion as the critics with respect to the reliability of God's Word.[12]

However, once much Old Testament narrative had been proven to be unreliable according to critical standards, scholars, both conservative and critical, were left with an unsatisfactory state of affairs. Of what use is an unreliable Bible? And so in order to salvage some meaning from the biblical account, not a few scholars turned their attention away from historical questions to literary approaches to the text. Old Testament narrative was now called a story and the importance of asking whether the events recorded actually occurred was downplayed. The matter of history was shunted to the side.[13] Genre studies became more important and room was made for categorizing some of the narrative as myth and legend.[14] The thinking was, and in many respects still is, that we need not be concerned with historicity. It is the *message* that counts.[15]

---

the context of a theistic set of background beliefs, need not exclude talk of divine intervention. Long, *The Art of Biblical History*, 134. But is this possible given the assumption of the autonomy of reason in the historical-critical method?

12. For Britain, see, e.g., Cameron, "Inspiration and Criticism," 129–59, esp. 146–159; Cameron, *Biblical Higher Criticism*, 279–80. For America, cf. Marsden, *Understanding Fundamentalism and Evangelicalism*, 122–25, 144–45, 150–52.

13. See, e.g., Longman, "History and Old Testament Interpretation," 105–7, the discussion in Bartholomew and Goheen, "Story and Biblical Theology," 162–65 and the helpful survey in Collins, "The 'Historical Character,'" 150–69. Frei argues that the realistic portrayal of events in the Bible does not necessarily mean it is history but it does carry a message. The narrative is a mode of theological reflection. Indeed (quoting Auerbach), the narratives should overcome our reality and we must fit our life into its world. Frei, *The Eclipse of Biblical Narrative*, 3, 9–11. Also see Bray, *Biblical Interpretation*, 485–86. On story in connection with N. T. Wright, see Frame, "N. T. Wright and the Authority of Scripture," 110–12.

14. This was one of James Barr's justifications for considering Old Testament narrative as story. See Barr, *The Scope and Authority of the Bible*, 1–17, discussed in Millard, "Story, History, and Theology," 37–64. Also see Barr, *The Concept of Biblical Theology*, 341–61.

15. It is of course obvious that downplaying the importance of historicity is unacceptable since the biblical message is meaningless if it is not historical (cf. 1 Cor 15:4). One therefore needs to be very careful in what manner one decides to call the

This brings us to another important feature of the methodology of validating truth claims, namely, its use of genre.

The Use of Genre

Understanding the genre of a narrative passage is of great importance and exegetes have always been cognizant of that. It is absolutely essential to determine the genre in order to interpret correctly. For example, recognizing Jotham's account of trees going to anoint a king as a fable is clearly necessary for a correct understanding of what the first part of Judges 9 is all about. The context also makes it obvious that Judges 9:8–15 is a fable. It is a short narrative, uses plants as characters, and teaches a moral lesson. Although this genre is rare in the Old Testament (2 Kgs 14:9 seems to be the only other example), it is readily recognizable and not controversial.

The current study of literary genre has, however, yielded an astonishing array of genres in the Old Testament. A standard work on biblical interpretation lists no less than ten varieties of Old Testament narrative genres, including such as: reports, heroic narrative, prophet story, farewell speech, proverb, and parable.[16] Another study claims as many as eleven sub-genres of the narrative genre of prophet legend, including such as "power demonstration narrative," "succession oracle narrative," and such like.[17] Alarm bells go off in my mind when all kinds of subtle distinctions are made, for I fear the imposition of our way of organizing and writing on the ancient text of Scripture. With so many proposals for genre being made, it is small wonder that scholars admit to the elusiveness of defining a genre.[18] The exercise has a good deal of subjectivity to it and is often governed by one's presuppositions. For these reasons the determination of a genre cannot function as *the* tool for determining and validating biblical truth. Indeed, the use of genre is often an abuse of genre in order to dehistoricize a narrative that is difficult for modern man to accept. At the most basic level, how one approaches the text in question is decisive for evaluating a narrative passage, its context, and its function. Especially important is whether one comes to the text as a skeptic or as a believer. One's basic faith presuppositions will affect how one

---

biblical account a story. See, e.g., the concerns raised by Childs, *Biblical Theology*, 20, 81, 722–23 and Blocher, "Biblical Narrative and Historical Reference," 102–22. Cf. the mediating position in Moberly, "Story in the Old Testament," 77–82.

16. Klein et al., *Introduction to Biblical Interpretation*, 323–40.

17. De Vries, *Prophet Against Prophet*, 52–71.

18. Long, *The Art of Biblical History*, 38–43.

determines and interprets the genre with a view to establishing whether fact or fiction is being presented.[19]

Three examples should suffice to illustrate these points. The first example concerns 1 and 2 Kings. Simon de Vries, in commenting on these books, notes that they record historical events. But when he comes to the narratives of Elijah and Elisha, he suggests that the genre is prophet legend or prophet story in which there is no room for historicity. Indeed, he compares them to Christ's parables.[20] The basis for such a decision is purely subjective. It appears that his assignment of genre may have been influenced by his rejection of the miracles recorded there.

Another example of the arbitrary nature of assigning genres is the account of David killing Goliath (1 Sam 17). Because 2 Samuel 12:19 appears to contradict this account, since it speaks of Elhanan the son of Jaareoregim, the Bethlehemite, killing Goliath, it has been suggested that the account of David killing Goliath was a folk tale. For this genre, it does not really matter who killed Goliath, whether David or Elhanan. The point of the story is to give glory to God who delivered his people in a wonderful way (1 Sam 17:47).[21] So Scripture is in error but the matter of historical accuracy is considered irrelevant. Such a solution is unsatisfying for there is no evidence that 1 Samuel 17 is a folk tale. The conflict between David and Goliath forms part of a larger historical narrative. The folk tale genre has been theorized to solve a problem. Other solutions are available which seek to honor Scripture.[22]

---

19. Long recognizes the crucial importance of presuppositions. Ibid., chapter 4 dealing with history and modern scholarship. See also Long, "How Reliable Are Biblical Reports?" 367–84.

20. The example is noted in Long, *The Art of Biblical History*, 180–84. De Vries lists 11 sub-genres under the genre "Prophet Legend" in *Prophet Against Prophet*, 53–56. This type of dehistoricizing jives with Alter's statements that "prose fiction is the best general rubric for describing biblical narrative." Alter, *The Art of Biblical Narrative*, 27. "There is a horizon of perfect knowledge in biblical narrative, but it is a horizon we are permitted to glimpse only in the most momentary and fragmentary ways." Alter, *The Art of Biblical Narrative*, 197. Cf. Osborne, "Historical Narrative," 680–81.

21. See the report which served the Gereformeerde Kerken in Nederland, *God met ons . . . over de aard van het Schriftgezag*, 65. For leaving the possibility open that the text is not historically accurate on the grounds of genre, see Van Bekkum, "Het Oude Testament als historisch document," 353–54.

22. Such as, e.g., considering on the basis of 1 Chr 20:5 that Elhanan actually killed Goliath's brother. See on this issue, e.g., the discussion of Long in Provan et al., *A Biblical History of Israel*, 221–25 and Walton, *Joshua, Judges, Ruth, 1 & 2 Samuel*, 477. The account is sometimes simply defined as a myth. Greenberg, *101 Myths of the Bible*, 276–79.

A final example is the account of the shadow turning back ten steps on the stairway of Ahaz as a sign to Hezekiah that God would heal him (2 Kgs 20:10–11; Isa 38:8). Because this was a miraculous event (2 Chr 32:24), doubt has been expressed about its historicity and the account has been called a prophetic legend or prophetic miracle story.[23] However, it is rather arbitrary to call this a legend or miracle story when it is found in the midst of historical narrative.[24]

These examples make clear that the determination of a genre can easily become a tool to dehistoricize a narrative passage. It is good to keep in mind the rule that Philips Long suggests: "If the larger narrative complex exhibits a historiographical intent, then, barring indications to the contrary, smaller units within the complex should be assumed to share in the historical impulse."[25]

The above examples also show that determining historicity on the basis of genre is at best a very subjective exercise and scholars often disagree with each other. However, the net result is that more and more Scripture tends to be designated as myth, legend, or metaphor on the basis of genre considerations. This trend is even noticeable in circles considered conservative. There are parts of Scripture which have always been regarded as historical narrative for almost two thousand years, but now genre categories are being imposed on them under the pressure of critical scholarship to make them less than historical.[26]

Another factor to consider when thinking of the proliferation of genre categories is that the study of genre and literary devices do not necessarily advance the exegetical cause beyond the traditional conservative approach of studying the text carefully, taking into consideration both the immediate and larger context. It is, for instance, interesting to note that Long's interpretation of 1 Samuel 8–13, which benefits from his expertise in genre studies,

---

23. See respectively Gray, *I & II Kings*, 243–45 and Nelson, *First and Second Kings*, 243–45.

24. Wiseman, *1 and 2 Kings*, 287.

25. Long, *The Art of Biblical History*, 180.

26. Some recent Dutch examples: Doedens questioned the historicity of Genesis 1 (an etiology?), in "Taal en teken van trouw," 71–108, esp. 103–106. De Bruijne asked whether understanding parts of narration in Scripture as metaphorical (Gen 6:1–4) may not "solve" certain historical issues: "Hermeneutiek en metaforie," 109–60 and "Er wordt verteld," 161–94. As noted earlier, Van Bekkum raised doubts about the truthfulness of David's slaying Goliath on the basis of genre considerations. Van Bekkum, "Het Oude Testament als historisch document," 353–54. He also denied that the sun stood still on the basis of literary conventions. See Van Bekkum, *From Conquest to Coexistence*, 283–95.

yields no significant new exegetical results compared to an older exegete such as C. J. Goslinga on the same passage.[27]

Finally, it should be noted that the exercise of establishing and validating truth claims through the use of genre designation does little to reach skeptical scholars. Someone who is critical of Scripture's claims will generally not be convinced by arguments for the truth value of a given portion of Scripture on the basis of genre. One could, for example, show that the passage is historical narrative, but if it contains a miracle, the modern skeptic will never accept the passage as historical for God's direct action in this world has been a priori excluded.

Another important feature of the methodology under discussion is its use of archaeology.

The Use of Archaeology

Archaeological discoveries have been a great blessing in biblical studies and we hardly need to dwell on that.[28] However, when it comes to using archaeology to validate truth in Scripture, one must be very careful. There are clear

---

27. Compare Long, *The Art of Biblical History*, chapter 6 in his treatment of 1 Sam 10:5; 13:2ff and 1 Sam 13:4, 8 with the exegesis of Goslinga, *Het Eerste Boek Samuël*, 223–24, 254, 256, 258. The point at issue is whether there are multiple accounts of Saul becoming king. The answer is no. But there are three steps in becoming king: designation, demonstration, and confirmation. Samuel anointed Saul and thereby *designated* him as king (1 Sam 10:1). In his first charge to Saul in 1 Samuel 10:7–8, Samuel hints that Saul should attack the Philistine garrison in Gibeah. This would provoke a response from the Philistines. But then Saul is to go to Gilgal and wait for seven days for Samuel to come and bring a sacrifice to the Lord (Long, *The Art of Biblical History*, 212–13). Saul, however, does not attack the Philistines at this point. But he does rescue Jabesh-gilead from the Ammonites (1 Sam 11). This provides the *demonstration* of his position as anointed one and the kingship is renewed (1 Sam 11:14). Saul's disobedience for not attacking the Philistines is finally undone in 1 Samuel 13 when Jonathan attacks the Philistines. In accordance with the earlier instructions received (1 Sam 10:7–8), when the Philistines would be attacked, Saul goes to Gilgal to wait for Samuel. Thus Saul faltered in his first charge which Jonathan ended up doing and he failed the next test in waiting for Samuel. Thus the *confirmation* of Saul's kingship which would have come through his obedience did not occur. Thus Saul was not fit to remain on the throne as theocratic king (1 Sam 13:13–14). Long solves the problem of what initially seems to be a confusing text by making use of a literary device called gapping (*The Art of Biblical History*, 216). But Goslinga, through careful contextual exegesis came to the same conclusion without resorting to this literary device.

28. One thinks of such outstanding finds as the Black Obelisk of Kalakh which shows Jehu or his envoy submitting to the Assyrian king Shalmaneser III (858–823 BC) or the Cyrus cylinder, describing how Cyrus captured Babylon in 539 BC, not to mention the Dead Sea Scrolls. For a handy summary of important findings now in the British Museum, see Barnett, *Illustrations of Old Testament History*.

limitations to archaeology which we need to be aware of. Let me mention only two:

Archaeology can elucidate and supplement the Old Testament and so help our exegesis, but it can never be used as a means to prove the Bible. To place such a high premium on archaeology invites questions such as "what about those areas in the Old Testament where archaeology has made no contribution? Are they to remain open to doubt?"[29]

A second limitation is the fact that the interpretation of archaeological finds depends very much on one's presuppositions. For example, there are at least three schools of thought on Israel's entering Canaan, all based on the same archaeological evidence. The one school says it was a military conquest as Scripture indicates; another says Israel infiltrated peacefully into Canaan, as archaeology is said to confirm; and yet another thesis is that there was a peasant revolt.[30] And then there are, of course, the so-called minimalist and maximalist approaches which interpret archaeological findings in relation to Scripture in vastly different ways.[31] Archaeological arguments will not sway the skeptic. One need only, for example, browse through book reviews of Kenneth Kitchen's study, *On the Reliability of the Old Testament*, to see how scholars react to his book according to their presuppositions. They are generally not swayed by his archaeological arguments to change their position.[32] In other words, we do not need to use the methodology of validating truth claims through archaeology in the hope of winning over skeptics. The problem of skepticism is often one of unbelief.

Archaeology as a discipline cannot conclusively validate or prove biblical truth to the satisfaction of all concerned. Positing a certain amount of probability is not good enough when judging the truth of Scripture. This takes us to the next problem of following a methodology of determining truth claim and truth value by the use of genre and archaeology.

---

29. Cf. Na'aman, "Does Archaeology Really Deserve the Status?" 165–83.

30. See, e.g., Long in Provan et al., *A Biblical History of Israel*, 139–47. Also see Yadin, "Biblical Account of the Israelite Conquest," 16–23 and, e.g., Shanks, "Letter from a Hebrew King?" 52–56. See further Brandfon, "The Limits of Evidence," 5–43.

31. The example of the "house of David" inscription is a case in point as the very different interpretations indicate. Cf., e.g., Kitchen, *On the Reliability of the Old Testament*, 36–37, 509–10 and Davies, "The Beginnings of the Kingdom of Judah," 54–61.

32. See, e.g., the review by Lemche, "On the Reliability of the Old Testament," 375–77. Similarly, Grabbe raised doubts about the historicity of Joshua in a negative review of Van Bekkum, *From Conquest to Coexistence* which bolsters Joshua's historicity, in Grabbe, review of *From Conquest to Coexistence*, 66. For a similar hostile treatment of another conservative work, see Grabbe, "The Big Max," 215–34. The authors of the book reviewed give a rebuttal in the next chapter.

The Lack of Certainty

The process of evaluating the truth claim of a biblical historical narrative according to our resources and logic never leads to the assured conclusion that the event or events really happened.[33] For example, the most definitive events in Israel's history, the exodus and conquest, were questioned once the influence of the Enlightenment was felt in Old Testament studies. The result today is that with all the available biblical and archaeological evidence, views on the historicity of the exodus and conquest vary widely. There are scholars who in faith accept the biblical account and reject modern skepticism but use all the scholarly tools available to them to understand the biblical text as well as possible and so write a modern history of Israel.[34] However, there are also those academics who do not accept the biblical account as it is but subject it to historical tests to determine what actually happened. Those who do this, however, end up with widely diverging view points and some even deny the exodus took place at all even though they all use the same historical and archaeological resources. When Scripture's claims need to be validated by human reason, there is no certainty that the outcome is trustworthy and true. Autonomous man's attempt to reconstruct what he thinks may actually have happened ends up with only a probability of what took place and therefore the results of different investigations will vary significantly.[35]

Not surprisingly, when conservative scholars play by the same rules as the critical scholars in an attempt to convince them of the validity of the biblical account, their conclusion is also only one of more or less probability, and they acknowledge that.[36] Such a lack of certainty is inherent in the method. By human reckoning there is no such thing as absolute proof for any past historical event and to attempt to build a history on that basis is simply impossible.[37] To have absolute surety one needs to accept Scripture's self-testimony as reliable.[38] It is of course true that exegetical results of a

---

33. See, e.g., Provan in Provan et al., *A Biblical History of Israel*, 54–56.

34. So, e.g., Merrill, *Kingdom of Priests*, 15–19, 57–140 and Wood, *A Survey of Israel's History*, 137–53.

35. For a survey of modern scholarship on the exodus and conquest, see respectively Kitchen, "Exodus, The," 701–2 and Dever, "Archaeology and the Israelite 'Conquest,'" 545–58.

36. E.g., with respect to what Long calls "Israel's emergence in Canaan," his final, somewhat negative, conclusion is that "we see little reason that an attempt to write a history of Israel's emergence in Canaan should take a path radically different from the one that the biblical texts already suggest." Long in Provan et al., *A Biblical History of Israel*, 139, 192.

37. Provan et al., *A Biblical History of Israel*, 42–43.

38. A point acknowledged, e.g., by Long, *The Art of Biblical History*, 221. It is telling,

difficult text are not always clear cut and one's interpretation of how certain events relate to each other can be uncertain.[39] However, there need be no doubt that the events in question did occur. But that certainty is only possible by a true faith. No academic argument can convict one that what Scripture says is trustworthy and true. The work of the Holy Spirit is needed.[40]

Another point to note is that with the perceived need to validate biblical accounts, the average Bible reader becomes dependent on the specialist with respect to the reliability of the historical narrative which he or she is reading. After all, the conclusions which specialists in literary analysis or archaeology reach are eventually reflected in resources for studying the Bible. However, readers of Scripture should be convicted of the truth of what they read by the inspired text of the historical narrative and not because some human authority has concluded that an event is believable or not.

In sum, when it comes to accepting or not accepting the truthfulness of biblical accounts that clearly intend to recount history, one's presuppositions are absolutely crucial. The attempt to objectively validate the truth claims of biblical narration by whatever method never ends in a positive affirmation acceptable to all. As those who hold to the trustworthiness of Scripture we must recognize that also in the academic world there is a struggle between belief and unbelief. There is no neutrality in biblical studies and we should not pretend that there is. The antithesis is a reality also in the workplace of the scholar studying Scripture.[41] We therefore need to build a hermeneutic that is positive and goes beyond trying to validate biblical truth and so serve the people of God. The Word has been given for their edification.

This brings us to the positive part of this presentation, a hermeneutical proposal.

---

however, that after considering the biblical evidence of Joshua and Judges with respect to the settlement in the land of Canaan, Long concludes in such a way that the historicity is less than certain. He writes: "*Historically*, the general picture seems plausible enough but at this point remains unproven, since internal coherence, while a necessary condition of historicity, is not a sufficient condition.... The texts of Joshua and Judges do appear to make historical truth claims, and so for those who assume the truth value of the Bible's truth claims, this appearance may suffice." Provan et al., *A Biblical History of Israel*, 168 (italics are in the original text).

39. Calvin often used the terms "probably" or "we may conjecture" when seeking answers to questions not directly addressed by Scripture or when trying to reconstruct exactly what happened on the basis of sparse biblical information, but he never doubted the recorded facts. Parker, *Calvin's Old Testament Commentaries*, 91, 96. Also see, e.g., the probable conclusion to the extended example in Long, *The Art of Biblical History*, 222–23.

40. See note 57.

41. See, e.g., Poythress, *Inerrancy and the Gospels*, 81–83, 100–104.

Interpreting Narrative Passages

I would now like to outline how I think we, as believing scholars, should approach biblical narrative.

Returning to the Plain Sense of Scripture

In our exegetical methodology we should return to the so-called pre-critical practice which accepted Scripture's claims with a believing heart and see where the exegesis and interpretation of the passage takes us from there. In the words of John Calvin: "Let us know, then, that the true meaning of Scripture is the natural and obvious meaning; and let us embrace and abide by it resolutely. Let us not only neglect as doubtful, but boldly set aside as deadly corruptions, those pretended expositions, which lead us away from the natural meaning."[42] Scripture should not be approached with suspicion, as if it is guilty of transmitting some wrong information, until we are satisfied by the court of our human judgment that it is telling the truth. In other words, I am arguing for the plain reading of Scripture's narrative in faith. Faith seeks understanding. Only then does the ancient text of God's Word have a credible message for us today. Instead of speaking of truth claim and truth value, we should speak of understanding the obvious meaning of the text. If historical facts seem to conflict, we should try to make sense of what is written rather than discounting the narrative or parts of it.

I fully realize that this approach puts us at odds with critical scholarship and our post-modern times, but it is precisely for that reason that those with a high view of Scripture need to continue to develop a hermeneutic that does justice to the unique character of the Word of God and is molded by that Word. This does not exclude entering into the dilemmas that post-modern academia puts before us in order to confront them. We can answer their arguments point by point. But that is a defensive operation. Ultimately our exposition and defense of Scripture will rest on totally different presuppositions. In the end, it will come down to the conviction of faith rather

---

42. Calvin, *The Epistles of Paul*, 85. The natural and obvious meanings "echo the objectivity and constancy" of the true meaning. The literal sense "anchors us firmly in the text. The meaning is contained in the words." Parker, *Calvin's New Testament Commentaries*, 64. Also see Gignilliat, "Paul, Allegory, and the Plain,"135–46; Opitz, "Oecolampadius, Zwingli and Calvin," 440–41. John Calvin's exegetical method with its stress on the literal text is more in continuity with medieval biblical interpretation than a precursor to so-called "critical" exegesis. See Muller, "Biblical Interpretation," 8–13.

than being convicted only by logic and what seems reasonable in our day and age.[43]

We need to build a biblical hermeneutic that is not beholden to the mold of Enlightenment categories and dilemmas. To prevent misunderstanding, we must not be afraid to learn and benefit from critical scholarship where it has made valuable contributions. For example, we can benefit from a current emphasis on the literary character of the Old Testament and so have a renewed appreciation for the beauty, selectivity, and subtlety of God's Word.[44] But, at the same time we need to keep in mind our own faith presuppositions and recognize that also in scholarship there is no such thing as neutrality. Indeed, our theology should inform our exegesis. They are basic to our presuppositions.[45]

A present challenge, especially for beginning students of Scripture, is that it is becoming increasingly difficult to discern where an author's loyalty lies. John Frame has correctly noted that often it is not easy to classify books as liberal and conservative or faithful to Scripture because many authors "seek to avoid, disguise, or suppress the antithesis between Christianity and liberalism."[46] But you cannot have a dual allegiance.

---

43. Kuyper and more recently Alvin Plantinga have stressed the difference between scholarship that subjects itself to the plain teaching of Scripture and that which does not. Kuyper: "But we emphatically assert that these two kinds of people [regenerate and unregenerate] devote their time and their strength to the erection of two different structures, each of which purposes to be a complete building of science. If, however, one of these two is asked, whether the building, on which he labors, will truly provide us what we need in the scientific realm, he will of course claim for himself the high and noble name of science, and withhold it from the other." Kuyper, *Encyclopedia of Sacred Theology*, 110. Also see Plantinga, "Two (or More) Kinds of Scripture Scholarship" (or Plantinga, *Warranted Christian Belief*, chapter 12).

44. See, e.g., Silva, "The Case for Calvinist Hermeneutics," 254–59. Also by way of example, see Provan, "Hearing the Historical Books," 258–67.

45. "My theological system should tell me how to exegete." Silva, "The Case for Calvinist Hermeneutics," 261. Silva gives three reasons for this statement in subsequent pages: 1. "Systematic theology is the attempt to reformulate the teaching of Scripture in ways that are meaningful and understandable to us in our present context." 2. "The unity of Scripture demands that we see the whole Bible as the context of any one part." 3. Whether we admit it or not, everyone exegetes according to his theological presuppositions.

46. Frame, *The Doctrine of the Word of God*, 343–44, also see the entire appendix of which these pages are a part. De Boer asks whether the Theological University of Kampen still sets itself up antithetically as it did in the past in his speech, "Is met *Woord op Schrift* Kampen op drift?" (12), delivered on the study day, "De kracht van het Woord" at the Theologische Universiteit Kampen on January 23, 2010. At the time of writing, this address was still unpublished. The reality of the antithesis was clearly recognized by an earlier generation of Kampen scholars. See, e.g., Van Bruggen, "Hermeneutics and the Bible," 166–67.

The Nature of the Old Testament Narrative

The historical narrative, stretching from Joshua to Kings, is prophetic literature. From earliest times, the Old Testament, the Hebrew canon, was referred to as the Law, the Prophets, and the Writings. The prophets include all the so-called historical books, running from Joshua to Kings. It is for this reason that the Lord Jesus often referred to the Old Testament by simply speaking of Moses or the Law and all the prophets (Matt 11:13; Luke 16:31; 24:27; John 1:45) or more fully as "the Law of Moses and the Prophets and the Psalms" (Luke 24:44).[47]

The fact that Scripture refers to what we often call historical books as prophetic is important to note. Acknowledging this prophetic identity has several implications. It indicates that in Scripture there is no such thing as history writing for its own sake, that is, history writing which has as its purpose to relay as objectively as possible a series of historical causes and effects. What is recounted to us in Scripture stresses God's activity and plan in the history of his people. Such divine involvement in the affairs of humans includes many miracles.

In the biblical narrative God is ultimately the main character. It is therefore not surprising that scholars have noticed in biblical narrative a certain reticence about giving a lot of information about human character description and development. Only what is of special significance for the account is given in some detail, such as the length of Absalom's hair (2 Sam 14:26; 18:9) and Bathsheba's beauty (2 Sam 11:2). For the rest, the details in biblical narrative are typically relatively sparse.[48] Furthermore, the biblical account often leaves out material that you would expect an author to give, a phenomenon called "gapping."[49] These features of the biblical narrative are understandable when one realizes that the accounts are not about people in the first place, but about God and his covenantal relationship with his people. In every narration, God is the chief character and the prime agent.[50] It is *his* account and his revelation to his people. The narratives are structured to that end.

---

47. All Scripture quotations in this article are translated by the author himself.

48. Longman, "Biblical Narrative," 73, the classic essay in Auerbach, *Mimesis*, 3–23, and Alter, *The Art of Biblical Narrative*, 143–62.

49. Longman, "Biblical Narrative," 77 and Long, *The Art of Biblical History*, 214–16.

50. See, e.g., De Graaf, *From Creation to the Conquest of Canaan*, 19. This theocentric emphasis runs through the entire work of De Graaf as he relates the biblical narrative. In the case of a book like Esther, the absence of God's name does not diminish the fact that God is in control. He providentially provides so that the old enemy Amalek in the person of Haman is defeated in his struggle against the covenant people of God. See, e.g., Longman and Dillard, *An Introduction to the Old Testament*, 221–22.

And so prophetic history writing is subservient to the overriding goal of God's self-revelation to Israel and to us today. This revelation speaks of his granting salvation to his people. But deliverance from the foe cannot be taken for granted. God is the God of the covenant and the facts are therefore placed within the framework of God's demands. He responds with blessing those who obey him and with judgment for those who disobey. This prophetic history writing therefore called God's people back to obeying the Lord (cf. Ps 78). What the author wanted to stress, such as the sin of Achan, is described in great detail (Josh 7) and what is considered less important is omitted entirely (e.g., the civic good that Saul and Omri must have done for their people). There is no pretense of so-called objectivity or completeness from a historical perspective. These are prophetic books with a clear message for God's people, containing within it different styles of writing (narrative, poetry, parable) all subsumed under the over-riding prophetic purpose of the whole.[51]

This type of prophetic history writing is found nowhere else in the ancient Near Eastern world. It is characterized by sovereign God working purposely toward a goal. This characterization gives the accounts of different events a unity and cohesion that is lacking in the narratives of ancient Israel's contemporaries. Ancient Near Eastern polytheistic religions pictured the gods as immanent in nature. When they did intervene in history it was only to maintain certain norms. Consistent with a cyclical view of history there was no movement to an overriding goal. Historical accounts were typically written to glorify a particular ruler or to give legitimacy to a certain dynasty and truth was not of paramount concern.[52]

With this recognition of the disparity between Old Testament history writing and that found elsewhere in the ancient world comes the need to be careful how one uses these extra-biblical writings in order to understand Scripture. Only in Scripture do we find a unity and meaningfulness of history from the beginning of time to its end. Indeed, as God's true revelation

---

51. See, e.g., Aalders, *De geschiedschrijving in het Oude Testament*, 160–61 and Woudstra, "Event and Interpretation in the Old Testament," 53–55. For current discussion on truth of the event and truth of the interpretation see Osborne, "Historical Narrative," 682–83.

52. On the unique historiography of Israel, see Porter, "Old Testament Historiography," 130–31. Also see Woudstra, "Event and Interpretation in the Old Testament," 56–57; Maier, "Truth and Reality," 201–6, and the cautionary notes of Long, *The Art of Biblical History*, 43–48. The uniqueness of Israel's historiography can be maintained in spite of the challenge from Albrektson, *History and the Gods*. This challenge was answered by Lambert, "History and the Gods," 170–77 and Lambert, "Destiny and Divine Intervention," 65–72. With respect to the historical reliability of ancient near eastern historical documents, see Laato, "Assyrian Propaganda," 198–226.

to his people, this literature stands in a class by itself and should be treated as such.

In this connection, it should also be noted that the modern critical dilemma of the history of Israel's faith (what Israel believed happened, *Heilsgeschichte*, which is non-verifiable) and what actually happened as reconstructed by the modern scholar (*Historie*, which is verifiable) is just that: a modern dilemma, and a false one at that. History was one for Israel. God worked his salvation in real time and space. The biblical account of the past is not the believing community's creation, but God's doing as recorded by his prophets under the guidance of his Spirit for instruction and direction.

And therefore to evaluate this revelation according to the canons of modern so-called objective scientific history writing does injustice to the Word of God. Scripture never claims, for example, to be comprehensive, objective, or always in chronological order. That does not always happen.[53] But what it states can be understood within its own context and accepted as true.

Key Elements for a Biblical Hermeneutic

In summary, here are several key elements for a biblical hermeneutic of Old Testament narrative passages, along with some implications:[54]

1. Approach the reading and interpretation of Scripture with a believing heart.

God's Word teaches that one cannot rightly discern Scripture if one is not enabled by the Holy Spirit (1 Cor 2:13–14; 2 Cor 3:14–15; Heb 4:2). Faith

---

53. E.g., Judges 10:7 gives the appearance that the Philistine oppression occurred prior to that of the Ammonites. However, the 40 year Philistine oppression (Judg 13:1) probably occurred after the oppression of the Ammonites. The main reasons are: 1. The Ammonites are mentioned second in Judges 10:7–8 because their oppression is described in the passage immediately following. The Philistines are not mentioned again until Judges 13:1 where the phraseology suggests an oppression subsequent to that of Ammon. 2. Ammonite power seems to have extended west of the Jordan according to Judges 10:9 which would have been unlikely if the Philistines were occupying the West Jordan region at the same time. 3. The loss of 42,000 men by Ephraim in their struggle with Jephthah after his defeat of Ammon (Judg 12:1–6) would certainly have invited the conquest of the West Jordan region by the Philistines later that year. For other examples, see Aalders, *Oud-Testamentische kanoniek*, 162.

54. For a classic Reformed exposition of basic hermeneutical principles, see Greijdanus, *Schriftbeginselen*, 100–145.

and prayer are needed.⁵⁵ The correct discernment of Scripture includes knowing the narrative in a way different from any abstract scholarly work. It means appropriating and experiencing it as part of our own history. It is our God who is active in the Old Testament accounts, working also for our salvation. He now confronts us, also in the narrative passages, with his Word. We need to respond in faith and appropriate his Word. This process of appropriation has been called "inhabiting the story."⁵⁶ Faith does not question whether the account is true. We positively accept it as such. It is part of our knowing God and his revelation. Indeed, the verification of Scripture comes by the internal testimony of the Spirit.⁵⁷

The need for the guidance of the Holy Spirit also applies to the science of exegesis. "The fear of the Lord is the beginning of knowledge" (Prov 1:7), also in seeking to understand Old Testament narrative. If we study Scripture using the assumptions of modern critical scholarship, we will not hear God speaking to us and we will invariably end up doing injustice to the Word of God. To put it differently, if we begin with the presuppositions of unbelief we will end up with the conclusions of unbelief.⁵⁸ This brings us to a second point.

2. Biblical presuppositions must shape our approach.

Such presuppositions include the unity and perspicuity of Scripture as well as its sufficiency. As those living in the world of post-Enlightenment scholarship, this is difficult to do. We live in the midst of a postmodern culture.

---

55. See, e.g., Maier, *Biblical Hermeneutics*, 50–51. Calvin on 1 Corinthians 1:20: "Man, with all his acuteness, is as stupid for obtaining of himself a knowledge of the mysteries of God, as an ass is unqualified for understanding musical harmonies." Also De Greef, "*De ware uitleg*," 196–97. For a recent reminder of the importance of prayer for interpreting Scripture, see Spears, "Preaching the Old Testament," 402–8.

56. Wright, "Inhabiting the Story," 495–98.

57. *Belgic Confession*, Article 5. "We believe without any doubt all things contained in them, not so much because the church receives and approves them as such, but especially because the Holy Spirit witnesses in our hearts that they are from God, and also because they contain the evidence of this in themselves; for even the blind are able to perceive that the things foretold in them are being fulfilled." See also Calvin's *Institutes*, 1.7.4, Kraus, "Calvin's Exegetical Principles," 9, and, e.g., the study of Van den Belt, *The Authority of Scripture*, and Murray, "The Attestation of Scripture," 42–54.

58. See Young, *Thy Word is Truth*, 191 and the entire chapter. When speaking of the clarity of Scripture, Van Bruggen notes: "The catholic truth is so clear in the Bible that it does not depend on any hermeneutical discussions. . . . We must avoid giving the impression that orthodox faith depends upon hermeneutical decisions. Unbelief defends itself with hermeneutical decisions! Don't take over that way of reasoning." Van Bruggen, "Hermeneutics and the Bible," 162.

But, as Fred Klooster stated some years ago: "Scripture must be interpreted through the spectacles of Scripture; the pre-understanding with which the interpreter approaches Scripture must wholly conform to Scripture. This hermeneutic circle must be consciously embraced."[59]

We should therefore also use terminology that reflects our presuppositions. For example, instead of speaking of Deuteronomic History which is loaded with all sorts of dubious presuppositions, we should, if possible, speak of prophetic history or the Former Prophets, as writings reflecting the covenant demands of the Lord with his people. Other terms that should be avoided in giving a positive explanation of Scripture include: Deutero-Isaiah, Yahwist, Elohist, Hexateuch, and Priestly Code.[60] By adopting such terminology one can unwittingly take over some of the presuppositions of such vocabulary. This brings us to the next point.

3. Deal with the canonical text and context as the church has received it.

We have not received traditions, text units, and contexts as reconstructed by critical scholarship, but a canonical text. If we follow the lead of critical scholarship we end up in speculative reconstructions and interpretations, including the determination of genre, which can distance us from the received text.[61]

3.a. In dealing with *the canonical text*, one needs to recognize that the biblical narrative is "resident in the text and not under or behind it. In other words, the 'story' is identified with the literal or grammatical sense."[62] Critical scholars of the previous three centuries as well as today did not and do not accept the literal sense of Scripture as the truth. They sought and still seek to get behind the current text to get the "real" facts. And so what the text really means is now governed by historical research, which can be quite

---

59. Klooster, "The Role of the Holy Spirit," 465. Similarly Young, *Thy Word is Truth*, 192–93 and Poythress, *Inerrancy and the Gospels*, 83–86. Also see Grier Jr., "The Apologetical Value," 71–76.

60. A handy resource for brief descriptions of Deuteronomic History, Deutero-Isaiah and other critical terms is Soulen and Soulen, *Handbook of Biblical Criticism*, 46 and elsewhere *sub voce*.

61. Dealing with the canonical text as the church received it does not, of course, deny the need and legitimacy of doing text criticism where the textual evidence warrants it.

62. Muller and Thompson, "The Significance of Precritical Exegesis," 339–40.

speculative, and the literal sense of the text in itself has lost all significance. The text is no longer canonical and therefore authoritative.[63]

But the canonical text is the text that has been given to us and that should be the object of our study and not some hypothetical diachronic reconstruction of the supposed real facts lying behind the text.[64]

3.b. With respect to the *canonical context*, it is important to consider the nature and purpose of the book in which the passage being studied is found. For example, the books of Kings and Chronicles cover similar ground but do it quite differently. Their selection and emphasis is determined to a great extent by the purpose for which these two very different books were written. We need to appreciate such factors when seeking to understand the history writing given in quite different ways in these books.

Furthermore, the canonical context includes factoring in how one part of Scripture interprets or makes use of another part. Scripture is a unit and so when Christ speaks of Jonah as a historical figure who was in the belly of the fish (Matt 12:40), any doubt about the historicity of this event is settled. Or when the Old Testament narrates that God opened the mouth of Balaam's donkey so that it spoke (Num 22:28–30) and the greater canonical context confirms that (2 Pet 2:16), then one must put away any doubts about the historicity of this event and not try to deny it by assigning the genre of fable to it.[65] What the larger canonical context says about a historical narrative is far more important than what recent archaeological or genre studies have come up with. The hermeneutical principle of the Word of God interpreting itself must be maintained. This brings us to the next point.

4. Determine the genre.

It is obvious that to determine the meaning of a passage one must be aware of the genre of the text in question. However, since the determination of genre has often been used as a tool to judge a passage as less than historically accurate, we need to approach deciding on the genre of a given passage with a good deal of biblical wisdom. We must be very careful that our explanation of a text is not dependent on a genre which we have imposed on Scripture and which does not arise from Scripture. Decisive for determining genre should be the content and the immediate and wider context of the passage.

---

63. See Childs, "The Sensus Literalis," 87–92.
64. Cf. Ibid., 92–93.
65. As done, e.g., by Levine, *Numbers 21–36*, 139.

5. Be sensitive to the prophetic character of the history.

The narrative running from Joshua through Kings is prophetic history. One needs to factor in their unique characteristics as historical writings when determining the message or meaning of the events described.[66] Scripture explains itself, also with respect to the significance of events it describes.[67]

Because of the passage's prophetic character and purpose we should be careful which historical questions we ask Scripture to answer. The Old Testament was not given to us to recreate a complete history of Israel according to what we consider scientific standards. That was not its purpose. It is God's revelation for the salvation of his people. It is therefore an abuse of Scripture to expect or try to derive historical material from it which it does not claim to present.

6. Accept as historically true whatever Scripture plainly affirms to be so.

I realize full well that there are challenging passages which bear investigation and study; but it should be done in submission to the Word.[68] Again, faith seeks understanding. The supposedly sure results of historical-critical research are anything but that. Their conclusions with respect to historicity will continue to change as any survey of Old Testament scholarship will

---

66. Long has a point in noting, as others have also done, that "it is one thing to believe the Bible to be true; it is another to understand what it says." *The Art of Biblical History*, 29. However, this point should not be overstressed. Calvin, for one, saw the event or biblical narration and its meaning as one and the same (Van Leeuwen, "The Quest for the Historical Leviathan," 149). "Calvin is at pains to make clear that word and spirit are not to be separated, but only through the biblical text does the Spirit illumine. Similarly, the illumination of the reader toward the edification of the church is integral to the proper study of scripture. Although the literal sense is insufficient apart from the Spirit, Calvin does not distinguish a spiritual sense from the literal as if it belonged to a second stage of interpretation." Childs, *Biblical Theology*, 48. Similarly, Childs, "The Sensus Literalis," 87. It is important to note that Scripture itself tells us the importance and significance of the events it recounts. Cf. the Mount Sinai covenant renewal, the conquest of Jericho, the enthronement of David, etc. On another level, truth and meaning cannot always be separated from each other. One cannot speak about the meaning of the gospel without speaking about truth. Veling, "Geen Eigenmachtige Uitlegging," 16.

67. Maier, "Truth and Reality," 203–5. Also see previous footnote.

68. Typically perceived difficulties like the talking donkey with Balaam and the account of David killing Goliath (a folktale, or was it someone else?) come up. See on these and other examples, for instance, *De Bijbel in de beklaagdenbank*, 30–45 and Van Bruggen, *Het kompas van het Christendom*, 77–79, 217–29. Regarding parallel accounts of Kings and Chronicles, see Dillard, "Harmonization: A Help and a Hindrance," 151–64.

show.⁶⁹ After all, if you put your trust first in man's autonomous reason then you get no certainty, only ever changing solutions.⁷⁰ And with no certainty of the facts, any message becomes less than sure as well.

If a work like Judges, for example, sets itself up as historical, then we accept its historicity.⁷¹ There need to be compelling arguments, especially from Scripture itself, to consider a pericope as less than or other than a real historical account. As noted earlier, if a larger narrative complex exhibits a historiographical intent, then, barring strong indications to the contrary, we can assume that smaller units within that complex have a similar intent.⁷²

Accepting the historical veracity of the Old Testament does not mean negating current archaeological and literary scholarship. These can be useful tools in the hermeneutical task. But a final determination as to the evaluation and interpretation of archaeological and literary research must jive with the clear statements of Scripture. And one must bear in mind the limitations of archaeology.

On the other hand, any historical detail that is given can be accepted as authoritative. For example, we cannot fault Scripture for not telling us the name of Egypt's Pharaoh (1 Kgs 3:1; 9:16; 11:17–22) prior to the specific mention of Shishak (1 Kgs 11:40). Such information was not considered important for the purpose of the account. But, what is recorded of the anonymous Pharaohs can be accepted as accurate. Omri, a king apparently renowned in the ancient world who is even mentioned in the Moabite Mesha inscription (about 835 BC), has only eight verses for his rule (1 Kgs 16:21–28). For the purpose of the author of Kings, he was not important for his history. But what Scripture records about him can be accepted as true. We would like to have more information on what precisely happened when the sun's shadow went back ten steps on the stairway of Ahaz (2 Kgs 20:11; Isa 38:8; cf. Josh 10:13). But Scripture is silent and we need to respect that. We submit to the clear testimony of Scripture and accept this event for what it is—a miracle.

7. Strive for a unified understanding of the passage in question.

This means taking into account all the various aspects of the text. Modern scholarship often defines and sets over against each other different

---

69. See, e.g., the surveys of Whitelam, "The History of Israel: Foundations of Israel," 376–402, and Younger Jr., "Early Israel in Recent Biblical Scholarship," 176–206.

70. See Young, *Thy Word is Truth*, 195–208.

71. See, e.g., Merrill, *Kingdom of Priests*, 141–50.

72. Long, *The Art of Biblical History*, 180. See note 26 above.

dimensions of the text, such as the historical, the literary and the theological, when interpreting Scripture. We should not set the one over against the other but integrate them, just as the biblical text has integrated them in one unified whole. For example, a passage that recounts history also has literary qualities as well as a theological message. The one dimension should not be contrasted over against the other or ignored.[73] This integrated reading also includes taking the canonical context seriously, including as relevant the New Testament. To interpret the accounts of the conquest in Joshua, for example, without any reference to the promises given to Abraham in Genesis 12 and elsewhere would exclude what should be included. Although the one is part of the Prophets and the other part of Torah, they are both part of the Old Testament canon and should be treated within that larger context.

8. Hear the message of the text.

The narratives of the past have been "written down for our instruction" (1 Cor 10:11). The interpretation of historical narrative, therefore, should never simply be a scholarly exercise. God's Word, also the historical narrative, has a message which needs to be heard. It has rightly been said that to hear the message we need to know where the passage we are dealing with fits into the grand narrative stretching from Genesis to Revelation.[74] In my view, the redemptive-historical approach, as championed, for example, by Sidney Greidanus and recently also set forth by Richard Gaffin, is best suited to deal with prophetic history. This hermeneutic takes seriously key characteristics of prophetic history, namely that God's revelation is rooted in real history, is a unified history, and tells of God's acts of salvation with an ultimate focus on the coming of the promised Savior.[75]

---

73. See also for integrative reading, e.g., Long, *The Art of Biblical History*, 167–68. A critical commentary will, e.g., often concentrate on text critical and historical issues and virtually ignore theological concerns or the message of the passage for today. For an overview of the issues, see Bartholomew, "Hermeneutics," 401–5. A recent example is the comment of Hershel Shanks: "The conquest tradition in the Book of Joshua is . . . better seen as a literary, theological account, rather than an historical one." Shanks, "What Brings You Here?" 6. "The Reformers' achievement [Luther and Calvin] was to offer an interpretation of the literal sense which . . . held together the historical and theological meaning." Childs, "The Sensus Literalis," 87. Also, Pitkin, "John Calvin and the Interpretation of the Bible," 356.

74. See, e.g., Provan, "Hearing the Historical Books," 268–76.

75. Greidanus, *Preaching Christ from the Old Testament*. An important historical study on this hermeneutic is Greidanus, *Sola Scriptura*. Also see Gaffin Jr., "The Redemptive-Historical View," 89–110. This approach is consistent with Calvin's treating Old Testament history as history of the church awaiting the advent of its Head. Parker,

To discern the message one must listen and listen to the text with a view to the original audience and our current context. What the text actually says is crucial and we must learn to listen to it on its own terms, keeping in mind the clarity and sufficiency of Scripture, and submitting to it in faith. Good exegesis concentrates on the text and listens, taking into full account its context and genre.[76] In our exegesis we need to follow the best of the so-called grammatico-historical method as the Reformers did before us. And while doing our exegesis, we recognize the sovereignty of God, who is able to intervene in the history and affairs of men as the faithful God of the covenant.[77]

In Conclusion

The current postmodern culture challenges us with its mantra that there are no truths, only truth claims. But we must not be intimidated by that. As a recent intellectual convert to Christianity put it, at least two decades of postmodern research has equipped intellectuals with powerful methods to question the reliability of truth-claims and procedures of evidence. But the powerful legacy this bequeaths to contemporary intellectuals should not create its own hegemony of intellectual expectation, one which categorically trades in truth for doubt and faith for skepticism.[78] As believing scholars we have every right and duty to oppose the "epistemological imperialism" of critical scholarship.[79] But in the long run, we must do biblical scholarship on our terms.

History has shown that to engage with critical scholarship on their terms in deciding what is historically trustworthy is a fatal flaw for it means that only logical arguments based on currently available resources are possible. Any arguments brought into the discussion, therefore, have to stand and fall solely on their own logical merit. In such a discussion one cannot appeal to one's faith in the veracity of Scripture.[80] Not surprisingly, this ap-

---

Calvin's Old Testament Commentaries, 83–90, 101.

76. Cf. Maier, *The End of the Historical-Critical Method*, 335–36. A volume that stresses listening is Bartholomew and Beldman, eds., *Hearing the Old Testament*, especially chapters 10 to 15.

77. See also on hermeneutics and God's sovereignty Silva, "The Case for Calvinist Hermeneutics," 264–69.

78. Butterfield, *The Secret Thoughts of an Unlikely Convert* (Kindle Edition), Chapter 2, the King Solomon talk.

79. The phrase is from ibid.

80. See footnote 12 above. Interestingly, Long affirms that the historical-critical method as such, if applied in the context of a theistic set of background beliefs, need

proach has meant that less and less Old Testament narrative is being considered historically trustworthy.

Approaching the biblical text of what is obviously a historical narrative with the notion that its truth value needs to be validated does not arise from a high view of Scripture but from unbelief. Scripture's historical narratives are not to be subjected to our approval or disapproval with respect to their truthfulness but accepted in faith. As Professor Gaffin put it: "The divine authorship and consequent authority of Scripture, on the one hand, and the historical-critical method, with its commitment to autonomy, on the other, exclude each other."[81]

Sometimes it is suggested that the clear facts that are now known to a modern Old Testament scholar necessitate a reappraisal of whether certain information or events pictured in the Old Testament are really historically true.[82] We need to be very careful as to what academia considers to be an established fact. Quite often it is an interpretation of an archaeological find or a desire to impose one's understanding of a chronology on the biblical data. As those with a high view of Scripture, we need to assume the accuracy of the biblical account, also when it comes to dates and time frames.[83] If there are truly difficulties in reconciling with the Bible what we know from the ancient world at the time of the passage in discussion, it is better to say *non liquet*, it is not clear, and await further clarification from future research.[84] Scripture does not pretend to give an exhaustive history and we cannot expect Scripture to answer all our historical questions because that is not the purpose of the Word. But under no circumstance can we compromise Scripture's own testimony and our confession that God's Word is true and impose an interpretation that does violence to the clear intent of the text.

We need not fear that in taking the received text seriously and the Bible's presentation of history as true we will ever be disappointed or let down. Numerous critical hermeneutical approaches and decisions have

---

not exclude talk of divine intervention. Long, *The Art of Biblical History*, 134.

81. Gaffin Jr., "The Redemptive-Historical Response," 180. It is of interest to note that the famous evangelical Old Testament Scottish scholar, William Robertson Smith embraced the historical-critical method, but was unable to integrate his faith with critical scholarship. He was left with a dualistic compromise. Cameron, *Biblical Higher Criticism*, 212–14, 229–62, 267–69.

82. Cf. Bavinck, *Modernisme en orthodoxie*, 12.

83. A classic example is the discussion around the historicity and date of the exodus and conquest. See, e.g., Wood, "The Rise and Fall of the 13th-Century Exodus-Conquest Theory," 475–89; Hoffmeier, "What is the Biblical Date for the Exodus?" 225–47; Wood, "The Biblical Date for the Exodus is 1446 BC," 249–58.

84. For positive purposes in meeting biblical difficulties, see Poythress, *Inerrancy and the Gospels*, 106–13.

been abandoned in the past because the realization dawned that they did not do justice to the Word and certainly did not get one closer to the biblical message. If our position today in upholding the historicity of all of Scripture may seem untenable it will eventually be vindicated. God's Word is truth (John 17:17).[85]

Finally, it is remarkable that after centuries of biblical criticism in universities and seminaries, the average Christian in the pew still holds to the basic historical facts of Scripture and is by and large not affected by all the scholarship that raises doubts about the veracity of all or parts of the biblical narrative. Apparently the clear meaning of Scripture and the testimony of the Spirit that the Word is from God are still more convincing than critical scholarship would like to let on.[86] As believing scholars, let us take note and develop our own style in studying the Word.

Let me conclude with these words from John Murray:

> Let us not refuse any of the parcels of enlightenment on many aspects of truth which even this confused generation may bring us. But let us beware of the controlling framework of modern thinking lest its patterns and presuppositions become our own, and then, before we know it, we are carried away by a current of thought and attitude that makes the sufficiency and finality of Scripture not only extraneous but alien to our way of thinking.[87]

Bibliography

Aalders, G. Ch. *De geschiedschrijving in het Oude Testament: Rede bij de 48e herdenking der stichting van de Vrije Universiteit te Amsterdam Op 20 Oct. 1928*. Kampen: Kok, 1928.

———. *Oud-Testamentische kanoniek*. Kampen: Kok, 1952.

Albrektson, Bertil. *History and the Gods. An Essay on the Idea of Historical Events as Divine Manifestations in the Ancient Near East and in Israel*. Lund: Gleerup, 1967.

---

85. For example, there is no longer any consensus on the Documentary Hypothesis and historical facts mentioned in the Bible which were once considered doubtful have now been verified to be true. See, e.g., Arnold, "Pentateuchal Criticism, History Of," 629–30; Young, *Thy Word is Truth*, 195–208, Wenham, "Pondering the Pentateuch," 116–44 and Provan et al., *A Biblical History of Israel*, chapters 1–3.

86. On the fact that Christians by and large do not buy into critical scholarship, see Plantinga, "Two (or More) Kinds of Scripture Scholarship," 40–57 (also Plantinga, *Warranted Christian Belief*, 401–21), where he shows that the underlying presuppositions and results of higher criticism don't inspire confidence. So, people stick to traditional ways of understanding Scripture.

87. Murray, "The Finality and Sufficiency of Scripture," 22.

Alter, Robert. *The Art of Biblical Narrative*. Revised and updated. New York: Basic Books, 2011.
Arnold, B. T. "Pentateuchal Criticism, History Of." In *Dictionary of the Old Testament: Pentateuch*, edited by T. Desmond Alexander and David W. Baker, 622–31. Downers Grove, IL: InterVarsity Press, 2003.
Auerbach, Erich. *Mimesis: The Representation of Reality in Western Literature*. Fiftieth anniversary ed. With an introduction by Willard R. Trask and Edward W. Said. 1953. Princeton, NJ: Princeton University Press, 2003.
Barnett, R. D. *Illustrations of Old Testament History*. London: British Museum Publications, 1966.
Barr, James. *The Concept of Biblical Theology. An Old Testament Perspective*. Minneapolis, MN: Fortress, 1999.
———. *The Scope and Authority of the Bible*. London: SCM, 1980.
Bartholomew, Craig G. "Hermeneutics." In *Dictionary of the Old Testament Historical Books*, edited by Bill T. Arnold and H. G. M. Williamson, 392–407. Downers Grove, IL: InterVarsity Press, 2005.
Bartholomew, Craig G., and David J. H. Beldman, eds. *Hearing the Old Testament: Listening for God's Address*. Grand Rapids, MI: Eerdmans, 2012.
Bartholomew, Craig G., and Mike W. Goheen. "Story and Biblical Theology." In *Out of Egypt: Biblical Theology and Biblical Interpretation*, edited Craig Bartholomew et al., 144–84. Milton Keynes UK / Grand Rapids, MI: Paternoster Press / Zondervan, 2004.
Bavinck, H. *Modernisme en Orthodoxie*. Rede gehouden bij de overdracht van het rectoraat aan de Vrije Universiteit op 20 october 1911. Kampen: Kok, n.d.
Blocher, Henri. "Biblical Narrative and Historical Reference." In *Issues in Faith and History*, edited by Nigel M. de S. Cameron, 102–22. Edinburgh: Rutherford House, 1989.
Brandfon, Fredric. "The Limits of Evidence: Archaeology and Objectivity." *Maarava* 4:1 (1987) 5–43.
Bray, Gerald. *Biblical Interpretation: Past and Present*. Downers Grove, IL: InterVarsity Press, 1996.
Butterfield, Rosaria Champagne. *The Secret Thoughts of an Unlikely Convert* (Kindle Edition). Pittsburgh, PA: Crown and Covenant, 2012.
Calvin, John. *The Epistles of Paul the Apostle to the Galatians, Ephesians, Philippians and Colossians*. Edited by D. W. Torrance and T. F. Torrance. Translated by T. H. L. Parker. Calvin's Commentaries. Grand Rapids, MI: Eerdmans, 1965.
———. *Institutes of the Christian Religion*. Edited by John T. McNeill. Translated by Ford Lewis Battles. 2 vols. Library of Christian Classics 20–21. Philadelphia: Westminster, 1960.
Cameron, Nigel M. de S. *Biblical Higher Criticism and the Defense of Infallibilism in 19th Century Britain*. Texts and Studies in Religion. Lewiston, NY: Edwin Mellen Press, 1987.
———. "Inspiration and Criticism: The Nineteenth-Century Crisis." *Tyndale Bulletin* 35 (1984) 129–59.
Childs, Brevard S. *Biblical Theology of the Old and New Testaments: Theological Reflection on the Christian Bible*. Minneapolis, MN: Fortress, 1992.
———. "The Sensus Literalis of Scripture: An Ancient and Modern Problem." In *Beiträge Zur Alttestamentlichen Theologie. Festschrift Für Walther Zimmerli Zum*

70. Geburtstag, edited by Walter Zimmerli et al., 80–93. Göttingen: Vandenhoeck und Ruprecht, 1977.

Collins, John J. "The 'Historical Character' of the Old Testament in Recent Biblical Theology." In *Israel's Past in Present Research: Essays on Ancient Israelite Historiography*, edited by V. Philips Long, 150–69. Sources for Biblical and Theological Study 7. Winona Lake, IN: Eisenbrauns, 1999.

Davies, Philip R. "The Beginnings of the Kingdom of Judah." In *Israel in Transition 2: From Later Bronze II to Iron IIA (c. 1250–850 BCE): The Texts*, vol. 521, edited by Lester L. Grabbe, 54–61. Library of Hebrew Bible/Old Testament Studies. New York: T&T Clark, 2010.

De Bijbel in de beklaagdenbank: Antwoord op het rapport "God met ons" van de Gereformeerde Kerken in Nederland over de aard van het Schriftgezag. Hilversum: Stichting de Evangelische Omroep, 1981.

De Bruijne, A. L. Th. de. "Er wordt verteld; er is geschied: de bijbel in beeld 2." In *Woord op schrift. Theologische reflecties over het gezag van de bijbel*, edited by C. Trimp, 161–94. Kampen: Kok, 2002.

———. "Hermeneutiek en metaforie: de bijbel in beeld 1." In *Woord op schrift. Theologische reflecties over het gezag van de bijbel*, edited by C. Trimp, 109–60. Kampen: Kok, 2002.

De Graaf, S. G. *From Creation to the Conquest of Canaan. Promise and Deliverance 1.* Translated by H. Evan Runner and Elisabeth Wichers Runner, with an introduction by H. Evan Runner. St. Catharines, ON: Paideia Press, 1977.

De Greef, W. *"De Ware Uitleg": Hervormers en Hun Verklaring Van de Bijbel*. Leiden: J. J. Groen en Zoon, 1995.

De Vries, Simon J. *Prophet Against Prophet: The Role of the Micaiah Narrative (I Kings 22) in the Development of Early Prophetic Tradition*. Grand Rapids, MI: Eerdmans, 1978.

Dever, William G. "Archaeology and the Israelite 'Conquest.'" In *Anchor Bible Dictionary*, edited by D. N. Freedman, 3:545–58. New York: Doubleday, 1992.

Dillard, Raymond B. "Harmonization: A Help and a Hindrance." In *Inerrancy and Hermeneutic: A Tradition, a Challenge, a Debate*, edited by Harvie M. Conn, 151–64. Grand Rapids, MI: Baker, 1988.

Doedens, J. J. T. "Taal en teken van trouw: over vorm en functie van Genesis 1." In *Woord op schrift. Theologische reflecties over het gezag van de bijbel*, edited by C. Trimp, 71–108. Kampen: Kok, 2002.

Frame, John M. *The Doctrine of the Word of God*. With a foreword by J. I. Packer. A Theology of Lordship. Phillipsburg, NJ: P&R, 2010.

———. "N. T. Wright and the Authority of Scripture." In *Did God Really Say? Affirming the Truthfulness and Trustworthiness of Scripture*, edited by David B. Garner, 107–28. Phillipsburg, NJ: P&R, 2012.

Frei, Hans W. *The Eclipse of Biblical Narrative*. New Haven, CT: Yale University Press, 1974.

Gaffin Jr., Richard B. "The Redemptive-Historical Response." In *Biblical Hermeneutics: Five Views*, edited by Stanley E. Porter and Beth M. Stovell, 174–87. Downers Grove, IL: IVP Academic, 2012.

———. "The Redemptive-Historical View." In *Biblical Hermeneutics: Five Views*, eds Stanley E. Porter and Beth M. Stovell, 89–110. Downers Grove, IL: IVP Academic, 2012.

Gignilliat, Mark. "Paul, Allegory, and the Plain Sense of Scripture: Galatians 4:21–31." *Journal of Theological Interpretation* 21 (2008) 135–46.
God met ons . . . over de aard van het Schriftgezag. Kerkinformatie dubbel-speciaalnummer. Leusden: Informatiedienst, 1981.
Goslinga, C. J. *Het Eerste Boek Samuël*. Commentaar Op Het Oude Testament. Kampen: Kok, 1968.
Grabbe, Lester L. "The Big Max: Review of *A Biblical History of Israel*, by Ian Provan, V. Philips Long, and Tremper Longman, III." In *Enquire of the Former Age: Ancient Historiography and Writing the History of Israel*, vol. 554, edited by Lester L. Grabbe, 215–34. Library of Hebrew Bible / Old Testament Studies. New York: Bloomsbury, 2011.
———. Review of *From Conquest to Coexistence*, by Koert van Bekkum. *Journal for the Study of the Old Testament* 36:5 (2011) 66.
Gray, John. *I & II Kings*. 2nd ed. 1964. Old Testament Library. Philadelphia: Westminster, 1970.
Greenberg, Gary. *101 Myths of the Bible: How Ancient Scribes Invented Biblical History*. Naperville, IL: Sourcebooks, 2003.
Greidanus, Sidney. *Preaching Christ from the Old Testament: A Contemporary Hermeneutical Method*. Grand Rapids, MI: Eerdmans, 1999.
———. *Sola Scriptura: Problems and Principles in Preaching Historical Texts*. Kampen: Kok, 1970.
Greijdanus, Seakle. *Schriftbeginselen ter Schriftverklaring en historisch overzicht over theorieën en wijzen van Schriftuitlegging*. Kampen: Kok, 1946.
Grier Jr., James M. "The Apologetical Value of the Self-Witness of Scripture." *Grace Theological Journal* 1:1 (1980) 71–76.
Hoffmeier, James K. "What is the Biblical Date for the Exodus? A Response to Bryant Wood." *Journal of the Evangelical Theological Society* 50 (2007) 225–47.
Johnson, Alan F. "The Historical-Critical Method: Egyptian Gold or Pagan Precipice?" In *Quo Vadis, Evangelicalism? Perspectives on the Past, Direction for the Future*, edited by Andreas J. Köstenberger, foreword by Roger Nicole, 91–108. Wheaton, IL: Crossway, 2007.
Kaiser, Walter C., Jr. *A History of Israel: From the Bronze Age Through the Jewish Wars*. Nashville, TN: Broadman & Holman, 1998.
Kitchen, K. A. "Exodus, The." In *Anchor Bible Dictionary*, edited by D. N. Freedman, 2:700–708. New York: Doubleday, 1992.
———. *On the Reliability of the Old Testament*. Grand Rapids, MI: Eerdmans, 2003.
Klein, William W., et al. *Introduction to Biblical Interpretation*. Rev. ed. Dallas: Word, 2004.
Klooster, Fred H. "The Role of the Holy Spirit in the Hermeneutic Process: The Relationship of the Spirit's Illumination to Biblical Interpretation." In *Hermeneutics, Inerrancy, and the Bible*, edited by Earl D. Radmacher and Robert D. Preus, 449–72. Grand Rapids, MI: Zondervan, 1984.
Kraus, Hans-Joachim. "Calvin's Exegetical Principles." *Interpretation* 31 (1977) 9–18.
Kuyper, Abraham. *Encyclopedia of Sacred Theology: Its Principles*. Reforming Science, 1897; rev. ed. 2008.
Lambert, W. G. "Destiny and Divine Intervention in Babylon and Israel." In *The Witness of Tradition: Papers Read at the Joint British-Dutch Conference Held at*

Woudschoten, edited by M. A. Beek et al., 65–72. Oudtestamentische Studiën 17. Leiden: Brill, 1972.

———. "History and the Gods: A Review Article." *Orientalia* 39 (1970) 170–77.

Lemche, Niels Peter. "On the Reliability of the Old Testament." *Journal of the American Oriental Society* 124:2 (2004) 375–77.

Levine, Baruch A. *Numbers 21–36*. AB 4A. New York: Doubleday, 2000.

Long, V. Philips. *The Art of Biblical History*. Foundations of Contemporary Interpretation, 5. Grand Rapids, MI: Zondervan, 1994.

———. "How Reliable Are Biblical Reports? Repeating Lester Grabbe's Comparative Experiment." *Vetus Testamentum* 52 (2002) 367–84.

Longman, Tremper, III. "Biblical Narrative." In *A Complete Literary Guide to the Bible*, edited by Leland Ryken and Tremper Longman III, 69–79. Grand Rapids, MI: Zondervan, 1993.

———. "History and Old Testament Interpretation." In *Hearing the Old Testament: Listening for God's Address*, edited by Craig G. Batholomew and David J. H. Beldman, 96–121. Grand Rapids, MI: Eerdmans, 2012.

Longman, Tremper, III, and Raymond B. Dillard. *An Introduction to the Old Testament*. 2nd ed. Grand Rapids, MI: Zondervan, 2006.

Maier, Gerhard. *Biblical Hermeneutics*. Translated by Robert W. Yarbrough. Wheaton, IL: Crossway Books, 1994.

———. *The End of the Historical-Critical Method*. Translated by Edwin W. Leverenz and Rudolph F. Norden. St. Louis: Concordia, 1977.

———. "Truth and Reality in the Historical Understanding of the Old Testament." In *Israel's Past in Present Research: Essays on Ancient Israelite Historiography*, edited by V. Philips Long, 192–206. Sources for Biblical and Theological Study 7. Winona Lake, IN: Eisenbrauns, 1999.

Marsden, George M. *Understanding Fundamentalism and Evangelicalism*. Grand Rapids, MI: Eerdmans, 1991.

Merrill, Eugene H. *Kingdom of Priests: A History of Old Testament Israel*. Grand Rapids, MI: Baker, 1987.

Millard, A. R. "Story, History, and Theology." In *Faith, Tradition, and History: Old Testament Historiography in Its Near Eastern Context*, edited by A. R. Millard et al., 37–64. Winona Lake, IN: Eisenbrauns, 1994.

Moberly, R. W. L. "Story in the Old Testament." *Themelios* 11:3 (1986) 77–82.

Muller, Richard A. "Biblical Interpretation in the Era of the Reformation: The View from the Middle Ages." In *Biblical Interpretation in the Era of the Reformation: Essays Presented to David C. Steinmetz in Honor of His Sixtieth Birthday*, edited by Richard A. Muller and John L. Thompson, 3–22. Grand Rapids, MI: Eerdmans, 1996.

Muller, Richard A. and John L. Thompson. "The Significance of Precritical Exegesis: Retrospect and Prospect." In *Biblical Interpretation in the Era of the Reformation: Essays Presented to David C. Steinmetz in Honor of His Sixtieth Birthday*, edited by Richard A. Muller and John L. Thompson, 335–45. Grand Rapids, MI: Eerdmans, 1996.

Murray, John. "The Attestation of Scripture." In *The Infallible Word: A Symposium by the Members of the Faculty of Westminster Theological Seminary*, 1–54. Philadelphia: Presbyterian and Reformed, 1946.

———. "The Finality and Sufficiency of Scripture." In *The Claims of Truth*, 16–22. *Collected Writings of John Murray* 1. Edinburgh: Banner of Truth, 1976.

Na'aman, Nadav. "Does Archaeology Really Deserve the Status of a 'High Court' in Biblical Historical Research?" In *Between Evidence and Ideology: Essays on the History of Ancient Israel Read at the Joint Meeting of the Society for Old Testament Study and the Oud Testamentisch Werkgezelschap, Lincoln, July 2009*, edited by Bob Becking and Lester L. Grabbe, 165–83. Leiden: Brill, 2011.

Nelson, Richard D. *First and Second Kings*. Interpretation. Atlanta, GA: John Knox Press, 1987.

Opitz, Peter. "The Exegetical and Hermeneutical Work of John Oecolampadius, Huldrych Zwingli and John Calvin." In *Hebrew Bible / Old Testament: The History of Its Interpretation. Volume 2: From the Renaissance to the Enlightenment*, edited by Magne Sæbø, 407–51. Göttingen: Vandenhoeck & Ruprecht, 2008.

Osborne, Grant R. "Historical Narrative and Truth in the Bible." *Journal of the Evangelical Theological Society* 48 (2005) 673–88.

Parker, T. H. L. *Calvin's New Testament Commentaries*. Grand Rapids, MI: Eerdmans, 1971.

———. *Calvin's Old Testament Commentaries*. Edinburgh: T. & T. Clark, 1986.

Pitkin, Barbara. "John Calvin and the Interpretation of the Bible." In *A History of Biblical Interpretation.* , edited by Alan J. Hauser and Duane F. Watson, 341–71. *The Medieval Through the Reformation Periods* 2. Grand Rapids, MI: Eerdmans, 2009.

Plantinga, Alvin. "Two (or More) Kinds of Scripture Scholarship." In *"Behind" the Text: History and Biblical Interpretation*, edited by Craig Bartholomew et al., 19–57. Scripture and Hermeneutics Series 4. Carlisle, U.K. / Grand Rapids, MI: Paternoster / Zondervan, 2003.

———. "Two (or More) Kinds of Scripture Scholarship." *Modern Theology* 14 (1998) 243–78.

———. *Warranted Christian Belief*. New York: Oxford, 2000.

Porter, J. R. "Old Testament Historiography." In *Tradition and Interpretation: Essays by Members of the Society for Old Testament Study*, edited by G. W. Anderson, 125–62. Oxford: Clarendon Press, 1979.

Poythress, Vern Sheridan. *Inerrancy and the Gospels: A God-Centered Approach to the Challenges of Harmonization*. Wheaton, IL: Crossway, 2012.

Provan, Iain. "Hearing the Historical Books." In *Hearing the Old Testament*, edited by Craig G. Bartholomew and David J. H. Beldman, 254–76. Grand Rapids, MI: Eerdmans, 2012.

Provan, Iain, et al. *A Biblical History of Israel*. Louisville, KY: Westminster John Knox, 2003.

Shanks, Hershel. "Letter from a Hebrew King?" *Biblical Archaeology Review* 6:1 (1980) 52–56.

———. "What Brings You Here?" *Biblical Archaeology Review* 39:4 (July/August 2013) 6.

Silva, Moisés. "The Case for Calvinist Hermeneutics." In *An Introduction to Biblical Hermeneutics: The Search for Meaning*, by Walter C. Kaiser, Jr and Moisés Silva, 250–69. Grand Rapids, MI: Zondervan, 1994.

Soulen, Richard N., and R. Kendall Soulen. *Handbook of Biblical Criticism*. 3rd ed. revised and expanded. Louisville, KY: Westminster John Knox, 2001.

Spears, Aubrey. "Preaching the Old Testament." In *Hearing the Old Testament*, edited by Craig G. Bartholomew and David J. H. Beldman, 383–409. Grand Rapids, MI: Eerdmans, 2012.

Van Bekkum, Koert. *From Conquest to Coexistence: Ideology and Antiquarian Intent in the Historiography of Israel's Settlement in Canaan*. Culture and History of the Ancient Near East. Leiden: Brill, 2011.

———. "Het Oude Testament als historisch document: een verkenning van de omslag in de visie op de oudtestamentische geschiedschrijving." *Theologia Reformata* 46 (2003) 328–55.

Van Bruggen, Jakob. "Hermeneutics and the Bible." In *Proceedings of The International Conference of Reformed Churches, June 20–27, 2001, Philadelphia, U.S.A.*, 161–72. Neerlandia, AB: Inheritance, 2001.

———. *Het kompas van het Christendom: Ontstaan en betekenis van een omstreden Bijbel*. Kampen: Kok, 2002.

Van den Belt, Henk. *The Authority of Scripture in Reformed Theology*. Studies in Reformed Theology. Leiden: Brill, 2008.

Van Leeuwen, Raymond C. "The Quest for the Historical Leviathan: Truth and Method in Biblical Studies." *Journal of Theological Interpretation* 5 (2011) 145–58.

Veling, K. "Geen eigenmachtige uitlegging: Moderne hermeneutiek en de omgang met de Bijbel." Rede uitgesproken bij de aanvaarding van het ambt van buitengewoon hoogleraar in de geschiedenis van de wijsbegeerte aan de Theologische Universiteit van De Gereformeerde Kerken in Nederland te Kampen op 7 december 1987. Kamper Bijdragen. Barneveld: De Vuurbaak, 1988.

Walton, John H. *Joshua, Judges, Ruth, 1 & 2 Samuel*. Zondervan Illustrated Bible Backgrounds Commentary (Old Testament). Grand Rapids, MI: Zondervan, 2009.

Wenham, Gordon J. "Pondering the Pentateuch: The Search for a New Paradigm." In *The Face of Old Testament Studies: A Survey of Contemporary Approaches*, edited by David W. Baker and Bill T. Arnold, 116–44. Grand Rapids, MI: Baker, 1999.

Whitelam, K. W. "The History of Israel: Foundations of Israel." In *Text in Context: Essays by Members of the Society for Old Testament Study*, edited by A. D. H. Mayes, 376–402. Oxford: Oxford University Press, 2000.

Wiseman, Donald J. *1 and 2 Kings*. Tyndale Old Testament Commentaries. Downers Grove, IL: InterVarsity Press, 1993.

Wood, Bryant G. "The Biblical Date for the Exodus is 1446 BC: A Response to James Hoffmeier." *Journal of the Evangelical Theological Society* 50 (2007) 249–58.

———. "The Rise and Fall of the 13th-Century Exodus-Conquest Theory." *Journal of the Evangelical Theological Society* 48 (2005) 475–89.

Wood, Leon J. *A Survey of Israel's History*. Revised and enlarged ed. Revised by David O'Brien. 1970. Grand Rapids, MI: Zondervan, 1986.

Woudstra, Marten H. "Event and Interpretation in the Old Testament." In *Interpreting God's Word Today*, edited by Simon Kistemaker, 49–72. Grand Rapids, MI: Baker, 1970.

Wright, Stephen I. "Inhabiting the Story: The Use of the Bible in the Interpretation of History." In *"Behind" the Text: History and Biblical Interpretation*, edited by Craig Bartholomew et al., 492–519. Scripture and Hermeneutics Series 4. Carlisle, U.K. / Grand Rapids, MI: Paternoster / Zondervan, 2003.

Yadin, Yigael. "Is the Biblical Account of the Israelite Conquest of Canaan Historically Reliable?" *Biblical Archaeology Review* 8:2 (1982) 16–23.

Young, Edward J. *Thy Word is Truth*. Grand Rapids, MI: Eerdmans, 1957.

Younger Jr., K. Lawson. "Early Israel in Recent Biblical Scholarship." In *The Face of Old Testament Studies: A Survey of Contemporary Approaches*, edited by David W. Baker and Bill T. Arnold, 176–206. Grand Rapids, MI: Baker, 1999.

5

"For the Word of YHWH will certainly come true" (1 Kgs 13:32)

Some remarks on the Reformed Hermeneutics of Biblical Historical Narrative

Koert van Bekkum

Levels of debate

Reading the Bible and trying to relate the stories about Adam, Abraham, Moses, Joshua, and David to history and to our own life—whether it is in the church, in the seminary, or in the field of secular biblical studies—is to enter an arena. There is always discussion about which interpretation is right and which is wrong. Moreover, the debate is not only about reading itself. It is also a battle between methods, traditions, and worldviews, and deep down even a spiritual battle between the Holy Spirit and Satan, the father of all lies.

Today, Christians entering this arena by interpreting biblical historical narratives will observe that three types of primary data are being discussed: first, the Bible itself as it was transmitted through the ages by the believing community, i.e., the Hebrew, Aramaic, and Greek texts and their ancient and modern translations; second, the ancient Near Eastern texts as they have been discovered and deciphered during the last two centuries; and third, the non-textual material remains from the Southern Levant and their neighboring lands as uncovered in excavations since the late nineteenth century.

If we take these three types of data and see how they are discussed and used in the arena of reading the Bible historically, three levels of debate can be distinguished. It (a) is a discussion between craftsmen and women searching for a right interpretation of the texts and the material culture; (b) regards a comparison and competition between diverse historical descriptions and explanations of the past, both in ancient sources and modern reconstructions; and (c) reflects a debate between diverse philosophical, political, and religious worldviews. As we all know, to have the right presuppositions on this last level does not mean that you also offer the right interpretation. If someone does not know how to read the rim of an Iron Age cooking pot or a biblical sentence in English or Hebrew, he or she will most likely fail in interpreting it. At the same time, however, it is evident that worldviews and definitions of the relation between the sources heavily influence our way of reading.[1]

Reformed hermeneutics

The question is: what hermeneutical considerations should guide a Reformed scholar in entering this arena? In fact, the answer is quite simple. Reformed theology accepts the Scriptures as the divine Word of God and is willing to do justice to all revelation, both special and general. According to the Reformed confessions, salvation history starts with creation and is directed at the renewal of all creation. Consequently, Reformed scholars not only study historical biblical narrative and history because it comprises a large part of the Bible and in order to discover some truths about their own souls, but also because the description of God's acts in history reveals something about God himself. These stories offer the framework of the lives of all members of humankind as well as of the universe as a whole. It therefore touches our experiences, hopes, and fears. "This is," to quote a recent Canadian worship song, "the story of the Son of God / Hanging on the cross for me, / But it ends with a bride and groom / And a wedding by a glassy sea."[2]

---

1. For how these three levels can be detected in the recent debates about ancient Israel in the SBL/EABS-section "European Seminar of Historical Methodology" (1996–2012), see Van Bekkum, "'The Situation Is More Complicated,'" 216–26.

2. The City Harmonic, "Holy (Wedding Day)."

Consequently, at the first level, Reformed scholars should try to be first-rate craftsmen in the linguistic and archaeological interpretation of the texts and material culture. Only in this way we can consider, for instance, the recent suggestion that the reference in Revelation 4:6 and 15:2 to the "glassy sea"[3] contains an allusion to an ancient Near Eastern image, suggesting that no sea or dragon from the waters can do any harm because the sea is frozen.[4] In that case, the glassy sea not only symbolizes the Lord's purity and holiness, but also the powerlessness of Satan in the presence of God.

This striving for excellence also applies to the second and third level of the debate. In order to make a proper use of historical explanations and methods, it is important to understand them and to be aware of their limitations. All too often it is stated that the Bible is wrong while in fact the biblical and non-biblical perspectives complement one another. Archaeology, for instance, makes it likely that the reign of the kings Omri and Ahab of Israel was successful from an economic perspective. As such, however, this does not mean—as is often stated[5]—that their negative portrait in the Book of Kings fails to do justice to their accomplishments, for archaeology is simply not able to offer a theological assessment of their rule.

In addition, it is even more significant on this second and third level to define the relation between the diverse sources in the debate. For Reformed scholars, the *sola scriptura* is very important in this respect, although not as a formal theory but as a vital standard helping to find the right way in seeking answers to our exegetical queries. It is undesirable and happily also impossible to formulate a hermeneutical foundation freeing biblical interpretation from all non-biblical influences. Special and general revelation are related, and the Bible is both divine and human. That should be appreciated and not be denied, neither explicitly nor implicitly.

At the same time, no pope, no way of human reasoning, no widely accepted interpretation, no confession or theologian may determine our exegesis beforehand. The biblical text should always be able to speak for itself. Accordingly, it is crucial to consider whether all exegetical possibilities and methods are able to do justice to the text and to Scripture as a whole.[6]

---

3. All Scripture quotations in this article are from the New International Version (NIV84).

4. Thanks are due to Marjo Korpel and Johannes de Moor, who allowed me to cite from the preliminary manuscript of their forthcoming book *Adam, Eve, and the Devil.*

5. See, e.g., Finkelstein, *The Forgotten Kingdom.*

6. Cf. Van Bekkum et al., "Gereformeerde bijbelwetenschap en Bijbelse hermeneutiek," 251–53.

Triangle of biblical historical narrative

What does this mean in practice for the hermeneutics of biblical historical narrative? As divine revelation written by men, the books of Genesis to 2 Kings and of Chronicles, Ezra, and Nehemiah build a bridge between the past and their audience. History is retold, elucidated, and used: "Listen, this is what has happened, and this is what it means for you!" Together these three elements form what one could call the triangle of biblical historical narrative: (1) the *past*, in which God acted; (2) a divinely inspired *text*, representing that past and giving it its meaning and message with the help of literary devices; and (3) the *audience*, which is influenced by the past and which is defined by the text as being part of that same reality in which God acts.

The three elements of this triangle belong together. But as the history of interpretation shows, the specific historical and cultural context of the interpreters determines which element gets the most attention. The Reformers simply assumed that God acts in history. As humanist scholars they primarily directed their attention to the text and its rhetorical effect, for the text is the *viva vox Dei*, God's living word.[7] Later, with the Enlightenment and the emergence of modernism, the idea of God's acting in history became contested. Accordingly, the attention shifted to the reconstruction of the past. Bishop James Ussher did so on the basis of the biblical text, Julius Wellhausen with the instrument of skeptical historical criticism, and William Foxwell Albright with the empirical methods of traditional biblical archaeology.[8] In the end their humanly reconstructed views of (redemptive) history largely determined their reading of the Bible, and, despite all principial differences, this focus on history as an interpretative framework also affected the Presbyterian and Neo-Calvinist interpretation of Scripture.[9]

Nowadays, in postmodern times, most attention is paid to the audience. Biblical historical narrative is read ahistorically with the help of reader-response criticism[10] or historically by stating that the text does not

---

7. Cf., e.g., Backus, "Bible: Biblical Hermeneutics and Exegesis," 152–58; Balke, *Calvijn en de Bijbel*.

8. Ussher, *Annales veteris testamenti*; Wellhausen, *Prolegomena zur Geschichte Israels*; Albright, *From Stone Age to Christianity*.

9. See, e.g., Marsden, *Reforming Fundamentalism*, 13–52; Hart, *Defending the Faith*, 5–9, 170; Harinck, ed., *De kwestie-Geelkerken*.

10. See, e.g., Alter, *The Art of Biblical Narrative*; Sternberg, *The Poetics of Biblical Narrative*; Bar-Efrat, *Narrative Art in the Bible*.

refer to a past but is to be understood as a total social fact reflecting the ideological views of a certain group.[11]

In my view, it would be wise to admit that we are children of our time and that our theological considerations are affected by our cultural circumstances. Nevertheless, Scripture and tradition teach us to hold together text, history, and audience. In this light, we should try to connect the best of the early modern, modern, and postmodern interpretation of historical biblical narrative. Historical matters matter to faith.[12] So there is every reason to oppose skeptical, naturalist interpretations of Scripture and the idea that biblical historical narrative is only a literary work of art. But the Reformers rightly located the *norma normans*, or normative rule of theology, in biblical historical narrative itself, the *viva vox Dei*, and not in history or in our perception of biblical history.

This observation is also of great help in the recent discussion about the way Scripture refers to history. *Sola scriptura* means that neither historical perceptions taught by our teachers in elementary school nor certain historicist presuppositions but the text itself should determine the way in which it refers to the past. Accordingly, it is necessary that we further develop the traditional historical-grammatical approach in order to refine our historical understanding of Scripture. We need to ask the question: *in what way* does this text refer to history? Interestingly, narrative criticism and a proper use of the postmodern stress on literary devices can be of a great help in this area. Let me try to explain what I mean by asking your attention for a story about two prophets, two donkeys, and a lion in the long biblical chapter of 1 Kings 13.

Two Prophets, Israel, and Judah

1 Kings 12:34—13:34 tells about King Jeroboam and his altar in Bethel, about a "man of God from Judah" and an "old prophet from Bethel." It is a strange story offering a fascinating portrait of its main characters and a beautifully designed plot, using repetitions and signal words in order to communicate its message. Nine times, for instance, the story mentions "the Word of YHWH," and fourteen times a verb occurs that is translated in the NIV as "to pull back," "to be restored," "to return," "to turn back," "to bring

---

11. See, e.g., Lemche, *The Israelites in History and Tradition*; Thompson, *The Bible in History*; Davies, *Memories of Ancient Israel*.

12. Cf. Hoffmeier and Magary, eds., *Do Historical Matters Matter to Faith?*

back," "to come back," or "to repent."¹³ In response to the Word of the Lord, people turn in all kinds of directions.

Traditional historical criticism tried to cut the story into pieces, although later it was also admitted that this is impossible.¹⁴ Karl Barth devoted an excursus to it in his *Church Dogmatics*,¹⁵ which formed the start of a whole series of synchronic interpretations.¹⁶ It is not the goal of this article to offer a full exposition of the story. But a few striking elements may suffice.

This chapter occurs at a crossroads in the Book of Kings. It all started so beautifully. Solomon was exactly the successor David needed: faithful to the Lord, wise, and powerful. But over time things went wrong. His many women made him commit idolatry, the areas surrounding Israel started to rebel (1 Kgs 11), and, when he died, the population was fed up with the heavy tax load (1 Kgs 12:14, cf. 4:7–19). YHWH had offered a way out in Jeroboam. Once he stood at the head of the administration in the northern tribal areas. But now that the tribe of Judah has broken its ties with the north, YHWH is with him . . . if he is as faithful to him as King David was. Then Jeroboam will enjoy all the riches in his area (1 Kgs 11:35–39). That is the situation. So the question is: what will now happen to Israel and Judah?

We know the story. From a political point of view, what Jeroboam is doing is very understandable. But he ignores what Ahijah, the prophet, had said to him: even though the glory of Solomon has come to an end, there will always be a light for David in the city YHWH has chosen (cf. 1 Kgs 11:36). Accordingly, he creates a new state cult by upgrading the heights for YHWH in Dan and Bethel.¹⁷ Then, at the opening ceremony in Bethel, the man of God comes from Judah and cries out against the altar. An incident in which his hand is withered and restored offers Jeroboam the opportunity to repent. But his response is negative. The only thing he and the old prophet strive for is to make the verdict of the man of God a verdict without consequences by inviting him for dinner. In the ancient Near East, eating together means that you are no longer allowed to do any harm to the person with

---

13. 13:1, 2, 5, 9, 17, 18, 20, 26, 32 (דבר יהוה, cf. 13:4, 11, 33); 13:4, 6, 9, 10, 16, 17, 18, 19, 20, 22, 23, 26, 29, 33 (שׁוב).

14. E.g. De Vries, *1 Kings*, 168–70; Würthwein, *Das Erste Buch der Könige*, 166–72. Cf. Noth, *1 Könige*, 291: "im einzelnen macht das Ganze den Eindruck literarischer Einheitlichkeit; und dieser Eindruck bestätigt sich bei genauerer Untersuchung."

15. Barth, *Kirchliche Dogmatik II/2*, 434–53 (ET: Barth, *Church Dogmatics 2/2*, 393–409). Cf. Bosworth, "Revisiting Karl Barth's Exegesis of 1 Kings 13," 360–83.

16. See, e.g., Van Winkle, "1 Kings XII 25—XIII 34," 101–114; Walsh, *1 Kings*, 171–221; Mead, "Kings and Prophets," 191–205; Bodner, *Jeroboam's Royal Drama*, 97–119.

17. See, e.g., Kruyswijk, *"Geen gesneden beeld,"* 138–145.

whom you share a meal.[18] But this also fails. The man of God is killed by a lion, and the old prophet has to admit: "The Word of YHWH will certainly come true." End of story.

According to most exegetes, this is a story about judgment. And it is. But there is more at stake. Why is the "good guy" killed in the end, while the "bad guy" remains alive? What is the function of the donkeys and the lion? The answer to this question is in the phrase and verb I already mentioned, and it starts to unfold in verse 19. The old prophet, totally against his will, starts to cry out the Word of YHWH. The man of God from Judah had stood at the altar and spoken against it. Now the old prophet of God sits at the table and suddenly he speaks against the man of God: "Thus says YHWH!" And like the man of God at the altar, he emphasizes his verdict with a sign: "You will not be buried with your ancestors."[19]

The Word of YHWH does not depend on human behavior, and it seems that the animals, more than the human beings, realize themselves that its remarkable power exceeds everything. The lion is hungry, but he does not eat the man of God. Its instinct tells the donkey to run away, but it is standing still out of respect for the man of God and his prophecy.

The Word of YHWH cannot be silenced. Finally, the old prophet understands this. The story tells nothing about his integrity. What matters is what he says: the Word of YHWH spoken by this man will certainly come true: "Bury me close to him," for he knows that the future of Israel depends not on the sanctuary at Bethel but on the words of YHWH about David and the temple in Jerusalem (1 Kgs 13:31–32).

1 Kings 13 tells a strange story at a crossroads in the Book of Kings. If it is read in a literary way—that is, from the perspective of the end of the book, from the perspective of exile as it occurs in 1 Kings 17 and 25—it turns out to be a very sad and threatening story. This is the beginning of the end.

---

18. An anthropological approach to the meaning of hospitality in the Ancient Near East and an interesting suggestion regarding Elisha's reply to the king of Israel not to kill the Arameans but to give them bread and water (2 Kgs 6:22) is offered by the Italian Assyriologist Mario Liverani: "Transformed from prisoners into guests, the Aramean soldiers are allowed to live and are sent back unhurt to their comrades, who will be forced in their turn—given the reciprocal character of the law of hospitality—to stop the siege and renounce any hostile action against Israel." Liverani, *Myth and Politics*, 14.

19. A series of allusions involving 13:1–10 and 20–25 parallels the paragraphs about Jeroboam and the old prophet and stresses the remarkable fact that the old prophet from Bethel is in his turn used as a means of revelation: "standing at the altar" (1, עמד על־המזבח) and "sitting at the table" (20, ישבים אל־השלחן); "cry out against the altar" and "cry out against the man of God" (2 and 21, קרא על); "This is what YHWH says" (2 and 21, כה אמר יהוה); the sign of the altar that is torn down (4) and the man of God who will not be buried with his ancestors (22); and the threefold repetition of "by the way" (9–10 and 24–25, בדרך).

YHWH will warn again and again. But he will do what he says: King Josiah will destroy the sanctuary at Bethel (2 Kgs 23). Eventually even Jerusalem will be devastated and Judah carried away to Babylon. Who would not fear YHWH because of his Word?

Representations

The end of the Book of Kings also sheds a surprising light on two other elements in the story, that is, on the prophets and animals. As literary characters, these men of God are described in a remarkable way. All the individual prophets in the Book of Kings are mentioned by name, but these two are anonymous.[20] They are real, historical human beings, for the narrative is clearly referential and prophetic in nature. Accordingly, the story has no meaning if they did not utter their words. But at the same time these prophets represent more than just themselves. The man of God from Judah represents Judah, and the old prophet from Bethel is Israel. Israel willingly chooses a path other than the Lord intended. Judah speaks its verdict against Israel because of this. But in the end even Judah will not escape divine judgment.

This clear representational effect of the description of the prophets gives in its turn rise to another issue regarding the characters in the story. What about the animals? Is it possible that ancient Israelites listening to the story would associate them too immediately with a well-known person or entity? The attestations of a lion in the books of the prophets in the context of the judgment of God offer a very clear answer. The lion is YHWH himself (Hos 5:14; Amos 3:8).[21] His heart goes out to his people. But in the end he does not hesitate again to execute judgment—even on Judah.

And the donkey? Maybe the fact that the donkey *stands* next to the dead man of God, just as king Jeroboam *stands* next to the altar, conveys a suggestion (1 Kgs 13:1, 23). The king behaves like an ass! Even after all this, Jeroboam does not change his evil ways. He is so stubborn! (1 Kgs 13:33–34). And the lion, YHWH himself? He lets it happen. He does not strike—not yet.

Finally, in this textual ambiguity the reader also encounters God's mercy. YHWH cries out his judgment. And when it comes true and he does

---

20. Cf. Nathan (1 Kgs 1:8); Ahijah (11:29); Jehu (16:7); Elijah (17:1, cf. 18:22); Elisha (19:16); Micaiah (22:16); Jonah (2 Kgs 14:25); Isaiah (19:2). The exceptions are groups of prophets or anonymous prophets described as belonging to a group of prophets (1 Kgs 18:4; 21:13, 35; 22:6; 2 Kgs 2:3; 3:13; 4:1, 38; 5:22; 6:1; 9:1; 23:2).

21. Cf. Isa 38:13; Jer 49:19; 50:44; Hos 13:7; Lam 3:10.

what he once said, in the time of Josiah of Judah, there is also respect for the man of God from Judah. The king orders to let his bones and those of the old prophet alone (2 Kgs 23:17–18).

That is what is at stake here: the Lord will do what he says. His Word will *make history*. But if that is true, if the Word of God indeed creates a new reality, then that will also be the case with that other motif in the Book of Kings: the motif of the light of David in the city YHWH has chosen, the motif of the Messiah, who will be King forever. That message of mercy is also part of this story. It is a message of mercy for Israelites in exile. They themselves are tangible proof of the truth of the Word of YHWH. The exile has come. But if that is true, the Messiah also will not fail!

Conclusion: 1 Kings 13 as literary historiography

The clue to 1 King 13 is in verse 32: "The Word of YHWH will certainly come true." This narrative is not only about the fate of the kingdom of Israel. It also about Judah and about the power of the Word of YHWH in general, and it is even about the future of the Davidic king.

A closer look at the story shows that literary devices in biblical historical narrative are more than just ornamentation. The divinely inspired writers of these biblical books used them to elucidate history and to formulate their message.

1 Kings 13 describes what actually happened. But at the same time the literary devices create a world of its own that can be applied to a much longer historical narrative. The focus is not on the precise historical details, but on the meaning of what has happened and its far-reaching consequences for the future of Israel and Judah.

A beautiful example of this can be found in the final words of verse 32, in the reference to "all the shrines on the high places in the towns of Samaria." In the context of the Book of Kings, this phrase refers primarily to the shrines and high places built by king Omri and king Ahab, who brought Jezebel of Sidon and the Baal of the Sidonians to Samaria, the new capital of Israel (1 Kgs 16:24, 31). This introduced a horrible form of idolatry that eventually also affected Judah (2 Kgs 21:3). In this form these shrines did not yet exist in the time of Jeroboam, and that poses a question: did the man of God refer to Samaria? Of course, that cannot be excluded. In my view, however, it is more logical to assume that, inspired by the Holy Spirit, the scribes of the Book of Kings included this reference in their literary composition.²² In this way they were able to make explicit the far-reaching consequences of this divine judgment over the Israelite state cult.²³

Look what has happened, and you will confess: "The Word of YHWH will certainly come true."

Bibliography

Albright, William Foxwell. *From Stone Age to Christianity*. Baltimore, MD: John Hopkins Press, 1946.
Alter, Robert. *The Art of Biblical Narrative*. London: Allen and Unwin, 1981.
Backus, Irena. "Bible: Biblical Hermeneutics and Exegesis." In *The Oxford Encyclopedia of the Reformation*, Vol. 1, 152–58. Oxford: Oxford University Press, 1996.
Balke, Willem. *Calvijn en de Bijbel*. Kampen: Kok, 2003.
Bar-Efrat, Shimeon. *Narrative Art in the Bible*. JSOTS 70. Sheffield: The Almond Press, 1989.
Barth, Karl. *Church Dogmatics 2/2*. Edinburgh: T. & T. Clark, 1957.
Barth, Karl. *Kirchliche Dogmatik II/2*. Zollikon-Zürich: Evangelischer Verlag, 1942.
Bodner, Keith. *Jeroboam's Royal Drama*. Oxford: Oxford University Press, 2012.
Bosworth, David. "Revisiting Karl Barth's Exegesis of 1 Kings 13." *Biblical Interpretation* 10 (2002) 360–83.
The City Harmonic. "Holy (Wedding Day)." *I Have A Dream (It Feels Like Home)*. Kingsway, 2011.
Davies, Philip R. *Memories of Ancient Israel. An Introduction to Biblical History— Ancient and Modern*. Lewisville, KY: Westminster John Knox Press, 2008.
DeVries, Simon J. *1 Kings*. WBC. Waco, TX: Word Books, 1985.
Finkelstein, Israel. *The Forgotten Kingdom. The Archaeology and History of Northern Israel*. SBLANEM 5. Atlanta, GA: Society of Biblical Literature, 2012.
Harinck, George, ed. *De kwestie-Geelkerken. Een terugblik na 75 jaar*. Ad Chartasreeks 5. Barneveld: Vuurbaak, 2001.
Hart, Darryll G. *Defending the Faith. John Gresham Machen and the Crisis in Conservative Protestantism in Modern America*. Baltimore, MD: Johns Hopkins Press, 1994.

---

22. According to Noth, *1 Könige*, 291, verse 32 is one of the few later additions to the story. This, however, is unlikely in light of the fact that it contains the conclusion of the main motif of the narrative, that is, the fulfillment of the "Word of YHWH" (דבר יהוה, 13:1, 2, 5, 9, 17, 18, 20, 26).

23. For similar considerations, see, e.g., Van Gelderen, *De boeken der Koningen*, 61–62. Van Gelderen maintains that the name "Samaria" was added by a writer from the time of King Hezekiah or Manasseh, because such an addition should have taken place before the fulfillment of the prophecy during the reign of King Josiah (2 Kgs 23). In my view this is indeed possible but not absolutely necessary. The prophets were not always able "to find out the time and circumstances to which the Spirit of Christ in them was pointing" (1 Pet 1:11–12). Consequently, an explication of the name "Samaria" dating after the destruction of Jerusalem can still be a clarification of the real consequences of the prophecy by the man of God from Judah, without creating a *vaticinium ex eventu* as suggested by, e.g., Wellhausen, "Die Composition der historischen Bücher," 244.

Hoffmeier, James Karl, and Dennis Robert Magary, eds. *Do Historical Matters Matter to Faith? A Critical Appraisal of Modern and Postmodern Approaches to Scripture.* Wheaton, IL: Crossway, 2012.

Korpel, Marjo and Johannes de Moor. *Adam, Eve, and the Devil: A New Beginning.* OBO 260. Fribourg: Academic Press, 2014.

Kruyswijk, Adriaan. "*Geen gesneden beeld.*" Franeker: T. Wever, 1962.

Lemche, Niels Peter. *The Israelites in History and Tradition.* Library of Ancient Israel. Lewisville, KY: Westminster John Knox Press, 1998.

Liverani, Mario. *Myth and Politics in Ancient Near Eastern Historiography.* Edited and Introduced by Zainab Bahrani and Marc Van De Mieroop. London: Equinox, 2004.

Marsden, George M. *Reforming Fundamentalism. Fuller Seminary and the New Evangelicalism.* Grand Rapids, MI: Eerdmans, 1987.

Mead, James K. "Kings and Prophets, Donkeys and Lions: Dramatic Shape and Deuteronomistic Rhetoric in 1 Kings XIII." *Vetus Testamentum* 49 (1999) 191–205

Noth, Martin. *1 Könige.* BKAT IX/1. Neukirchen: Neukirchener Verlag, 1968.

Sternberg, Meir. *The Poetics of Biblical Narrative: Ideological Literature and the Drama of Reading.* Bloomington, IN: Indiana University Press, 1987.

Thompson, Thomas L. *The Bible in History: How Writers Create A Past.* London: Jonathan Cape, 1999.

Ussher, James. *Annales veteris testamenti, a prima mundi origine deducti.* London: ex officina J. Flesher. & prostant in ædibus G. Bedell, prope januam Medii Templi in platea dicta Fleetstreet, 1650.

Van Bekkum, Koert. "'The Situation Is More Complicated.' Archaeology and Text in the Historical Reconstruction of the Iron Age IIA Southern Levant." In *Exploring the Narrative. Jerusalem and Jordan in the Bronze and Iron Ages: Papers in Honour of Margreet Steiner*, edited by Eveline van der Steen, et al., 216–26. LHB / OTS 583. London: Bloomsbury T&T Clark, 2014.

Van Bekkum, Koert, et al. "Gereformeerde bijbelwetenschap en Bijbelse hermeneutiek." In *Nieuwe en oude dingen. Schatgraven in de Schrift,* 243–55. Apeldoornse Studies 62 / TU-Bezinningsreeks 13. Barneveld: Vuurbaak, 2013.

Van Gelderen, Cornelis. *De boeken der Koningen, dl 2.* Korte Verklaring. Kampen: Kok, 1936.

Van Winkle, D. W. "1 Kings XII 25–XIII 34: Jeroboam's Cultic Innovations and the Man of God from Judah." *Vetus Testamentum* 46 (1996) 101–14.

Walsh, Jerome T. *1 Kings.* Berit Olam. Collegeville, MN: Liturgical Press, 1996.

Wellhausen, Julius. *Prolegomena zur Geschichte Israels.* Berlin: Georg Reimer, 1878.

Würthwein, Ernst. *Das Erste Buch der Könige,* Bd. 1. Göttingen: Vandenhoeck & Ruprecht, 1977.

6

The Structure of Jeremiah
Confessional Integrity and Quality Control

Jannes Smith

Introduction

This paper has three parts. The first part will present a hypothetical structure for the book of Jeremiah. The second part will introduce and apply some critical methods to test the validity of the hypothesis. In particular I will introduce rhetorical criticism and outline its relevance and effectiveness as a testing tool. The third part will outline the profits and perils of using critical methods and suggest what sorts of things a Reformed Old Testament scholar can and cannot say. In short, I hope to use the structure of the book of Jeremiah as a hermeneutical test case for the interplay of confessional integrity and quality control.

The structure of the book of Jeremiah is a difficult problem. As Dillard and Longman put it, "The materials are not in a chronological sequence and do not seem to follow a coherent plan—or at least, if there is some inner logic to the arrangement, it has escaped interpreters."[1] In part the difficulty

---

1. Longman and Dillard, *Introduction to the Old Testament*, 326. In his article on "Jeremiah," Louis Stulman writes that "the vast majority of scholars during the 20th cent. have come to the conclusion that Jeremiah is void of any meaningful structure" (220).

may have to do with the compositional history of the book itself. We know from chapter 36 that Baruch wrote a second, expanded version after King Jehoiakim burned the first one. In chapter 51 Jeremiah instructed Seraiah to drop a written version of the oracle against Babylon into the Euphrates after he had read it aloud.[2] Chapter 51 closes with the colophon, "The words of Jeremiah end here," but someone at some point added chapter 52 as an appendix of sorts.[3] Furthermore, the book ends with a Jewish community divided over two locations: some, including the prophet himself, living in Egypt, others residing in Babylon, where Daniel is said to have had access to a written copy (Dan 9:1–2). Who finished the book, and when, and how much work it took, is difficult to determine. Complicating matters still more, at an early stage there were two versions of the book. Besides the familiar Masoretic version, there is an alternate version, about one eighth shorter, found in the Septuagint translation.[4] The sequence of chapters is also different in the two versions, the main difference being that the oracles against the nations, in chapters 46–51 of the Masoretic text, are located after 25:13 in the Greek, and in a different order.[5] For the sake of time I'll limit

---

2. To navigate the wide range of interpretations of this passage one should consult McLane, "Jeremiah's Instructions," 697–706.

3. For an analysis of this chapter and references to pertinent literature, see Smith, "Jeremiah 52," 55–96.

4. Lacking about 2700 Hebrew words, as calculated by Graf, *Der Prophet Jeremia*, xl-lvii, and Giesebrecht, *Das Buch Jeremia*, xxv-xxxiv. Since one would hardly expect a translator to change the sequence of the book, and since Hebrew fragments of both the Masoretic and Septuagint text types have been found at Qumran, it appears that there was more than one Hebrew version of the book at an early stage of its history. Among major treatments of the relationship between LXX and MT Jeremiah are Janzen, *Studies*; Soderlund, *Greek Text of Jeremiah*; Stipp, *Das masoretische und alexandrinische Sondergut*. Which version is older, or whether both coexisted at a very early stage, is difficult to say, and scholars are divided. Leslie Allen views the location of the oracles in the LXX as secondary, "explained by the insertion of an independent scroll of foreign oracles that belonged to the Jeremian tradition," but fails to suggest why said scroll should have been inserted there. Allen, "Jeremiah," 435. For Jack Lundbom, on the other hand, "The location in the LXX is the earlier, containing both a superscription (25:13a) and a subscription (LXX 32:13). In the MT these have been combined in 25:13." Lundbom, *Jeremiah 1–20*, 98.

5. The following passages are absent in the Greek: 8:10b–12; 10:6–8, 10; 17:1–5a; 25:14; 29 (LXX 36):16–20; 33 (LXX 40):14–26; 39 (LXX 46):4–13; 52:28–30. In MT the sequence of oracles is Egypt (46), the Philistines (47), Moab (48), Ammon (49:1–6), Edom (49:7–22), Damascus (49:23–27), Kedar and Hazor (49:28–33), Elam (49:34–39), and Babylon (50:1—51:58). In LXX the sequence is Elam (25:14—26:1), Egypt (26:2–28), Babylon (27:1—28:58), the Philistines (29:1–7), Edom (29:8–23), Ammon (30:1–5), Kedar (30:6–11), Damascus (30:12–16), Moab (31). Hazor is lost in translation because the Greek has *aulē* "court," from *ḥaṣēr* rather than *ḥaṣôr* (30:11). Note too that whereas the Masoretic text has Jeremiah's commission to make the nations drink of

myself to the familiar Masoretic version, but it's good to be aware of the complexity of the book's textual history.

A variety of structures have been proposed, but time fails me to summarize them.[6] My own hypothesis may be summarized in three points. The first is that the book introduces Jeremiah as a prophet with a double audience: he is called both a prophet to his own people (1:5–10) and a prophet to the nations (1:16–19). Correspondingly, the material which follows is of two kinds: oracles and narratives intended for Judah and oracles against the nations. The former, those intended for Judah, are found in chapters 2 through 45 and the oracles against the nations in chapters 46 through 51. The second point is related to the first, namely that both the oracles and narratives intended for Judah and the oracles against the nations are introduced as a *rîb* or covenant lawsuit (2:9; 25:31).[7] Thirdly, it is fascinating to observe that the book on the one hand shows a lack of concern for historical sequence, particularly in the second half, and on the other hand a high concern for historical specificity—again, particularly in the second half—suggesting the work of a compiler who, though sensitive to chronology, opted for a non-chronological arrangement of the material. In short, my hypothesis is that the material of chapters 2 through 45—that is, the oracles and narratives intended for the covenant people of Judah—has been arranged according to the order of the Decalogue, for the purpose of building a legal case that would demonstrate commandment by commandment how the people of Judah had broken God's covenant and forfeited their land.

Jeremiah as Decalogical Lawsuit

We come, then, to the arrangement of Jeremiah's contents, specifically of chapters 2 through 45. These chapters may be divided into a number of sections containing oracles and narratives that illustrate sin against successive

---

YHWH's cup in 25:13–38, in the Septuagint it is found in chapter 32:1–24, at the close of the oracles against the nations.

6. Stulman offers a highly structured proposal, that the (Masoretic version of the) book divides "into two major sections," 1–25 and 26–52, "producing a two-part prophetic drama. Each part comprises five acts held in place by an introduction and a conclusion." "Jeremiah," 221. A convenient summary of major twentieth-century positions may be found in Brueggemann, *To Pluck Up*, 7–10; Carroll, "Surplus Meaning," 195–216; Carroll, "Century's End," 217–31; Diamond, "The Jeremiah Guild," 232–48. A recent collection of papers representing the state of the question is Kessler, *Reading the Book of Jeremiah*.

7. For a clear instance of a *rîb* introducing a legal case, followed by material supporting the case and a closing divine judgment, see Mic 6:1–16.

commandments.[8] What complicates matters, to be sure, is that the sections are not mutually exclusive: sins against a particular commandment can be found in other sections as well. That is to say, what marks the structure of the book as decalogical is not that each section *only* contains sin against its corresponding commandment, but rather that each section illustrates sin *especially* against a particular commandment, and that the overall sequence persistently follows that of the Decalogue.

Chapters 2 through 4 collect ample evidence for the sin of idolatry. The section begins by recalling Israel's early devotion to the LORD who brought them out of Egypt and through the desert. The noun *'Elôhîm* is used five times for gods other than Yahweh, and 4:1 urges the people to remove their abominations "from before" the LORD, echoing the wording of the first commandment. Other expressions for idolatry include "walking after vanity" (2:5) and "after that which does not profit" (2:8), becoming distant from God (2:5), "loving strangers" (2:8), "exchanging one's Glory for what does not profit" (2:11), "forsaking the spring of living water for broken cisterns" (2:13), behaving like a "prostitute" (2:20, 3:1–3, 4:30) or an unfaithful wife (3:1, 20), "saying to wood, 'You are my father,' and to stone, 'You have begotten me'" (2:27).[9] It is in apparent response to this idolatry, and in this section alone, that God is referred to as "Father" (3:4, 19).[10]

Whether the prohibition against making images constitutes a second commandment or a second part of the first has been the subject of long-standing debate. In Jeremiah, one consideration for treating them separately is the use of the phrase "to visit upon" (*pqd 'al*) for judgment upon Israel's children in chapter 5:7–9. The phrase is also found in 5:29, 9:9, and 11:22.[11] The word for "image" (*pesel*) occurs but twice in Jeremiah, the first time in 10:14, and a related noun (*pasîl*) occurs for the first time in this section as well (8:19). The phrase "bow down and serve," occurs for the first time in 8:2 together with the verb "to love," producing an unmistakable allusion to the second commandment. Chapter 7 describes the corruption of the temple worship; at the end of that pericope the LORD refers to his people as a "generation under his wrath" (*dôr 'ebratô*). In 9:24 one finds the first of

---

8. I have attempted to divide sections along natural breaks in the text, but as Carroll notes, "Each section or description of that section may be disputed as to extent of division or accuracy of the summary of its contents. Each reader will offer a different assessment of the contents of a section, and in some cases there will be disagreement about the precise point where a block may begin or end." Carroll, *Jeremiah*, 17.

9. Translations of the Hebrew are my own.

10. On Jeremiah's use of this title, see Van Dam, "Call me Father," 77–88.

11. On the phenomenon of recurring phrases in Jeremiah, see especially Parke-Taylor, *Formation*.

only two passages in Jeremiah where God is said to "show kindness" (*'asah ḥesed*).[12] Chapter 10 offers a detailed description of image-making, and in chapter 11 Jeremiah pronounces God's judgment on the men of Anathoth in words reminiscent of the second commandment: "Behold, I am punishing them (*hinĕnî pôqēd 'alêhem*). The young men will die by the sword, their sons and their daughters will die by famine" (11:22). The section ends in Jeremiah 12:1–13 where the LORD responds to the prophet's challenge to prove his justice by punishing the wicked.

The evidence for a section corresponding to the third commandment is comparably weak. Fuller evidence for the adjacent sections corresponding to the second and fourth commandments prompts one to look for it in the area of 12:14 to 17:18. The expression "to take someone's name in vain," does not occur in Jeremiah at all, perhaps not surprisingly since one finds it only in the Decalogue itself (Exod 20:7, Deut 5:11). In 14:9, Jeremiah has the people say, "You are in our midst, O LORD, and your name is called over us; do not leave us." More relevant, perhaps, is 13:11: "'For just as a belt is tied around a man's waist, so I tied the whole house of Israel and the whole house of Judah to myself,' declares the LORD, 'to be a people and a name and praise and glory for me, but they have not listened.'" In other words, Jeremiah's ruined belt, unfit to be worn around his waist, was a fitting image for the dishonor which Israel's behavior had brought to God's name. Finally, a phrase nearly unique to the book of Jeremiah is "to prophecy in someone's name."[13] Of the nine times in which this phrase is found in Jeremiah, six times it is used of false prophets who used God's name to lend authority and authenticity to their false predictions; i.e. they associate his name with lies. The first two of these six occurrences are found in 14:14, 15.[14] Such misuse of God's name effectively hampered Jeremiah's claim to authentic prophecy in 15:16: "Your words appeared, and I ate them, and they became my joy, my heart's delight, because your name is called over me." For God to defend his name and to defend his prophet are one and the same, and thus it is no surprise that the sole use of the verb "to curse" (*qll*) is found in 15:10 where the prophet bewails his existence: "Woe to me, my mother, that you bore me, a man whom the whole land blames and condemns; I haven't lent and I haven't borrowed, but they're all cursing me!"

Much more obvious is the connection of the next section to the fourth commandment. It begins in 17:19 where the LORD commanded Jeremiah to station himself at the gates of Jerusalem and to deliver an oracle urging

---

12. The other is 32:18, which even more clearly echoes the second commandment.
13. Outside of Jeremiah it occurs only in Zechariah 13:3.
14. The remaining four are found in 23:25, 27:15, and 29:9, 21.

obedience to the Sabbath commands, followed by contingent well-being for obedience (24–26) and disaster for disobedience (27). Chapters 18 through 20 lack further references to Sabbath legislation but do express Judah's clear choice for disobedience and consequently contain some of the prophet's most passionate pleas for divine judgment.

A significant message of chapters 21 through 25 seems to be that Judah's final kings would lose the land due to their failure to honor their father Josiah. One reads in 22:11–12, for example: "For thus says the LORD concerning Shallum son of Josiah, who became king in place of his father Josiah and has gone away from this place: 'He will never return to it; indeed he will die in the place where they have led him captive, and he will not see this land again.'" In other words he would forfeit the blessing of long days in the land that God had given to his people. His brother Jehoiakim would receive an even worse fate—the burial of a donkey—for failing to follow his father's example of defending the cause of the poor and needy. Of his father is twice said (22:15, 16) that it went well with him ($ṭôb\ lô$), an allusion to Deuteronomy's wording of the fifth commandment, "that it may go well with you" ($yîṭab\ lak$). Jehoiachin would be cast into a foreign land, together with his mother, never to return. The land is told to regard him as a failure, a man without children to inherit his throne (22:24–30). Chapter 24 differentiates, however, between the Jews exiled with Jehoiachin and those who remained with Zedekiah: God would bring the former back to the land, he would build them and plant them and be their God, but the latter would forever forfeit the promise accompanying the fifth commandment: "I will send the sword, famine, and plague against them until they are destroyed from the land I gave to them and their fathers" (24:10). The section ends in 25:1–14 with the prophecy that the land would be laid waste for seventy years until the LORD would bring judgment upon the land of Babylon.

In the second half of chapter 25 Jeremiah is instructed to make the nations drink of the cup of God's wrath and to announce God's case against them. It is at this point that the Septuagint inserts the oracles against the nations, but the Masoretic text places them at the end of the book and continues in chapters 26 through 28 with a section related to the sixth commandment. While the verb for "murder" ($rṣḥ$) does not occur, in chapter 26 the prophet was charged with a capital offence. He responded to those who put him on trial, "If you put me to death, you will bring the guilt of innocent blood on yourselves, and on the city and on those who live in it" (26:15). That is to say, to execute him would have been tantamount to murder. Chapter 26:23 records the murder of the prophet Uriah at the hands of Jehoiakim, and interestingly, the section ends with the death of the false prophet Hananiah at the word of Jeremiah (28:15–17). Given that the narrative jumps more than a decade from the beginning of Jehoiakim's reign in 26:1 to the beginning of Zedekiah's reign in 27:1,[15] this section supports the notion that the material is arranged not chronologically but topically, here by grouping the death or near-death experiences of various prophets.

Chapters 29 through 31 relate easily to the seventh commandment. The verb "commit adultery" (*n'p*) occurs in this section (29:23), though not for the first time (3:8, 9; 5:7; 7:9; 9:1; 23:10, 14). Jeremiah's letter to the exiles instructs them to marry and have sons and daughters and give their children in marriage. At the end of the letter the false prophets are said to have committed adultery with their neighbors' wives. Chapter 31 twice refers to God's people as "Virgin Israel" (*betûlat yiśra'el*).[16] Particularly the second occurrence uses language reminiscent of marital fidelity: "Return, Virgin Israel, return to these your towns! How long will you waver, unfaithful daughter? For the LORD will create something new in the land: a female will surround a male" (31:21b-22). The same chapter compares the new covenant to a marriage relationship, "unlike the covenant which I made with their fathers when I held them by the hand, bringing them out of the land of Egypt, my covenant which they broke, though I was a husband to them (*ba'altî bam*), declares the LORD." Verses 33–37 then give God's pledge of lasting faithfulness to his people.

Like the third commandment, evidence for the eighth is sparse, and it is certainly the weakest link in the chain of commandments. For example, the verb "to steal" (*gnb*) is attested in the book (2:26; 7:9; 23:30; 48:27; 49:9), but not where the proposed arrangement might lead one to expect it. In chapters 32 and 33 one finds evidence that is circumstantial at best, for example in the godly character of the prophet who follows legal process to buy a field that becomes a pledge of a future time when business would again be transacted in the land (32:43-44), and in the recurring phrase, "I will restore their fortunes" (32:44; 33:11, 26), which uses an idiom for restitution in case of theft or loss of property (*šûb*).

Much better attested are allusions to the ninth commandment in a lengthy section running from chapter 34 to 45. It begins in 34 with the treachery of Zedekiah *cum suis*, who renege on their sworn promise to set the slaves free. Chapter 35 jumps back in time to the reign of Jehoiakim to illustrate the virtues of loyalty and honesty via the example of the Rechabites. In 37 Jeremiah is falsely accused of deserting to the Babylonians, and in 38 Zedekiah's officials testify to the king that he was hurting the morale

---

15. Assuming, of course, that the correct reading in 27:1 is not Jehoiakim but Zedekiah. Cf. 28:1.

16. Jeremiah 31:4, 21. The expression is otherwise found only in 18:31 and in Amos 5:2.

of the people, but Ebed-Melech showed him love by gaining the king's permission to rescue him from the cistern into which they had lowered him. The chapter ends with Zedekiah consulting the prophet in secret: Jeremiah warns him about treacherous friends (22), while the king instructs him to lie about the purpose of their conversation (24–27). In chapter 39 the LORD proved Jeremiah's word true by bringing the Babylonians into the city, and in the following chapter Nebuzaradan vindicated and released him (40:2–4). Gedaliah swore an oath to reassure the remaining residents of the Babylonians' goodwill (40:9) but then died for his naivety, refusing to believe the testimony of those who warned him that his life was in danger. The section ends as it began, with a people whose word has become altogether untrustworthy: they appeal to God as true and faithful witness to their oath that they would accept his direction (42:5), but renege on their promise when the direction given is unpalatable to them. They falsely accuse Jeremiah of duplicity and conspiracy (43:3) and compel him to accompany them to Egypt. There the refugee community becomes the recipient of a concluding message of disaster and doom. Indeed the entire section serves to contrast the faithfulness of God's word with the unreliability of God's people; upright and honest men are rare—Jonadab the Rechabite, Ebed-Melech the Cushite, and Baruch the son of Neriah—but each of these three men receives a prophetic assurance of God's favor and protection (35:19; 39:17; 45:5).

There is no section corresponding with the tenth commandment, and the verb "to covet" does not occur in the book. Its absence is not surprising, however: since the tenth commandment forbids an attitude or intent rather than an action, the sin of coveting is not quantifiable in the evidentiary sense necessary for building a legal case against God's people. To put it differently, if intent precedes action, then the fact that the other commandments have been broken is sufficient evidence that the tenth has as well.

The final section of Jeremiah comprises prophetic oracles, all of which predate the destruction of Jerusalem, supporting the hypothesis of a compiler whose concern was not chronological but topical. These oracles constitute evidence to support a second legal case, this time against a variety of nations surrounding Israel. This second legal case is introduced in 25:31, and it is therefore interesting that in the Septuagint these oracles run from 25:14 to the end of chapter 32, right between the sections here identified with the fifth and the sixth commandments, while the Masoretic text places them at the end of the book. Furthermore, the LXX order, though different from the Masoretic, does not affect the decalogical sequence that I've outlined, nor does it interrupt a section associated with a particular command.[17]

---

17. That is to say, the versification for the sections associated with commandments

From that perspective the literary structure I've proposed for the Masoretic text remains intact for the Septuagint version as well.

Testing the Hypothesis

In summary, I have presented the hypothesis that chapters 2 through 45 have been arranged according to the order of the Decalogue, for the purpose of building a legal case that would demonstrate commandment by commandment how the people of Judah had broken God's covenant and forfeited their land. Now, one *could* decide to leave it at that, and be content to adopt the hypothesis as a working model for studying the book or for preaching a series of sermons on it, or for supplying Scripture readings to accompany a series of sermons on Lord's Days 34-44 of the Heidelberg Catechism. However, an OT scholar working in an ecclesiastical seminary should go a step further and test the hypothesis by asking critical questions and ensuring that responsible methodology has been followed to arrive at the hypothesis, recognizing that a working model may be modified or rejected after further research has been done. Among the many questions that could be asked of my hypothesis are the following three: Firstly, was there indeed a compiler who arranged the book into final form after the sequential pattern of the Decalogue? Secondly, is the lawsuit that's introduced in chapter 2 intended to apply to the entire section running from chapter 2 through 45, and is the lawsuit introduced in chapter 25 intended to apply to all the oracles against the nations, or do both occurrences of *rîb* apply only to their immediate contexts? Thirdly, do the sections that I've aligned with particular commandments divide into pericopes in a defensible manner?

Over the course of the past century and a half, critical tools have been developed and refined to address precisely these kinds of questions. I think, for example, of form criticism, rhetorical criticism, and delimitation criticism.[18] To be sure, it cannot be taken for granted that a Reformed OT scholar should or is even allowed to make use of such tools. To cite a well-known authority from our own heritage, Abraham Kuyper, in his 1881 rectoral address at the Free University of Amsterdam, defended the thesis that the Scripture criticism of his day would "bleed the church's theology to death,

---

one through five is the same in the Greek as in the Hebrew (Jer 2:1—25:13), and the content of the sections associated with commandments six through nine, while placed after the oracles of the nations, follows the same order as the Masoretic text (LXX 33–51 = MT 26–45).

18. For an orientation to delimitation criticism, see Korpel and Oesch, *Delimitation Criticism*.

rob the church of her holy Scriptures, and deliver the church helplessly into the arms of the most unbearable, though intellectual, clericalism."[19] Kuyper's words are still well worth reading, though it should be noted that they are not timeless: he spoke of "hedendaagsche Schriftcritiek," *en de Schriftcritiek van toen is wel een beetje anders als die van tegenwoordig.* Scripture criticism has not stood still in the 133 years that have passed since 1881.[20] For example, earlier approaches tended to focus on oral and written traditions behind the text, while later methods are more concerned with understanding the text with a view to its final form, its structure, its recipients, and its interpretive history. Criticism has become a catchall for a wide variety of hermeneutical approaches to the text, such that the word today means little more than a particularly defined reading strategy. Soulen and Soulen's *Handbook of Biblical Criticism* has entries for no fewer than twenty-two varieties, and that is far from a comprehensive list.[21] It's become quite common for writers of dissertations to introduce their methodologies as new forms of criticism. The traditional distinction between higher and lower criticism is now discouraged because it does injustice not only to the current variety within Biblical criticism but also to the importance and complexity of textual criticism.[22] All of this is not to suggest that Kuyper be disregarded as passé, but simply to observe that one cannot assume that his warnings apply without modification to the current situation or that they rule out the use of all critical methodologies whatsoever. I'll return to Kuyper in my closing comments, but first I'd like to discuss one particular approach that can yield fruitful answers to the sorts of questions I've raised on the structure of the book of Jeremiah, namely rhetorical criticism.

---

19. Kuyper, *De hedendaagsche Schriftcritiek*, 6. I thank Prof. J. Geertsema for supplying me with a copy of this address. From the same period, and in a similar vein, though far less convinced of the ability of Scripture criticism to do real damage, is Warfield's inaugural address, in which he addressed the following question: "Is the church doctrine of the plenary inspiration of the New Testament endangered by the assured results of modern Biblical criticism?" "Inspiration and Criticism," 419–42.

20. See, e.g., Berkouwer, *Probleem der Schriftkritiek*, 6–7.

21. Soulen and Soulen, *Handbook*.

22. See, e.g., the following comment in Soulen and Soulen, *Handbook*, 121: "Lower criticism is an unhappy term, now of infrequent parlance, characterizing textual criticism in contrast to so-called higher criticism, i.e., all other forms of Biblical criticism. The term has fallen into disuse because of its pejorative sound coupled with the increasing acknowledgment that textual criticism is both important and complex."

Rhetorical Criticism

James Muilenburg first introduced "rhetorical criticism" to OT scholarship in his 1968 Presidential Address to the Society of Biblical Literature.[23] A few years later, one of Muilenberg's students, Jack Lundbom, applied this tool to the book of Jeremiah in his 1973 dissertation.[24] These two scholars understand rhetorical criticism as a means of identifying the structural and stylistic features of Biblical texts and tracing how these features shape its literary units and illuminate the writer's intent. It is not concerned with the sources or historical development or forms of the text, but it focuses on the text as it is composed. In that respect, it offers a corrective to form criticism: rather than interpret a passage on the basis of pre-established genre categories or forms, it seeks to let the rhetorical features of the text speak for themselves.[25] The first point on its agenda is to divide the text into literary units, that is, to identify where a pericope begins and ends, based on the placement of ancient Hebrew paragraph markers as well as literary features such as superscriptions, messenger formulas, shifts from poetry to prose and vice versa, and the use of *inclusio*s and chiasms. Once a literary unit has been identified, the second step is to study its structural features, such as refrains, rhetorical questions, and discourse markers, in order to analyze how the pericope develops and what it achieves. A third step is to identify stylistic features such as wordplays, metaphors, similes, repetition, accumulation, as well as keywords and catchwords that tie various literary units together. The fourth and final step is to pull the results of this research together to gauge how the speaker is interacting with the audience, what sort of response the text is trying to elicit.[26]

It is not difficult to see how rhetorical criticism can serve as a useful tool for testing the hypothesis I've presented. In the first place it can help to evaluate the validity of the work that I have done. In particular, its concern for dividing the text into literary units in a methodologically responsible manner addresses a lynchpin of my argument. Would rhetorical criticism confirm or contradict the sectional delimitations I have suggested? As mentioned, one criterion is the placement of Hebrew paragraph markers, because these often correspond with spaces in the Dead Sea Scrolls, indicating that they represent very ancient divisions of the text.[27]

---

23. Muilenberg, "Form Criticism and Beyond," 1–18.
24. Lundbom, *Jeremiah*.
25. Soulen and Soulen, *Handbook*, 184.
26. Lundbom, *Jeremiah*, xxxiii–xlii.
27. Ibid., xxxiv.

Let me go through a few examples. I suggested that the section corresponding with the second commandment ends in 12:13, and that a new section begins at 12:14. Chapter 12:14 does have a closed paragraph marker (*setumah*, marked by ס), and it also begins with what Lundbom calls a messenger formula ("Thus says the LORD"),[28] but according to the *petuḥot* or open paragraph markers (marked by פ) the section runs from 11:1 to 13:27, so the evidence is ambivalent. Similarly, I suggested that a section corresponding to the fourth commandment begins at 17:19. It too has a closed paragraph marker before it, but the *petuḥot* are found earlier and later, at 17:11 and 17:27. There too it can be argued that the messenger formula in 17:19 is enough of a structure marker to begin a new section. The same is true of 34:1, which begins the section corresponding to the ninth commandment: it too lacks a *petuḥah* but begins with a messenger formula. It should be noted, however, that the sections divided according to Hebrew paragraph markers and messenger formulas are smaller subsections of the divisions that I have proposed, and I haven't yet found rhetorical markers that confirm the larger decalogical sections I've proposed. To be sure, I haven't had time to look at other structural features such as chiasms and *inclusio*s, but it is already sufficiently clear to me that the division of the book needs further attention in order for my hypothesis to be sustained.

A second benefit of rhetorical criticism is to alert me to work that still needs to be done. One example is the need to study keywords and repeated formulas that might serve to tie the book together. Obvious candidates are the verbs listed in 1:10: "to uproot," "to tear down," "to destroy," "to overthrow," "to build," and "to plant." Various configurations of these verbs are repeated at intervals throughout the book,[29] but the intervals do not clearly correspond with the sections that I've proposed. In short, rhetorical criticism can profitably be used as a kind of quality control to ask critical questions of one's hypotheses.

Confessional Integrity

All of this is not to suggest that rhetorical criticism can be used without peril: it's an approach that arose within the context of form criticism, and it builds upon the findings of source and tradition-historical criticism. That brings me to the final section of my paper, on maintaining confessional integrity. Here I'd like to propose four theses:

---

28. Ibid., xxxv.
29. Cf. 12:14–17, 18:7, 24:6, 31:28, 42:10, and 45:4.

1. While bearing in mind Kuyper's warning words about the detrimental impact of the Scripture criticism of his time, a confessional hermeneutic does not *a priori* rule out the use of all critical approaches to Scripture. Some degree of responsible biblical criticism is beneficial not because the Scriptures need it but because its interpreters do, in order to ensure a sufficient measure of quality control for their research so that they can both verify and falsify their theories.

2. Kuyper warned that Scripture criticism could lead to "unbearable clericalism," and indeed, one of the disadvantages of adopting critical methods is the impression that Bible study is an activity for the intellectual elite, for which the layman is unqualified. Such an impression runs counter to the spirit of the Reformation, which gave the Bible back to the people, to whom it belongs. At the same time, however, if I as a theology professor am going to give guidance to the churches and suggest to a Bible study group how I think the book of Jeremiah should be read, or to an audience of ministers how I think the book should be preached, then I owe it to the churches to make sure that my theory can stand up to critical scrutiny.

3. In the current proliferation of critical methodologies it can be tempting to develop tools that justify reading into Scripture what one wants to find there. That temptation should be resisted: one is more likely to test a hypothesis objectively by making use of existing tools than by developing one's own tools.

4. One of the perils of rhetorical criticism is that the scholar becomes preoccupied with literary features to the point of losing sight of the book's character as divine revelation. Critical study must not become an end in itself, but must remain a means to a greater end, namely to better understand what God's word is saying to the church.

Conclusion

In conclusion, this paper intends not so much to solve the problem of the structure of Jeremiah as to propose how a Reformed OT scholar might participate in the conversation of those who wrestle with such problems. I've presented the material in a "stream of consciousness" fashion, taking you along on the path of discovery and difficulty, in order to illustrate the challenges of navigating between the profits and perils of critical scholarship. In the midst of such challenges one needs trustworthy conversation partners, and therefore I'm thankful for the opportunity to do this kind of exploratory research within the context of an ecclesiastical seminary where there are close contacts with godly, Reformed colleagues, allowing for ongoing interaction between the disciplines, within the bounds of confessional subscription, and also in the context of vibrant congregations that keep us grounded in the faith through the means of grace, fellowship, and prayer.

Bibliography

Allen, Leslie C. "Jeremiah: Book of." In *Dictionary of the Old Testament Prophets*, edited by Mark J. Boda and J. Gordon McConville, 423–41. Downers Grove, IL: IVP Academic, 2012.

Berkouwer, Gerrit C. *Het Probleem der Schriftkritiek*. Kampen: Kok, n.d.

Brueggemann, Walter. *To Pluck Up, To Tear Down: A Commentary on the Book of Jeremiah 1–25*. International Theological Commentary. Grand Rapids, MI: Eerdmans, 1988.

Carroll, Robert P. "Century's End: Jeremiah Studies at the Beginning of the Third Millennium." In *Recent Research on the Major Prophets*, edited by Alan J. Hauser, 217–31. Recent Research in Biblical Studies 1. Sheffield: Sheffield Phoenix Press, 2008.

———. *Jeremiah*. Old Testament Guides. Sheffield: JSOT Press, 1989.

———. "Surplus Meaning and the Conflict of Interpretations: A Dodecade of Jeremiah Studies (1984–1995)." In *Recent Research on the Major Prophets*, edited by Alan J. Hauser, 195–216. Recent Research in Biblical Studies 1. Sheffield: Sheffield Phoenix Press, 2008.

Diamond, A. R. Pete. "The Jeremiah Guild in the Twenty-First Century: Variety Reigns Supreme." In *Recent Research on the Major Prophets*, edited by Alan J. Hauser, 232–48. Recent Research in Biblical Studies 1. Sheffield: Sheffield Phoenix Press, 2008.

Giesebrecht, Friedrich. *Das Buch Jeremia*. Handkommentar zum Alten Testament. 2nd ed. Göttingen: Vandenhoeck & Ruprecht, 1907.

Graf, Karl H. *Der Prophet Jeremia erklärt*. Leipzig: T.O. Weigel, 1862.

Janzen, J. Gerald. *Studies in the Text of Jeremiah*. Harvard Semitic Monographs 6. Cambridge, MA: Harvard University Press, 1973.

Kessler, Martin, ed. *Reading the Book of Jeremiah: A Search for Coherence*. Winona Lake, IN: Eisenbrauns, 2004.

Korpel, Marjo C. A., and Josef M. Oesch, eds. *Delimitation Criticism: A New Tool in Biblical Scholarship*. Pericope 1. Assen: Van Gorcum, 2000.

Kuyper, Abraham. *De hedendaagsche Schriftcritiek in hare bedenkelijke strekking voor de gemeente des levenden Gods*. Amsterdam: J. H. Kruyt, 1881.

Longman, Tremper, III and Raymond B. Dillard. *An Introduction to the Old Testament*. 2nd ed. Grand Rapids, MI: Zondervan, 2006.

Lundbom, Jack R. *Jeremiah: A Study in Ancient Hebrew Rhetoric*. 2nd ed. Winona Lake, IN: Eisenbrauns, 1997.

———. *Jeremiah 1–20: A New Translation with Introduction and Commentary*. Anchor Bible 21A. New York: Doubleday, 1999.

McLane, William. "Jeremiah's Instructions to Seraiah (Jeremiah 51:59–64)." In *Pomegranates and Golden Bells: Studies in Biblical, Jewish, and Near Eastern Ritual, Law and Literature in Honor of Jacob Milgrom*, edited by D. P. Wright et al., 697–706. Winona Lake, IN: Eisenbrauns, 1995.

Muilenburg, James. "Form Criticism and Beyond." *JBL* 88 (1969) 1–18.

Parke-Taylor, Geoffrey H. *The Formation of the Book of Jeremiah: Doublets and Recurring Phrases*. SBL Monograph Series 51. Atlanta: SBL, 2000.

Smith, Jannes. "Jeremiah 52: Thackeray and Beyond," in *BIOSCS* 35 (2002) 55–96.

Soderlund, Sven. *The Greek Text of Jeremiah: A Revised Hypothesis*. JSOT Supplements 47. Sheffield: JSOT Press, 1985.

Soulen, Richard N., and R. Kendall Soulen, *Handbook of Biblical Criticism*. 4th ed. Louisville, KY: WJK Press, 2011.

Stipp, Hermann-J. *Das masoretische und alexandrinische Sondergut des Jeremiabuches*. Orbis Biblicus et Orientalis 136. Göttingen: Vandenhoeck & Ruprecht, 1994.

Stulman, Louis. "Jeremiah, Book of." In *The New Interpreters Dictionary of the Bible*, edited by K. D. Sakenfeld et al., 3:220–35. Nashville: Abingdon Press, 2006–2009.

Van Dam, S. Carl. "Call me Father! The Grief and Desire of a Loving Father." In *Living Waters from Ancient Springs: Essays in Honor of Cornelis Van Dam*, edited by Jason Van Vliet, 77–88. Eugene, OR: Pickwick Publications, 2011.

Warfield, Benjamin B. "Inspiration and Criticism." In *The Inspiration and Authority of the Bible*, edited by S.G. Craig, 419–42. Grand Rapids, MI: Baker, 1967.

7

1 Timothy 2:12–15

Is Paul's Injunction about Women still Valid?

Gerhard H. Visscher

Shortly after I committed to speak on this topic a report was published by a committee mandated by the GKN(v) Synod of 2011 to investigate whether women may be admitted to the office of elder, deacon, and minister of the Word. It is entitled *Rapport Deputaten M/V in de kerk* (*The Report of deputies male/female in the church*). The *Report*, to the surprise of many on this side of the ocean, answered that "the position that besides men, women may also serve in the offices of the church . . . fits within the breadth of what can be affirmed as Biblical and Reformed."[1] In the *Report* addressed to Synod Ede 2014, the committee examined some of the hermeneutical issues, wrote about the relevant NT texts, made many good comments, and then concluded that it is legitimate for women to function in all the offices. While it is not necessary for women to do so in all churches, there should really be no objection, they said. In the *Report*, the conclusion is drawn that the culture in which Paul wrote was very unique, as is today's modern European culture, and it is thus problematic to suggest that Paul's voice should stand in the way in our day.

---

1. Bakker et al, *Rapport Deputaten*, decision 2, page 33. There was also a dissenting minority report.

With respect to the question being asked tonight, the Dutch committee has answered with a firm "no." Paul's injunction is not valid or normative any longer. I will argue, however, that if we use the same redemptive-historical hermeneutic that we use everywhere else with respect to Scripture, and listen to it regardless of whether we like its results, we will arrive at a firm "yes."

There are a number of components that are necessary to see if we are to understand what Paul has to say about women and their role in the life of the church. There are obviously many texts of the New Testament that have a bearing upon the role of women, but with respect to women in office, particularly 1 Corinthians 11, 14 and 1 Timothy 2 are critical.

1 Corinthians 11, 14

The first thing we need to do is pause along the way in Corinth in order to understand what Paul is saying about women in 1 Corinthians 11 and 14. The difficulty with understanding the first letter to the Corinthians is that we actually lack so much information about the original context. Reading 1 Corinthians is like listening to one side of a phone conversation, or one set of letters in a conversation; we are never quite sure what is being said or understood from the other side. One of the persons, however, who may have done the most to bridge that gap is Bruce W. Winter, the former director of Tyndale House, Cambridge,[2] a scholar who came to my attention also because the Dutch *Report* refers to him. Winter, a Greco-Roman historian, wants to bring some details from that world to the attention of New Testament scholars.[3] Having waded through the material presented by Winter and others,[4] the following are significant components in answering the question before us.

Winter argues that around 44 BC a new type of woman emerged in Roman circles: women who could retain their own property, claim their own means to sexual pleasure, terminate their marriage, receive back a portion of their dowry, compete with men in ways unheard of before, and stand up against the former indiscreet and adulterous practices of their husbands.[5]

---

2. At the time of publication of *After Paul Left Corinth* (2001) and *Roman Wives, Roman Widows* (2003), Winter was the director of the Institute for Early Christianity in the Graeco-Roman World, Tyndale House, Cambridge.

3. Winter complains that NT scholars are not adequately familiar with the Greco-Roman world on this point. *Roman Wives*, xii, 21.

4. Winter, in turn, acknowledges (*Roman Wives*, 3n8) a degree of dependence on the work of Fantham et al., "The 'New Woman,'" 280–93.

5. *Roman Wives*, 21–22.

Winter cites a wealth of evidence for this "New Woman" from writers from the late Roman Republic and the early first century AD, and shows that these practices extended throughout the empire, also in the area of Corinth and Ephesus.[6] Says Winter,

> The "new" wife or widow in the late Roman Republic and early Empire was the one whose social life was reported to have been pursued at the expense of family responsibilities that included the complex running of households. Life beyond their household could involve illicit liaisons that defied the previously accepted norms of marriage fidelity and chastity.[7]

Of great interest in all of this is the fact that at several points the Emperor becomes concerned about the eventual effects of these New Women on the empire and actually issues legislation to curtail them. Decrees from Caesar Augustus in 17 BC, says Winter, "prescribed moral conduct, financial disadvantages in remaining single, the procreation of children with resulting career advantages, and dress codes for wives; it proscribed marriage between certain classes, and punished inactivity on the part of husbands who ignored their wife's extramarital liaisons."[8] This so-called *lex Julia* was also careful to ensure that prostitutes and women convicted of adultery were distinguished in their dress; it did so by forbidding them to wear the marriage veil.[9] This comprehensive legislation was revised and strengthened to some degree again in AD 9 in the *lex Papia*, and it all had a lasting effect throughout the NT era. Augustus was more than a legislator; he was "an adept promoter of traditional Roman values"[10] that had lasting effect throughout the empire. One scholar asks: "What difference did the Augustan legislation make? It may have persuaded upper class men to marry earlier than they might otherwise have done.... Women in both classes were given new reasons to want to be wives and prolific mothers."[11] Obviously we

---

6. Ibid., 22–38. See also Wood, *Imperial Women*. There appears to be little opposition to the views of Bruce W. Winter; the only significant criticism I could find was from Lynn H. Cohick, who suggests that "the existence of the 'new woman,' who was sexually promiscuous and upset the balance of propriety in Rome and beyond, is more a poetic fiction and a political smear than a historical reality." Cohick, *Women in the World of the Earliest Christians*, 75. This seems, however, to be in conflict with the vast amount of material referenced by Winter and others; referring to it as "poetic fiction" also appears odd as emperors and rulers hardly seek to pass legislation regarding fictional events.

7. *Roman Wives*, 5.

8. Ibid., 39. Cf. Bauman, *Women and Politics*, 105.

9. See Winter, *Roman Wives*, 43, and McGinn, *Prostitution*, 162

10. *Roman Wives*, 56.

11. Treggiari, *Roman Marriage*, 80.

cannot deal with all of this tonight, but among the vast amount of information passed on by Winter and others is a delightful quote from Seneca; it strikingly reflects much of the tension around women in his day as well as some of the notes that Paul and Peter touch on in the NT. He writes to his mother around AD 41–49:

> Unlike the great majority of women, you never succumbed to immorality, the worst evil of our time; jewels and pearls have not moved you; you never thought of wealth as the greatest gift to the human race; you have not been perverted by the imitation of worse women who lead even the virtuous into pitfalls; you have never blushed for the number of children, as if it taunted you with your years; never have you, in the manner of other women whose only recommendation lies in their beauty, tried to conceal your pregnancy as though it were indecent; you have not crushed the hope of children that were being nurtured in your body; you have not defiled your face with paints and cosmetics; never have you fancied the kind of dress that exposed no greater nakedness by being removed. Your only ornament, the kind of beauty that time does not tarnish, is the great honour of modesty.[12]

"In classical antiquity, you were what you wore."[13] In a world that clearly wished to identify its citizens in terms of classes, the most obvious way to do so was to develop a distinctive dress code for everyone and to ensure that at dinners, theaters, and other public gatherings a certain dress protocol would be observed.[14]

With respect to clothing then, it is of interest that since the year 2000, a significant amount of new material has also been put forth by ancient historians which throws new light on the significance of women wearing veils in 1 Corinthians 11.[15] This material suggests that at stake here was not the status of all women, but particularly married women. The veil that Paul speaks about is the wedding veil: "the veiled head was the symbol of the modesty and chastity expected of a married woman."[16] The wives praying and prophesying with their heads uncovered were following the practices of these "new" Roman women who were defying the traditional practices.[17]

---

12. Seneca, *ad Helviam*, 16:3–4, as quoted by Winter, *Roman Wives*, 60.
13. McGinn, *Prostitution*, 162.
14. Winter, *Roman Wives*, 4–5.
15. Ibid., 77–96.
16. *Roman Wives*, 80.
17. Ciampa and Rosner, *First Corinthians*, 520.

The "omission of the veil by a married woman was a sign of her 'withdrawing' herself from the marriage."[18] This is also what 1 Corinthians 11:5 is referring to; in the background there is the fact that in the Roman world a woman who was found to be guilty of adultery was to have her hair cut off, and so Paul is arguing: if she will not cover her head, "it is the same as having her head shaved" (11:5).[19] Augustus' legislation sought in fact to distinguish carefully between the modest wife, the adulteress, and the prostitute.[20] Indeed, you "were what you wore."

So, if we pause here and consider the significance of this beyond what the Greco-Roman historians normally do, what we have is this: Paul is essentially agreeing with Augustus in terms of the nature of the family and the role of women, but he is doing so for different reasons. Both the origin and the goal of his approach are different. The apostle is arguing that Christian women, especially married women, should see their roles differently—not just for the sake of the well-being of society but especially for the well-being of the church and the cause of the Gospel. Elsewhere he has argued that in God's New Society (to borrow a phrase from John Stott),[21] husbands have to love their wives (Eph 5:25), and wives need to respect their husbands (Eph 5:22); here he expands especially on the latter. In his culture, the marriage veil was part of the honor that a Christian wife would give her husband. He is not saying: God requires all married women to wear a veil throughout the ages. But he is saying: God requires all married women throughout the ages to respect their husbands, and in our culture they cannot do that without wearing a veil. It is impossible for women to appear as Christian women without doing this in certain contexts.

More specifically then regarding the 1 Corinthians passages, it is rather curious that Paul argues, on the one hand, that women can prophesy (11:5, 13) yet, on the other hand, they must "remain silent" and not be "allowed to speak . . . for it is disgraceful for a woman to speak in the church" (14:34, 35). While the last phrase of verse 35 appears to be rather general, the best position that helps us to work through this apparent contradiction is one which sees the 1 Corinthians 14 passage as speaking in the context of the sifting of prophecy in the early Church. What we need to realize here is that in the biblical picture, the lines of authority do not flow from the OT prophets to the NT prophets in the early church, but from the OT prophets to the

---

18. Winter, *Romans Wives*, 81.

19. All Scripture quotations in this article are from the New International Version (NIV84).

20. Ibid., 84.

21. Stott, *Ephesians*.

NT apostles. The apostles are understood to be speaking with the authority of the Word of God. Whether NT prophets, who often had to interpret a revelation, were actually speaking the Word of God with authority needed to be judged and weighed by others.[22] And so what Thiselton says is, in my judgment, the best interpretation here: this "almost certainly refers to contributions from *women who seek to join in the sifting* or *testing of a claim to speak with prophetic activity.*"[23] So Paul is saying in 1 Corinthians that while women can pray and prophesy in the services, when it comes to speaking with any kind of authority, they should be silent.

1 Timothy 2

This, in turn, brings us to the 1 Timothy 2 passage where Paul extends the lines somewhat and has other things to say about women and worship.

In 1 Timothy 2 Paul is again speaking about matters of worship (3:15) and again has much to say about the conduct of men (2:8) and women in worship (2:9, 10). Strikingly, in this culture where "you were what you wore," he cannot do that without speaking about the attire of the women (2:9, 10); it is noteworthy here that also Augustus had sought to curb excess with respect to jewelry and clothing.[24]

Here, however, Paul expands on what women should not do in worship. Consistent with what he says in 1 Corinthians about women being silent in authoritative matters, he says that he, the apostle (1 Tim 1:1), does "not permit a woman to teach or to have authority over a man;" again he emphasizes that "she must be silent" in this regard (2:12). And notice how he affirms his role as a "herald and apostle" in 2:7 just before the disputed verses—that the "I" of 2:12 is not the "I" of Paul the individual, but of Paul the apostle sent by God, is clear from 2:7.

Despite an array of attempts to prove that 1 Timothy 2 had some kind of specific contextual situation that limits the significance of the passage,[25] the fact is that if Paul wanted to say that he certainly could have done so easily. Instead, a plain reading of 1 Timothy 2 understands Paul as saying that, when it comes to public worship, women should not teach or have authority

22. For more on this, see Grudem "Prophecy," 11–23.

23. Thiselton, *First Corinthians,* 251; emphasis mine. See also D. A. Carson who says: "a strong case can be made for the view that Paul refused to permit any woman to enjoy a church-recognized teaching authority over men (1 Timothy 2:11ff.), and the careful weighing of prophecies falls under that magisterial function." Carson, "'Silent in the Churches,'" 152. Cf. Schreiner, *New Testament Theology,* 775.

24. Winter, *Romans Wives,* 103.

25. See Kroeger, *I Suffer Not a Woman.*

over a man. Much of the exegetical gymnastics that happens with respect to this verse, I suspect, is not due to a lack of clarity on the part of the author or the text, but to the reader's lack of willingness to accept the message. The most significant difficulty of these verses is probably the exact meaning of the verb for "have authority over" (αὐθεντέω) because of its rare occurrence, but Al Wolters has shown that the NIV 1984 is correct here.[26] The text of 1 Tim. 2:13-15 itself, if it were speaking about a different subject, would not be considered so difficult from a lexical, grammatical and syntactical point of view; the main difficulty is really that many in our world do not like the message it conveys.

To be sure, the prohibition is not absolute. Priscilla and Aquila obviously taught Apollos privately (Acts 18:26). Priscilla, Euodia, and Synteche were in some way "co-workers" with Paul (Rom 16:3, Phil 4:3). Paul tells Titus to tell the older women to teach the younger women, and to "teach what is good" elsewhere. And believers are called upon to "teach one another" (Col 3:16). However, in 1 Timothy 2 Paul is referring to the public and authoritative teaching that happens in worship (see also 1 Tim 4:13, 16; 6:2; 2 Tim 4:2; Titus 2:7). In other words, the task that the dying Paul will pass on to young Timothy is the exclusive prerogative of the men whom God calls. In my judgment, Douglas Moo is correct when he says that the two verbs "to teach" or "to have authority over" are not referring to one action but two, although the two are closely related. Says Moo:

> Although teaching in Paul's sense here is authoritative in and of itself, not all exercising of authority in the church is through teaching, and Paul treats the two tasks as distinct elsewhere . . . (3:2, 4-5; 5:17) . . . in 1 Timothy 2:12, Paul prohibits women from conducting either activity, whether jointly or in isolation, in relation to men.[27]

But how do we know that Paul's words apply also today? How do we know that he's not just concerned again about what the citizens of the Roman world will say if he allows women to preach? What changes everything here is the fact that Paul appeals to creation, and whenever people like Paul or our Lord Jesus appeal to creation, the church is being told about principles that span the cultures of all ages.

---

26. For affirmation that αὐθεντέω does mean "to have authority over . . . ," see Wolters, "ΑΥΘΕΝΤΗΣ and its Cognates," 727. In a subsequent article, Wolters argues that the words do "not designate a despot or a tyrant, but simply a superior or person in authority." Wolters, "An Early Parallel of αυθεντειν," 684. He also notes that the ingressive sense of the verb ("assume authority," as in the 2011 NIV), while possible, is not necessary.

27. Moo, "What does it mean," 187. Cf. Schreiner, "An Interpretation," 133.

At this point, I must say, I take issue with the Dutch *Report*, as they speak rather disparagingly about what has been called "creation ordinances." The *Report* suggests that references to creation in 1 Timothy 2 have less authority than actual references to OT scriptural texts. For instance, the *Report* states that "such a reference to a historical event, even when they are about the beginning of history, is not a normative appeal to God's regulations."[28] In response, I would argue that an *inspired* author does not need another OT scriptural text to give his words weight since he himself is inspired. Moreover, when such an author references an event in the creation or the fall as the grounds for his injunction, that has particular weight and is not irrelevant to "God's regulations" as it tells the reader what is according to God's original intention (creation) or against his will (fall).

The *Report* denies that a reference to Adam and Eve in Paradise should have some kind of special significance ("een bepaalde meerwaarde") and that it should be regarded as a "virtually timeless theological concept."[29] In response to this, I would point out that "creation ordinances" have long had a special place in the history of revelation and in Reformed theology and ethics.[30] They do not take on a life of their own,[31] but they are particularly noteworthy when Holy Scripture appeals to them.

As an introductory hermeneutics textbook says:

> Creation ordinances refer to principles for how people should live that God established prior to the Fall of humanity into sin. Presumably, such principles remain part of the redemptive ideal

---

28. Bakker, *Rapport Deputaten*, 24. The *Report* also refers to 1 Peter 3:5–6 (Gen 18:12) to show that such creational references do not always carry weight. For example, women have not referred throughout history to their husbands as "lord." This, however, ignores the fact that Genesis 18 is a reference to that special creation-fall narrative of Genesis 1–3, and that the point of 1 Peter 3 is not that women should call their husbands "lord" as Sarah did (3:6) but that they should be subject to their husbands (3:1, 5) as Sarah was.

29. Ibid., 23–24.

30. See Murray, *Principles of Conduct*.

31. The *Report* refers, for example, to the fact that Paul can say that "it is good for a man not to touch a woman," even though marriage is a "creation ordinance," and to the fact that Christians worship on the first day of the week even though Exodus 20:11 references the last day of the week as a day of rest. Bakker, *Rapport Deputation*, 24. These comments ignore the fact that it is biblically recognized that creation principles do not have authority of their own, but when someone like Jesus (Matt 19) or Paul uses Adamic or Paradisiac references it is considered to have a special authority which clinches the argument because it refers to God's original intention. With respect to the examples above, if a NT biblical writer would actually say "all people must marry because marriage happened in Paradise," or "we must worship on the last day of the week because that is what they did at creation," those would be pretty convincing arguments.

for Christians as they are progressively renewed in God's image after their salvation.[32]

Similarly, in a very interesting paper on dealing with the redemptive-historical method, Dan Doriani discusses the 1 Timothy 2 passages and says:

> Today . . . and at first impression Paul's dictum—"I do not permit a woman to teach"—seems irrational and outdated. But the form of Paul's argument forbids that we rest on first impressions, for the command is grounded in creation. When Jesus appealed to creation regarding divorce, he considered it a conclusive argument (Matt 19:4, 8). The same holds for David in Psalm 8, Solomon in Proverbs 8:22–36, Isaiah in 40:18–25, Paul in 1 Corinthians 11:3–10, and Hebrews in 2:5–15. Paul's claim that male leadership rests in creation means his teaching rests on something essential to men and women. Scripture says the order of creation will not change until Jesus returns to judge and restore creation.[33]

In my view then, and I suspect in the view of the majority of Reformed scholars, Paul gives his controversial injunction in 1 Timothy 2:12 special weight when he says: "*For* Adam was formed first, then Eve. *And* Adam was not the one deceived; it was the woman who was deceived and became a sinner. But women will be saved through childbearing—if they continue in faith, love and holiness with propriety." Paul gives one reference to creation, another to the manner in which the fall occurred, and then makes a general reference to what has been the predominant role of women from the beginning. While the manner in which Paul speaks in verse 15 ("saved through childbearing") may not be a way in which we would choose to describe a woman's role in this twenty-first century, in that first century context with its controversy over the "New Woman" world, it fits right in. What is Paul saying? He is saying: from the beginning godly women have realized that the task of raising children and bringing forth a new generation of believers is not peripheral in the history of redemption; rather, it is essential. It is what God intended from the beginning. There is, by the way, a very recent article by Andrew B. Spurgeon which suggests that in 1 Timothy 2:13–15, Paul is doing nothing other than retelling the narrative of Genesis 2:4—4:1.[34]

---

32. Klein, *Introduction*, 493.
33. Doriani, "A Redemptive-Historical Model," 112.
34. Spurgeon, "1 Timothy 2:13–15," 543–56.

And it is noteworthy that such references are not just found here. Notions of how things were in the beginning permeate also the Corinthians passage. For example, Paul says things like the woman is the glory of man and man is the image and glory of God (7). He also refers to woman coming from man (8).

It is not really surprising that Paul should refer to creation and the fall at this point since he is talking about male and female and their roles throughout history.[35] And what our world needs so desperately to hear is that male and female, marriage and family—these did not come about through sociological development or an evolutionary process. They were God's idea from the beginning. At creation, God revealed what male and female, and marriage look like. Here sexuality began. And he revealed what leadership in marriage looks like and what it does not. Our world, with its twisted ideas about sexuality and marriage, needs more of this rather than less. We need, simply, to accept the fact that along with all the variety and beauty of creation, God has ordained it that male should be different than female, and that they are made that way, physically, emotionally, psychologically, and in innumerable more ways—including the fact that one should take more of a leadership role in the home and in the church. Today, those God-ordained differences should be accentuated rather than blurred. The church that projects the clear lines of Genesis 2 and 3 into today's culture and proclaims the whole Word of God, including the call for males to be leaders, has a vibrant message for today's culture, but it has nothing more to say when it caves into the fickle moods and changing attitudes of every civilization's culture.

---

35. It is noteworthy that Thomas R. Schreiner, in "Women in Ministry," suggests (287) that Genesis contains "six indications Adam had a special responsibility as a leader," and they, not necessarily of equal weight or clarity, are:

1. God created Adam first, and then he created Eve.
2. God gave Adam the command not to eat from the tree of the knowledge of good and evil.
3. God created Eve to be a helper for Adam.
4. Adam exercised his leadership by naming the creature God formed out of Adam's rib "woman."
5. The serpent subverted God's pattern of leadership by tempting Eve rather than Adam.
6. God approached Adam first after the couple had sinned, even though Eve sinned first.

Other Comments

The other major difficulty I have with the *Report* is its approach to culture. Christianity has always seen itself as a force that shapes culture by the power of the Gospel, and it has done that, no doubt, in an inestimably powerful way throughout history. But now we are being told that Paul's culture is so unique, and ours so unique, that the message proclaimed to the one cannot be regarded as normative for the other.

Without wishing to be alarmist, I really want to ask my respondent whether that is not going down a regrettable hermeneutical path? As Reformed people we have a long history of appreciating the redemptive-historical approach to Holy Scripture, which has always involved determining the principles that span the ages. But if Paul's world is so unique that the biblical principles cannot bridge the two, how then can we move from the Old Testament world to the New Testament world and to our world? How do we then determine the relevance of Scripture at all? Is it still relevant? Despite an attempt to suggest that this report is following the hermeneutics of the previous generation,[36] I sense a significant and far-reaching shift and fear the consequences.

Instead, I would urge the people of God on both sides of the ocean to go forth in the confidence that the living and active Word of God which is able to divide soul and spirit, joints and marrow (Heb 4:12) is also able to be read through the illumination of the Holy Spirit in such a way[37] that context and background help, rather than hinder, us in understanding the abiding principles of the Word of God.

Lastly, it has struck me that in each of these passages, as controversial as they may be today, the Spirit-inspired apostle becomes very emphatic. It happens when he writes to Timothy before (2:7) and after (3:15) the disputed words, and even in the midst of them (2:12). It also happens when he writes in 1 Corinthians 11:16, "If anyone wants to be contentious about

---

36. The authors of the *Report* suggest that hermeneutically they are taking an approach that is in practice no different from that of Drs. J. van Bruggen and J. Douma when they both argue for an understanding of the verb "obey" that is more nuanced because of sensitivity to modern culture. There is however a significant difference between pleading for a more nuanced use of words in a later culture and suggesting that these concepts are no longer normative for a culture.

37. I would refer the reader to the fine work of Daniel M. Doriani, "A Redemptive-Historical Model," and Andreas J. Köstenberger and Richard Patterson, *Invitation to Biblical Interpretation*. The volume in which Doriani's essay appears discusses at length various approaches to determining abiding principles through the various cultures. In his essay, Doriani proposes a method not unlike that described here. In the latter book, the authors argue for a hermeneutical approach that takes history and literature seriously as it attempts to move from ancient to modern cultures.

this, we have no other practice—nor do the churches of God," and in 14:37, "If anybody thinks he is a prophet or spiritually gifted, let him acknowledge that what I am writing to you is the Lord's command." Reformed churches not only pause and reflect when appeals are made to God's creation; they also sit up and take notice when, under the inspiration of the Holy Spirit, the Lord's servant becomes so solemn.

Bibliography

Bauman, R. A. *Women and Politics in Ancient Rome*. London: Routledge, 1992.

Bakker, Peter, et al. *Rapport Deputaten M/V in de kerk: Mannen and vrouwen in dienst van het Evangelie*. 2013. Online: http://www.synode.gkv.nl/download/64/. (ET also online: http://www.synode.gkv.nl/download/473/).

Ciampa, Roy E., and Brian S. Rosner. *The Pillar New Testament Commentary: First Letter to the Corinthians*. Grand Rapids, MI: Eerdmans, 2010.

Clouse, Bonnidell, and Robert G. Clouse, eds. *Women in Ministry: Four Views*. Downers Grove, IL: InterVarsity Press, 1989.

Cohick, Lynn H. *Women in the World of the Earliest Christians: Illuminating Ancient Ways of Life*. Grand Rapids, MI: Baker, 2009.

Doriani, Daniel M. "A Redemptive-Historical Model." In *Four Views on Moving Beyond the Bible to Theology*, edited by Gary T. Meadors. Counterpoints. Grand Rapids, MI: Zondervan, 2009.

Fantham, Elaine, et al. *Women in the Classical Period*. Oxford: Oxford University Press, 1994.

Grudem, Wayne. "Prophecy—yes, but Teaching—no: Paul's Consistent Advocacy of Women's Participation without Governing Authority." *Journal of the Evangelical Theological Society* 30.1 (March 1987) 11–23.

Hawley, Richard, and Barbara Levick, eds. *Women in Antiquity: New Assessments*. London: Routledge, 2003.

Klein, W.W., et al. *Introduction to Biblical Interpretation, Revised Edition*. Nashville: Nelson, 2004.

Köstenberger, Andreas J., and Richard Patterson. *Invitation to Biblical Interpretation: Exploring the Hermeneutical Triad of History, Literature, and Theology*. Grand Rapids, MI: Kregel, 2011.

Köstenberger, Andreas J., and Thomas R. Schreiner, eds. *Women in the Church: A Fresh Analysis of 1 Timothy 2:9-15*. 2nd ed. Grand Rapids, MI: Baker, 1995.

Kroeger, Catherine Clark, and Richard Clark Kroeger. *I Suffer Not a Woman: Rethinking 1 Timothy 2:11-15 in Light of Recent Evidence*. Grand Rapids, MI: Baker, 1992.

McGinn, T. A. J. *Prostitution, Sexuality and the Law in Ancient Rome*. Oxford: Oxford University Press, 1998.

Moo, Douglas. "What does it mean not to Teach or Have Authority Over Men? 1 Timothy 2:11-15." In *Recovering Biblical Manhood and Womanhood: A Response to Evangelical Feminism*, edited by John Piper and Wayne Grudem, 176–92. Wheaton, IL: Crossway, 1991.

Murray, John. *Principles of Conduct*. Grand Rapids, MI: Eerdmans, 1971.

Piper, John, and Wayne Grudem, eds. *Recovering Biblical Manhood and Womanhood: A Response to Evangelical Feminism.* Wheaton, IL: Crossway, 1991.

Schreiner, Thomas R. *New Testament Theology: Magnifying God in Christ.* Grand Rapids, MI: Baker, 2008.

———. "Women in Ministry." In *Two Views on Women in Ministry.* Rev. ed., edited by James R. Beck, 175–236. Grand Rapids, MI: Zondervan, 2005.

Spurgeon, Andrew B. "1 Timothy 2:13–15: Paul's Retelling of Genesis 2:4–4:1." *Journal of the Evangelical Theological Society* 56.3 (September 2013) 543–56.

Stott, John R. W. *God's New Society: The Message of Ephesians.* The Bible Speaks Today. Downers Grove, IL: InterVarsity Press, 1979.

Thiselton, Anthony C. *First Corinthians: A Shorter Exegetical and Pastoral Commentary.* Grand Rapids, MI: Eerdmans, 2006.

Treggiari. S. *Roman Marriage: Iustic Coniuges from the Time of Cicero to the Time of Ulpian.* Oxford: Clarendon, 1991.

Winter, Bruce. *After Paul Left Corinth: The Influence of Secular Ethics and Social Change.* Grand Rapids, MI: Eerdmans, 2001.

———. *Roman Wives, Roman Widows: The Appearance of New Women and the Pauline Communities.* Grand Rapids, MI: Eerdmans, 2003.

Wolters, Al. "ΑΥΘΕΝΤΗΣ and its Cognates in Biblical Greek." *Journal of the Evangelical Theological Society* 52.4 (December 2009) 719–29.

———. "An Early Parallel of αυθεντειν in 1 Tim. 2:12." *Journal of the Evangelical Theological Society* 54.4 (December 2011) 673–84.

Wood, S.E. *Imperial Women: A Study in Public Images, 40 B.C–.A.D. 69.* Leiden: Brill, 1999.

Paul's Injunction about Women

A Response

Rob van Houwelingen

My Canadian colleague has accurately reported the contribution of Bruce Winter in his book on the new Roman woman. In my response I will confine myself to 1 Timothy 2, which according to the title was his main topic. I really appreciate it that we are on speaking terms here.

By the way, what my colleague says about 1 Corinthians 11 reveals that in my view the title of his paper does not ask the right question. Is Paul's injunction about Corinthian women, namely that they have to wear a head covering, still valid today—yes or no? For what reason are we to assume that Paul does not say that all married women are required to wear a veil through the ages? What would be our response if someone were to argue that such a head covering is still required, the way Christian women in Eastern Europe are used to wearing a kerchief? So the real question should be: in what way do we, Christians of the twenty-first century, have to deal with Paul's injunctions about women?

First, I want to make some remarks about the meaning of 1 Timothy 2, using material from my research on the Pastoral Epistles.[1] After that, I will discuss the significance of this passage for Christians today, using material in the *Report of deputies male/female in the church*.

---

1. Van Houwelingen, "Power"; Van Houwelingen, *Timoteüs en Titus*. I wish to thank Dr. Myriam Klinker-De Klerck and Dr. Hans Schaeffer for their helpful comments on an earlier draft of this contribution.

Part One: Meaning

1.1 Observations

At the outset, we have to notice that in 1 Timothy 2 Paul does not use arguments arising from particular, local circumstances when he regulates the behavior of men and women in the Christian congregation. Although Ephesus was dominated by its Artemis cult, in comparison with contemporary world cities, its situation was not exceptional.[2] From Rome the type of the "free women" became more and more fashionable, in particular among the well-to-do.[3] This tendency could have been the reason for Paul's specific instructions to Timothy, the pastor of the congregation in Ephesus.

As far as we know, the apostle does not derive his line of thought from a Jewish tradition of interpretation. It is his original retelling of the Genesis narrative. He points to the historical role of Eve at creation, at the fall, and in redemption. By doing so, Paul places his church order, which aims at rest and peace within the congregation (1 Tim 2:1-2), in a redemptive-historical framework.

1.2 Authority

The meaning of the verb αὐθεντεῖν in verse 12 is difficult to establish. Before the New Testament period this word was used only sporadically. H. S. Baldwin has done extensive lexicographical research on this word; he distinguishes a progressive range of five basic meanings: to rule, to control/to dominate, to exercise authority, to act independently, and, in later texts, to commit murder.[4] The fact that Paul combines such an unusual term with the much more frequently used verb διδάσκειν indicates his intention to make a complementary nuance in meaning as clarification.[5] For a neutral

---

2. Winter, *Roman Wives*; Baugh, "A Foreign World"; contra the position of Gritz, *Paul*.

3. Winter seems to overstate his case. In Asia Minor the prominence of women was most noticeable on the western coast. Trebilco, *Jewish Communities*, 104-26; Trebilco, *The Early Christians*, 11-52 and 507-28.

4. Baldwin, "An Important Word," 39-51.

5. Köstenberger endeavors to prove that the Greek construct with οὐδέ coordinates activities of the same order, that is to say, activities that are either both viewed positively or negatively by the writer. He likes to value positively both teaching as well as exercising authority, so that Paul is denying both activities to the woman though they are worthwhile in themselves. Köstenberger, "A Complex Sentence," 53-84. Payne disputes the view of Köstenberger, demonstrating that syntactic constructions with οὐκ + οὐδέ + ἀλλά are normally used to combine two elements over against something else

expression such as "exercising authority" Paul would have had other verbs at his disposal.⁶ Within the framework of the male/female relationship in the church, the activity of teaching has a negative connotation: women with an authoritarian attitude should not abuse the teaching-learning situation by trying to overrule the men. This would disturb the desired "rest" of the worship service.⁷

To understand the situation the apostle is addressing, we have to realize that at that time three developments were taking place, and each development strengthened the impact of the other two. The first one was the ambition of rich women to physically (by clothing) and verbally (by teaching) assert themselves over against the other gender. That was a form of taking control which could cause serious unrest during worship services. The second was the possibility that such women would be stirred up by false teachers into doing exactly that. Those false teachers were looking to promote their heretical views (hence the charge in 2 Tim 3:6 of "capturing silly women").⁸ The third was the emergence of a trendy type of "free woman" from Rome. This trend probably also started to infiltrate the Christian congregation at Ephesus, functioning as a sort of role model for independence. In the context of a teaching-learning situation in which men and women together received instruction in the Christian doctrine, the male/female relationship was particularly sensitive. That is the reason why Paul disapproves of all hunger after power, due to the fall into sin. The Christian congregation should not give any room to thinking in terms of power!

(Polybius, *The Histories* XXX 5, 8; Josephus, *Jewish Antiquities* 7, 127). Paul uses such a construction in eleven cases: Rom 2:28-29; 9:6-7, 16; 1 Cor 2:6-7; Gal 1:1, 11-12, 16-17; 4:14; Phil 2:16-17; 2 Thess 3:7-8; 1 Tim 2:12 (cf. John 1:13). The only instance in which two distinct elements can be discerned (2 Cor 7:12) still shows a self-evident relation between the two. Payne paraphrases: "I am not permitting a woman to teach and [in combination with this] to assume authority over a man." Payne, "1 Tim 2.12 ," 235-53. Klinker-De Klerck argues that teaching was contrary to the subordinated position of women. Klinker-De Klerck, *Als vrouwen het Woord doen*, 93-95.

6. The dictionary of Louw and Nida describes the semantic field to which αὐθεντεῖν belongs: Louw and Nida, "Control, Rule." The ancient Lexicon of Hesychius lists, among others, ἐξουσιάζειν and αὐτοδικεῖν as synonyms.

7. Blomberg points out that in this letter Paul more often uses partly synonymous words or expressions. Thus in this case διδάσκειν gets more color by αὐθεντεῖν ἀνδρός. Paul does not allow women to tell men what to do. Blomberg, "Neither Hierarchalist nor Egalitarian," 329-72. For more lexicographical research on the meaning of the verb αὐθεντεῖν, see Knight III, "ΑΥΘΕΝΤΕΩ," 143-57; Wilshire, "The TLG Computer," 120-34; Wolters, "A Semantic Study," 145-75; Belleville, "Teaching and Usurping Authority," 205-23.

8. All Scripture quotations in this article are from the New International Version (NIV84).

1.3 Adam and Eve

A good understanding of the structure of the text, and therefore also its meaning, is achieved when one takes verses 13 and 14 together with verse 15a as belonging to Paul's reference to the history of Adam and Eve.[9] This is what the text shows:

1. The subject of verse 15a is the same as in verse 14: "the woman" (ἡ γυνή; note the use of the definite article) who in verse 13 was called Eve (the name Adam later gave her).

2. The term τεκνογονία in verse 15a, unique in the New Testament, refers to Genesis 3:16 (LXX: τέξῃ τέκνα: "you will give birth to children") and Genesis 4:1 (LXX: ἐκτησάμην ἄνθρωπον: "I have brought forth a man").

3. The plural of the verb is used in verse 15b, not earlier; thus grammatically verse 15a must be connected to the preceding sentence.

We see that in regard to the proper male/female relationships within the Christian church, Paul refers back to the beginning of mankind: the creation, the fall, and the redemption of the first human couple, Adam and Eve. Surprisingly enough, he considers primeval history from the perspective of the woman! Thus considered, Genesis tells us the story of human weakness. Eve was created after Adam; the woman let herself be fooled and therefore fell into transgression. She, however, shall find salvation in her motherhood (in verse 15a the translation should be "she," i.e., Eve).

This, of course, does not mean that Adam would not be guilty of the fall into sin. Neither does it mean that man would not stand in need of redemption. It does mean, however, that women of the congregation will be able to find their origin as well as their destiny as daughters of Eve. To take control of men would be to reverse the order in which man and woman were created. It would also promote deception that leads to sin against God, endangering the redemption through Jesus Christ. Therefore Paul's direction is: to continue in faith, love, and holiness, together with prudence, the virtue that was already mentioned in verse 9. In this way the term σωφροσύνη ("propriety") encompasses the entire instruction for women.[10]

---

9. Cf. Mulder, "'En daarna Eva,'" 174–200; Wall, "1 Timothy 2:9–15," 81–103; Towner, *The Letters*, 233; Spurgeon, "1 Timothy 2:13–15," 543–56.

10. According to Malherbe, this term comprises characteristics such as orderliness or decency and neatness; it has to do with self-respect, a sense of good judgment, and controlling the tongue; in brief, σωφροσύνη exactly fits in the context of 1 Tim 2:8–15. Malherbe, "The *Virtus Feminarum*," 45–65. In the next pericope, Paul uses the related term σώφρων for one of the virtues of a (male) overseer (1 Tim 3:2; cf. Titus 1:8).

Part Two: Significance

2.1 Reformed hermeneutics

Now we have to ask the question: what is God saying to us today through this passage of the apostle Paul in his letter to Timothy? Reflection on the search for meaning has always been taking place—also in the case of the Bible. Previously, however, this happened less explicitly. At the present time the process of coming to an understanding of meaning is itself being examined and described; this is what we call "hermeneutics." Reformed hermeneutics can be appropriately defined as

> ... critical reflection on the totality of the process of understanding the text, including exegesis. Exegesis, then, is the craft of text interpretation, one element of the whole process of understanding. In all of this, we believe in the guidance of the Holy Spirit, who leads us in the truth, enlightens our minds, and gives us insight into the Word of God.[11]

Two diagrams can show, perhaps in an oversimplified schematic form, what happens when Christians read the Bible. The first, smaller triangle represents the text in its original context, and for its first reader(s). In our case, the text of 1 Timothy 2 was written by Paul to his co-worker Timothy in the context of the Ephesian congregation, let us say somewhere in the middle of the first century AD. Ten years ago I started a workshop at the annual *Schooldag* (Schoolday) at Kampen on "reading the Bible contextually" by drawing only this triangle. I thought this would be enough. We have to read just as Timothy did, as if looking over his shoulder. However, some participants of this workshop, particularly some who served as ministers in a congregation, were not satisfied and challenged me to develop my position. After all, we have to discern between the "meaning" and the "significance" of the text, according to the introductory hermeneutical handbooks used in both Hamilton and Kampen.[12] And this simple triangle concerned no more than meaning.

---

11. Citation of the Deputies for Church Unity (Bakker et al, *Rapport Deputaten*, 20). Cf. Thiselton, *Hermeneutics*, 4: "Hermeneutics explores *the conditions and criteria that operate to try to ensure responsible, valid, fruitful, or appropriate interpretation.*"

12. Klein et al., *Introduction to Biblical Interpretation*; Kaiser, Jr., and Silva, *Introduction to Biblical Hermeneutics*.

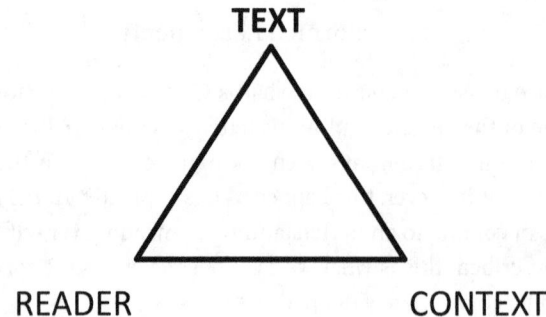

So we have to draw a second, larger triangle around the first one. Now, the text of 1 Timothy 2 is still central, but we, too, are readers, and the text functions in our context also. There are many examples of such larger triangles: such as the time of Luther, the Netherlands in 1950, or Kenya today.

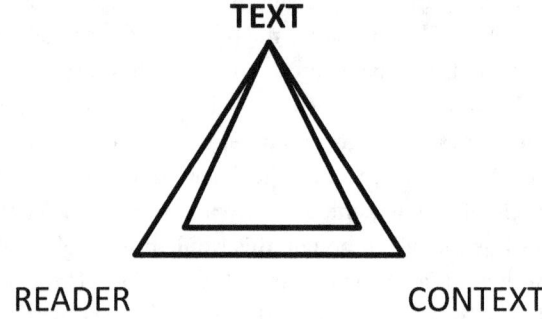

Together the diagrams aim to show how the reading of a text develops during the passage of time, opening new dimensons. The order of the triangles is essential. The text must be analysed within the smaller triangle first, before coming to its function in the larger triangle. It is important, therefore, to make a distinction between the two. Sometimes the reader may allow the two triangles to coincide; to do so could lead to two errors. The first error is to apply the smaller triangle (the meaning of the text in its original context) directly to our situation; the second error is to begin with the larger triangle (the significance of the text in our context) and to interpret this back into the earlier situation.

2.2 Paul's motivations

Paul writes with the authority of an apostle of Jesus Christ. He is an inspired author. This authority applies both to Timothy and to us. God speaks in the Bible to people from the past as well as of today. That is beyond debate. Still, we have to be aware of some main differences between our context and that of Paul. Let me only mention the essential topic, exactly the point that has been neglected by my colleague.[13] Paul's instruction is one for the church, but what he strives for in the church was substantially no different from what leading moral philosophers of his time, such as Seneca and Musonius Rufus, also advocated. The stipulation that women ought to be silent in church was consistent with the accepted and prevailing social situation of his time. In our time this command runs counter to the accepted social situation. Since the separation of church and state, the church has been pushed aside, out of the public domain. Paul, with his proscriptions in the first century AD, was still able to make links with a non-Christian environment. In the twenty-first century, however, we with these same proscriptions create, or strengthen, an isolation from society that might unnecessarily hinder the progress of the proclamation of the Gospel.

Paul appears to have a two-fold drive which motivates his proscriptions. On the one hand, he draws from the account of creation, explicitly referring to the history of Genesis 1–3. We should keep in mind that in doing so he aims to preserve the established order, *both* in the *church* and in *society*. On the other hand, he also uses practical arguments that play a more implicit role. He has regard for the internal structure of the church (peace and order) as well as its external, missionary influence (its public image, what is honorable/shameful).

We therefore can distinguish two kinds of motivations, and, in the concrete application of Paul's instructions in ever-changing contexts, it is important that we understand what drives him. Apparently, Paul was sufficiently flexible in his thinking (pastorally, rhetorically, and theologically) that for him various motivations were not mutually exclusive; rather, they supported and complemented each other.[14] In our context as regards male-female relationships, these motivations could easily become a hindrance to each other.[15] Take, for example, the biblical concept of "submission" (Greek: ὑποτάσσειν). The apostle Paul used this term within the framework of a

---

13. A list of topics can be found in Bakker et al, *Rapport Deputaten*, 18.

14. Cf. Van Spanje, *Inconsistency in Paul?*

15. Perhaps we could handle such conflicting arguments in the same way as we have handled the classic problem of the collision of duties or obligations.

certain ordering of society, while today it evokes a negative perception of the church among outsiders.[16] What would Paul say in our society?

As for the "creation order argumentation," my colleague states rightly that "God has ordained it that male should be different than female." However, to be different is not the same as being authoritative and subordinate—"including," my colleague suggests, the fact that men "should take more of a leadership role in the home and in the church." I have to note that "leadership role" is a modern concept, different from "authority" in biblical times. The use of this modern term marks a shift in the argumentation. Moreover, there is one important element missing here: society. In modern society we (without any problem) accept women in all kinds of leadership roles, even the leading position of the former queens of the Netherlands. Is that not against the creation order?

Paul brings forward a whole palette of arguments, without giving any indication as to which one, for him, carries the most weight. The question arises whether others have not subsequently assigned a greater value to the creation order argument, so that the idea of "the creation order" has become a virtually timeless theological concept.[17] This question remains unanswered by my colleague, but when he responds to the *Report* by stating that creation ordinances have long had a special place in Reformed theology and ethics he simply confirms what the *Report* suggests.[18] Moreover, he admits that creation ordinances "do not take on a life of their own." That is exactly what the *Report* wants to say, no more and no less. We have to reckon with creation (Genesis 1–2), but also with the fall and redemption (Genesis 3). And precisely this last element requires an orientation towards the coming Kingdom as well.

2.3 The relevance of Scripture

My colleague asks, somewhat rhetorically, "How do we then determine the relevance of Scripture at all? Is it still relevant?" These are fundamental

---

16. More on this motif: Du Toit, "Sensitivity," 1–7.

17. Of particular relevance are the arguments of Giles, "A Critique," 195–215.

18. Even Calvin affords the critical remark that the ranking argument that Paul puts forward in verse 13 is not strong. He comments: "Yet the reason which Paul assigns, that woman was second in the order of creation, appears not to be a very strong argument in favour of her subjection; for John the Baptist was before Christ in the order of time, and yet was greatly inferior in rank. But although Paul does not state all the circumstances which are related by Moses, yet he intended that his readers should take them into consideration" (*Commentaries*, 68–69).

questions indeed. Of course Scripture is relevant, but how do we deal with it? We have to listen carefully to what the Spirit says to the churches.

Let us take the example of the apostles' decree (Acts 15). The decision of the Jerusalem council concerning Gentile believers—that they had to abstain, among other things, from meat with blood still in it and from sexual immorality—was officially written down in Jerusalem and sent to Antioch, delivered by Paul and Silas to the other churches in the southern part of Asia Minor to be obeyed (Acts 16:4). It is echoed in Paul's letters, for example when he writes: "For you know what instructions we gave you by the authority of the Lord Jesus. It is God's will that you should be sanctified: that you avoid sexual immorality" (1 Thess 4:2-3; cf. 5:22).[19] This instruction was meant for non-Jewish believers like us. It was by no means an incidental measure, since it is rooted in basic principles of creation life (blood, the seat of life, belongs to God as the Creator),[20] and it was generally observed during the first centuries, yet most Christians today do not feel bound by this biblical rule. Nobody in the Reformed tradition has serious objections against eating blood pudding or rare steak.

Does this mean that Scripture has no relevance for us today? No, because we have to take into consideration the unique redemptive-historical situation in which the apostolic decree originated. Two Christian cultures—an older culture (represented by the mother church in Jerusalem) and a younger one (represented by the daughter church at Antioch)—had to match with each other. Therefore the following was decided: Gentile Christians need not become Jewish, but neither can they stay half Gentile. So they may be asked to break radically with paganism. Pagan is all idolatry, which can be expressed in sacred prostitution, eating raw meat (known from the Dionysus cult), and drinking blood. Nowadays blood pudding and rare steak do not smell like idols anymore. To put it positively, what Christians through the ages can learn from this instruction is that Christ is sufficient. Being united with him results in a different attitude.[21]

---

19. Other echoes of the apostles' decree can be found in Acts 21:25; 1 Corinthians 8-10; Galatians 5:19-21; 1 John 5:21; Revelation 2:14 and 20. Compare Bauckham, "James and the Jerusalem Church," 464-65. For the redemptive-historical setting, see Van Houwelingen, ed., *Apostelen*, 54-60. For the setting in antiquity, see Öhler, ed., *Aposteldekret*. For the communal setting, see De Villiers, "Communal Discernment," 132-55.

20. "The Decree obliges Gentile Christians to live a life according to the most basic elements of God's order of creation." Deines, "The Apostolic Decree," 186. No wonder the Jews violently protested when Jesus, who had presented himself as the bread of life, said that the true and imperishable life is fed by eating his body and drinking his blood (John 6:52-59).

21. See Haak, *Metamorfose*, 65-72.

We are used to dealing with Paul's instructions about the holy kiss and the remarrying of widows in the same way. Why not with his command for women to be silent in the church?[22] That women are in an equal position with men is no longer perceived as offensive in our society. What we can learn from 1 Timothy 2 today is that in church life, peaceful living is essential. Therefore Paul demands Christians to live a "normal" life. Human relationships are sensitive and vulnerable. Jesus Christ, child of Adam and Eve and Son of God, was born in the world to save sinners and to sanctify the male/female relationship, which means purging it from the impact of evil.

This way of dealing with Scripture requires readers who are genuine disciples.[23] The slippery slope argument has never been very convincing. And fear is a bad counsellor, although I can fully understand my colleague's worry about the relevance of Scripture. That is also my concern.

A helpful metaphor was introduced in 1991 by N.T. Wright.[24] Suppose there exists a Shakespeare play whose fifth act has been lost. Only four acts and the first scene of the fifth are known, giving hints of how the play is supposed to end. How could the actors play the whole drama without a complete script for the final part? If they are familiar with Shakespeare, they are able to improvise, but they are not free to produce their own text. The best that can be required of them is an "entering into the story as it stood, in order first to understand how the threads could appropriately be drawn together, and then to put that understanding into effect by speaking and acting with both *innovation* and *consistency*."

Let us for a moment consider Holy Scripture as a Holy Script, taking into account the redemptive-historical perspective. It tells the great story

---

22. The American philosopher Nicholas Wolterstorff, who stands in the Reformed tradition, has warned against an arbitrary use of Bible texts and a selective application of principles in regard to the relation between men and women. Wolterstorff, "The Bible and Women," 202–9.

23. Of course, much more could be said regarding this theme, but the present contribution claims to be only a response. Kevin J. Vanhoozer compares the reader of the Bible with someone who stands at a well. It is one thing to study the water in the well, to look at the reflection of your own face, or to analyse its chemical composition, and quite another thing to drink. The reader at the well, in order to be nourished, must draw from and drink of the text. To "drink" here means to accept and to appropriate. The reader has a responsibility to receive the text according to its nature and intention, resulting in a creative echo of the text. Vanhoozer, "The Reader," 283.

24. Wright, "How Can the Bible Be Authoritative?" 7–31; Wells, *Improvisation*; Vanhoozer, *The Drama of Doctrine*. Vanhoozer correctly adds to this metaphor the element that you do not choose your own role—your role is defined by your identity in Christ. Such role definitions are most appropriately understood within a vital Christian community.

of God, who is both the author and the main actor. As Bible readers we are involved in his story. The four known acts are (simply put): Creation, Fall, Israel, Jesus. Act five contains the whole period to the Eschaton, but from the New Testament we know only the first scene, and we have a visionary description of the rest, namely the book of Revelation. So we find ourselves within the scope of the Bible, although the canon has been closed. Our performance has to be faithful to the previous acts. You have to play your role in line with the entire story and with the other actors.

Thus, the Bible has to be our spiritual property, carefully carried in our hearts. We seek fellowship with God in his Word by maintaining a personal relationship of faith with him and his Son Jesus Christ, as living members of a congregation that is finding her way with the light of the Bible and under the guidance of the Holy Spirit. Then, from the texts to which we are giving significance, God will come to us, in order to give significance to our lives.

Bibliography

Bakker, Peter, et al. *Rapport Deputaten M/V in de kerk: Mannen en vrouwen in dienst van het evangelie*. 2013. Online: http://www.synode.gkv.nl/download/64/. (ET also online: http://www.synode.gkv.nl/download/473/).

Baldwin, H. S. "An Important Word: Αὐθεντέω in 1 Timothy 2:12." In *Women in the Church: An Analysis and Application of 1 Timothy 2:9–15*. 2nd ed., edited by Andreas J. Köstenberger and Thomas R. Schreiner, 39–51. Grand Rapids, MI: Eerdmans, 2005.

Bauckham, Richard. "James and the Jerusalem Church." In *The Book of Acts in Its First-Century Setting*. Volume 4: *Palestinian Setting*, edited by Richard Bauckham, 415–80. Grand Rapids, MI: Eerdmans, 1995.

Baugh, S. M. "A Foreign World: Ephesus in the First Century." In *Women in the Church: An Analysis and Application of 1 Timothy 2:9–15*. 2nd ed., edited by Andreas J. Köstenberger and Thomas R. Schreiner, 13–38. Grand Rapids, MI: Eerdmans, 2005.

Belleville, L. "Teaching and Usurping Authority. 1 Timothy 2:11–15." In *Discovering Biblical Equality: Complementarity without Hierarchy*, edited by R. W. Pierce and R. M. Groothuis, 205–23. Downers Grove, IL: InterVarsity Press, 2004.

Blomberg, C. L. "Neither Hierarchalist nor Egalitarian: Gender Roles in Paul." In *Two Views on Women in the Ministry*, edited by J. R. Beck and C. L. Blomberg, 329–72. Grand Rapids, MI: Zondervan, 2001.

Calvin, John. *Commentaries on the Epistles of Timothy, Titus, and Philemon*. Translated by William Pringle. Grand Rapids, MI: Eerdmans, 1948.

Deines, Roland. "The Apostolic Decree: Halakhah for Gentile Christians or Concession to Jewish Taboos?" In *Acts of God in History*, edited by Christoph Ochs and Peter Watts, 121–88. Tübingen: Mohr Siebeck, 2013.

De Villiers, Pieter G. R. "Communal Discernment in the Early Church." In *The Spirit That Guides: Discernment in the Bible and Spirituality*, edited by Pieter G. R. de

Villiers, 132–55. Acta Theologica Supplementum 17. Bloemfontein: Sun Media, 2013.

Du Toit, Andrie B. "Sensitivity Towards the Reaction of Outsiders as Ethical Motivation in Early Christian Paraenesis." *HTS Theological Studies* 68.1 (2012) 1–7. Online: http://dx.doi.org/10.4102/hts.v68i1.1212.

Giles, Kevin. "A Critique of the 'Novel' Contemporary Interpretation of 1 Timothy 2:9–15 Given in the Book, *Women in the Church*, Part II." *Evangelical Quarterly* 72.3 (2000) 195–215.

Gritz, Sharon Hodgin. *Paul, Women Teachers, and the Mother Goddess at Ephesus: A Study of 1 Timothy 2:9–15 in Light of the Religious and Cultural Milieu of the First Century*. Lanham, MD: University Press of America, 1991.

Haak, C. J. *Metamorfose. Intercultureel begeleiden van kerken in een niet-christelijke omgeving*. Zoetermeer: Boekencentrum, 2002.

Kaiser, Jr., Walter C., and Moisés Silva. *Introduction to Biblical Hermeneutics: The Search for Meaning*. Rev. and expanded ed. Grand Rapids, MI: Zondervan, 2007.

Köstenberger, Andreas J. "A Complex Sentence: The Syntax of 1 Timothy 2:12." In *Women in the Church: An Analysis and Application of 1 Timothy 2:9–15*. 2nd ed., edited by Andreas J. Köstenberger and Thomas R. Schreiner, 53–84. Grand Rapids, MI: Eerdmans, 2005.

Klein, William W., et al. *Introduction to Biblical Interpretation, Revised and Updated*. Nashville: Thomas Nelson, 2004.

Klinker-De Klerck, Myriam. *Als vrouwen het Woord doen. Over Schriftgezag, hermeneutiek en het waarom van de apostolische instructie aan vrouwen*. Barneveld: De Vuurbaak, 2011.

Knight III, G. W. "ΑΥΘΕΝΤΕΩ in Reference to Women in 1 Timothy 2.12." *New Testament Studies* 30 (1984) 143–57.

Louw, J. P., and E. A. Nida. "Control, Rule." In *Greek-English Lexicon of the New Testament Based on Semantic Domains*. Vol. 1–2, Domain 37, edited by J. P. Louw and E. A. Nida. Cape Town: Bible Society of South Africa, 1989.

Malherbe, A. J. "The *Virtus Feminarum* in 1 Timothy 2:9–15." In *Renewing Tradition: Studies in Texts and Contexts in Honor of James W. Thompson*, edited by M. W. Hamilton et al., 45–65. Eugene, OR: Pickwick Publications, 2007.

Mulder, M. C. "'En daarna Eva.' Over het schriftberoep van Paulus, met name in 1 Timoteüs 2: 11–15." In *Vrouwen op een zij-spoor? Emancipatie van de vrouw en het verstaan van de Schrift in gereformeerd perspectief*, edited by J. M. Aarnoudse et al., 174–200. Amsterdam: Buijten & Schipperheijn, 1988.

Öhler, Markus, ed. *Aposteldekret und antikes Vereinswesen: Gemeinschaft und ihre Ordnung*. Tübingen: Mohr Siebeck, 2011.

Payne, P. B. "1 Tim 2.12 and the Use of οὐδέ to Combine Two Elements to Express a Single Idea." *New Testament Studies* 54 (2008) 235–53.

Trebilco, Paul. *The Early Christians in Ephesus from Paul to Ignatius*. Tübingen: Mohr Siebeck, 2004.

———. *Jewish Communities in Asia Minor*. Cambridge: Cambridge University Press, 1991.

Spurgeon, Andrew B. "1 Timothy 2:13–15: Paul's Retelling of Genesis 2:4—4:1." *Journal of the Evangelical Theological Society* 56.3 (2013) 543–56.

Thiselton, Anthony C. *Hermeneutics: An Introduction*. Grand Rapids, MI: Eerdmans, 2009.

Towner, P. H. *The Letters to Timothy and Titus*. The New International Commentary on the New Testament. Grand Rapids, MI: Eerdmans, 2006.
Vanhoozer, Kevin J. *The Drama of Doctrine: A Canonical-Linguistic Approach in Christian Theology*. Louisville, KY: Westminster John Knox Press, 2005.
———. "The Reader in New Testament Interpretation." In *Hearing the New Testament: Strategies for Interpretation*. 2nd ed., edited by Joel B. Green, 259–88. Grand Rapids, MI: Eerdmans, 2010.
Van Houwelingen, Rob, ed. *Apostelen. Dragers van een spraakmakend evangelie*. Commentaar op het Nieuwe Testament. Kampen: Kok, 2013.
Van Houwelingen, Rob. "Power, Powerlessness and Authorised Power in 1 Timothy 2:8–15." In *Power in the New Testament*, edited by Pieter G. R. de Villiers and Annette Merz. Leuven: Peeters, 2014. [forthcoming]
———. *Timoteüs en Titus. Pastorale instructiebrieven*. Commentaar op het Nieuwe Testament. Kampen: Kok, 2012.
Van Spanje, T. E. *Inconsistency in Paul? A Critique of the Work of Heikki Räisänen*. Tübingen: Mohr Siebeck, 1999.
Wall, R. W. "1 Timothy 2:9–15 Reconsidered (Again)." *Bulletin for Biblical Research* 14 (2004) 81–103.
Wells, Samuel. *Improvisation: The Drama of Christian Ethics*. Grand Rapids, MI: Brazos Press, 2004.
Wilshire, L. E. "The TLG Computer and Further Reference to ΑΥΘΕΝΤΕΩ in 1 Timothy 2.12." *New Testament Studies* 34 (1988) 120–34.
Winter, Bruce W. *Roman Wives, Roman Widows: The Appearance of New Women and the Pauline Communities*. Grand Rapids, MI: Eerdmans, 2003.
Wolters, Al. "A Semantic Study of αὐθέντης and Its Derivatives." *Journal of Greco-Roman Christianity and Judaism* 1 (2000) 145–75.
Wolterstorff, Nicholas. "The Bible and Women: Another Look at the 'Conservative' Position." In *Hearing the Call: Liturgy, Justice, Church, and World*. Edited by Mark R. Gornik and Gregory Thompson, 202–9. Grand Rapids, MI: Eerdmans, 2011.
Wright, N.T. "How Can the Bible Be Authoritative?" *Vox Evangelica* 21 (1991) 7–31. Online: http://ntwrightpage.com/Wright_Bible_Authoritative.htm.

Paul's Injunction about Women
A Rejoinder

Gerhard H. Visscher

First of all, I wish to concede to my esteemed Kampen colleague that in my paper I went further afield into Corinthians than my title suggested. But that was because I felt you cannot really understand Paul's injunction to Timothy in 1 Timothy without understanding this baffling passage in 1 Corinthians 11 and the overall cultural context.

Regarding my colleague's question about what I would say to those who insist on women wearing veils today, I believe Paul is not saying that throughout all ages God requires all married women to wear veils, but he is saying that throughout the ages women need to respect their husbands. In Paul's culture, that meant a veil. In our culture, that might show itself in many and various ways.

My colleague asks about my position on women in society. I believe, as mentioned previously, that Paul's instructions about women are focused on worship contexts. That may have consequences for society, but that is not really Paul's concern. In 1 Timothy 3:15, Paul says to Timothy: "I am writing you these instructions so that . . . you will know how people ought to conduct themselves in God's household, which is the church of the living God, the pillar and foundation of the truth."

I thank our brother for the instruction about the triangles, and assure him that we use similar models in our instruction in Hamilton. I think he will agree that it is also through a better understanding of the first, smaller triangle that we, in the larger triangle, come to understand the text, and that there is a third possible error, namely, to suggest that the biblical writer says to people in the larger triangle something completely different from what he says to people who have been in the smaller triangle.

At one point my colleague suggests that women being silent in church was consistent with "the accepted and prevailing social situation of his time." I have suggested that it was not quite so. "Feminists" of that time were beginning to reshape the culture, and maybe the church, in a way that Paul is concerned about. He also suggests that submission was more acceptable to women at that time than it is today. I doubt it; precisely because women wanted to do otherwise Paul speaks to them about submission.

My colleague suggests that the word αὐθεντεῖν is difficult. He refers to Baldwin. I refer to Wolters also in footnote 25. I would also refer to the Bauer-Danker lexicon, the lexicon for NT study, which says the word means: to assume a stance of independent authority, give orders to, dictate to. My colleague suggests that the two verbs, this one and the verb "to teach" should be understood as "women with an authoritarian attitude should not abuse the teaching-learning situation by trying to overrule the men." I am not convinced. For one thing, the two verbs "to teach" and "to have authority over" are about as far apart from each other as they can be in the Greek text, with the word "teach" even "fronted for emphasis," as we say in Greek grammar, and they are separated with a "nor."[1] Paul forbids two things in worship: a) for women to teach in worship, and b) for women to have authority over a man. Those may be overlapping circles, but they still are two circles. I believe that Paul had other better ways of saying what our brother suggests he says, if he wanted to. Besides, what my Kampen colleague suggests that Paul forbids for women is forbidden for men as well. Preachers of the gospel must preach with authority because that's the nature of preaching but abusing authority in the teaching-learning situation is forbidden of men as well.

Furthermore, I do not believe that my colleague, the Dutch *Report*, and I are all on the same page when it comes to creation ordinances. The *Report* is attempting to deny much of the force of verses 13-15 by denying that a reference to creation has a special significance and suggesting that Paul's words would have carried more clout if he had referred to Scripture instead. As I said earlier, it is not every aspect of creation in and of itself that is normative, but when an inspired author such as Paul backs up his argument with a reference to creation, he is making a reference to what God has wanted of mankind from the very beginning and what he still wants today of our culture and all cultures. Male and female are entirely equal when it comes to their status as children of God—that is the message of Galatians 3:28 (cf. 1 Peter 3:7, "heirs with you")—but that does not deny that in the

---

1. See also Köstenberger, "A Complex Sentence Structure," 81–104.

context of the home and of the church, their roles are distinct at times, with men called to be "loving leaders" in both, and women called to submit to godly leadership. References to the events of Genesis in 1 Timothy 2:13–15 make clear that this is, and will be, God's will for all times and all cultures.

Bibliography

Danker, Frederick W., and Bauer, Walter. *A Greek-English Lexicon of the New Testament and other early Christian literature*. Chicago, IL: University of Chicago Press, 2000.

Köstenberger, Andreas J. "A Complex Sentence: The Syntax of 1 Timothy 2:12." In *Women in the Church: An Analysis and Application of 1 Timothy 2:9–15*. 2nd ed., edited by Andreas J. Köstenberger and Thomas R. Schreiner, 53–84. Grand Rapids, MI: Eerdmans, 2005.

8

Christian Ethics and God's Use of the Bible

Ad L. Th. de Bruijne

1. Introduction: between foundationalism and relativism

In November 2013 the General Synod of the *Christelijke Gereformeerde Kerken* in the Netherlands judged homosexual relationships to be incompatible with Scripture.[1] In response, the chairman of Contrario, an association of Reformed homosexuals, declared that the church should allow for different choices, because of the divergent interpretations of biblical passages concerning homosexuality.[2] This brings us to my theme: the relationship between ethics and the Bible. In what way does the Bible guide us in the area of ethics?[3]

The reaction of Contrario's chairman reveals that nowadays the traditional use of the Bible is experiencing a crisis that affects many orthodox and evangelical churches in the Western world.[4] Conventional ethical use of

---

1. Bruins, "CGK wijzen homorelatie af."
2. Bruins, "Verlegenheid over homobesluit."
3. Many studies deal with these questions. Among these are Bilkes, *Theological Ethics*; Birch and Rasmussen, *Bible and Ethics*; Cosgrove, *Appealing to Scripture in Moral Debate*; Curran and McCormick, *The Use of Scripture*; Fowl and Jones, *Reading in Communion*; Spohn, *What Are They Saying About Scripture and Ethics?*; Verhey, *Remembering Jesus*.
4. Honey, "Litmus Test," *Christianity Today*, Nov 2009, 17; Chamberlain, "Younger Evangelicals," 327–41; Gagnon, "Biblical Witness on Homosexual Practice," 19–130;

the Bible depended on exegesis. In order to uncover God's will with regard to a subject, we have to explain those Bible texts in which this subject is raised. For example, when we do so with regard to the theme of divorce we find a clear biblical disapproval, but at the same time we have to allow for two exceptions: adultery and desertion by an unbelieving spouse. With these biblical tools we, in principle, can manage the whole field of divorce ethics.[5]

This exegetical approach is deeply rooted in the ecclesial tradition, but in modern times it encountered a shift that orthodox Christians are not always aware of. It was mixed with a modern foundationalist epistemology, which stresses the importance of incontrovertible axioms, exact data, and rational certainty.[6] Thus, basic biblical norms—especially the Ten Commandments—were interpreted as axioms. Texts from Scripture provided the exact data. And sound reasoning was seen as the route to reaching true conclusions. On some issues, such as homosexuality, these conclusions could be derived directly from exegesis. Other themes—like the expansion of the second cause for divorce to all situations of willful desertion—required some intermediate steps.

Thomas and Olson, "Evangelical Elites' Changing Responses," 239–72; Olson and Thomas, *Sexual Moral Reasoning*.

5. For overviews of this classical approach, see Van Dam, *Divorce and Remarriage*, and Douma, *Echtscheiding*.

6. Rauser, *Theology in Search of Foundations*, 25–55; Wolterstorff, *Reason Within the Bounds of Religion*; Phillips, *Faith After Foundationalism*; Grenz and Franke, *Beyond Foundationalism*; Van Bekkum and Rouw, eds., *Geloven in zekerheid*; Cunningham, *Christian Ethic*, 5–15; Murphy, *Theology in a Postmodern Age*; Kuyper, *De heedendaagse schriftcritiek*. Cf. Oliver O'Donovan's self-description of his earlier "puritan" ethical practice. O'Donovan, *Resurrection and Moral Order*, vii–viii. Jack Rogers traces the roots of this orthodox method to the nineteenth-century combination of Reformed Scholasticism and Scottish Common Sense philosophy, which created a paradigm for many Reformed and Evangelical Christians. Rogers, *Jesus, the Bible and Homosexuality*, 29–32; see also Rogers and McKim, *The Authority and Interpretation of the Bible*. Allen Verhey makes a comparable point in "The Holy Bible and Sanctified Sexuality," 31–45. This foundationalist vision can be detected in the presuppositionalist position of Cornelius van Til as well as in his speaking about law and commandments as the "absolute standard" that God revealed. Van Til, *In Defense of the Faith*, 145. The same counts for aspects in the vision of Carl F. H. Henry, although he acknowledges more ethical dimensions in the Bible than only commandments Henry, *Christian Personal Ethics*, 265ff.. See also John Murray, who like Henry draws wider perspectives, yet uses the expression "system of truth" Murray, *Principles of Conduct*, 202; also Wayne Grudem, who despite his attention to the necessity of a biblical worldview, still follows this mode of reasoning in his treatment of political-ethical questions. Grudem, *Politics According to the Bible*. The same counts for the evaluation of homosexuality in Schmidt, *Straight and Narrow*.

This combination of the traditional appeal to the Bible with modern foundationalism has rendered Christian ethics vulnerable to postmodernism. The famous analysis of late modernity that Alisdair MacIntyre offered in the eighties suits Reformed and evangelical communities today.[7] Absolutes turn into relativity. Belief in a universal truth succumbs to a myriad of individual options. And many opt for emotion instead of reason. From the outset my ethical ambitions have been determined by my awareness of these tendencies, which I already sensed during my ministry in the city church of Rotterdam in the nineties.[8] I consider this to be a development posing a great risk. But to fight it effectively Reformed Christians should acknowledge that they themselves have contributed to it by combining faith in Scripture with a foundationalist model. Only by revising their view on the relationship between Bible and ethics may they hope to take the wind out of threatening skeptical sails.

2. From unshaken certainty to tempted faith

In the first place, a better vision of moral certainty is required. We cannot deny that the believing reason (*ratio*) increasingly fails to establish one single interpretation and application that everyone accepts. Often alternative views remain that also contain more or less plausibility. Regarding the grounds for divorce, for example, Jakob Van Bruggen has proposed a translation of Matthew's passages about adultery which leaves undecided the question whether they can function as exception clause, while David Instone-Brewer perceives behind Paul's command to remain unmarried after divorce a specific Corinthian background which contradicts the use of this command as a universal rule.[9] Again, concerning homosexuality Van Bruggen writes that Paul's choice of terms in Romans 1 indicates that he is referring to heterosexuals who consciously seek homosexual intercourse.[10]

The fact that in the past Reformed Christians were often unanimously certain about a particular interpretation was caused not only by exegesis and sound reasoning but also by other factors. They all participated in the same tradition, experienced the same influences, shared the same outlook on reality, and respected the same authorities. Therefore the erosion of consensus today should not only be considered a sign of a weakening lifestyle. Our

7. MacIntyre, *After Virtue*, 1–78.
8. De Bruijne, "Ethics and Spirituality," 5–8.
9. Van Bruggen, *Het huwelijk gewogen*, 55–62; Instone-Brewer, *Divorce and Remarriage*.
10. Van Bruggen, *Romeinen*, 45.

once closed traditions have opened up, so that Reformed Christians have become familiar with possibilities that previously remained at a distance. Our reflection on the relationship between Bible and ethics should reckon with factors such as the narrative we inhabit, the tradition that has formed us, the authorities that we acknowledge, and the experiences we undergo.[11] If we ignore them and just stick to the classical claims, we indirectly and unintentionally foster the relativistic idea that biblical meaning is ambiguous and that you are therefore justified in legitimizing your own preferences.

One serious requirement for our reflection will be to rediscover that the trust of faith does not coincide with rational certainty. Psalm 119 is about the ethical power of God's word. The poet does not appear as confident possessor of all the answers. He is a stranger, continually in danger of getting lost and begging for God's directing signs. Yet he knows the Torah. But the application of its content in specific situations is not evident at face value. In order to find direction, one has to meditate on this Torah as intensively as happens in this song. Only God himself could give the once spoken word afresh so that it shows us the way in the specific situation we encounter today.[12] In much the same mode 2 Peter 1 characterizes God's Word as a light shining in a dark place. Many things in our lives remain in the dark. Full daylight has not yet come. But the Bible provides enough light for the next step in the right direction. A third way exists between modernist-colored orthodox certainty and postmodern relativism. It consists of *trusting* that God through the Bible spreads enough light. This trust leads to *boldness* to expect God's word, and *courage* to take the best possible next step, and at the same time it calls for *modesty*, for we advance only step by step and should not forget that we can also be mistaken.[13]

3. From "scriptural data" to "salvation-historical narrative"

Secondly, the Bible should not be used primarily as a source of "scriptural data" for ethics. This is something the Dutch Reformed salvation-historical tradition could already have taught Reformed Christians. And for systematic theology it has done so. Already decades ago it was acknowledged that doctrine should not be based on isolated biblical proof texts (as often happened

---

11. Mouw, *The God Who Commands*; Hauerwas, *The Peaceable Kingdom*; Black, *Christian Moral Realism*.

12. Brock, *Singing the Ethos of God*, 85, 183; O'Donovan, "Scripture and Christian Ethics," 121–29.

13. Vanhoozer, "The Trials of Truth," 120–56; Vanhoozer, *First Theology*, 231–35.

in the Reformed past) but that it should be rooted in the whole of God's historical revelation. In Benne Holwerda's well-known phrase: salvation history *founds* and not only *illustrates*. For ethics, however, these insights were hardly harvested. Only in the eighties Cornelis Trimp stressed that, above all, the Bible contains the story of the historical ways the Triune God in Christ chose to go with his people. Therefore, also ethics should not in the first place operate with biblical data but be founded upon this salvation-history.[14] Jacob Kamphuis stressed this same point with his explanation of the key ethical appeal in Old and New Testament, namely: "be holy because I am holy." He proposed a historical dimension in the concept of God's holiness.[15] Accordingly, ethics consists of making God's eschatological goal at the end of history into our own and of following him on his ways towards this goal. These promising first steps, however, received no follow-up.

Yet, this would have been fully justified from the perspective of the New Testament itself. The apostles always place their ethical exhortations in the context of a presentation of God's works.[16] They all operate from the same unifying story of God's works and words in Christ. In the New Testament this apostolic tradition shines through in terms like "doctrine," "gospel," "word," and "truth."[17] The apostles did not build their ethics by logical reasoning from a supposed foundational Ten Commandments, nor did they systematize ethical data from the Scriptures. Instead, their main stress was to teach Christians who were underway to God's kingdom to respond appropriately to the works of God in Christ. Today as well, that should be the basic question when dealing with the relationship between Scripture and ethics. What attitude or practice within the given circumstances will do optimal justice to the aims of the work of the Triune God, which ultimately can be summarized as the coming of his kingdom?

4. Ethics with the apostles and with Christ

Third, Reformed ethics should refine its view on the practical ethical instructions that the apostles offer. Primarily these instructions form an access route to the underlying apostolic truth about God's work in Christ.

---

14. Trimp, *Heilsgeschiedenis en prediking*, 12–17, 67–69, 103–5; modest beginnings in Schilder, *Dictaten Kompendium der ethiek I-VI*. For the debate about salvation history, see also Greidanus, *Sola Scriptura*.

15. Kamphuis, *Aantekeningen*, 30.

16. O'Donovan, "Evangelicalism and the Foundations of Ethics," 96–107; O'Donovan, *Resurrection*, 25.

17. Van Bruggen, "Het apostolisch evangelie," 168–216.

They show how this truth became the guiding source for a variety of practical situations in the first century. Those applications, therefore, contain a contingent element. They raise themes that were current in their context and leave out others. Our main task is not to repeat the instantiations but to connect the narrative of God's work in Christ to situations and questions we face today.

With this I certainly do not want to imply that we can ignore the apostolic instantiations. After having been located in this wider perspective, these fulfill two ethical functions. When contexts and phenomena from those days and today are sufficiently similar, they still constitute direct normative instructions for us. This, for example, can be said about Paul's guidelines for divorce in a mixed marriage (1 Cor 7:12–16). However, should circumstances then and now differ too much, this would be wrong. Nevertheless, then the apostolic instruction still performs an exemplary function. Drawing on their method of connecting the phenomenon in their time to God's works in Christ, we should learn to do the same with the phenomenon in our context. Thus, Paul's prohibition to consult secular judges to rule between Christians cannot always be applied today (1 Cor 6:1–3). Different from those times, today churches are legally embedded as recognized structures within the civil society of a once Christian culture. Such legal aspects regard civil courts, which often respect the specific character of the church. Meanwhile, also today Paul's words teach us to be as reluctant in this as possible. Calvin likewise applied the biblical rejection of taking interest not directly to his own economic context because it differed too much from the biblical one.[18] In the same way, texts about homosexuality may not be applied automatically to our context. First we need to consider whether they really touch upon the same phenomena as we encounter today.[19]

This independent way of using biblical instructions is justified by the content of the apostolic tradition. It certainly and prominently contained Christ's ethical teachings from the Sermon on the Mount. After his resurrection, Jesus, depicted in the gospel of Matthew as a new Moses who at the same time is more than Moses, commanded the apostles to instruct his upcoming worldwide community of followers to keep these ethical teachings. With that aim, Matthew explains, he gathered them deliberately once again on the hill that some years before set the stage for his Sermon on the Mount (Matt 28:16–20).[20] Just as Moses' Torah showed God's ways for

---

18. Calvin, *De Profetieën van Ezechiel*, 5–9 in chapter 18.

19. This is even done by Robert A. Gagnon, a convinced adherent of the position that rejects homosexual intercourse, in *The Bible and Homosexual Practice*, 341.

20. Van Bruggen, *Matteüs*, 474.

covenantal life in Canaan, so Jesus' Torah prepares for the life of the coming kingdom over which he now will be inaugurated as the highest authority. Yet unlike Moses' law, Jesus' ethics is not given as a complete package covering all spheres of life. On the one hand this is due to the fact that Christ does not abolish Moses' instructions but includes the existing Torah in his own teachings. On the other hand Jesus relocates Moses' law in the new context of his kingdom. This may lead to corrections, as in Jesus' words about the divorce letter and creation (Matt 19:4-9). It could also cause a deepening and widening of perspective, as in the command to love the enemy. But in any case, only for a limited range of subjects does Jesus himself make the consequences of this new context already explicit. As becomes clear in connection with the theme of the oath, these subjects were especially relevant to the Jewish context of his days (Matt 5:33-37). In the new covenant he does not provide a second exhaustive model of ethical guidelines for all fields of life, as was the case in Moses' Torah. Apparently, with respect to what is not elaborated, New Testament believers should imitate what Jesus explicitly has shown for some themes. They should locate their lives and Moses' instructions in the perspective of the kingdom and draw out the fitting ethical consequences. Sometimes we need to build on Moses, sometimes we have to relativize him.

Only this justifies, for example, Sunday observance.[21] This neither follows necessarily from Moses' commandment nor forms part of Jesus' explicit instructions. It was developed in a church that had learned from the apostles to maintain all that Jesus had commanded. With New Testament Christian maturity the church on this point imitated Jesus' teaching. It transferred Moses' commandment into the new context of the kingdom. It is not coincidental that from the days of its beginning Sunday observance has been a difficult subject for Reformed Christian ethics, which more or less tended towards foundationalism. Today this results in an increasingly relativistic reaction that spoils God's gift of the Sunday. Sunday observance does not form the exceptional case in the law because of the New Testament's silence on the subject. On the contrary, it can be considered as paradigmatic for the use of the law and of Scripture as such within Christian ethics. Such free and mature ecclesial choices are indispensable in finding God's route to the kingdom today. It was already Luther who stated that Christians are free to create new Decalogues.[22]

---

21. Douma, *The Ten Commandments*, 109-60.

22. Gremels, "Freiheit vom Gesetz, im Gesetz," 142, 150-52, referring to Luther, *Thesen de fide*.

5. Practical relevance: God's way with new and old themes

Choosing a starting-point in the grand salvation-historical biblical narrative, instead of in isolated instructions, proves important when dealing with the numerous ethical items on which the Bible contains no direct guidance, subjects such as the environment, bio-industry, and free-market capitalism. Working within the paradigm of biblical instructions, Christians tend to grant such items less weight than those that are specifically mentioned. Sometimes the visions that they form about them are not even explicitly Christian in character, and concerning these they more easily tolerate ethical differences within the church. We then, however, forget the contingency of the fact that the Bible does not raise these topics. It cannot be inferred that they are less important, but only that in biblical times they were not an issue. These themes, too, should be approached from God's works and words in Christ in order to find out what is pleasing to God and what attitude and practice best suits God's purposes and coming kingdom in the given situation.

Even when the Bible does speak about an ethical theme, this should remain the first question. For even then contingency plays a role, so that we cannot assume beforehand that the Bible says all there is to say about a given topic. What was written is partly due to the inducements of its time. What was not important then is not automatically covered. For example, the fact that the Bible contains two situations in which marital separation is possible does not necessarily mean that new situations can never come into view. Such a conclusion would be based on the unfounded assumption that any potential problem was already included in the specific circumstances which the apostles addressed. As a result, reasoning would become either forced or unfair. For example, either abuse should then be construed as desertion or we should reject it as being a possible reason for divorce since the Bible does not mention it. Besides, in Paul's days abuse was probably not perceived to be as insurmountable for the continuation of a marriage as it is today.[23] In much the same way as Paul brought the narrative of God's work in Christ to bear on the dilemmas of his day, the church must continue to do so in the new circumstances that she faces.

This, again, is also important for the theme of "homosexuality." The key question should be: how can we deal with homosexuality in a manner that does justice to God's salvation-historical course in Christ with man and woman, and with sexuality, from creation to the coming kingdom?[24] With

---

23. However, Instone-Brewer claims that the Jews accepted abuse as ground for divorce and that neither Jesus nor Paul denied this (*Divorce*).

24. De Bruijne, "Vriendschap voor christenhomo's," 57–70.

such a point of entrance into the field, we can no longer, like the chairman of Contrario, hide behind the fact that the specific texts concerning homosexuality are interpreted differently, so that any choice could be legitimate and should be acknowledged. Moreover, with this key question we uncover an extra criterion for judging between different ways of dealing with the texts. They have to be in harmony with this overall framework. On the other hand, also with respect to homosexuality, we should acknowledge the contingent nature of the biblical texts. What they do say and do not say is connected with their own contexts. Problems that were not at stake then, but are pressing today, are not automatically answered with the content of those texts. Indeed, the most difficult questions we face are absent from the perspective of the apostles. Scripture, for example, nowhere addresses the intense struggles of gay and lesbian Christians originating within the Christian community and then discovering their unwanted and yet inevitable disposition. In the same way, the Bible nowhere deals with causes and characteristics of homosexuality. Many of our urgent questions are not answered directly with biblical instantiations. We have to reflect on them ourselves from the perspective of God's work in Christ.

In my view, differences of ethical opinion among Christians are mostly caused not by different explanations of texts but by underlying conceptions of God himself, of his work through the ages, and of reality.

6. Manifold modes of scriptural data

In the preceding paragraphs I already stressed that specific ethical content in Bible passages continues to keep its function, even while stressing the priority of the salvation-historical narrative. The latter even helps to uncover more potential in concrete texts than the traditional model. My predecessor, Jochem Douma, has pointed out that Christians should not only search direct normative guide texts in the Bible, but also indirect signposts and guards, and even models. Other ethicists proposed comparable distinctions.[25]

These refine our use of the Bible in ethics. First, they stimulate us to process biblical passages only in the mode in which they speak. For instance, we should not interpret examples as rules. It would be wrong to interpret Acts 4:32–37 as a command to sell our property, but this passage does provide a stimulating example. Secondly, they offer new possibilities of shaping our ethical reflection with biblical content. For difficult situations

---

25. Douma, *Grondslagen Christelijke ethiek*, 97–122; Hays, *Moral Vision*, 208–9. See also Nullens and Michener, *The Matrix of Christian Ethics*, 189–224.

about ending possibly senseless medical treatments, the Bible contains no direct commands. However, biblical perspectives on the nature and place of suffering do offer a directional framework. And the idealist notion of a world government that has been proposed by contemporary politicians and philosophers and even by the Pope, is not addressed directly in biblical texts but still collides with biblical wisdom teaching that concentrations of power surpass human capacities and, beyond that, offer free passages to demons.[26]

In the same way, our reflection on homosexuality should take into account more biblical data than only directly normative texts—for example, that it is not good to be alone, but at the same time that remaining unmarried can be God's calling; that it is better to marry than to burn, but also that following Jesus always implies bearing the cross; that Christian friendship sometimes surpasses marital love; that a eunuch is welcome in God's church; that sexual sin causes specific damage (Gen 2:18; 1 Cor 7:9, 2, 26; Luke 14:26–27; 2 Sam 1:26; John 15:15; Acts 8:38; 1 Cor 6:18).

7. Knowing reality as well

This approach to the place of the Bible in ethics implies that the Bible alone is not enough. Already to be able to compare phenomena and contexts then and now, requires knowledge of our own culture and of the biblical surroundings. When dealing with Scripture we all operate with an image of its context and of our own context, although often unconsciously. Knowing the Bible always interacts with the knowledge of created reality. The *sola scriptura* of the Reformation never meant that the Bible should function in a vacuum, but that it should be acknowledged as the ultimate criterion. According to Article 2 of the Belgic Confession, even knowledge of God involves knowledge of reality. How much more should this be the case when it comes to good and evil and reality itself!

Therefore, when using the Bible we should be receptive to facts and realities. For the case of homosexuality this means that it is wrong to produce moral judgments without dealing with homosexuals themselves and opening our hearts to listen to their life stories and experiences. Likewise we should honestly consider possible results of scientific research.[27] At the same time, the Bible keeps the final word. It forms—in Calvin's phrase—the spectacles through which we see the reality that we come across. When gay men tell us about their stable relationship of love and faithfulness which

---

26. Donadio and Goodstein, "Pope Urges Forming New World Economic Order"; Küng and Schmidt, eds., *A Global Ethic and Global Responsibilities*.

27. Jones and Yarhouse, *Homosexuality*.

they manage to combine with following Jesus, we must take them seriously, but without considering their experience to be automatically normative. It must be interpreted in the light of Scripture.[28]

8. God's use of the Bible

Thus far in my argumentation I have spoken about "our use" of the Bible in ethics. However, priority should be given to God's use of the Bible in the lives of his children. According to Lord's Day 25 of the Heidelberg Catechism, the preaching of the Word is a means of grace of which the Spirit forms the subject. That confession should also guide us with respect to Scripture, which preserves this Word through the ages.[29] This priority of the Spirit is decisive for the relationship between Scripture and ethics. Through his Word, God himself equips Christians with what they need for a God-fearing life (2 Tim 3:16). Scripture is not primarily supplier of ethical building blocks or even of the great story of God's works. It is the powerful recreating Word of God, in which Christ himself is invested.[30] Whatever the Bible ethically achieves, the first thing it does is to unite people to Christ. By doing this, the Spirit changes the attitude of their hearts and minds. We grow, as 1 Corinthians 2:16 says, into the mind of Christ. Only in that way are Christians able to develop affinity with the intentions of the Spirit. Christ is characterized as "God's wisdom and power" (1 Cor 1:24). Therefore, above all, the Spirit through the Bible grants us wisdom to discern the good and strength to put it into practice. This is foremost a spiritual and not only a cognitive reality. In passing, I note that here lies an important point of entrance for an approach that has often been absent from Reformed ethics, namely that of virtue or character. With Scripture, God's Spirit trains us not in the first place by giving us the right insights but by forming our character after the pattern of Jesus himself (2 Pet 1:4-8; Col 3:10, 12).[31]

These operations of the Spirit occur also when we are dealing with texts in which the specific ethical item that concerns us is not at issue. It is similar to preaching. All kinds of instantiations in the situation of a given congregation may arise from texts that did not explicitly seem to contain them beforehand. Thus an important element in my approach to the environmental issue arose on the occasion of a sermon about Jesus' parable of

---

28. This is lacking in the description of reality in Ganzevoort et al., *Adam en Evert*, 43–63.
   29. Van den Brink and Van der Kooi, *Christelijke dogmatiek*, 496–501.
   30. Calvin, *Institutes*, 3.2.6.
   31. Wright, *After You Believe*, 27–71.

the man who built his house on sandy ground and then saw it being swept away by the flood of God's judgment (Matt 7:24–27). And my suspicion that it is not right when we already in advance aim at compromise when dealing with homosexuality was confirmed when I meditated on the first verses of Psalm 37: "Trust in God and do good."[32] The use of the Bible in ethics is not just a question of the right insights but foremost of a receptive spiritual attitude. Whoever does not open himself to God and his Word, continually praying for wisdom, should not expect to receive ethical insight. Even impressive biblical reasoning can camouflage disobedience. On the other hand, questionable arguments can accompany a receptive attitude which God rewards by showing the right direction. Our understanding of good and evil is proportionally related to our pious approach to Scripture, personally as well as ecclesially and theologically. Could here perhaps emerge a deeper-lying spiritual cause of the increasing insolubility of ethical debates in Western Christianity? If so, also the answer would have to commence at this spiritual level.

9. The nature of ethical understanding: the gift of discernment

Because, as we saw, God should be considered the decisive subject of the ethical use of Scripture, ethical insight cannot be produced by method alone. Insight is given and has to be received. Accordingly, it displays a specific character. The traditional foundationalist approach betrays an ideal of knowledge modeled after the natural sciences. However, as Gadamer has shown, interpreting music, paintings, culture, and texts involves more than analysis and logical reasoning. Such knowledge is partly intuitive and aesthetic in character. It is a way of seeing. We form a picture of the whole and recognize whether an interpretation fits or not.[33] Ethics, too, requires such recognition. What attitude and practice suits God's work in Christ or fits specific biblical moral data? The Bible itself uses such terms as "discernment," "sensibility," and "ethical experience" (Rom 12:1–2; Phil 1:9–10; Heb 5:14). In contemporary ethics this has been compared rightly with the

---

32. Brock shows that this way of reaching ethical conclusions in a direct spiritual wrestling with all kinds of biblical passages through which the Spirit shapes our understanding was in fact usual among Christian theologians in all ages. To prove this, he analyses Augustine, Luther, and Bonhoeffer. Brock, *Singing*, 189–91, 248.

33. Thiselton, *Hermeneutics*, 1–16; Spohn, *Go and Do Likewise*, 55, 80, 153, 158; Vanhoozer, *First*, 347–48.

operation of metaphors. Two different fields of meaning interconnect in such a way that we learn to see the one in terms of the other.[34]

To find this type of insight, Christians need each other in the church. The Western model of knowledge, in its orthodox version too, tacitly assumes an individualist pattern: equipped with the right principles derived from faith, with clear data and with sound reasoning, any individual should be able to deduce correct conclusions. As a matter of fact, it is precisely the caricature of *this* model that confronts us today in postmodern individualist arbitrariness. However, God uses his Word as means of grace always in the context of the church. The ethical messages of New Testament prophets, for example, were uttered and tested in the congregation. Especially today, we need an ecclesial ethics to respond to individualism.[35] The gifts of the Spirit—also those gifts that contribute to ethical understanding—are given and meant to function in the context of Christ's body. Listening to God should be a communal practice. And when opinions differ, Augustine said Christians should choose what serves love. Only ecclesial love provides a context for finding God's direction.[36]

This ecclesial ethics stands in clear opposition to the message of Contrario's chairman. He claimed legitimacy for different choices in advance and thereby unconsciously ruled out the possibility that God uses Scripture to provide his church with shared insights concerning homosexuality. Today we urgently need to rediscover the narrow path between such postmodern permissiveness and our traditional orthodox rational certainty. Only this path of faith, boldness, courage, humility, and love will bring us closer to God's purpose, even with regard to the theme of homosexuality.

Bibliography

Augustine. *City of God and Christian Doctrine*. In *A Select Library of the Nicene and post-Nicene Fathers of the Christian Church, volume 2: St. Augustine's City of God and Christian Doctrine*, edited by Philip Schaff. Grand Rapids, MI: Eerdmans, 1993.

Bilkes, Laurens W. *Theological Ethics and Holy Scripture: The Use of Scripture in the Works of James M. Gustafson, R. Paul Ramsay, and Allen D. Verhey*. Heerenveen: Groen, 1997.

Birch, Bruce C., and Larry L. Rasmussen. *Bible and Ethics in the Christian Life*, revised and expanded edition. Minneapolis, MN: Augsburg Fortress, 1989.

---

34. Hays, *Moral Vision*, 298–305.

35. De Bruijne, "Navolging en verbeeldingskracht," 195–237; Hays, *Moral Vision*, 304–6.

36. Augustine, *On Christian Doctrine*, Book III, Chapter 15, 23.

Black, Rufus. *Christian Moral Realism: Natural Law, Narrative, Virtue and the Gospel.* Oxford: Oxford University Press, 2000.

Brock, Brian. *Singing the Ethos of God: On the Place of Christian Ethics in Scripture.* Grand Rapids, MI: Eerdmans, 2007.

Bruins, Gerald. "CGK wijzen homorelatie af," *Nederlands Dagblad*, November 27, 2013.

———. "Verlegenheid over homobesluit," *Nederlands Dagblad*, November 30, 2013.

Calvin, John, *De Profetieën van Ezechiel hoofdstuk I-XX.* Translated into Dutch by J. Lugtigheid. Kampen: Kok, 1903.

———. *Institutes of the Christian Religion in Two Volumes.* Edited by John T. McNeill. Translated by Ford Lewis Battles. Philadelphia: Westminster Press, 1960.

Chamberlain, Pam. "Younger Evangelicals: Where Will They Take the Christian Right?" *Christian Higher Education* 8. 4 (Sept–Oct 2009) 327–41.

Cosgrove, Charles H. *Appealing to Scripture in Moral Debate: Five Hermeneutical Rules.* Grand Rapids, MI: Eerdmans, 2002.

Cunningham, David S. *Christian Ethics: The End of the Law.* London: Routledge, 2008.

Curran, Charles E., and Richard A. McCormick. *The Use of Scripture in Moral Theology.* New York: Paulist Press, 1984.

De Bruijne, A. L. Th. (Ad). "Ethics and Spirituality." *Lux Mundi* 28. 1 (2009) 5–8.

———. "Navolging en verbeeldingskracht." In *Woord op schrift: theologische reflecties over het gezag van de bijbel*, edited by C. Trimp, 195–237. Kampen: Kok, 2002.

———. "Vriendschap voor christenhomo's." In *Open en kwetsbaar. Christelijk debat over homoseksualiteit*, edited by Ad de Bruijne, 57–70. Barneveld: De Vuurbaak, 2012.

Donadio, Rachel and Laurie Goodstein. "Pope Urges Forming New World Economic Order to Work for the 'Common Good.'" *New York Times*, July 7, 2009. No pages. Online: http://www.nytimes.com/2009/07/08/world/europe/08pope.html?_r=0

Douma, Jochem. *Echtscheiding.* Amsterdam: Bolland, 1982.

———. *Grondslagen Christelijke ethiek.* Kampen: Kok, 1999.

———. *The Ten Commandments: Manual for the Christian Life.* Translated by Nelson D. Kloosterman. Phillipsburg, NJ: Presbyterian and Reformed Publishing, 1996.

Fowl, Stephen, E., and L. Gregory Jones. *Reading in Communion: Scripture and Ethics in Christian Life.* London: SPCK, 1991.

Gagnon, Robert A. *The Bible and Homosexual Practice: Texts and Hermeneutics.* Nashville: Abingdon Press, 2001.

———. "Why the Disagreement over the Biblical Witness on Homosexual Practice? A Response to Myers and Scanzoni, *What God Has Joined Together?*" *Reformed Review: A Theological Journal of Western Theological Seminary, Holland, Michigan* 59. 1 (2005) 19–130.

Ganzevoort, Ruard, et al. *Adam en Evert: de spanning tussen kerk en homoseksualiteit.* Kampen: Ten Have, 2010.

Greidanus, Sidney. *Sola Scriptura: Problems and Principles in Preaching Historical Texts.* Eugene, OR: Wipf & Stock, 2001.

Gremels, Georg. "Freiheit vom Gesetz, im Gesetz, und durch das Gesetz. Die Position Luthers und der christlich-jüdisches Dialog." In *Kirche und Synagoge. Ein lutherisches Votum*, edited by Folger Siegert, 127–152. Göttingen: Vandenhoeck & Ruprecht, 2012.

Grudem, Wayne. *Politics According to the Bible: A Comprehensive Resource for Understanding Modern Political Issues in Light of Scripture.* Grand Rapids, MI: Zondervan, 2010.

Hauerwas, Stanley. *The Peaceable Kingdom: A Primer in Christian Ethics.* London: SCM, 1984.

Hays, Richard B. *The Moral Vision of the New Testament: A Contemporary Introduction to New Testament Ethics.* New York: HarperCollins, 1996.

Henry, Carl F. H. *Christian Personal Ethics.* Grand Rapids, MI: Eerdmans, 1957.

Honey, Charles. "The Litmus Test: Trustee ban on advocacy stirs up Calvin faculty." *Christianity Today* 53.11 (Nov 2009) 17.

Instone-Brewer, David. *Divorce and Remarriage in the Bible: The Social and Literary Context.* Grand Rapids, MI: Eerdmans, 2002.

Jones, Stanton L., and Mark A. Yarhouse. *Homosexuality: The Use of Scientific Research in the Church's Moral Debate.* Downers Grove, IL: InterVarsity Press, 2005.

Kamphuis, J. *Aantekeningen bij J.A. Heyns Dogmatiek 1–2.* Kampen: Van den Berg, 1982.

Kirk, Andrew, and Kevin J.Vanhoozer. *To Stake a Claim: Mission and the Western Crisis of Knowledge.* Maryknoll, NY: Orbis Books, 1999.

Küng, Hans, and Helmut Schmidt, eds. *A Global Ethic and Global Responsibilities: Two Declarations.* London: SCM, 1998.

Kuyper, Abraham. *De heedendaagse schriftcritiek in haar bedenkelijke strekking voor de gemeente des levenden Gods.* Amsterdam: Kruyt, 1881.

MacIntyre, Alisdair. *After Virtue: A Study in Moral Theory.* 2nd ed. Notre Dame: University of Notre Dame Press, 1984.

Mouw, Richard J. *The God Who Commands.* Notre Dame: Notre Dame University Press, 2000.

Murphy, Nancey C. *Theology in a Postmodern Age.* 2nd ed. Prague: International Baptist Theological Seminary of the European Baptist Federation, 2003.

Murray, John. *Principles of Conduct: Aspects of Biblical Ethics.* London: Tyndale Press, 1957.

Nullens, Patrick, and Ronald T. Michener. *The Matrix of Christian Ethics: Integrating Philosophy and Moral Theology in a Postmodern Context.* Downers Grove, IL: InterVarsity Press, 2010.

O'Donovan, Oliver. "Evangelicalism and the Foundations of Ethics." In *Evangelical Anglicans: Their Role in the Church Today,* edited by R. T. France and Alistair E. McGrath, 96–107. London: SPCK, 1993.

———. *Resurrection and Moral Order: An Outline for Evangelical Ethics.* 2nd ed. Grand Rapids, MI: Eerdmans, 1994.

———. "Scripture and Christian Ethics." *Theologia Reformata* 48 (2005) 121–29.

Olson, Daniel V.A., and Jeremy N. Thomas. *Sexual Moral Reasoning in American Evangelicalism.* West Lafayette, IN: Purdue University, 2012.

Phillips, D. Z. *Faith after Foundationalism.* London: Routledge, 1988.

Rauser, Randal. *Theology in Search of Foundations.* Oxford: Oxford University Press, 2009.

Rogers, Jack. *Jesus, the Bible, and Homosexuality: Explode the Myths, Heal the Church.* Louisville, KY: Westminster John Knox Press, 2006.

Rogers, Jack B., and Donald K. McKim. *The Authority and Interpretation of the Bible: An Historical Approach.* San Francisco: Harper & Row, 1979.

Schilder, Klaas. *Dictaten Kompendium der ethiek I–VI*. Compiled by G. J. Bruijn. Kampen: Van den Berg, 1980.

Schmidt, Thomas E. *Straight and Narrow? Compassion and Clarity in the Homosexuality Debate*. Downers Grove, IL: InterVarsity Press, 1995.

Spohn, William C. *Go and Do Likewise: Jesus and Ethics*. New York: Continuum, 2007.

———. *What Are They Saying About Scripture and Ethics?* New York: Paulist Press, 1984.

Thiselton, Anthony C. *Hermeneutics: An Introduction*. Grand Rapids, MI: Eerdmans, 2009.

Thomas, Jeremy N., and Daniel V. A. Olson. "Evangelical Elites' Changing Responses to Homosexuality 1960–2009." *Sociology of Religion* 73. 3 (2012) 239–72.

Trimp, C. *Heilsgeschiedenis en prediking. Hervatting van een onvoltooid gesprek*. Kampen: Van den Berg, 1986.

Van Bekkum, Koert, and Rien Rouw, eds. *Geloven in zekerheid. Gereformeerd geloven in een postmoderne tijd*. Barneveld: De Vuurbaak, 2000.

Van Bruggen, Jakob. "Het apostolisch evangelie als geloofsbelijdenis." In *Apostelen. Dragers van een spraakmakend evangelie*, edited by P. H. R. van Houwelingen, 168–216. Kampen: Kok, 2010.

———. *Het huwelijk gewogen: 1 Korinthe 7*. 4th impression. Amsterdam: Bolland, 1979.

———. *Matteüs. Het evangelie voor Israël*. Kampen: Kok, 1990.

———. *Romeinen. Christenen tussen stad en synagoge*. Kampen: Kok, 2006.

Van Dam, Cornelis. *Divorce and Remarriage in the Light of Old Testament Principles and Their Application in the New Testament*. Winnipeg, MB: Premier Publishing, 1996.

Van den Brink, G., and C. van der Kooi. *Christelijke dogmatiek: een inleiding*. Zoetermeer: Boekencentrum, 2012.

Vanhoozer, Kevin J. *First Theology: God, Scripture, and Hermeneutics*. Downers Grove, IL: InterVarsity Press, 2002.

———. "The Trials of Truth. Mission, Martyrdom and the Epistemology of the Cross." In *To Stake a Claim: Christian Mission in Epistemological Crisis*, edited by Andrew Kirk and Kevin J. Vanhoozer, 120–56. Maryknoll, NY: Orbis, 1999.

Van Til, Cornelius. *In Defense of the Faith. Christian Theistic Ethics* 3. Phillipsburg, NJ: Presbyterian and Reformed Publishing, 1970.

Verhey, Allen D. "The Holy Bible and Sanctified Sexuality: An Evangelical Approach to Scripture and Sexual Ethics." *Interpretation* 49. 1 (1995) 31–45.

———. *Remembering Jesus: Christian Community, Scripture, and the Moral Life*. Grand Rapids, MI: Eerdmans, 2002.

Wolterstorff, Nicholas. *Reason Within the Bounds of Religion*. 2nd ed. Grand Rapids, MI: Eerdmans, 1984.

Wright, N.T. *After You Believe: Why Christian Character Matters*. New York: HarperOne, 2010.

Christian Ethics and God's Use of the Bible
A Response

Theodore G. Van Raalte

Ad de Bruijne has chosen a very pertinent topic and made a valuable contribution to our discussion of Reformed hermeneutics. The interpretation of Scripture in Reformed ethics is a very concrete and practical matter and thus an excellent way to test our hermeneutical rules, models, and methods. I share and applaud De Bruijne's concern to fight off the postmodern relativistic, individualistic, and emotive approach to ethics. I thank him for helping me think about the relationship between the broad themes of salvation history and the various texts of the Bible in a more isolated sense.

De Bruijne introduces the topic with the observation that "the traditional use of the Bible is experiencing a crisis ... [in] many orthodox and evangelical churches in the Western world."[1] He supports this with reference to a response to a recent Synod decision in the Netherlands and adds in a footnote a number of recent relevant popular and academic articles. Throughout most of his essay De Bruijne opposes what he calls a "modern foundationalist epistemology" combined with "the traditional appeal to the Bible." He contrasts this "modernist-colored orthodox certainty" with "postmodern relativism" and then argues for a third way between them, namely, a "salvation-historical narrative" approach. He states that whereas the salvation-historical tradition has taken root in dogmatics, so that dogmaticians no longer use the Bible "primarily as a source of 'scriptural data,'" we have yet to learn the same for ethics. Unless we do so, we will not "take the wind out of threatening skeptical sails" of postmodernism. Indeed,

1. Unsourced quotations in this response refer to Ad de Bruijne's presentation.

"[we] should acknowledge that [we ourselves] have contributed to [the postmodern problem] by combining faith in Scripture with a foundationalist model." De Bruijne thus justifies advancing a salvation-historical method of Scripture interpretation in the field of ethics. I appreciate his concern that our ethics be rightly grounded.

One could of course argue that the "traditional use" of the Bible has always been going through a crisis, whether on account of the Montanist view of prophecy in the early church, or on account of the medieval developments concerning papal authority and the role of tradition, or on account of Socinian and Enlightenment rationalism, or, finally, on account of the postmodern view of language and truth. The question then would be whether the traditional use of the Bible—a use that has survived so many other challenges—could not survive the most recent postmodern challenges. I would argue that it most certainly can and is.

I begin with the question of foundationalism. De Bruijne states that "modern foundationalist epistemology . . . stresses the importance of incontrovertible axioms, exact data and rational certainty."

If De Bruijne means simply Cartesian foundationalism and the highly positive role assigned to reason in the Enlightenment we can no doubt join him in specifying various errors spawned by this movement. But it seems that De Bruijne means to include the early modern foundationalism employed by Reformed theologians such as Calvin (1509-64), Chandieu (1534-91), Beza (1519-1605), and Zanchi (1516-90), and continued by the Reformed Orthodox thereafter up through Bavinck, for he generalizes to what is "traditional" and even seems to challenge the common practice of using the Ten Commandments to systematize the scriptural data on ethics, something practiced by his own predecessor in ethics at Kampen. I would like to present the briefest summary of the foundationalism and logic employed by our Reformed forefathers in their theology, church polity, and ethics. I consider their approach to the use of reason in theology to be universally valid because such logic derives from the nature of things (realism) and is assumed in Scripture.

One could, in this matter, go back to Augustine who viewed logic, rhetoric, arithmetic, and even astronomy as studies that derive from the nature of things and thus represent things *discovered* rather than things invented by humans. He maintained that pagan insights into these matters not only could be used, but ought to be, just as the Lord commanded the Israelites to despoil the Egyptians when leaving Egypt under Moses (Exod 11:2).[2]

---

2. Augustine, *Teaching Christianity*, Book II.25.38–II.42.63. All Scripture quotations

Let us consider the "axioms, exact data, and rational certainty" which De Bruijne questions: In fact, the Reformed theologians sought to conform their arguments to logic and thus appealed explicitly to grounds, axioms, foundations, or principles.[3] They also paid attention to "exact data" in terms not just of words but also of the aspects, moods, and tenses of verbs, the etymological and cultural nuances of terms, and the precise relationship of words, clauses, and sentences, especially as specified by syncategorematic terms. As for rational certainty, I would suggest that it is precisely by conforming to the canons of reason that we can be certain that our theological definitions reflect the truth of Scripture (laws of identity, non-contradiction, and excluded middle). After all, we necessarily employ reason when we draw both direct and deduced conclusions from Scripture as well as when we afterwards test whether or not they conform to Scripture. This is an unavoidable aspect of language as it seeks to reflect and interact with reality. And, when the apostles frequently used the verb *ginosko* (to know), as in "we know that in all things God works for the good of those who love him . . ." they did not eviscerate the rational elements from "we know" but assumed them. Surely the rational is not sufficient for our knowledge of Scripture, but it is absolutely necessary, given the very nature of Scripture as written communication conveying propositional truth.

Further to the notion of foundations, let us consider the important question our forefathers had to answer, namely, whether the authority of the Scripture "is grounded in the approval of the church" or in God himself and his self-authenticating written Word.[4] Or, note the text wherein the church is called "the pillar and foundation of the truth" (1 Tim 3:15). Calvin affirms that this foundation is doctrine, a doctrine passed on to us in Holy Scripture.[5] Similarly, commenting on Ephesians 2:20 where the church is said to be built on the foundation of the apostles and prophets, Calvin writes that the foundation means doctrine.[6] He is polemicizing against the Roman Catholics who prefer to make persons the foundation rather than their teaching. In no way does Calvin question the very idea of the foundation metaphor; certainly he never polemicizes against it as the postmodernists do. Our own Belgic Confession maintains that we receive all the canonical

---

in this article are from the New International Version (NIV 84).

3. Calvin, *Institutes*, 1.11.21, 3.3.15, 3.17.1–3,9–10, 4.10.21; Van den Belt, *Authority of Scripture*, 123–4; Muller, *Post-Reformation Reformed Dogmatics*, vol. 1: 430–55.

4. For an example see Calvin, *Institutes*, 4.9.14; compare his comments on John 17:20. Calvin, *Commentary on John*, 181–82.

5. Calvin, *Commentaries on Timothy, Titus, and Philemon*, 89–90.

6. Calvin, *Commentaries on Galatians and Ephesians*, 242–43. Compare his *Institutes*, 1.7.2.

books "for the regulation, *foundation*, and confirmation of our faith" (BC 5). Thus, we must not jettison foundations when expressing concerns about "foundationalism."

Allow me to proceed to the example of Chandieu, who wrote with greater precision than Calvin. In 1566, when he published the first defense of Reformed synodical church polity at the request of the French National and Provincial Synods, Chandieu clearly distinguished the authority of different parts of Scripture as regards church polity (we could apply the same principles as regards ethics). Chandieu weighted the passages: weightiest are the direct commands; weighty are the doctrines and their implications; less weighty are the examples; of even less weight are the more ambiguous examples from early church practice; and of least weight are arguments from expediency (contrary to what De Bruijne suggests, these distinctions were well known for centuries).[7]

Chandieu's more scholastic works in the 1580s made the role of Scripture in theological argument very clear: in its entirety Scripture is the *principium* or foundation of all theological argument and its particular texts may indeed function as *principia* (foundations, principles) of the various doctrines.[8] He worked this way precisely to make clear that his arguments rested on Scripture and not on logic. Logic functioned, rather, as the tool or instrument of all knowledge, not its foundation. In his voluminous correspondence Beza highly recommended such works of Chandieu.

The *principia* were also called *axiomata* (axioms) and these indeed functioned as a *fundamentum* (foundation) but at no time was any of this foundation drawn from outside of Scripture itself, as would happen later in the Enlightenment.[9]

What we are saying was neatly summarized in the Westminster Confession of Faith in 1648: "The whole counsel of God concerning all things necessary for His own glory, man's salvation, faith and life, is either expressly set down in Scripture, or by good and necessary consequence may be deduced from Scripture" (1.6).

Our own Reformed confessions have always assumed the same thing. For instance, Article 10 of the Belgic Confession speaks of Christ as truly divine and uses this expression: "He is the Son of God, not only from the time that he assumed our nature but from all eternity, as the following testimonies, when compared with each other, teach us." We then encounter

---

7. Chandieu, *La confirmation de la discipline*, 42–52, 75–82, 88–108, 150, 155, 205.

8. See especially his introduction in Sadeele, *Locus de Verbo Dei scripto*. See also Sinnema, "Chandieu's Call," 159–90; Van Raalte, "Chandieu: One of the Fathers of Reformed Scholasticism?"

9. Muller, *Post-Reformation Reformed Dogmatics*, 1:432.

statements from Moses, John, the letter to the Hebrews, and Paul. Following this we confess, "Therefore *it must necessarily follow* that he who is called God, the Word, the Son, and Jesus Christ, did exist at that time when all things were created by him." The phrase "it must necessarily follow" indicates a consequence, entailment, deduction, or implication. The sequence of statements offered must lead to the conclusion that follows. There is a cause and effect of some kind going on, and, if the reasoning has the right foundation and follows the right method, the conclusion will follow by "good and necessary consequence." Other similar examples can be found elsewhere in the confessions of faith, all of which obviously precede René Descartes.[10]

Now I would like to step back from these historical remarks to focus on what I consider to be a false dilemma in De Bruijne's presentation, namely, the dilemma between the trajectories/themes/motifs and the actual injunctions of Scripture. God is one; the Holy Spirit has authored one Bible, which is united in all its parts. If we rightly discern the themes of Scripture (such as creation, fall, redemption, consummation) they will in no way contradict the actual injunctions and ethical commands found therein. The themes and commands work in concert, the latter helping us make the practice of the former concrete and actual. Pitting the one against the other is dangerous for our faith.

Indeed, the "whole historical revelation" of God comes to us by way of various sayings. As long as the sayings and particulars are used according to their proper contextual meaning, they certainly may function as "proofs."

While it is true that the apostles didn't "build their ethics by logical reasoning from a supposed foundational Ten Commandments, nor did they systematize ethical data from the Scriptures," we must realize that God was not using them to write textbooks in Ethics. We, however, now have a need to teach Ethics as a formal discipline and thus we need to systematize our knowledge, much like Jochem Douma did in *De Tien Geboden*. More fundamentally, however, we must agree, based on the apostolic appeal to the law in Romans 13:8–14, James 1:22—2:13, and 1 John 3, that the apostles most certainly assumed and taught the authority of the Ten Commandments and expected Christians to put them into practice.

---

10. Other examples from the Belgic Confession: "For since the soul was lost as well as the body, it was necessary that he should assume both to save both" (Art. 18). "For it must necessarily follow, either that all we need for our salvation is not in Jesus Christ or, if it is all in him, that one who has Jesus Christ through faith, has complete salvation" (Art. 22). "This church has existed from the beginning of the world and will be to the end, for Christ is an eternal King who cannot be without subjects" (Art. 27). Compare the Heidelberg Catechism, Lord's Days 5–6.

It's somewhat ironic that while appealing to the salvation-historical narrative for the building of a Christian ethic, De Bruijne also speaks of Jesus as the new Moses giving his new law, namely, the Sermon on the Mount. Not only do I disagree that Jesus is the new Moses in this sense—for Jesus is not undermining Moses, but simply explaining and deepening what Moses taught—but also I strongly disagree that the Ten Words are not useful for life in the kingdom of Jesus. Our own catechism, in line with the history of the church of many centuries, confesses the normative role of the Ten Words as the rule of thankful living for the redeemed children of God (Lord's Days 34–44).

Further, if we are *not* going to maintain this central place for the Ten Words, we will need to develop some clear guidelines to ensure that we start and stop in the right places as we "connect the narrative of God's work in Christ to situations and questions we face." We need to guard ourselves against subjectivity, and we need to be able to declare, "thus says the Lord."

I would like to close with appreciation for two things: the first is De Bruijne's insistence that no right ethical conclusions can be reached apart from faith. I agree that unbelievers are unable to appreciate the *significance* of the biblical injunctions, even if they might rightly discern the meaning of Scripture intellectually. As God's children we are uniquely gifted with the Holy Spirit, who will guide us into all truth.

The second item of appreciation I would like to single out is De Bruijne's conclusion that he could not endorse the objections raised against the decisions of a recent Reformed Synod regarding homosexuality. This was heartening. However, I wonder whether he might re-examine the nature of his conclusion, that is, what constituted it. De Bruijne states, "And my suspicion that it is not right when we already in advance aim at compromise when dealing with homosexuality was confirmed when I meditated on the first verses of Psalm 37: 'Trust in God and do good.'" It seems to me that by pointing to this text De Bruijne suggests that his own conviction arose neither from a consideration of the precise texts of Scripture that deal with homosexuality nor from a careful employment of reason. Rather, the conviction came upon him when he was looking at a different place, and meditating on the theme of trusting God and doing good.

I suspect that his description is incomplete. This text, I would suggest, could only have helped him because he was *already* familiar with all the particular texts of Scripture that do openly speak about homosexuality. So, basically, if he thinks homosexual practices and nurtured homosexual desires are sin, he has reached this conclusion in much the regular, traditional way. Perhaps one thinks that postmodern homosexuals will be more convinced by a conclusion that does not appear to have followed the path of reason.

In fact, both the academy and life in general rely heavily upon reasoned grounds. We ask, "Why did you do that?" and we expect grounds for the action. Only by providing sufficient grounds can the rational faculty of the soul be satisfied and offer guidance to the will and passions. The traditional way of employing reason may not be appreciated when it undermines one's desires, but it still is able to survive the postmodern challenge.

In the scientific discipline of Ethics, as taught at a seminary in particular and as thought out by us for practical application—whether in medical ethics, penal justice, civic order, or ecclesiastical discipline—we need clear direction, developed in a commonly agreed manner, with decisions and positions that are biblically and rationally defensible. An answer that appeals to the freedom and intuition of the artisan is far too subjective. Decisions made in this way cannot be rationally defended and thus cannot satisfy either the questions of opponents or the questions that one may raise at a later time. All that can be said is, "I felt that way then" rather than "Here are the grounds for the position I took at that time. They still hold."

To bring my response back to the beginning, I conclude with a consideration of De Bruijne's title: "Christian Ethics and God's Use of the Bible." At first this had me rather puzzled, but I finally decided that he must mean God's way of using the Bible in our lives to bring us to the right ethical positions. In this regard I have no dispute that a text from Psalm 37 about trusting the Lord might be the means God uses to bring us to the conviction that we must resolutely follow his expressed will on some specific matter. But as noted, I would argue that we actually already knew the substance of the matter from elsewhere in Scripture. The more difficult question, however, is how to relate God's use of the Bible as means of instructing and convicting us to our own use of the Bible in forming conclusions about ethics. That is to say, if "God's use of the Bible" at times seems to be somewhat indirect (De Bruijne's example of God's use of Psalm 37 in his own life), does this mean that our own use of the Bible to arrive at convincing Christian ethical positions should also be more or less indirect? Should we refer primarily to themes and motifs when we study ethical topics and seek to convince others, especially postmoderns? Or should we still be able to say, "Thus says the Lord," because he himself has pronounced distinct and clear commands that speak to the issue?

Though wisdom may dictate that in one or another situation it be best to lead another to realization of God's will in a somewhat indirect way, I maintain that faithful listening to God's voice in ethics must include all the relevant scriptural data, especially those texts that speak directly to the issue. At the end of the day we must bow the knee, for God's Word in all its facets is the foundation of our faith and life.

Bibliography

Augustine. *Teaching Christianity: De Doctrina Christiana*. Translated by Edmund Hill. New York: New City Press, 1996.

Calvin, John. *Commentaries on the Epistles of Paul to the Galatians and Ephesians*. Translated by William Pringle. Grand Rapids, MI: Baker, 1984.

———. *Commentaries on the Epistles to Timothy, Titus, and Philemon*. Translated by William Pringle. Grand Rapids, MI: Baker, 1984.

———. *Commentary on the Gospel According to John, second volume*. Translated by William Pringle. Grand Rapids, MI: Baker, 1984.

———. *Institutes of the Christian Religion*. Edited by John T. McNeill. Translated by Ford Lewis Battles. Philadelphia: Westminster Press, 1960.

[Chandieu, Antoine de]. *La confirmation de la discipline ecclesiastique, obseruee es eglises reformees du royaume de France. Avec la response aux obiectiones proposees alencontre*. [Geneva: Henri II Estienne], 1566.

Sadeele, A. [Antoine de Chandieu]. *Locus de Verbo Dei scripto, adversus humanas traditiones, theologice et scholastice tractatus*. Morges: J. Le Preux, 1580.

Sinnema, Donald. "Antoine de Chandieu's Call for a Scholastic Reformed Theology (1580)." In *Later Calvinism: International Perspectives*, edited by W. Fred Graham, 159–90. Kirksville, MO: Sixteenth Century, 1994.

Muller, Richard A. *Post-Reformation Reformed Dogmatics: The Rise and Development of Reformed Orthodoxy, ca. 1520 to ca. 1725*. Four vols, 2nd ed. Grand Rapids, MI: Baker, 2003.

Van den Belt, Henk. *The Authority of Scripture in Reformed Theology: Truth and Trust*. Leiden: Brill, 2008.

Van Raalte, Theodore G. "Antoine de Chandieu (1534–1591): One of the Fathers of Reformed Scholasticism?" Ph.D. diss., Calvin Theological Seminary, 2013.

9

A Soteriological Perspective on Our Understanding

Hans Burger

Introduction

Theological reflection on hermeneutics needs reflection on participation in Christ, for in Christ we find all treasures of wisdom and knowledge (Col 2:3) and the renewal of our understanding. By describing some of the dangers that Dutch Neo-Calvinists encounter I will show the influence of modern foundationalism. Having done so, I will propose to take our participation in Christ as a hermeneutical starting point. I will develop this theme further in four steps, (a) showing the dynamics of sin and salvation, (b) emphasizing what is given in Christ, but also the importance of (c) formation, in (d) a longing for a renewed understanding.

The influence of modern foundationalism

With regard to hermeneutics, Dutch Neo-Calvinists are faced with two dangers. On the one hand, the case of the Dutch theologian Harry Kuitert exemplifies the domino effect: when the first stone falls, the other stones fall as well. And so we see people lose their faith. People start doubting a little in a seemingly harmless way, but more and more they lose their Christian beliefs and their faith. Kuitert's rational quest for certain knowledge started with the Enlightenment criticism of metaphysics and the empirical reality of human religiosity. In the end, he lost the Reformed heritage in which he grew up.[1] On the other hand, we see separation after separation within Reformed churches. A predominantly rational focus on "truth" leads to conflicts, the loss of Christian community, new divisions, and the inability to deal with diversity.[2]

It seems that Reformed people coming from a *bevindelijke*, experiential, or more Puritan background, are faced less with these two dangers. Often they are better able to maintain Christian fellowship. In the Netherlands we see this in the *Christelijke Gereformeerde Kerk* (CGK)[3] as well as in the *Gereformeerde Bond* (Reformed Alliance) within the Protestant Church (PKN).[4] Furthermore, they seem less vulnerable to the domino effect.

What is the reason for this? And as for their ancestors, the forefathers of the people we now find in the *Christelijke Gereformeerde Kerk* and in the *Gereformeerde Bond*, why did they dislike Abraham Kuyper? For now, one thing is important: they sensed that Abraham Kuyper was influenced by the enemy he opposed, by modernity. The anti-modern Kuyper was modern as well. He was a believing Christian, and at the same time a modern organizer belonging to Charles Taylor's "age of mobilization," working with Reformed principles and building on a Reformed foundation.[5]

One of the characteristics of modernity is its focus on epistemological questions and absolute certainty. We find here what has become known as

---

1. Van de Beek, *Van Kant tot Kuitert*, 225–38; Van den Brom, "Kuitert"; Geertsema, *Om de humaniteit*, 13–43.

2. As Herman Bavinck knew, the Protestant principle contains "een kerkontbindend element" (an element causing churches to break up or separate). Bavinck, *De katholiciteit*, 50.

3. Literally translated, *Christelijke Gereformeerde Kerk* is "Christian Reformed Church"; however, by comparison, the North American counterpart to the CGK is the Free Reformed Church of North America.

4. The *Gereformeerde Bond* is an alliance of congregations within the much larger Protestant Church of the Netherlands (PKN).

5. Bratt, "Abraham Kuyper: Puritan, Victorian, Modern"; Bratt, *Abraham Kuyper*, xiv–xvii; Taylor, *A Secular Age*, 459. On the *Hervormde* (original Dutch Reformed State church), J. H. Gunning, Jr., and Abraham Kuyper, see Balke, *Gunning and Hoedemaker*, 67–106; Mietus, *Gunning en Kuyper*. The *hervormde* Ph. J. Hoedemaker shared Kuyper's views of Scripture. See Veenhof, "Openbaring." The *Gereformeerde Bond* (see note 4 above) as well shared many of Kuyper's concerns. On the similarities and differences between Kuyper and the *Gereformeerde Bond*, see Graafland, "Beproefde trouw," esp. 67–69. With regard to the doctrine of Scripture, see Van den Brink, "De Bijbel als geloofsboek." On Kuyper and the *Christelijke Gereformeerde Kerk* (see note 3 above), see Van 't Spijker, "Enkele hoofdlijnen," 9–46. Bavinck was sensitive to these problems; cf. Bavinck, "Als Bavinck nu maar eens," 50, 58, 62, 66.

foundationalism.⁶ According to foundationalism, rational knowledge must be based on a solid and firm foundation.

It is too easy to accuse Neo-Calvinism of clear-cut foundationalism. However, in Kuyper's rectoral address, "The Biblical Criticism of the Present Day," we can detect traces of foundationalism.⁷ Here Kuyper clearly focuses on absolute, determined, certain knowledge. This focus is accompanied by a formal defense of the authority of Scripture. The content of the gospel of Jesus Christ itself does not play a role in Kuyper's argument.

For now, it is not necessary to agree about the historical question whether Neo-Calvinists are foundationalists. Suffice it to say that in the popular theology of ordinary Dutch Christian believers the foundationalist model is present. The Bible is our foundation. If we cannot trust the Bible for absolute certain knowledge, then everything is subjective. In this popular theology Jesus Christ or our faith in him are not mentioned!

That Jesus Christ does not play a role in Kuyper's argument is important. The more you follow a foundationalist model, the more you focus on absolute certain knowledge and on an epistemological foundation, and the more you follow a modern path, forgetting that Jesus Christ is our only solid foundation. Now we encounter the first problem of foundationalism. Within the New Testament, we do find the foundation metaphor.⁸ Here it is primarily a soteriological and ecclesiological metaphor. Christ is the church's foundation or its cornerstone. The metaphor primarily concerns life, salvation, community. Within this soteriological and ecclesiological framework, epistemological questions are implied as well, but to a smaller degree than a modern framework suggests. Therefore the first problem of foundationalism is its focus on epistemological questions, where the standard answers have a formal character, without reference to the gospel and to Jesus Christ.

Thus, theologically speaking, foundationalism focuses on epistemological questions. It has a tendency to forget salvation, Christian fellowship, and, most importantly, Jesus Christ. This corresponds remarkably well to

---

6. According to foundationalism, propositions with the status of "knowledge" are (i) self-evident to reason and can function as foundation of our knowledge, or (ii) justified by a foundational proposition. See Van den Brink, *Almighty God*, 11–13; Hoogland, "Orthodoxie," 135–36; Sarot, "Christian Fundamentalism," 259–61; Van den Toren, *Breuk en brug*, 56–59; Wolterstorff, *Reason Within the Bounds of Religion*, 28–30.

7. Kuyper, *The Biblical Criticism of the Present Day*. See Burger, "Kuyper's Anti-Revolutionary Doctrine." And further, Van Keulen, *Bijbel en dogmatiek*, 20–67.

8. *Themelios* (foundation) we find in Rom 15, 20; 1 Cor 3:10–12 (see further Luke 12:32–33; 1 Tim 6:19; 2 Tim 2:19); Eph 2:20. *Akrogoonaios* (cornerstone): Eph 2:20; 1 Pet 2:6. *Hedraiooma* (foundation): 1 Tim 3:15.

the second danger I mentioned: a predominantly rational focus on "truth," making it vulnerable to a spirit of separation.

Another problem of foundationalism is the self-fulfilling prophecy it contains. According to foundationalism, knowledge will be either absolutely certain or absolutely subjective. Here we sense the Cartesian anxiety.[9] Hence, if the quest for absolute certainty fails, we have nothing, and relativism and subjectivism loom. Here we find the domino effect, the first danger I mentioned. But this domino effect necessarily follows only as long as foundationalism is accepted as a true theory.

The difference between Reformed people coming from a Neo-Calvinist background and those from a *bevindelijke*, experiential group, can be summarized—in a rough and somewhat unfair manner, but for the sake of argument—as the difference between foundationalism and experiential religion. When this *bevindelijkheid*, this experience of God, is focused on union with Christ or on the work and the fellowship of the Holy Spirit, it will be less vulnerable to the domino effect as well as to an ongoing process of separation. The Cartesian anxiety will disappear, for we are Christ's church. Living in the fellowship of the Holy Spirit, we will "make every effort to keep the unity of the Spirit through the bond of peace" (Eph 4:3).[10]

Consequently, we need to be conscious of the dangers of the foundationalist model and eliminate foundationalist traces. Instead, we need to reinforce other elements in Neo-Calvinism, such as union with Christ and pneumatology, and consider their hermeneutical implications more seriously.[11]

I have an additional reason for this proposal. In the days that the Netherlands was still a pillarized society, our own Reformed pillar provided a safe, well-ordered world. Without pillars the situation changed rapidly. Nowadays we need to face the factual plurality in Dutch society, a plurality that has destabilizing effects on everyone, Christians included.[12] Why should I be a Christian? Why not an atheist, or a Muslim? To counter such pressure in our Dutch pluralist society, we need more than a foundationalist model. We need reflection on the moral, spiritual, and hermeneutical formation of individual Christians; we need a vital Christian community where faith, love, and hope are nourished. We need to be in Christ.

---

9. The term "Cartesian anxiety" comes from Bernstein, *Beyond Objectivism and Relativism*.

10. All Scripture quotations in this article are from the New International Version (NIV84).

11. See, e.g., Bolt, *A Theological Analysis*; Burger, *Being in Christ*, 87–139.

12. Cf. Taylor, *A Secular Age*, 435, 505, 526.

The epistemological non-foundationalism I am defending here does not entail anti-realism. If God acts to save us in Christ and if he in Christ renews our minds, we need some kind of realism, a "complex pragmatic realism." In our Christian life we do refer to a language-independent reality and make explicit or implicit truth claims, even if we help to shape reality with our words and if we can refer to the difference between this reality "out there" and our language only by linguistic means. Further, epistemological reflection on the role of Scripture remains indispensable. In our search for truth the canonical Scriptures should have the decisive voice, for these texts grant access to God and his saving truth.[13]

Participation in Christ as a hermeneutical starting point

Accordingly, we need to rediscover the implications of participation in Christ for our understanding and for hermeneutics.

Within the dynamics of sin and salvation

To understand the implications of participation in Christ, we need to see its negative background, the problems caused by sin from which Christ saves us.

Sin starts with disobedience to God. This disobedience damages our relationship with God and changes our being: a fundamental instability now characterizes our existence, an instability oscillating between pride and fear. To find new stability, we justify ourselves and worship idols. Stubborn, cowardly, or power hungry, we try to maintain our egos. Each human being has become, as Martin Luther said, a *homo incurvatus in se*: sinners are condemned to being curved inward on themselves.

---

13. Burger, *Being in Christ*, 6–7, 20–23; Dalferth, *Existenz Gottes*, 30–130; Dalferth, *Gedeutete Gegenwart*, 118–32, 181–92; Gunton, *The Actuality of Atonement*, 36–52; Van den Brink, *Almighty God*, 25–33; Patterson, *Realist Christian Theology*, 30–31, 51–52. Vanhoozer, *The Drama of Doctrine*, 77–112. For a helpful overview of different theories of truth, see Brümmer, *Theology and Philosophical Inquiry*, 169–81. Echeverria offers a critical discussion of the position of Van den Toren (comparable to the epistemological non-foundationalism I am defending here). See Echeverria, "Divine Revelation and Foundationalism." He consents to Van den Toren's plea for epistemological non-foundationalism, but still pleads for a historically conscious foundationalism. Note further that after rejecting modern foundationalism, different theologians still defend a "non-foundationalist foundationalism" (Colin Gunton) or a "modest foundationalism" (J.P. Moreland and Garrett DeWeese; and further Ad de Bruijne). See De Bruijne, "Geworteld en dan opgebouwd"; Gunton, *The One*, 129–35; Moreland and DeWeese, "The Premature Report."

This has epistemological and hermeneutical implications: egoism, as pride or as anxiety, blinds us to the truth; it causes us to be blind to others, blind to reality, and blind to God. Our own interests misguide our knowing and understanding. We encounter conflicts, misunderstandings, wrong interpretations, false judgments, lies, misguided speculations.

However, Jesus Christ gives us a new, justified identity in a restored relationship with God. Consequently, the *homo incurvatus in se* finds himself being renewed in Christ. Dying and rising with Christ, we are taken up in the process of sanctification and transformation. Conversion and sanctification have hermeneutical implications.[14] Nevertheless, the consequences of sin do not disappear entirely and all at once.[15] As "our best works in this life are all imperfect and defiled with sin" (Heid. Cat., L.D. 62), so is our understanding. We all have our blind spots and live partly with distorted views. Consequently we need each other within the body of Christ.[16] Only together with all the saints, may we "grasp how wide and long and high and deep is the love of Christ," and "know this love that surpasses knowledge" (Eph 3:18–19). As long as Christ has not returned yet, whatever we have reached in our Christian lives, in our churches, and in theology has not reached completion. We need to keep striving for a full understanding of God's truth.

From what is given in Christ

As far as I know, I am someone from a gentile background. Without Christ, I would have been among those who are "excluded from citizenship in Israel and foreigners to the covenants of the promise, without hope and without God in the world" (Eph 2:12).

But baptised into Christ and believing in him, I came to share in his identity, in his story, in his relationship with God his Father, in the story of Israel. As a consequence, I find back my place in God's story as member of God's eschatological people. Only by participation in Christ does it make

---

14. Cf. Burger, "Hermeneutiek en bekering."

15. In his *Encyclopedie der Heilige Godgeleerdheid*, Abraham Kuyper does consider sin and its epistemological questions. However, after the introduction of the *palingenesie* (regeneration), it seems as if all problems have disappeared. With a new foundation, a new building of Christian science can be constructed, no longer hindered by consequences of sin. Kuyper does not reflect on the ongoing effects of sin for Christian science. See Kuyper, *Encyclopedia*, 59–182.

16. It is important to keep in mind that we are created as embodied, speaking, and historical beings. Consequently the necessity of hermeneutics is not caused by sin but is a consequence of our creation with a body in space, in time, using language.

sense to read those books of Israel and Jesus' apostles as God's Holy Word that concerns me as well. And this is true of all gentile believers.

Only from Christ do we learn to read the Scriptures in an appropriate way. He needs to open our minds to make us understand the Scriptures. As followers of Christ we have come to understand that Jesus Christ, the Word of God that became flesh, is the fulfillment of the Scriptures of Israel. Believing in Christ, we discover that he is the promised seed of Abraham, the fulfillment of the Law, the son of David, the one who inaugurates the new covenant. Only in Christ, the Scriptures become books full of saving knowledge of the one true God. We need to see this in the right order: Christ is our Savior, not these books.

It is because of God that we are "in Christ Jesus, who has become for us wisdom from God—that is, our righteousness, holiness, and redemption" (1 Cor 1:30). In him we receive wisdom and knowledge, a new justified identity as children and heirs of God, a life that is sacrificed to God, a life that is transformed as part of the new creation. In this process of transformation we receive the mind of Christ, while the Holy Spirit lives in our hearts to guide us in all truth. This gift of life, of union with Christ, of the fellowship of the Holy Spirit within Christ's body—all these gifts precede our efforts to read and understand the Scriptures ourselves. We are not justified by our reading of the Scriptures or by our hermeneutics, but by faith in Christ Jesus.

I think we need to rediscover this in the Netherlands. Would you recognize such a need in your own context? The gift of Christ and of the truth, the bond of love, the fellowship of the Holy Spirit—they precede our theological discussions. We are sinners. We make mistakes—all of us, even if we read the Scriptures. But to be able to handle differences of opinion, we first of all need God's unifying work. This is not a plea for relativism. But I simply want to emphasize that we are not united by our works, by our efforts to understand the Bible correctly, but by faith in Christ Jesus. As Paul writes in Ephesians 4, "Only if we make every effort to keep the unity of the Spirit through the bond of peace" (3), only then we will "all reach unity in the faith and in the knowledge of the Son of God and become mature" (13). It is only through Christ that "the whole body, joined and held together by every supporting ligament, grows and builds itself up in love" (16). Without always consciously and explicitly taking our starting point in Christ, our churches in the Netherlands will shatter. It is important to ask ourselves how we practice this: keeping the given unity, approaching our problems and disagreements together, in order to reach the unity of faith and become mature.

Actively aiming at formation

It is not just because we are living in a secular, pluralist context that we need formation. Every sinner needs to be sanctified—which includes our moral, hermeneutical, and spiritual formation.

This process of transformation starts with conversion. We need to convert from our idols and our wrong images of God. We need conversion from our misunderstandings of Scripture; from our wrong conceptions of our world, and of our neighbors; from old ways of thinking, wrong concepts and interpretations, false narratives; from our misguided self-images: pride, self-hatred, repression, self-delusion, etc. We have to make a change from an old, self-centered life towards a new, God-centered life. And in a process of transformation we learn new ways of thinking, using good concepts and correct interpretations, and telling true narratives. The new reality of God's kingdom breaks through. Here we see how the transformation of our understanding and the transformation of our life are inseparably related.

We need to learn how to see everything in the light of God's judgment as proclaimed in Christ when God vindicated Jesus by his resurrection from the dead, and declared through the power of the Holy Spirit that he was the Son of God. This vindication of Jesus Christ is also the hermeneutical starting point of the transformation of our understanding—our understanding of everything. Without the resurrection we could not learn to read the Scriptures in the light of Christ. Without it, we could not learn what it implies that Christ has been raised for our justification, for our self-image and for the images of our brothers and sisters in Christ. Most importantly, without the resurrection we could not come to know God as our Father, as our judge who hates evil but foremost is a true Savior who will renew the entire creation.

Converted to Christ, justified in him, our ego-structures will be renewed. This transforms our attitudes. We receive the attitude of Christ, and he is formed in us. What letters in a book never can do, Christ can do by his Word and Spirit. He can transform us and renew our minds.

Nevertheless, the Holy Scriptures and the community of the church both play an important role in this process of formation. Scriptures and church need each other. Consequently, it is necessary to say something about the *sola scriptura* and the Roman Catholic position. Without the Scriptures, the church will disappear. That is the truth of the *sola scriptura*. Without the church, the Scriptures cannot play a formative role. That is the truth of the Roman Catholic position. But we need more than the text of the Scriptures and the community and tradition of readers. We need the grace of God as well, to bring us close to himself, to keep us in Christ Jesus and to instil the truth of the Scriptures in our hearts.[17] The *sola scriptura* needs the other *solas*: the *sola gratia* of the acts of the triune God himself to give us the grace to understand his truth; the *sola fide* of the perspective of faith by which we can understand the Scriptures, which is alive in the church and handed over in the tradition of the church; and the *solus Christus* as the unifying heart and as the content of all the other three: Christ alone is the Word of God, in Christ alone we receive grace, in Christ alone we believe.

Within this equilibrium we receive our formation by listening to the Scriptures and by living in the community of the church. Both the canonical texts of the Scriptures as well as the canonical practices of the church play their formative role.[18] Listening to the Scriptures will bring us to participation in the church and its practices. Participating in these practices will deepen our understanding of the Scriptures. Hence we need to ask: do we really participate in Christ, by listening to the Scriptures and by participation in our imperfect Christian communities, so that we are transformed more and more to Christ-likeness and renewed in the image of God?

Longing for a new understanding

We read the Scriptures in order to receive not only a Christian worldview, but also a Christian self-image and a Christian image of God. The Neo-Calvinist tradition knows about a renewal of our understanding that is more than just the renewal of the understanding of the Scriptures. Consequently, ideas we find in twentieth-century German hermeneutical philosophy—that we always understand something as something, or that processes of understanding are everywhere—are not foreign to our own tradition.

We read the Scriptures, longing for a new understanding—not just a new understanding of the Scriptures, but a new understanding of God, of our world, and of ourselves and our neighbors—in the light of Scripture. We long for a new understanding of our world, ourselves, and our times *coram deo*.[19] Salvation is not identical with this new understanding. Salvation is more: salvation will be a public reality only when Christ has returned, when

---

17. Mark Alan Bowald emphasizes that in theological hermeneutics we need to reflect on God's triune presence and agency, on the text, and on the readers who are transformed by the encounter with the living Christ in his word. See Bowald, *Rendering the Word*, 167–68, 172, 174–81.

18. Vanhoozer, *The Drama of Doctrine*, 211–237, 374–380.

19. Dalferth emphasizes the new understanding of God, world, and self *coram deo*. See, e.g., Dalferth, *Radikale Theologie*, 15–21, 242–44, 254–80. O'Donovan, working in the field of Christian ethics, mentions three moments of our moral awareness: self, world, and time. See O'Donovan, *Self, World and Time*, 6–17.

we are all raised from the dead in a new spiritual body, and when we see new heavens and a new earth. However, salvation still has hermeneutical implications.

To clarify these implications, Paul Ricoeur's distinction between the world *behind* the text, the world *of* the text, and the world *in front of* the text is clarifying.[20] We have the texts of the Bible with the speech acts they embodied and still embody. These texts give us access to the acts of God in the past. However, when we know the stories about the past acts of God, we discover his work in the present as well. Being able to refer to the triune God and to identify his acts with words that the Scriptures have taught us, we also pray for the renewal of our world *in front of* the text. What we long for now, by getting well acquainted with the world *of* the texts of the Bible, is finding out about the world *behind* the text of the Bible—God's acts in Christ and in the Holy Spirit—so that by God's present acts our world, the world *in front of* the text, is more and more conformed to God's purpose and glory.

As a consequence, new God-given perspectives emerge and are nourished in our lives and communities. We live in these perspectives: new perspectives on God, world, self, and neighbor.

A new perspective will not change everything. We meet others with their perspectives. Sometimes we disagree, sometimes we learn from them. Together we share the same reality. Our bodies and diseases, our physical reality, our societies and histories—we share them, live in them, study them in science. From each perspective we can learn true knowledge. Hence we have to learn to distinguish between what is true and what is not—in the light of Jesus Christ. That is: clothed with the new man, with new attitudes, new regulative beliefs,[21] a new direction of our lives[22]—learning to know with a new heart. Until Christ comes: then I shall know fully, even as I am fully known.

Bibliography

Balke, W. *Gunning en Hoedemaker. Samen op weg.* 's-Gravenhage: Boekencentrum, 1985.

Bavinck, Herman. 'Als Bavinck nu maar eens kleur bekende.' *Aantekeningen van H. Bavinck over de zaak-Netelenbos, het Schriftgezag en de situatie van de*

---

20. See, e.g., Thiselton, *New Horizons in Hermeneutics*, 358–68.
21. Wolterstorff, *Reason within the Bounds of Religion*, 69–70, 76–84.
22. Van Woudenberg, *Gelovend denken*, 38, 46–51, 56–62.

Gereformeerde kerken (november 1919). Edited by G. Harink et al. Amsterdam: VU Uitgeverij, 1994.

———. *De katholiciteit van Christendom en kerk: Rede bij de overdracht van het rectoraat aan de Theologische School te Kampen op 18 december 1888*. Kampen: G. Ph. Zalsman, 1888.

Bernstein, Richard J. *Beyond Objectivism and Relativism: Science, Hermeneutics, and Praxis*. Philadelphia: University of Pennsylvania Press, 1983.

Bolt, John. *A Theological Analysis of Herman Bavinck's Two Essays on the Imitatio Christi: Between Pietism and Modernism*. Lewiston, NY: The Edwin Mellen Press, 2013.

Bratt, James D. *Abraham Kuyper: Modern Calvinist, Christian Democrat*. Grand Rapids, MI: Eerdmans, 2013.

———. "Abraham Kuyper: Puritan, Victorian, Modern." In *Kuyper Reconsidered: Aspects of His Life and Work*, edited by C. van der Kooi et al., 30–41. Amsterdam: VU Uitgeverij, 1999.

Brümmer, Vincent. *Theology and Philosophical Inquiry: An Introduction*. London: Macmillan, 1981.

Bowald, Mark Alan. *Rendering the Word in Theological Hermeneutics: Mapping Divine and Human Agency*. Aldershot / Burlington, VT: Ashgate, 2007.

Burger, Hans. *Being in Christ: A Biblical and Systematic Investigation in a Reformed Perspective*. Eugene, OR: Wipf and Stock, 2008.

———. "Hermeneutiek en bekering." In *Charis: Theologische opstellen, aangeboden aan prof. dr. J.W. Maris*, edited by A. Baars et al., 57–66. Heerenveen: Groen, 2008.

———. "Kuyper's Anti-Revolutionary Doctrine of Scripture." In *Neo-Calvinism and the French Revolution*, edited by James Eglinton and George Harinck, 127–42. London: T&T Clark, 2014.

Dalferth, Ingolf U. *Existenz Gottes und christlicher Glaube. Skizzen zu einer eschatologischen Ontologie*. Beitrage zur evangelischen Theologie 93. München: Kaiser, 1984.

———. *Gedeutete Gegenwart. Zur Wahrnehmung Gottes in den Erfahrungen der Zeit*. Tübingen: Mohr Siebeck, 1997.

———. *Radikale Theologie*. Forum Theologische Literaturzeitung 23. Leipzig: Evangelische Verlagsanstalt, 2010.

De Bruijne, A. L. Th. "Geworteld en dan opgebouwd wordend in Hem." In *Filosofie en Theologie. Een gesprek tussen christen-filosofen en theologen*, edited by K. van Bekkum et al., 155–63. Amsterdam: Buijten en Schipperheijn, 1997.

Echeverria, Eduardo J. "Divine Revelation and Foundationalism: Towards a Historically Conscious Foundationalism." *Josephinum Journal of Theology* 19 (2012) 2, 283–321.

Geertsema, Henk G. *Om de humaniteit. Christelijk geloof in gesprek met de moderne cultuur en filosofie*. Kampen: Kok, 1995.

Graafland, C. "Hoe en waarom kwam de Gereformeerde Bond rond de eeuwwisseling op?" In *Beproefde trouw. Vijfenzeventig jaar Gereformeerde Bond in de Nederlands Hervormde Kerk*, edited by J. van der Graaf, 13–95. Kampen: Kok, 1981.

Gunton, Colin E. *The Actuality of Atonement: A Study of Metaphor, Rationality and the Christian Tradition*. Edinburgh: T & T Clark, 1994.

———. *The One, the Three and the Many. God, Creation and the Culture of Modernity. The 1992 Bampton Lectures*. Cambridge: Cambridge University Press, 1998.

Hoogland, Jan. "Orthodoxie, moderniteit en postmoderniteit." In *Filosofie en theologie. Een gesprek tussen christen-filosofen en theologen*, edited by K. van Bekkum et al., 132–54. Amsterdam: Buijten en Schipperheijn, 1997.

Kuyper, Abraham. *The Biblical Criticism of the Present Day*. Translated by J. H. de Vries. *The Bibliotheca Sacra* 61. 243. Andover, MA: Bibliotheca Sacra, 1904.

———. *Encyclopedia of Sacred Theology: Its Principles*. New York: Charles Scribner's Sons, 1898.

Mietus, Leo. *Gunning en Kuyper in 1878. A. Kuypers poliemiek tegen "Het leven van Jezus" van J.H. Gunning Jr. Een theologiehistorische bijdrage*. Velp: Bond van Evangelische Gemeenten in Nederland, 2009.

Moreland, J. P., and Garret DeWeese. "The Premature Report of Foundationalism's Demise." In *Reclaiming the Centre: Confronting Evangelical Accommodation in Postmodern Times*, edited by Millard J. Erickson et al., 81–107. Wheaton, IL: Crossway Books, 2004.

O'Donovan, Oliver. *Self, World and Time: An Induction*. Ethics as Theology 1. Grand Rapids, MI: Eerdmans, 2013.

Patterson, Sue. *Realist Christian Theology in a Postmodern Age*. Cambridge: Cambridge University Press, 1999.

Sarot, Marcel. "Christian Fundamentalism as a Reaction to the Enlightenment." In *Orthodoxy, Liberalism, and Adaptation: Essays on Ways of Worldmaking in Times of Change from Biblical, Historical and Systematic Perspectives*, edited by Bob Becking, 249–67. Leiden: Brill, 2011.

Taylor, Charles. *A Secular Age*. Cambridge, MA: The Belknap Press of Harvard University Press, 2007.

Thiselton, Anthony C. *New Horizons in Hermeneutics. The Theory and Practice of Transforming Biblical Reading*. London: HarperCollins, 1992.

Van de Beek, A. *Van Kant tot Kuitert. De belangrijkste theologen sinds 1800*. Kampen: Kok, 2009.

Van den Brink, Gijsbert. *Almighty God: A Study of the Doctrine of the Omnipotence of God*. Studies in Philosophical Theology 7. Kampen: Kok Pharos Publishing House, 1993.

———. "De Bijbel als geloofsboek. De Gereformeerde Bond en de Schriftvisie." In *Uw Naam geef eer. Honderd jaar Gereformeerde Bond 1906–2006*, edited by P. J. Vergunst, 114–42. Zoetermeer: Boekencentrum, 2006.

Van den Brom, Luco. "Kuitert: een echt dolerend theoloog." In *Harry Kuitert: zijn God. Schrijvers, theologen en filosofen over de God van Kuitert*, edited by Martien Brinkman et al., 42–51. Kampen: Ten Have, 2004.

Van den Toren, Benno. *Breuk en brug. In gesprek met Karl Barth over postmoderne theologie en geloofsverantwoording*. Zoetermeer: Boekencentrum, 1995.

Vanhoozer, Kevin. *The Drama of Doctrine. A Canonical-Linguistic Approach to Christian Theology*. Louisville, KY: Westminster John Knox Press, 2005.

Van Keulen, Dirk. *Bijbel en dogmatiek. Schriftbeschouwing en schriftgebruik in het dogmatisch werk van A. Kuyper, H. Bavinck en G.C. Berkouwer*. Kampen: Kok, 2003.

Van 't Spijker, Willem. "Enkele hoofdlijnen van de geschiedenis van de Christelijke Gereformeerde Kerken sinds 1892." In *Een eeuw christelijk-gereformeerd. Aspecten* van *100 jaar Christelijke Gereformeerde Kerken*, edited by W. van 't Spijker et al. Kampen: Kok, 1992.

Veenhof, Jan. "Openbaring. Geschiedenis. Bijbel. Drie kernmomenten van de theologie van Hoedemaker in hun onderlinge samenhang." In *Hoedemaker herdacht*, edited by G. Abma et al., 135–54. Baarn: Ten Have, 1989.

Wolterstorff, Nicholas. *Reason Within the Bounds of Religion*. 2nd ed. Grand Rapids, MI: Eerdmans, 1999.

A Soteriological Perspective on Our Understanding

A Response

Alan D. Strange

It is fitting to be critical of the foundationalism spawned by the Aufklärung, whether Cartesian rationalism or Lockean empiricism, even as it is of the foundational-for-the-West philosophies set forth by Plato and Aristotle. The problem with all of these approaches is that they are autonomous, beginning not with God and his Word, but with man and his ability to reason and to make sensory data intelligible. If the twentieth century has proven anything, it has demonstrated that salvation does not lie in the employment of rationalistic pursuits, especially the scientific method. It is clear from the passage under consideration here, 1 Corinthians 2, that neither the mind nor the senses furnish man with what he needs; only the revelation of God does (1 Cor 2:9–10) through general revelation (Ps 19:1–6; Rom 1–2) and special revelation (Ps 19:7–11).

As Dr. Burger has pointed out, since the Enlightenment in particular, man has been obsessed with epistemology. When asked how we know what we know, secular man earlier has said that we know what we know through a stop-and-think method (in line with Plato and Descartes) or a look-and-see method (following after Aristotle and Locke). Hume's radical empiricist challenge awoke Kant from his dogmatic slumbers, but he and his successors continued an autonomous pursuit of truth, albeit untethered from metaphysics. When all of this failed, particularly the project of modernism, men turned to postmodernism, yielding skepticism and mere perspectivalism epistemologically.

Thus while I appreciate Dr. Burger's criticism of modernism, I do not think that the solution to the problem lies in embracing something that sounds altogether too much like some sort of Christian postmodernism, a coherentism or the like that seeks to dodge the "truth" question.[1] If the truth is not arrived at by the sort of "indubitable" method that Descartes sought to employ or by the phenomenology of Kant and Hegel, neither ought it to be conceived through the lens of Wittgenstein, Rorty, Derrida and others like them. As trenchant as some of the criticisms of these philosophers are with respect to foundationalism of the autonomous sort that we've been describing, the solution that they offer is simply not one that Christians can embrace, being also autonomous, not starting with God and revelation, but starting with the community and its beliefs. The creeds and confessions of the Christian church, as important and useful as they are, have purchase only as they *correspond* to the truth of the Word of God, the meaning of the Reformation's *sola scriptura* motto over against Rome's continuing claim that the church produces the canon and serves as its infallible interpreter. The locus of infallibility for the Reformers was not the church but the Word that the church confessed and by which it sought to be Reformed.

It is not surprising that Abraham Kuyper made common cause with the Enlightenment where he could, particularly before the issuing of the Nietzschean challenge. Kuyper obviously rejected the anti-supernaturalism of the Enlightenment (and the French Revolution) but did not have the full advantage of the criticism of modernism that neo-Calvinism as well as postmodernism would bring. Some of Kuyper's successors have developed a stringent critique of modernism without embracing the epistemic skepticism of postmodernism or the "weak tea" of critical realism,"[2] notably C. Van

---

1. Dr. Burger has clarified his position with respect to this, first in private correspondence and now in revising his paper, making it clear that he does not embrace a post-modern epistemology but a sort of "critical realism." While I think that critical realism falls short of the kind of biblical epistemology that I describe below in elucidating a Van Tilian epistemology, it is far better than his position seemed before he clarified his epistemology.

2. Reflected in M. Polyani, and theologically by T.F. Torrance, N.T. Wright and others. For the broader roots of such an approach, see Ramsperger's article on "Critical Realism," 261–63. The more modest foundationalism, as it's sometimes called, of Colin Gunton, J.P. Moreland, Kevin Vanhoozer and others, recognizes the problem with historic foundationalism while also acknowledging the difficulties inherent with coherentism or mere perspectivism. Burger's epistemology appears to be consonant with that sort of approach.

Til[3] and some of his students (V. Poythress,[4] J. Frame,[5] and S. Oliphint[6] especially). These neo-Calvinists developed Van Til's insights about the myth of neutrality, circular reasoning, perspectivalism, a covenantal apologetics and the like that would affirm both a vigorous view of truth, stemming from a biblical epistemology, and the conviction that such is understood rightly only within a shared Weltanschauung.

Simply to attack modernism and agree with a warmed-over postmodernism[7] is to give away the store and gain nothing in return. What we need, and have, in the best of neo-Calvinism, in seed-form in Kuyper and developed subsequently, is a vigorous understanding that Christ is not only the soteric Lord, but also the epistemic Lord, as implied in the all-comprehensive claims of 1 Corinthians 2, particularly as set forth in Richard B. Gaffin's article.[8] This means that Christianity (as set forth in the Word of God, particularly with respect to the ontological Trinity and the self-attesting Christ of Scriptures) serves as the necessary and indispensable precondition of the intelligibility, not only of the faith, but of all of reality (laws of logic, science, ethics, etc.). The way to go about proving the Christian faith, then, is not by a rationalistic or empiricistic method but transcendentally, taking God and his Word as that which enjoys revisionary immunity. The proof of the Christian faith is the impossibility of the contrary, because even the most virulent antitheism presupposes theism.

I would argue that we need to derive our epistemology from the Bible itself, which teaches us that we know what we know because God has revealed it to us, in general and special revelation, the genius of the whole of 1 Corinthians 1–2, which contrasts the supposed "wisdom" of this world with the true wisdom that comes only from God. Because of our sin and the resultant antithesis, man apart from God suppresses the truth in unrighteousness (Rom 1:18–32; Eph 4:17–19), distorting both general and special revelation. Because of God's common grace, however, fallen unregenerate man retains the broader image of God and can make sense of things (proximately if not ultimately) and function even in his fallen state (Gen 9:6; Rom 2:13). To be sure, what he needs to know for salvation cannot

---

3. See particularly Van Til, *Defense of the Faith*, and Van Til, *Survey of Christian Epistemology*.

4. Poythress, *Symphonic Theology*.

5. Frame, *Apologetics to the Glory of God*.

6. Oliphint, *Covenantal Apologetics*.

7. I affirm that a "critical realist" approach does not do this in the same way as does a more vicious postmodernism, yet in a measure, lacking the "radical" biblical epistemology of Van Til.

8. Gaffin, "Some Epistemological Reflections," 103–24.

be known without his being renewed and given the glasses of Scriptures (Ps 19:7–11). Moreover, man cannot rightly understand general revelation apart from such glasses, but will ultimately distort and misinterpret what he finds there; hence the folly of man's "wisdom" (even as man regards God's wisdom as folly).

I agree that we need a salvific approach; not one that is set over against truth, however, but that brings us to the truth. Truth, while it is given a rationalistic turn in man's autonomous definitions, is not given such thin definition in Scripture. For instance, modernism defines truth as propositional and postmodernism as personal. We are right to be critical of both definitions because they present us with a false dichotomy: they allege that truth is either/or but it is both/and. Truth is *both* personal *and* propositional, according to John 14:6—the *person* of Jesus Christ *is* the truth, as set forth in the inspired *propositions* of the Bible. It is the Word of God that furnishes us with the truth about him who is the Truth.

Jesus Christ is the living Word about whom the written word speaks. Both Christ and his word are identified, each are the Word of God, in perfect accord, and in the Incarnation, Jesus is the Word become flesh (John 1:14). The self-attesting Christ of Scripture is revealed in the self-attesting Word of God. He is the Truth. His word is the Truth (John 17:17) and it is by such truth that we are sanctified. There is no dichotomy between the Living Word and the written word that reveals him. He is true and his Word is true.

If the claim is, however, that truth, salvifically understood, is narrow in its focus, then the 1 Corinthians 2 text does not support that claim. As Paul puts it in 1 Corinthians 2:2, all of reality is reduced to Christ and him crucified (Paul was determined to know nothing but that), which becomes the lens through which we see all reality: we see all things through the prism of Christ and him crucified. Additionally, the work of the Spirit, crucial in this text, is said, likewise, not to be limited or limiting but comprehensive. Gaffin comments on the 1 Corinthians 2 passage:

> Virtually from its beginning the church has wrestled with the implications of this passage for determining the relationship of the gospel to non-Christian knowledge and reasoning. Consequently, there is a long line of efforts (e.g., as early as Clement of Alexandria, Aquinas and the medieval synthesis, Kant in the modern era) to define the scope of what Paul says here in order to make room for the more or less peaceful (Schräge: 'schiedlich-friedlich') coexistence of Christian and non-Christian wisdom. Repeatedly, especially beginning with the Enlightenment, attempts have been made to accommodate the exercise of human reason as in some sense autonomous.

All such efforts, however, run aground on the immovable rock of Paul's unqualified πάντα. Every attempt to read our passage in partial terms or to restrict its scope by categorical distinctions, of whatever kind, clashes with the sweeping totality of Paul's vision. The antithesis in view leaves no room for an amicable division of territory or a neutral terrain. The wisdom of God is eschatological; it opposes *all* the wisdom of this age, *all* human wisdom κατά σάρκα.

Especially popular but damaging has been the notion that the passage is limited to the 'religious' sphere, as if Paul's concern is 'spiritual' truth in distinction from other kinds ('secular'), which are beyond his purview. The pernicious consequences of this view are nowhere more palpable than in its highly influential Kantian version. The noumenal-phenomenal disjunction supposedly functions to circumscribe (pure) reason and limit its autonomous exercise, thus making room for faith and its free exercise. But the effect, as Western culture of the past 200 years makes all too evident, has been exactly the opposite. Increasingly, faith, especially faith in Christ and the Scriptures, has been marginalized and banished into irrelevance. The lesson is plain: give 'secular' (= autonomous) reason an inch and it will not rest content until it controls everything (which, by the way, simply demonstrates the truth of our passage). Or, as Paul might warn the church, 'all things are yours . . . or nothing is yours.'[9]

Dr. Burger is quite right to criticize a rationalism that is prior to and forms the grid for our reading of Scripture. Man is indeed a reasoning creature, and has been given senses that furnish real information. This is because God created man with the capacity for reason, but such reason is to be used ministerially not magisterially, not to judge God and his Word, or to provide the grid through which we understand it, but to recognize that God in his Word is our Judge to whom we must give an account. Thus while rightly criticizing rationalism, we must not make the opposite mistake and embrace irrationalism (as did Nietzsche in some sense), but rather make a ministerial and right use of reason.

We are wont, both personally and historically, to jump from the frying pan into the fire, or to swing from one extreme to the other. We see this, for example, in the arch-heretics of the first four to six ecumenical councils of the church: a swing between unity and diversity that fails either to account for the integrity of the theanthropic person or the two natures that he possessed without confusion, conversion, division or separation. So we

---

9. Gaffin, "Some Epistemological Reflections," 116–17.

avoid the Scylla of Nestorianism, on the one hand, only to founder on the Charybdis of Eutycheanism, on the other hand. Let us not seek to escape the clutches of foundationalism / rationalism / modernism only to fall prey to irrationalism and solipsism. We rightly decry the rationalism of a Descartes and the empiricism of a Locke, both of which in their own ways are foundationalist. We must not, in response, call for a combination of the two, but for a truly biblical epistemology that can account for the one and the many. To say that the choice, as we seem to find it here in Dr. Burger, is between foundationalism and some sort of critical realism, is to posit a false dichotomy. I would call for a third way—the kind of rigorous biblical epistemology we discover in what Scott Oliphint is now calling "covenantal apologetics."[10]

It is right to call for a Christocentric approach, but what does such mean? It means that we reject the false dichotomy of modernism and post-modernism. Surely the criticisms of foundationalism leveled by neo-pragmatism, post-structuralism, analytic philosophy and other postmodernisms bear weight, but the solutions offered end up in a relativism and skepticism that renders Scriptures and doctrine uncertain. Yes, we know analogically: thus our theology is not archetypal but ectypal. Because we don't know comprehensively (only God knows comprehensively) does not mean that we don't know sufficiently and truly. We know God and his Word not univocally, to be sure, but not equivocally, either. He has accommodated by deigning to speak to us and we can, as his image-bearers, and by his Spirit, understand him.

Just because we reject a Platonic notion of Truth (with a capital T) that is abstract does not mean that we properly reject Truth that is personal and propositional, and that finds ultimate expression in the Incarnation, to whom the written Word is our infallible and inerrant witness. The Word of God, considering its divine and thus authoritative origin, is infallible (the church has always confessed this) and since it is not capable of error (the meaning of infallible), it actually does not have any error (and is thus inerrant). This is not the product of an autonomous foundationalism, of a supposedly neutral Cartesian "search for certainty," but of what it means to have, by the Holy Spirit who inspired the Word, a heart to receive it, a mind that is, indeed, *the mind of Christ* (1 Cor 2:16).

---

10. As noted above in his recent (2013) book of the same title. See also Oliphint's *Reasons for Faith*, especially 83–166, and his *God With Us*.

Bibliography

Frame, John. *Apologetics to the Glory of God: An Introduction.* Phillipsburg, NJ: P&R Publishing, 1994.

Gaffin, Richard B. "Some Epistemological Reflections on 1 Cor 2:6–16." *Westminster Theological Journal* 57:1 (Spring 1995) 103–24.

Oliphint, K. Scott. *Covenantal Apologetics: Principles and Practice in Defense of Our Faith.* Wheaton, IL: Crossway, 2013.

———. *God With Us: Divine Condescension and the Attributes of God.* Wheaton, IL: Crossway, 2012.

———. *Reasons for Faith: Philosophy in the Service of Theology.* Phillipsburg, NJ: P&R Publishing, 2006.

Poythress, Vern Sheridan. *Symphonic Theology: The Validity of Multiple Perspectives in Theology.* Phillipsburg, NJ: P&R Publishing, 2001.

Ramsperger, A. G. "Critical Realism." In *The Encyclopedia of Philosophy* 2, edited by Paul Edwards, 261–63. New York: Macmillan and Free Press, 1972.

Van Til, Cornelius. *Defense of the Faith*, 4th ed. Edited by K. Scott Oliphint. Phillipsburg, NJ: P&R Publishing, 2008.

———. *Survey of Christian Epistemology (In Defense of Biblical Christianity)*, 2nd ed. Phillipsburg, NJ: P&R Publishing, 1980.

10

The Reader as Focal Point of Biblical Exegesis

Gert Kwakkel

"Meaning depends entirely on the individual reader reading himself or herself."[1] The idea expressed in this phrase may be considered an important characteristic of postmodern hermeneutics. Texts do not have meaning in themselves. They get their meaning or meanings from their readers. If there is no reader assigning a meaning to a text, there is no meaning at all.

Scholars working from this perspective naturally focus their interpretive research on the readers. In doing so, they differ from their predecessors before the Second World War, who concentrated on the authors of the texts and on authorial intention. Later on, in the second half of the twentieth century, the author-centered approach met competition from the synchronic interpretation, which focuses on the texts (as distinguished from the authors). Postmodern interpreters are content with neither of these approaches. Instead, they prefer to take the readers as their focal point. The rise of methods such as reader-response criticism (which analyzes how readers respond to the texts) and reception history (which inquires how the texts were interpreted and applied over the course of time) corresponds to this preference.[2]

The aim of this paper is to make a number of comments on the developments just mentioned. First, the claim that texts get their meaning from

---

1. Van Wolde, *Words Become Worlds*, 169. The quotation is part of Van Wolde's description of Stanley Fish's view, as set forth in Fish, *Text*.

2. For more details on postmodern biblical interpretation, see Adam, *What Is Postmodern Biblical Criticism?*; Lodge, *Romans 9–11*, x–xii, 1–32.

the readers will be evaluated in more general terms. Second, the results of the evaluation will be related to reading the Scriptures. Third, the question will be addressed whether focusing on the readers might be fruitful for biblical interpretation. Can interpreters who respect the Bible as the authoritative word of God derive any benefit from this approach?

The Reader and the Meaning of the Text

Christians adhering to the principle of *sola Scriptura* may be inclined to reject without further ado the claim that texts get their meaning from the readers. Is it not self-evident that every text has a meaning, that is, the meaning that the author intends to communicate? Another objection might be that the view that everybody can give any meaning to a text makes interpretation fully arbitrary and subjective. If, however, one is left with nothing but subjective interpretations, how can Christians know that their interpretation of the Bible is correct and corresponds to the truth revealed by God?

These reactions are fully understandable and worth considering. Yet it would be unwise simply to reject the claims of postmodern hermeneutics without further reflection. The scholars who make such claims are intelligent people. To a certain degree, they do have a point. Believers who accept the divine authority of Scripture may even take advantage of their insights.

In this connection, two examples taken from real life can provide some clarification. The first example is a clay tablet in cuneiform script from ancient Babylonia. The tablet was written by a scribe who wanted to communicate a message of some kind. The meaning of the text in cuneiform was clear to him and to all his contemporaries who were able to read the cuneiform script and knew the Babylonian language. For them, the text indeed had a meaning. For almost all people of the present time, however, it does not have any meaning at all. Only those who have followed university courses in cuneiform writing and Babylonian can read and understand the text.

It follows that a text needs competent readers. If there are no such readers, a text cannot transmit any meaning. It does not have the capacity to change that situation either. A text obviously cannot communicate its meaning just by itself. Some activity of one or more readers is required in order that the meaning may come across.

Furthermore, the example shows that the phrase "a text has a meaning" can be used in two different senses. Those who say that a text such as the clay tablet has a meaning independent of the reader focus on the message which the ancient author intended to encode in the text and which can be deciphered by competent readers. Those who state that the text does not have a meaning independent of the reader focus on the effect of the text: does the message encoded in the text reach the reader or not?[3] Maybe part of the dispute under consideration is due to these different understandings of the phrase "a text has a meaning."

The second example is a tax assessment. Suppose that somebody has just received a tax assessment in his mail box. He may open the envelope and say: "This is not serious. This document has not been sent by the tax office. This is just a joke played on me by my neighbor. He is kidding me! He wants to frighten me by putting this piece of paper in my mail box. Come, let me show him that I got his joke. I'll make a boat of this paper and put it in his hot tub."

Obviously, the text (i.e., the tax assessment) cannot do anything about this. In itself, it is merely a piece of paper, with patterns of ink or toner on it. If somebody decides to interpret it as a falsification, the text can only accept the fact that a similar meaning has been assigned to it. However, this situation cannot last forever. If the person who received the tax assessment persists in considering it a falsification, the tax inspector will come along. In the name of the law, the inspector will convict him of having committed an offense. Although he was duly informed about the amount of money he had to pay, he failed to do so. He may reply that he was convinced that the letter was a document made up by a neighbor who wanted to play a joke on him. Perhaps the tax inspector will only smile and point out that this was a wrong assumption. A person receiving a tax assessment is not in a position to assign his own meaning to the document. At any rate, the end of the matter will be that this person has to withdraw the meaning he had given to the tax assessment. Although the text itself could not do anything about it, the reader will have to accept the meaning intended by its author (i.e., the tax office) as the only legitimate meaning and pay his taxes.

This example shows once again that a text cannot fight for its own meaning. It does not have the power to guarantee that its message or the intention of the author is correctly communicated to the reader. The text itself is no more than paper and ink. It is a dead object. However, as the example of the tax assessment makes clear, a text usually functions in a societal framework. Human beings use texts in order to communicate messages to other persons.

In every society, customs and rules regarding the interpretation of texts apply. Most often these rules have not been formulated in official documents such as state laws. They are conventions, which can change from time

---

3. Cf. Fish, *Text*, 65: "The meaning of an utterance, I repeat, is its experience."

to time. Each society or culture may have its own customs and rules as to how texts should be read. Yet these conventions are agreed upon and may be supposed to be known in their own historical context. In the Netherlands, for example, tax assessments are mailed in blue envelopes and have a fixed layout and wording, including some kind of official signature. Except for the very rare case of falsification, people know how to recognize these texts and which meaning should be assigned to them.

A person's freedom to assign meanings to texts is not only guided by these societal conventions, it is also limited by the presence and activities of other persons. People can check and correct one another's interpretations. As can be gathered from the example of a tax assessment, there may be persons with authority and power who can supervise, or direct, the interpretation of the document. Some of them can even enforce sanctions upon those who read a text in a wrong way![4]

It seems, then, that the idea that texts do not have meanings or that readers are free to assign to them any meaning is related to a purely formal or materialistic approach to texts. That is to say that texts are dealt with as pieces of paper with patterns of ink, in abstraction from their function as means of communication in a given society. It may be helpful to consider texts in this way, in particular in academic or philosophical analyses.[5] Nevertheless it is clear that more than that must be said about texts if one wants to draw an accurate picture of their actual function.

To sum up, if texts are related to the societal framework in which they function as means of communication, one can correctly say that texts have meanings. Although texts in themselves cannot control the way in which they will be read, people do not enjoy absolute freedom of interpretation either. If, however, one prefers to treat texts as mere objects of paper and ink, one must formulate claims about the meanings of texts in terms of the activities of readers. In that case, a phrase such as "this text has that particular meaning" should be replaced with: "Competent readers will interpret the text in that particular way; by virtue of their training and by restraints imposed by societal conventions, they will be able to pick up the message that the author intended to communicate."

---

4. Cf. Fish, *Text*, 317–21; Van Wolde, *Words Become Words*, 170–72.

5. The question of whether this approach is due to academic rigor or to the influence of a materialistic philosophy such as Marxism is an interesting one, but far beyond the scope of this paper.

The Proper Context for Reading the Bible

Does the above also apply to the Bible? The Bible obviously differs from a Babylonian clay tablet or a modern tax assessment. Nevertheless it shares their inability to ensure that the message intended by the author will indeed reach the reader. In itself the Bible does not have the capacity to defend itself against wrong or arbitrary interpretations. Readers of the Bible can assign any meaning to it according to their preference. This is true as long as the Bible is dealt with as a mere object made of paper and ink or a set of printed pages. However, just as with a clay tablet or a tax assessment, things may change if the Bible is considered in its proper communicative context. What, then, is this proper communicative context?

First of all, the Bible functions in the context of God's creative and redemptive works. Before the Bible was written, God spoke and acted various times. The Bible is the authoritative record of these words and acts of God. It contains and presents the message which God wants to communicate to people all over the world.

Second, the Bible can be read by everyone, believers and unbelievers, individually or together. Yet it is primarily meant to be read and studied by God's people, in the Christian congregation, the church of Jesus Christ. In the church, the message of God is transmitted orally, by preaching, teaching, and counseling. Thus the gospel is handed down through the generations as the tradition of the church. Within that context, God has given the Bible as the absolute and authoritative norm for all communication of his message.

It should be realized that for many centuries the average Christian did not have a copy of the Bible which he could read at home. It was already a great thing for local congregations to possess a copy of all biblical books! The faith of the believers was mainly fed by listening to what was read and preached in church. Now that Christians have their own Bibles, it goes without saying that they should be eager to read these for themselves. Often they will be able to grasp the meaning correctly and benefit greatly from this. However, individual Bible reading should not be glorified at the expense of the Bible's function in the congregation. The church of Jesus Christ is still the most proper place for the Bible to be read. Christians should read the Bible together and help each other in understanding its message, for "together with all the saints" they will be able to grasp "the breadth and length and height and depth" (Eph 3:18).[6]

---

6. Cf. De Bruijne, "Samen met alle heiligen," 573–77, and "Navolging en verbeeldingskracht," 223–25. All Scripture quotations in this article are from the New International Version (NIV84).

This is the normal way in which the Holy Spirit works with the Word. He oversees and steers the process of reading, interpreting, and detecting the meaning of the texts. He does so by means of the talents he has given to the community of the saints. As has been pointed out, individual Bible reading may also be very fruitful. Yet the risk of misinterpretation is much less if the Bible is read in its proper context, that is, in the congregation of Jesus Christ, which has accepted it as the trustworthy record of God's redemptive words and acts.

Three consequences follow from this. First, if the Holy Spirit makes use of people's talents to help others in correctly understanding the Scriptures, Christians need not be afraid of accepting the help of specialists. In fact, they already do. To give just one example: most Christians are not able to read the Bible in its original languages. They use translations made by specialists. In most cases they are not in a position to check the work of the translators. On the basis of information provided by respected church leaders, they trust that the work has been done well. Of course, it is fully understandable that Christians do not want to be totally dependent on others when their relationship with God is concerned. Yet accepting the idea that one also depends on specialists need not be a problem if it is realized that this is how the Spirit works and as long as the specialists in question are willing to give account of what they have done.

Second, if Christians from different times find different things in the Bible, this need not be a problem either, as long as the core message remains the same. The Holy Spirit makes use of the Bible in order to enlighten Christians in their particular historical situations. Some elements from Scripture may be more relevant in one specific situation than in another. Psalm 119:105 says that the Word of God is a lamp to our feet and a light to our path. It helps believers to walk safely wherever they have to go. It is not a huge floodlight casting light upon all elements of the world, so that Christians know everything they desire to know. It does not resolve all riddles. For Bible readers living in the twenty-first century it is not necessary to know everything that Christians living in the twenty-second century will need to know. The Bible is sufficient to inform believers about what they must know in order to believe, to lead a Christian life, and to be saved (cf. Belgic Confession, Art. 7)—no less, but often no more than that either.

Third, to a certain extent arguments taken from common sense suffice to make it clear that people do not enjoy total freedom in assigning meanings to texts. In spite of misinterpretations of details, the message intended by the author can come across in a satisfactory way. If, however, one tries to demonstrate that people can really pick up the message intended by God in giving the Scriptures, more than common sense is needed. The argument presented above is based on belief in God and confidence in the work of the Holy Spirit. Ultimately, if the perspective of faith is totally left aside, there is no definitive epistemological basis for what Christians believe. Adherents of postmodern hermeneutics or others may claim that one can never be sure that the way in which Christians read the Bible really corresponds to God's intention. Arguments taken from common sense can be helpful to put this claim into perspective. At the same time it must be admitted that in the end the response can be formulated only by faith.

Reading the Bible from a Reader's Perspective

If the argument just presented is correct, the central question to which Bible readers must seek an answer is: What does God or what does the Holy Spirit intend to communicate through these texts? This section will examine a much smaller topic, namely the question whether the recent emphasis on the reader can contribute anything in this connection. Can it help interpreters to develop ideas about what God wants to communicate to his people by means of a given text?

As a concrete example I will use Ehud Ben Zvi's commentary on Hosea, published in 2005. In this commentary Ben Zvi often considers the question how readers may have read the text of the Book of Hosea. Traditionally, in commentaries on Hosea the prophet himself predominantly figures as the grammatical subject of the sentences in which the exegesis is presented (e.g., "here the prophet says . . ."). In more recent commentaries it may also be the editor of the book who receives critical attention. In Ben Zvi's commentary, the most common subject is the readers.

More precisely, Ben Zvi refers to readers living in the Persian province of Yehud (around Jerusalem) in the fifth or the fourth century BC. In his view, the Book of Hosea was written there in those days. The book may bear a relationship to the activities of the historical Hosea living in the eighth century BC, but according to Ben Zvi this is anything but certain. In any case, it is irrelevant to his exegesis. He consequently reads and interprets Hosea as a post-exilic book from Yehud. He analyzes how it may have been read and reread in that period.

Most likely conservative Bible readers will be uncomfortable with Ben Zvi's approach. Objections could be formulated, but that is not the issue at stake here. Even so, the commentary may help readers or interpreters who submit to the authority of the Bible as God's infallible Word to see a number of things more clearly.

This paper takes it for granted that the Book of Hosea is a record of the Word of God as it was received and transmitted by the prophet Hosea when he lived in the eighth century BC. Given this conviction, it is appropriate for exegetes to ask the question: "What did the prophet mean by saying this or that?" However, this does not suffice. More work has to be done.

In the case of Hosea, this can also be demonstrated from the book itself. The last verse of the book, Hosea 14:10[9], reads:

> "Who is wise? He will realize these things. Who is discerning? He will understand them. The ways of the Lord are right; the righteous walk in them, but the rebellious stumble in them."

The verse evidently is a subscript to the whole book. It may have been written by Hosea himself. It is more probable that it was added by someone else, for example, the person or persons who collected Hosea's prophecies and edited the book and who may also have formulated the introductory note at the beginning of the book (Hos 1:1).[7] Be that as it may, the point made by the verse is that the Book of Hosea is worth reading, not only by people living in Hosea's days but also by others who would live later. Most of these later readers lived after the fulfillment of several of Hosea's prophetic words. They had witnessed, for example, the fall of the Israelite capital Samaria in 722 BC, which the prophet had announced in Hos 14:1[13:16]. For such later readers, it still made sense to reflect upon the question how Hosea himself might have meant or understood his own messages. In addition, however, they also had to consider the question: "What is the wisdom that God wants to communicate to us by means of these prophecies, now that several of them have already been fulfilled? What is their lasting value for us?"

The subscript makes it clear that right from the beginning the Book of Hosea was also meant to be studied and meditated upon from that perspective. Therefore, it certainly makes sense for modern interpreters to inquire how this may have been done by later readers. In this connection it may be helpful to define groups of more recent readers, such as people living shortly after the fall of Samaria in 722 BC or after the fall of Jerusalem in 586 BC. What did these texts mean to those people? How might they have read them?

In fact, such interpretation in terms of how people may have read or understood biblical texts is not new at all. When commenting upon, for example, Paul's letters to the Corinthians, evangelical or conservative

---

7. On the work of the editors, see also Kwakkel, "Prophets and Prophetic Literature," 10–12.

exegetes not only try to answer the question as to what Paul meant in writing such and such, they also put themselves in the position of the Christians in Corinth and wonder how these people might have understood the words of the apostle.

In this context Ben Zvi's commentary can be of benefit to interpreters who disagree with his view on the composition and date of Hosea. More specifically, his commentary is beneficial in cases in which a given text apparently can be interpreted in two or even more different ways. In such cases, commentaries traditionally tended to focus on the question: "What did Hosea mean?" They made an effort to make the right choice. They pointed out why the other possibilities were improbable or even impossible. When confronted with such problems, Ben Zvi often entertains and accepts both or all possibilities. He argues that readers could have read the text in this way, but also in another.[8] In such cases, both interpretations can stand side by side. Together, they make up the meaning of the text for the present readers.

One may object that this approach could also be reframed as a quest for the intention of the author (in this case, Hosea). The objection applies in particular to texts in which double entendres are involved. This and similar textual elements can well be analyzed in terms of authorial intention (as has sometimes been done in more traditional commentaries such as C. Van Gelderen and W. H. Gispen's and Wilhelm Rudolph's)[9] without resorting to a readers' perspective. Yet taking the readers' perspective makes one more willing to consider these possibilities, if only for psychological reasons.

In conclusion, interpreters reading Scripture in the context of God's communication with his people should at least try to find the intentions of the human authors of the biblical books. At the same time, they must take into account that there can be more in the texts than the authors themselves realized. According to 1 Pet 1:10–11, the prophets did not always understand all the details of the revelations which the Spirit was giving them. Adding an analysis from the readers' perspective may be helpful in finding elements that go beyond the horizon of the authors. To be sure, the "beyond" should be in line with the intention of the human authors. The intention of the Spirit speaking through them should not be opposed to theirs. Yet the exegete should ultimately be interested in what *God* wanted to say through

---

8. See, e.g., Ben Zvi, *Hosea*, 126 (on Hos 6:7); 130–31 (on 5:11); 133 (on 5:1); 207–8 (on 10:1); 221–22 (on 10:12).

9. See, e.g., Van Gelderen and Gispen, *Het boek Hosea*, 254–55 (on Hos 7:6); Rudolph, *Hosea*, 124–25 (on 5:13).

the prophets, just as Matthew when quoting Hos 11:1 referred to "what the Lord had said through the prophet" (Matt 2:15).[10]

In conclusion, then, what is the benefit of the confrontation with the postmodern view that texts get their meaning from the readers? The results of this study can be summarized in two points.

1. The confrontation can help interpreters to develop a more accurate view of what is going on in the process of interpretation. Moreover, it can remind one of the fact that the Bible should be read in the context of God's communication with his people and in connection with the congregation of Jesus Christ.

2. More specifically, it has been shown that focusing on the reader may be a helpful tool in interpretation, in particular when it makes sense to go beyond what was meant or intended by the human authors of the biblical books.

Bibliography

Adam, A. K. M. *What Is Postmodern Biblical Criticism?* GBS New Testament Series. Minneapolis, MN: Fortress, 1995.
Ben Zvi, Ehud. *Hosea*. The Forms of the Old Testament Literature XXIA/1. Grand Rapids, MI: Eerdmans, 2005.
De Bruijne, A. L. Th. "Navolging en verbeeldingskracht: De bijbel in beeld 3." In *Woord op schrift: Theologische reflecties over het gezag van de bijbel*, edited by C. Trimp, 195–237. Kampen: Kok, 2002.
———. "Samen met alle heiligen." *De Reformatie* 70 (1994–1995) 573–77.
Fish, Stanley. *Is There a Text in This Class? The Authority of Interpretative Communities*. Cambridge, MA: Harvard University Press, 1980.
Kwakkel, Gert. "'Out of Egypt I Have Called My Son': Matthew 2:15 and Hosea 11:1 in Dutch and American Evangelical Interpretation." In *Tradition and Innovation in Biblical Interpretation: Studies Presented to Professor Eep Talstra on the Occasion of his Sixty-Fifth Birthday*, edited by W. Th. van Peursen and J. W. Dyk, 171–88. Studia Semitica Neerlandica 57. Leiden: Brill, 2011.
———. "Prophets and Prophetic Literature." In *The Lion Has Roared: Theological Themes in the Prophetic Literature of the Old Testament*, edited by H. G. L. Peels and S. D. Snyman, 1–13. Eugene, OR: Pickwick, 2012.
Lodge, John G. *Romans 9–11: A Reader-Response Analysis*. University of South Florida International Studies in Formative Christianity and Judaism 6. Atlanta: Scholars Press, 1996.
Rudolph, Wilhelm. *Hosea*. Kommentar zum Alten Testament XIII 1. Gütersloh: Mohn, 1966.
Van Gelderen, C., and W. H. Gispen. *Het boek Hosea*. Commentaar op het Oude Testament. Kampen: Kok, 1953.

---

10. On Matthew 2:15 and Hosea 11:1, see also Kwakkel, "'Out of Egypt.'"

Van Wolde, Ellen. *Words Become Worlds: Semantic Studies of Genesis 1-11*. Biblical Interpretation Series 6. Leiden: Brill, 1994.

11

Another Wax Nose?

Accommodation in Divine Revelation

Theodore G. Van Raalte

"This, no doubt, is what they mean by a saying common among them, in that Scripture is a nose of wax, because it can be formed into all shapes." (John Calvin, replying to the Council of Trent)[1]

Introduction

In Reformation times both sides were accusing the other of making Scripture a wax nose.[2] Today one may well wonder whether the dogmatic construct of accommodation in divine revelation has become a wax nose. Looking back and looking around, one may observe countless thinkers—many arguing from rather opposing foundations and toward rather contradictory

---

1. Calvin, *Tracts and Letters*, 3.69. Dr. Ronald Feenstra read an earlier version of this essay and I hereby acknowledge his helpful feedback. After the conference Dr. Jitse van der Meer also kindly read it and responded privately with questions and comments. While the views here expressed remain my own, I owe both scholars thanks for their careful reading and helpful comments. Note: only half of the essay was presented at the conference.

2. Porter, "The Nose of Wax," 155–74.

ends—vying for the principle that in giving scriptural revelation God accommodated his message to its recipients.

The debate has scriptural underpinnings: For example, does God really "repent," "relent," or "change his mind," as some Scripture texts describe him (Gen 6:6; Exod 32:14; 1 Sam 15:35)?[3] Or, does God have such a comprehensive plan that he never ultimately changes his mind, as other texts teach us (Num 23:19; Mal 3:6; Matt 10:29-30; Jas 1:17)? Again, must God "come down" to see what people are doing (Gen 11:5) or does he have comprehensive knowledge and presence (Ps 139; Jer 23:24)? Such diverse texts were reconciled by saying that the one set describes God as he is while the other set speaks about God in a manner that is accommodated to our capacity. They help us understand God and his attributes, even though they are not true of God if taken literally. Sometimes God seems to "lisp" or "stammer" because he speaks in terms intelligible to us instead of thundering from Mt. Sinai or using angelic language.[4]

Finding appeals by theologians to accommodation is not difficult: One may turn not just to the regulars—various church fathers, Augustine, Aquinas, Luther, Calvin, and the Lutheran and Reformed Scholastics;[5] but also to the discoverers—Copernicus, Galileo, and Kepler;[6] then to the higher critics of various shades—Socinus, Spinoza, Le Clerc, Lessing, Hume, Kant, Semler, and Herder;[7] and now even to evangelical feminists like Jann Clanton who argue that Jesus addressed God in the masculine as an accommodation to Jewish first-century patriarchal society,[8] or Letha Scanzoni, Nancy Hardesty, Virginia Mollenkott, Paul Jewett, Mary Evans, Ruth Tucker, Gilbert

---

3. All Scripture quotations in this article are from the New International Version (NIV84).

4. Calvin, *Institutes*, 1.13.1.

5. Rogers, "Charles Hodge and Accommodation," 225-42; Huijgen, *Divine Accommodation in Calvin*, 47-318; Benin, "Mere Stories and Ordinary Words," 84-90; Benin, *The Footprints of God*, 1-126, 177-212; De Jong, *Accommodatio Dei*, 22-49.

6. Scholder, *Birth of Modern Critical Theology*, 53-64.

7. Lee, "Accommodation," 335-48; Barentsen, "Validity of Human Language," 21-44; Woodbridge, "Recent Interpretations of Biblical Authority, Parts 2 and 3," 105, 111n31, 204; Frei, *Eclipse of Biblical Narrative*, 60-62; Benin, *Footprints of God*, 202-7; Scholder, *Birth of Modern Critical Theology*, 138-41; De Jong, *Accommodatio Dei*, 50-53; De Moor, "Problem of Revelation," 66-74, 139-51, 205-15. Pannenberg notes Leydekker's opposition in 1677 to the broadened notion of accommodation found in Wittich, Spinoza, and others. But, writes Pannenberg, "there was no halting the victorious march of the accommodation theory," i.e., in eroding the doctrine of inspiration, and in "loosening the older Protestant doctrine of the authority of scripture." Pannenberg, *Systematic Theology*, vol. 1: 34-36.

8. Clanton, *In Whose Image?* 10-11; compare a review of two works: Otto, review of Clanton, *In Whose Image?* and Heine, *Matriarchs, Goddesses, and Images of God*, 202-4.

Bilezikian, and Johanna Van Wijk-Bos who argue that biblical patriarchy as a whole was an evil that God simply accommodated in his revelation.[9] Today, argue the latter, we can strip away the accommodated elements. And if all the above does not suggest a wax nose, along come the open theists to contest the traditional use of accommodation regarding anthropomorphic language. "Just why are these texts considered "accommodated" and not the other set of texts?" they ask.[10] Deep questions of religious epistemology are at stake.[11]

Studying these diverse uses, one rarely finds theologians explicitly setting boundaries for their employment of accommodation, though a few notice the problem.[12] In my view, all theologians using accommodation do in fact employ some guidelines—written or unwritten—derived from their very reasons for employing the construct. What they "accommodate" depends on their core view of God, so the question is whether or not they employ "accommodation" appropriately, and also whether they apply the principle consistently and self-consciously.

---

9. As noted by Haas, "Patriarchy As An Evil," 322–23, 326, and by Cooper, *Our Father in Heaven*, 44–46. For Van Wijk-Bos's appeal to accommodation, see her book *Reformed and Feminist*, 65–66.

10. Sanders notes that Calvin and others are presupposing a particular understanding of God's sovereignty, immutability, and omniscience, which leads them to adopt certain texts as literal and reduce others to anthropomorphic. But, he asks, how can we get behind the text to know for sure what God is in himself and what is an accommodated revelation? Sanders wants "grounds" and a "criterion." Sanders, *The God Who Risks*, 67–69, 156. Coming from the other side, Paul Helm also recognizes the problem: "Which of these apparently inconsistent or incompatible sets of data is to take priority? Which data control the remainder?" Helm, *The Providence of God*, 51. Compare Caneday, "Putting God at Risk," 131–63.

11. One could add the philosopher William Alston who argues that even God's covenant and the idea of God having personal obligations are as metaphorically spoken as God stretching out his arm. The writers were simply choosing "the closest human analogue to what God was doing." See Wolterstorff, *Divine Discourse*, 100; compare Helm, *John Calvin's Ideas*, 201–4.

12. Dreyfus is one writer who sets forth the dangers of employing this hermeneutical device: he states that the biblical message can be stripped of its present-day authority by a rationalization that limits it to the specific time and place of its promulgation, or, conversely, the biblical message can be interpreted entirely through the lens of a modern-day philosophy, relegating all that does not comport with one's philosophical outlook to the status of accommodated revelation. Dreyfus, "Condescendance Divine," 106. Balserak writes of, "accommodation's ability to undermine the authority of the scriptures," but he denies that Calvin's use of the principle eroded Scripture's authority and truthfulness. Battles writes of the "danger . . . of making the whole Christian gospel an exercise in rhetoric," but he too denies this to be the case because the "accommodating language and the truth to which it points are really a unity." Balserak, *Divinity Compromised*, 163, 168; See also Battles, "God was Accommodating Himself," 37.

In this essay I will evaluate the use of accommodation from a Reformed confessional standpoint.[13] I will argue that in order for the doctrinal construct of divine accommodation in revelation to be fruitfully employed, exegetes in that tradition need to adopt some key guidelines for its use. I intend to advance: a) some key definitions and distinctions, clarifying the topic; and, b) some essential guidelines and boundaries, circumscribing the application of the concept. Outside of these boundaries, the principle of accommodation can undermine scriptural authority and thus become destructive to the very revelation and the very God Reformed theologians purport to explain.

The following section of this essay offers the aforementioned definitions and distinctions, in dialogue with historians who have studied how Reformed theologians used the accommodation concept (a). These definitions and distinctions will guide the discussion in the following section where I undertake an examination and evaluation of the diverging uses of accommodation noted at the outset of this essay—including, necessarily, a judgment about each practitioner's view of Scripture's authority. All of this will open the way for the last section, where I proceed with the list of aforementioned guidelines (b).

It will become evident that revelation and theology proper are intertwined such that one's starting point theologically will in large part govern one's application of the principle of accommodation.[14] Since theology proper depends on revelation, this sounds circular but in fact Reformed theologians in principle have no pre-theological or pre-biblical *principia* (principles).[15] That is to say, the most foundational theological principles are from the Bible, and must be, since we depend upon God to reveal himself to us. Whatever the case, it seems to me that if Scripture is revelation from God, one should draw the very rules and limits for interpreting Scripture from Scripture itself—*scriptura sui interpres* (Scripture is its own interpreter).

---

13. That is to say, I am assuming such confessional points as the first article of the Belgic Confession wherein God is described as a "simple and spiritual Being," etc., or as the fifth and seventh articles on Scripture or the eighteenth article regarding the incarnation. These are mentioned because of their pertinence to the topic at hand.

14. Selderhuis writes, "Calvin's concept of God . . . constrains him to this logic," i.e., of accommodation. Selderhuis, *Calvin's Theology of the Psalms*, 50.

15. Muller, *Post-Reformation Reformed Dogmatics*, 1:430–50.

Definitions and Distinctions

In the most comprehensive survey to date of the accommodation construct, Stephen D. Benin first offers this definition: "Accommodation/condescension is divine revelation in human terms; that is, divinity adapting and making itself comprehensible to humanity in human terms. It is the adaptation and adjustment of the transcendent to the mundane; it is the fine tuning of the divine order."[16] Later he adds, "That is, the sublime nature of divine revelation was too majestic and hence incomprehensible for humanity, and thus, in a merciful and compassionate act, the deity adjusted, modified, harmonized, and regulated his revelation to human limitations."[17] Richard Gamble draws the analogy of an Oxford English professor speaking in a childish manner to his two or three-year-old child.[18]

The church fathers use the terms "accommodation," "condescension," and "economy." Their early uses of the terms were apologetic—an answer to the Jews regarding the cessation of the Old Testament sacrifices in the New Testament church: God had accommodated his teaching to Israel on the only terms they could understand at that time, but now the time of maturity had arrived.[19] Thus, the earliest uses have to do with the relationship of the Old to the New Testament.

Another point from early uses involves the denial of any hypocrisy on God's part. In accommodating his message he in no way compromised its truth.[20] Although we "look through a glass darkly," we do receive true knowledge of God.[21]

For Augustine accommodation was not merely a concession on the part of God, but a necessity in the relationship between the unchanging and the changing.[22] Certain perfections of God required accommodation: indeed, there was from early times (e.g., Irenaeus) an exalted view of God as immutable, impassible, infinite, invisible, and incomprehensible that required conditioning his revelation to human capacity. A. D. R. Pol-

---

16. Benin, *Footprints of God*, 1. Gamble identifies the Creator–creature distinction as the basic reason why Calvin in his hermeneutics advances accommodation with respect to Scripture. Gamble, "Calvin as Theologian," 192.

17. Benin, "Mere Stories and Ordinary Words," 83.

18. Gamble, "Calvin as Theologian," 182.

19. De Jong, *Accommodatio Dei*, 16–22; Dreyfus, "Condescendance Divine," 97–98; Benin, *Footprints of God*, 1–30.

20. Battles, "God was Accommodating," 23; De Jong, *Accommodatio Dei*, 16.

21. Gamble, "Calvin as Theologian," 182–83.

22. Augustine, *Confessions*, 3.7.12–14; cf. Augustine, *Teaching Christianity*, 3.14.17; Benin, "Mere Stories and Ordinary Words," 84–90.

man presents something of Augustine's views: "When the Manichees object to Biblical references to God's jealousy and wrath, they simply fail to understand that there are no words to express God's inexpressible majesty. The Holy Spirit has been forced to use words with which we normally describe human failings."[23]

Aquinas, and even more Scotus, are good representatives of the widespread position that humans cannot know God *in se*, as he is in himself. We are dependent upon him to reveal himself to us, and even then his revelation does not convey his inner essence, which can only be known negatively. Luther's contrast of the hidden and revealed God likewise lends itself to the accommodation theory. Calvin's abundant use of accommodation complements and, to some extent, depends on both Scotus's and Luther's positions.[24]

The Protestant Scholastics used the term in much the same way, to refer to the manner or mode of God's revelation, namely that, "the gift of the wisdom of the infinite God [came] in finite form."[25] Their distinction between archetypal and ectypal theology, drawn from the medieval theologians, naturally advanced accommodation as its corollary, since one of the points of the distinction is that our knowledge of God is not self-acquired but derived from God. It must be such due to our finite capacities, and is given in a form accessible to us.[26]

Abundant studies exist regarding Calvin's use of the concept of accommodation; in fact, the varied analyses and categorizations offered by historians of Calvin beg for some structure. I intend to offer such a structure, not so much to explicate Calvin, but to explicate accommodation.

At the broadest level, drawing on the work of others, I distinguish ontological and soteriological accommodation.[27] Ontological accommodation should be understood as that kind of accommodation necessary for God to reveal himself to his human creatures apart from any consideration of

---

23. Polman, *St. Augustine*, 58.

24. Aquinas, *Summa Theologica*, 1a.12.11–12; Te Velde, *Aquinas on God*, 20–21, 42–43, 65–67; Muller, "Turretin," 198, 203–4; Muller, *Post-Reformation Reformed Dogmatics*, 1:227; Dreyfus, "Condescendance Divine," 99–100; De Jong, *Accommodatio Dei*, 26–30. For Calvin's relation to Aquinas' distinction of God *in se* and God *quoad nos*, see Helm, *Calvin's Ideas*, 13–34.

25. Muller, "*Accommodatio*."

26. Muller, "Turretin," 198, 203–4; Muller, *Post-Reformation Reformed Dogmatics*: 1:229, 262; 2:305; Muller, "John Cameron," 16.

27. See especially the early and lucid treatment in Dowey, *Knowledge of God*, 4–17, esp. 4. The same distinction operates frequently in Huijgen's work though he seems more likely to label the soteriological as pedagogical. Huijgen, *Divine Accommodation in Calvin*, 214, 252, 271–72, 294.

their fall into sin, whether in Paradise or the new creation.[28] God's being (his *ontos*) is infinite, but we are finite, and this will always be the case. Soteriological accommodation, however, is conditioned by human sin and is well illustrated in the saying of our Lord, that Moses permitted divorce in the Old Testament due to the *hardness of heart* among the covenant people (Matt 19:8).[29]

When we examine an instance of or a claim for accommodation, we do well to ask to which category it belongs. But why distinguish at all? First, this helps us appreciate that whereas in the new creation we will see God face to face without accommodation occasioned by our sin, some kind of condescension on God's part will still be necessary because we will still be finite. Similarly, describing the other end of history, the Westminster Confession 7.1 speaks of a "voluntary condescension" of God before the fall so that he could establish a covenant with us.[30] Second, distinguishing ontological from soteriological accommodation also prevents us from concluding that because all divine revelation is accommodated to human language (ontological), therefore a description of God as unchangeable is as accommodated as a description of God repenting (soteriological).[31] In Scripture, God's "repentance" only occurs in situations where human sin appears to undermine his purposes (soteriological) whereas God's immutability has correctly been confessed by the church to describe God as he is (ontological), albeit negatively.[32]

If the condescension is simply a matter of ontological accommodation, we can ask what limitations, inabilities, and finite capacities of humanity are being accommodated. If instead we have to do with soteriological accommodation, we can ask what human slowness, dullness, forgetfulness,

---

28. Gamble states that for Calvin God was accommodating himself even in his paradisal revelation, as well as on Mt. Sinai when speaking "face to face" with Moses. Why? Because he used our language and held back the fullness of his glory. I categorize this as ontological accommodation. Gamble, "Calvin as Theologian," 182.

29. Balserak criticizes the value of this distinction as a tidy explication of Calvin's thought (contra Dowey). As noted, this essay seeks to offer a systematic account that might help Reformed theologians treat accommodation, not to explicate Calvin's position as such. Balserak, *Divinity Compromised*, 42.

30. Schaff, *Creeds*, 3:616.

31. For an example where this error occurs, consider this: "In Calvin's exegesis . . . the problem is . . . that he does not consistently regard *all* Biblical texts as accommodated; so, not only the Biblical description of God's repentance is accommodated to our understanding, but also the Biblical description of God's unchangeability." Huijgen, *Divine Accommodation in Calvin*, 288.

32. See the Belgic Confession, article 1, which includes "immutable" as a perfection of our God. Schaff, *Creeds*, 3:383.

fickleness, stubbornness, selfishness, or deceitfulness is being accommodated. There are indeed occasions that involve both species in one act of accommodation, for instance, the system of Old Testament sacrifices. One may discern in the sacrificial system both an ontological aspect in God's act of slowly teaching his people about Christ and a soteriological aspect in tolerating for several millennia a system which could never take away sin (Heb 10:1–4). Nevertheless, the two categories—ontological and soteriological—may be distinguished as two *species* of the *genus* accommodation.

Each of these two species can be further subdivided into five identical *subspecies*. After reviewing the literature, I have adopted the following: (a) creation, (b) providence, (c) scripture, (d) incarnation, and (e) sacraments.[33] A few brief comments on each category will provide further details on the distinction between ontological and soteriological accommodation.

In ontological accommodation (a) creation is a sensory means of revealing the deity and power of the God who cannot be sensed. It exists as a thing caused by God, and he has shaped our minds so that we perceive in these majestic, orderly, and variegated effects their cause in him. This would especially be true in a world not disturbed by sin. Providence (b) likewise reveals him via the visible results and effects of his otherwise invisible actions, as he makes the sun rise, the plants grow, etc. Scripture (c) did not exist as such before sin, but God did accommodate some of his infinite knowledge to finite human speech. He gave commands in Genesis 1 and 2 and would have depended on human language to reveal himself. In some sense, the incarnation (d) may even play a role in God's accommodated revelation prior to the fall—Calvin, for example, states that even apart from the fall into sin humanity would have been too lowly to reach God without a mediator.[34] As for the sacraments (e), there were two trees which represented a special message from God. Calvin calls them sacraments (in a general sense).[35]

What happens when we view all the same subspecies of accommodation soteriologically, between the fall and the new creation? All of the former ontological facets hold true, but now other elements are added so that the message is accommodated to the instruction of humans about their

---

33. Van der Kooi identifies four kinds [for me: *subspecies*] of accommodation in Calvin: creation, scripture, incarnation, and sacraments. I have added providence/history as a distinct subspecies because: a) divisions of general revelation in Reformed theology include it; b) Balserak isolates this category in Calvin. Van der Kooi, "Within Proper Limits," 371–72; Balserak, "The God of Love," 187–91.

34. Calvin, *Institutes*, 2.12.1. The subsequent context of Calvin's remarks suggest that he was not necessarily envisioning the incarnation of the second Person of the Trinity when he speculated about such a "mediator."

35. Calvin, *Institutes*, 4.14.18; see also Huijgen, *Divine Accommodation in Calvin*, 214, 233–34.

sinful condition over against God's righteousness. Creation (a) now reveals more than God's greatness and glory: God's punishing wrath is revealed as the earth produces thorns and thistles; all things tend to destruction. All humans thus recognize something is wrong. Providence (b) comes with divine chastening of all sorts, which would not have been necessary before the fall—the obvious being earthquakes, floods, and fires, by which he tests his children's faith and jars unbelievers in their complacency. As for Scripture (c), God's words now need a permanent written record because of human dullness and deceitfulness. Scripture includes strong warnings so as to teach sinful souls. The incarnation (d) now focuses on the passion and death of Christ to reveal God's wrath against sin while simultaneously revealing God's love in an unparalleled way—God came in human form, making known to our senses in a tangible way the grace and truth of God (John 1:18). Finally, the sacraments (e) reveal the same by their emphasis on blood atonement, whether pointing ahead (OT) or back (NT). It is evident that after the fall into sin further accommodated elements were introduced by God so as to reach not just finite creatures, but *sinful* finite creatures. The distinction between the two species of accommodation underlines that we are doubly indebted to our God.

Of the five subspecies, Scripture reveals the greatest variety of soteriological accommodation. Four further *sub-subspecies* of accommodation can be detected in Scripture, namely, law, prayer, anthropomorphisms, and the historical progress of revelation. By these categories I am drawing together various analyses made by other authors, adding one: the history of revelation.[36] It seems to me that under the history of revelation one can place discussions of type/antitype, promise/fulfilment, and the movement from

---

36. Battles isolates in Calvin accommodation in law, prayer, and the sacraments. I will adopt the categories law and prayer, but maintain that the sacraments form a species parallel to Scripture, not a subspecies. Battles, "God Was Accommodating," 34–36. Wright detects accommodation in Calvin's elucidation of various civil and ceremonial laws of the Pentateuch and in other particular one-time commands such as to exterminate the Canaanites. Wright, "Accommodation and Barbarity," 417–22; Compare Balserak, *Divinity Compromised*, 163–90; Balserak, "Accommodating Act Par Excellence?" 417–21. Balserak distinguishes four kinds of accommodating responses of God to humans' limited capacity: when God instructs, when God legislates and commands, when God sanctions religious rites and practices and receives worship, and when God pastors his flock. Balserak's second and third categories offer a further division for "law," namely "worship." His detailed analysis of these categories also alerts us to the place of anthropomorphisms. Although ontological accommodation could, broadly speaking, be called anthropomorphic, Scripture's abundant use of specific anthropomorphisms requires separate treatment. Balserak's category of instruction appears rather broad, matching my species soteriological accommodation and its subspecies, while his pastoral category mostly belongs to providence. Balserak, *Divinity Compromised*, 59–98.

material (OT) to spiritual (NT). These motifs are typically included as examples of accommodation: for instance, Moses is a type of Christ (e.g., Heb 3:5-6); promises such as the restoration of David's throne or the gathering of the remnant are accommodated to the time, yet find a greater fulfilment in Christ's ascension and in Pentecost (e.g., Acts 2:16, 34); and where old covenant blessings were tied to the land of Israel, new covenant blessings extend these things to Christ's kingdom, the beginning of the new creation (e.g., Eph 6:3).

The category of law may be divided into the written law, specific one-time commands, and commands regarding worship. Many of these are arguably accommodated. Some one-time commands such as the command to exterminate the Canaanites Calvin calls barbarous, monstrous, and wicked except that God specifically commanded them, thus making them right in a specific time and place.[37]

Soteriological accommodation in prayer includes oaths and vows. Sometimes God indulged the sinful prayer requests of his people; other times he wanted to give them abundant blessings but had to hold himself back to prevent their idolatry. Such at least, is Calvin's exegesis. Similarly, God accommodated the fickleness of fallen humanity by permitting his name to be used for the firmness of oaths and vows.[38] He himself used an oath to confirm his words (Heb 6:17).

Anthropomorphisms after the fall include the ascription of negative emotions to God, such as wrath. Calvin sometimes remarks that the expression of God's wrath does not belong to his nature as such, since by nature God is gracious.[39]

It should be emphasized that the preceding taxonomy is not airtight and need not be, for that would not reflect actual usage.[40] It does, however, help us analyze the multi-faceted concept of accommodation, which in turn will help us evaluate whether the appeals of various scholars to the principle of accommodation are in line with traditional uses or not. Note that the categories of (a) law, (b) prayer, (c) anthropomorphic language, and (d) his-

---

37. Wright, "Accommodation and Barbarity," 416-22.
38. Balserak, "The God of Love," 181-87.
39. Selderhuis, *Calvin's Theology of the Psalms*, 165-67.
40. Wright concludes that what appears to be a "handy principle" in the *Institutes* issues in a "handful of practices" in Calvin's commentaries and sermons, practices which are "not always wholly consistent." Wright, "Accommodation and Barbarity," 415. Balserak concludes that the "images are probably not irreconcilable," even though they are disparate. Balserak, *Divinity Compromised*, 190. Huijgen takes up Wright's challenge and goes much farther in finding an "integrated portrait of Calvin's God." See Huijgen, *Divine Accommodation in Calvin*, 20, 317-18, 367-87.

tory of revelation are categories that can likewise explicate ontological accommodation, for in Paradise (a) God gave commands, (b) man sought his God, (c) God was said to "walk" in the garden, and (d) certainly God makes progress in his revelation from garden (Gen 2) to city (Rev 21–22) rather than revealing his entire plan at once to Adam and Eve.

Two Species of Accommodation
> **Ontological Accommodation**
> **Soteriological Accommodation**

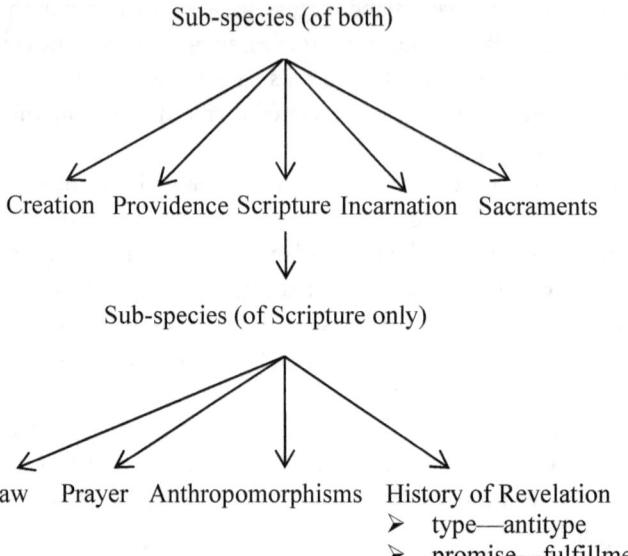

Sub-species (of both)

Creation   Providence   Scripture   Incarnation   Sacraments

Sub-species (of Scripture only)

Law   Prayer   Anthropomorphisms   History of Revelation
> type—antitype
> promise—fulfillment
> material—spiritual

As for the way in which this genus accommodation and its two species relate to revealing God, it is clear that they and all their subspecies function as *means*. The genus is simply a way of grouping the species for the sake of showing that they all serve the same ultimate goal: to reveal the unaccommodated God so that his people may have true communion with him. This point will be key to further discussion below.

Thus, accommodation is not an accommodation of the truth as such (the end), but of the means or modes of revealing this truth. To say it another way, we do not come to know and commune with an accommodated God but actually come to know and commune with the true God *by accommodated means*. In his acts of revelation God acknowledges and maintains the structure of his creatures who are made in his image by revealing himself in human language, via discursive logic, and in the Person of his

Son.[41] His revelation is necessarily accommodated to the finite, yet conveys what is true. Richard A. Muller's definition of the Protestant Scholastic term illustrates this: "The *accommodatio* or *condescensio* refers to the manner or mode of revelation, the gift of the wisdom of infinite God in finite form, not to the quality of the revelation or to the matter revealed."[42] Ford Lewis Battles makes a clear statement of this as well, regarding Calvin, when he writes, "The act of accommodating to our weakness is not mere rhetoric clothed with the physical, but divine energy, power, spirit, *channelled through* the physical."[43] The physical is the means by which the spiritual is revealed; Word and Spirit are joined; Calvin is not a mystic.

It should be added that God's revelation first of all concerns himself and the moral or spiritual relationship between him and his creatures.[44] Therefore the primary content involved in accommodated revelation is likewise *God*. In the classical understanding, appeals to accommodation would concern just that: revelation about the nature and will of God and the moral or spiritual standing of his people, not all sorts of lesser matters.[45] The same point holds true for the archetype/ectype distinction used by the medieval and post-reformation scholastics; the archetypal knowledge was God's knowledge *of himself* and the ectype our finite "copy" of this.[46] This theological point may seem minor, but in fact it is a major assumption within the language of the church fathers, medieval theologians, reformers,

---

41. This is not to say that God is fully or comprehensively known by us, but that what he allows us to know is true. In addition, I do not mean to say that God is known simply by the exercise of discursive logic, but that such language and logic are necessary elements in the true knowledge of God—a knowledge available only to true believers.

42. Muller, "*Accommodatio*." See also this statement, "The concept of accommodation, moreover, is found quite consistently among the Reformed orthodox both in their understanding of theology and revelation and in their discussions of the perfection of Scripture *as the finite perfection of an instrument suited toward a particular end*." Muller, *Post-Reformation Reformed Dogmatics*, 2:188; emphasis mine.

43. Battles, "God was Accommodating," 36; emphasis mine.

44. For this reason, "[I]t is the purpose of theology to teach savingly of God." Muller, "Turretin," 204.

45. Even Calvin's extensive and varied use of the concept in his Old Testament commentaries, ably explored

by Balserak, Wright, Zachman, and Huijgen nearly always has to do with God's nature and will, and his people's slowness and/or stubbornness in understanding and obeying (although Calvin's appeal to the ancient legal concept of *aequitas* [equity] as central to natural law also plays an important role here). Haas, *The Concept of Equity*, 49–126.

46. Besides literature in notes 22 and 24, see Klauber, "Turretin on Biblical Accommodation," 78. Note that Klaas Schilder contests the validity of the archetype/ectype distinction, and appears to contrast it with the principle of accommodation. De Jong, *Accommodatio Dei*, 89.

and post-reformation dogmaticians.[47] As Herman Bavinck and Cornelius Van Til would say, "We can only think God's thoughts after him." For them this statement indicated our absolute dependence on God and thus exuded humility.

In order to further promote clarity of analysis in the midst of the varying applications of the concept—both within the corpus of one writer like Calvin and across the varying perspectives outlined in the introduction of this essay—I intend in the next section to demarcate some of the similarities and differences between accommodation and phenomenological language, accommodation and biblical criticism of both the higher and lower sorts, and accommodation and cultural adaptation.

An Examination and Evaluation of the Varying Uses of Accommodation

If we assume a mainly uniform understanding of the principle of accommodation and the authority of Scripture from the church fathers, through the Middle Ages and Reformation, and into the era of Protestant Orthodoxy, we are on fairly safe ground.

But what about the Copernican revolution and Joshua 10:12–13? Is this the first bending of the wax nose? The question we might consider in this case is whether or not the shift from geocentrism to heliocentrism required recourse to the principle of accommodation to explain the passages in Joshua 10 or whether one might simply speak of phenomenological language.[48] Calvin, commenting on Psalm 136:7 stated, "The Holy Spirit had no intention to teach astronomy; and . . . he made use by Moses and the other Prophets of popular language . . . the Holy Spirit would rather speak childishly than unintelligibly to the humble and unlearned."[49] Similarly, one might argue that the passage of Joshua 10:12–13 is entirely right and true

---

47. See, for example, the language used in Muller, *Post-Reformation Reformed Dogmatics*, 1:262.

48. For Augustine the first rule of interpretation is that it must promote a love that flows out of faith, together with hope. Augustine, *Teaching Christianity*, 3.10.14–3.16.24 (176–80).

49. Calvin, *Commentary on the Psalms*, 184–85. See further: Balserak, *Divinity Compromised*, 167–68. Calvin offers no support to the arguments of Rogers and McKim, for he in no way considers Scripture to be in error. Woodbridge masterfully dismantled the historical claims of Rogers and McKim. See Rogers and McKim, *Authority and Interpretation*, and Woodbridge, "Biblical Authority," 165–236.

according to the normal standards of language, phenomenologically used.[50] In fact, according to Klaus Scholder, this was the main argument of Kepler![51]

It was Galileo Galilei, however, who made the move from accommodation regarding God and his will to accommodation regarding scientific questions.[52] My contention is that accommodation properly applies to the communication that occurs in the spiritual relationship between God and his people, a communication aimed at their salvation (see John 20:31). It does not apply to questions about the nature of scientific truth because God was not trying to reveal things about science as such.[53] Believers do not need to be scientists to receive scriptural truth. Our greatest need is not the development of esoteric and advanced revelation, but the humble submission of our hearts to the simple truth about God and ourselves. This does not mean the scriptures have nothing to say about the foundational principles of science or that its statements that touch on scientific matters are irrelevant or false. Each part of revelation is true according to the standards for truthful statements that would hold among the general public; each statement serves the greater truth of the whole; and each will support in-depth study and meditation as they are further probed.

I would add that Galileo's use of accommodation no longer answers to the proper role of the accommodation construct as identified in the previous section. In order for Joshua 10:12–13 to be an example of accommodated revelation, it should serve as a means which reveals a truth about God's nature or will, expressed anthropomorphically. But the passage is not like that. We do not encounter the "wisdom of infinite God in finite form" as regards the relationship of the sun and the earth. Indeed, how could we? For the relationship of the sun and the earth is a finite matter itself. No accommodation is required! Assuming the classical view of God, the only accommodated aspect of the text—its theological value—lies in the fact that

---

50. Woodbridge, "Evaluation of Rogers and McKim," 234. Phenomenologically speaking, we today would also say the sun stopped. After all, we still speak of the sun rising and setting. Synod Assen 1926 of the *Gereformeerde Kerken van Nederland*, dealing with Geelkerken's non-literal understanding of the snake in Genesis 3, determined that the Bible spoke, "in the language of naïve experience." The Synod opposed all arbitrariness in determining which Scripture passages are literal and which are figurative. De Jong, *Accommodatio Dei*, 108.

51. Although Kepler "supported" his argument with an appeal to the accommodation theory, his main argument was that Joshua described the events "as we experience them." Scholder, *Birth of Modern Critical Theology*, 55–58.

52. Scholder, *Birth of Modern Critical Theology*, 59.

53. This distinction between communication regarding salvation and matters of scientific truth does not correspond to Kant's divide between faith and knowledge because both of the former matters belong to the phenomenal realm, to use Kant's category.

God *listened to* a man in a hitherto unprecedented way and would *appear to us* to have altered his plan by lengthening the day. That is accommodated language, but speaking of the sun standing still has nothing to do with the theological category of accommodation. In my view, it is better to call this "the language of naïve experience" with the Synod of Assen, or, "phenomenological language."[54] We will return to Galileo momentarily.

The use of accommodation by the critical scholars of the Enlightenment was far more radical than that of Galileo and Kepler. Several authors note the origins of this Enlightenment use of accommodation lie with Faustus Socinus and are not continuous with the established tradition. Christoph Wittich, a Cartesio-Cocceian who popularized this view, made an appeal to accommodation as the way to bring Scripture into agreement with all of the 'clear and distinct' new findings in natural philosophy.[55] Similarly, Baruch Spinoza, in his *Theological-Political Tractate*, cast doubt on many of the narratives of Scripture, stating that the idea that all humanity was killed in the flood was "accommodated" knowledge, "revealed to Noah according to his capacity."[56] Retaining essentially only "moral guidance" from Scripture, Spinoza went on to state that "knowledge" of all matters, including God, derives from what he called philosophy. By "knowledge" he meant specific knowledge of a thing's essence. Thus, all of Scripture, except for its enduring moral message, was accommodated to the philosophy of its age. In his own day, thought Spinoza, reason had made knowledge in the order of Noah's rather outdated.

Johann Semler, like Spinoza, found many passages that did not measure up to reason, including accounts of miracles. Scripture contained these because the people to whom they were first revealed were yet infants whose reason was not as developed as Semler's. Revelation needed to be "clothed" with miracles in order to be accommodated to them.[57] Hans Frei lists a host of events—from Jesus' earthly ministry, to his casting out demons, his death

---

54. On this point, I question the statement of Klauber: "In addition, it should be noted that accommodation was designed not for the well-educated elite, but for the common people. *This explains the use of phenomenological* and anthropomorphic *language* in Scripture." Klauber, "Turretin on Accommodation," 77; emphasis mine.

55. Lee, "Accommodation," 336–39; Pannenberg, *Systematic Theology*, 3:34; Scholder, *Birth of Modern Critical Theology*, 124–27; compare Muller, *Post-Reformation Reformed Dogmatics*, 2:139. In subjecting Scripture's message to his own opinion of what was "reasonable," Spinoza was echoing the Socinian view of accommodation. Klauber and Sunshine, "Jean-Alphonse Turrettini," 14. Compare Woodbridge, *Evaluation of Rogers and McKim*, 204.

56. Spinoza, *A Treatise Partly Theological and Partly Political*, 42.

57. De Jong, *Accommodatio Dei*, 51; Semler's views were strongly opposed by Charles Hodge. Rogers, "Hodge and Accommodation," 234–39.

as penal atonement, and his teachings about the second coming—all as "typical instances of such time-conditioned conceptions ... to which the writers had 'accommodated' themselves," in Semler's view.[58]

It is not necessary to chronicle the views of Jean-Alphonse Turretin, son of the famous Francis Turretin, who questioned the historicity of Genesis 1–11, used accommodation as his defense, and so introduced not only Cartesianism's appeal to reason but also Socinianism's view of accommodation into the Academy at Geneva. Likewise, little needs to be said about Lessing, who also argued that all truths are ultimately truths of reason and who took to its climax the idea that all Scripture is accommodated in the Socinian sense. Revelation, he mused, belonged to a teaching process and may now be put behind us. In fact, natural light gets us to the same goal.[59]

How is it that "accommodation" became the weapon set on "loosening the older Protestant doctrine of Scripture"?[60] Is this simply the working out of one and the same principle? Is Arnold Huijgen correct to conclude that, "ultimately, a line can be drawn from Calvin's approach to Spinoza's"?[61]

Scholder traces the source of this higher criticism to the principle earlier introduced by Galileo. He quotes Galileo, "Therefore I think that the authority of Holy Scripture is directed mainly towards convincing men of such conceptions and principles which, because they transcend all human thought, cannot find belief through any science or any means other than through the revelation of the Holy Spirit," and observes that Galileo had stood on its head the principle that philosophy should be conformed to Scripture, even though Galileo only had in mind those items of Scripture which were "related to phenomena within the limits of human possibilities of knowledge." Scholder then asks who will lay down the limits that restrict scripture criticism to these phenomena. He concludes, "In fact, once the principle [proposed by Galileo] had been recognized, it was impossible to see where criticism would end."[62]

---

58. Frei, *Eclipse of Biblical Narrative*, 60–61.

59. See the literature listed in note 7, particularly De Moor. I add: Klauber and Sunshine, *Jean-Alphonse Turrettini*, 7–27. Compare Muller, *Post-Reformation Reformed Dogmatics*, 2:141, and contrast the opinion of Wright who asserts (but fails to argue) that there may be more formal similarity between Calvin and the younger Turretin than Klauber allows. Wright, "Accommodation and Barbarity," 424n10. Huijgen also argues for a line from Calvin to Spinoza, but limits this to the issue of anthropomorphisms. Huijgen, *Divine Accommodation in Calvin*, 387.

60. Pannenberg, *Systematic Theology*, 1:35.

61. Huijgen, *Divine Accommodation in Calvin*, 387.

62. Scholder, *Birth of Modern Critical Theology*, 60 (a recognition of the wax nose syndrome's cause). Note that this is not the slippery slope argument, but a tracing out

Scholder's is a valuable critique. In essence, Galileo says that whatever is attainable by reason in Scripture is subject to criticism. It did not escape the critics that this includes the entire history of writing and all of the narratives of Scripture. They declared it to be factual but not ostensive, that is, factual but not historical.[63] Before long, reason had apparently observed the regularity of the world in such wide measure that it could draw the negative conclusion that there were no miracles. The higher critical appeals to the principle of accommodation became subjective and lacked any criterion arising from Scripture itself.

The critics judged all non-moral issues to be accommodated to the mind of the writers, whose minds were part and parcel of the culture of their day. But this view actually runs directly counter to the earlier use of accommodation. In the earlier use it was precisely certain moral and spiritual requirements in Scripture that were accommodated! Accommodation applied to the spiritual Being of God, and to the moral and spiritual relationship of God and his people.

Note that in fact the higher critics could not take refuge under the umbrella of accommodation in its ontological form, because accommodation was about the infinite truths being clothed in finite dress, not about the finite truths of narrative history, nor about matters of rational investigation independent of revelation. As noted above, the latter are items that by their very nature do not need to be accommodated. I conclude that the higher critics appealed to the principle of accommodation directly contrary to its earlier purpose.

At the outset I also mentioned more recent appeals to accommodation. One of these looks to the cultural aspects of Scripture and notes a discontinuity between the patriarchy of the Bible and today's egalitarian culture and takes the latter as normative. It should be noted that "today's egalitarian culture" is a recent western phenomenon, by no means universal. The claim that God's revelation of himself in the male gender is accommodated belongs to the category of anthropomorphisms in Scripture whereas the (lesser?) claim that the teaching office should be open to women appeals to a cultural accommodation of patriarchy in the sense of the history of revelation. Proponents of both views would regard this accommodation to be sin-conditioned, soteriological.

Besides the foregoing categorization, how should the Reformed confessional approach evaluate these claims? First of all, on the question of God's gender, it is indisputable that both male and female were created in

---

of the corollary of Galileo's position.

63. Frei, *Eclipse of Biblical Narrative*, 261.

his image. But the meaning of "in his image" is thus beyond gender, and whether it even means something like "reflection" is debatable. Therefore, we cannot draw conclusions about God's nature on the basis of this "image." Besides, we must not reverse the scriptural imagery of the "image," which consistently reasons from the divine to the human and not vice versa. The most essential question to raise is whether or not there are any scriptural precedents for addressing God in the feminine. As Cooper argues, mother is a figure of speech for God, not a title or name like Father, King, and Lord, and not functionally equivalent to Father.[64] He admits that there are no scriptural precedents for addressing God in the feminine, yet concludes that it is possible as "secondary," "occasional," and "figurative" language for God, if kept within certain guidelines.[65]

In terms of accommodation, it seems to me that although masculine titles for God surely are ontologically accommodated to human finitude not only as using human language but also as employing finite concepts, it is categorically impossible for human finite creatures to go beyond these limitations. I have no reason to believe God would have used different language apart from the fall into sin, and there is no reason to think that God's use of human language as such introduces error.[66] Certainly in this era Scripture does not point us beyond these masculine titles. Appealing to changes in culture applies an external, arbitrary, and fickle standard.[67]

In contrast, evangelical proponents of 'women in office' more overtly appeal to Scripture. Although today's culture may be the occasion to examine the doctrine, Galatians 3:28 forms the backbone of their contention. It serves as an indication that gospel principles require egalitarianism. I agree with Guenther Haas who points out that while abusive patriarchy is an evil, to hold the same for patriarchy generally, undermines Scripture's authority. Haas concludes that holding patriarchy to be an evil as such, "appears to

---

64. Cooper, *Our Father in Heaven*, 115–32, 200.

65. Cooper, *Our Father in Heaven*, 277–78, and generally 277–94. Compare 270, where we read masculine terminology is essential and irreplaceable for God, though this does not mean that God is "ontologically masculine." "Mother" tells us something about what God is like, but not who he is (131–32).

66. Barentsen ably defends the view that "from the divine perspective, there is no great trouble in communicating divine eternal truth in changing human language." Comparatively, contra Barth, Christ's incarnation does not necessitate sin. Barentsen, "Validity of Human Language," 39–40.

67. Clanton writes, "Jesus referred to God as masculine because his Jewish disciples, steeped in their male-dominated culture, could not bear fuller revelation at that time (John 16:12). In our culture, which places greater value on females, we can understand the Spirit's leading us beyond referring to God as 'he.'" But herewith Clanton identifies the Spirit's leading with culture, not with Scripture. Clanton, *In Whose Image*, 11.

maintain the authority of the gospel principles, such as Galatians 3:28. But it clearly does not maintain the authority of the specific instructions found in the NT."[68] A tension is introduced into the unity of Scripture, for the same apostle who wrote Galatians 3:28 also wrote 1 Corinthians 11:3–16; 14:33–38 and 1 Timothy 2:11–14. In his mind these passages were not in conflict; he gives no indication that he regarded them to be accommodated to any culture. Quite the opposite (1 Cor 11:8–10, 14; 14:36; 1 Tim 2:13–14)!

If an appeal to accommodation would be in place, it would have to be along the lines of soteriological accommodation, specifically the history of revelation.[69] But here the history in view must be circumscribed by the revelation given. Drawing out principles from Scripture that need to be developed after the canon's closing and comparing these to intra-biblical developments is suspiciously arbitrary and runs the risk of developing a tradition that overrules scriptural commands.[70] If, on the other hand, the appeal is to culturally specific commands such as head coverings or hairstyles, the comparison is a stretch because the latter are rather minor differences. Moreover, culturally specific commands could be treated as applications of unchanging principles, rather than as revelational accommodation. In my view "ontological equality" is compatible with "functional subordination."[71]

We arrive, finally, at the deep questions introduced by open theism. Inasmuch as these depend heavily on alternative hermeneutics, the examination of Scripture that follows will have application to the previous comments about the relationship of one Scripture text to another.

Open theists ask the most difficult question of traditional theists who depend on the accommodation construct. "On what basis do these thinkers

---

68. Haas, "Patriarchy as an Evil," 332.

69. For example, "Given the patriarchal conventions of marriage and society in his time, it was probably not possible for him to endorse women teaching in any case." Cooper, *Cause for Division?* 53.

70. Cooper notes "social-political changes within Scripture" such as hairstyles, and then under the title "accommodation to culture within Scripture," he first specifies several culturally conditioned injunctions such as the holy kiss, raising hands in prayer, and female head coverings, and then moves on to several practices which God permitted for a time but later, within Scripture, abrogated (polygamy, divorce, and slavery). The difficult issue that needs to be addressed here is whether such intra-biblical changes establish a norm that may continue to be used today. May the church extend the principle to other issues on which Scripture is silent? In my opinion, this extension is unwarranted. In principle, such an extension tips the hand to the Roman Catholic position on tradition. Cooper, *Cause for Division?* 27–28.

71. The terms are from Gangel, "Biblical Feminism and Church Leadership," 58. I register my objections, however, to his view that "The theory of accommodation always undercuts the authority and inerrancy of the Scriptures" (59), for one ought to distinguish the Socinian from the orthodox use of accommodation.

claim that these biblical texts do not portray God as he truly is but only God as he appears to us? How can they confidently select one biblical text as an 'exact' description of God and consign others to the dustbin of anthropomorphism?"[72] Note that within traditional theism similar questions have been entertained, albeit sparsely.[73] For instance, one may ask with Frei, "On what grounds or by what criteria does one judge that a given text . . . means something other than what an author says . . . unless he gives us a special hint to that effect or uses obviously figurative language?"[74]

Traditionally, appeals to accommodation were not to be arbitrary; special revelation itself gave the impetus such that where one text speaks anthropomorphically it may need to be interpreted by others that explicitly and ultimately deny such things of God. A possible implicit consideration cannot overrule an explicit statement. Thus, for instance, we do not find any texts that amount to the argument, "You may think God does not change, but actually he does." Just the opposite (compare Exod 32:14 and Jonah 3:10 to Num 23:19, 1 Sam 15:29, Ps 33:1, Mal 3:6, and Jas 1:17)! Similarly, there are no texts that say, "You may think that God fills heaven and earth, but actually he is absent here or there." Just the opposite (compare Gen 11:5, 7 and 18:21 to 1 Kgs 8:27, Jer 23:24, Ps 33:13, 139:7,15,16, Prov 15:3, and Isa 66:1)! These contrasting texts have always been harmonized in the church by the principle of interpreting the less clear texts in light of the more clear texts. In this case "more clear" refers to what is stated explicitly and absolutely.

---

72. Sanders, *The God Who Risks*, 68. Caneday responds that, "It does not seem to occur to Sanders that others could ask this same question of him when he claims, 'Though God sustains everything in existence, he does not determine the results of all actions or events, even at the subatomic level' (p. 215). How did Sanders acquire such knowledge of God's activities at the 'subatomic level'?" Caneday, *Putting God at Risk*, 147.

73. For instance, when a proponent of open theism probes Calvin for an answer to the hermeneutical question why certain texts deserve priority, it seems impossible to find an answer. Calvin simply assumes the classical view of God. This assumption is noted by Huijgen, who in some respects wishes to correct Calvin. Huijgen, *Divine Accommodation in Calvin*, 355–61, 371, 373, 384.

74. Frei, *Eclipse of Biblical Narrative*, 62. Compare Helm, "How then is one to proceed in constructing from Scripture an account of divine omniscience or goodness, and with it an account of divine providence? Which of these apparently inconsistent or incompatible sets of data is to take priority? What data control the remainder?" Helm, *The Providence of God*, 51. Selderhuis analyzes Calvin on the Psalms: "The issue that arises from this—how the 'accommodated God' is related to the real God and how the one is distinguished from the other is—not treated as such by Calvin [sic]." Also, "[Calvin] avoids the discussion on what can in fact be said about God if, in his speech, he so strongly adapts himself to humans." Again, "[T]hese words reveal some of the questions in Calvin's conception of God: when God's countenance frightens us, is he then actually like that or is it but his mask?" Selderhuis, *Calvin's Theology of the Psalms*, 48, 134, 288.

Augustine unequivocally teaches this in *De Doctrina Christiana* and illustrates this point well in his *Enchiridion* when he discusses Romans 9:16, "So it comes not from the one who wills or runs, but from God who shows mercy."[75] The foregoing response to open theists is brief but it aims to meet them at the most foundational level.

Context also determines meaning. Thus, to hark back to Galatians 3:28, nothing in the context would indicate that the text is offering a corrective to any earlier texts (as Christian feminists suggest), but only to the view that justification could be by human works. In that context no social status holds any higher value for salvation. Galatians 3:28 does not explicitly deny what seems to be implicit in other texts; the most that might be said is that it might implicitly deny what is explicitly said in other texts (e.g., 1 Cor 14:33b–35; 1 Tim 2:11–14). But even this admission would challenge the Reformed confessional understanding of Scripture's unity. Thus, from within a Reformed confessional standpoint wherein the Scripture's inspiration, infallibility, authority, and sufficiency are confessed, this position is not permitted.

Guidelines for the Employment of Accommodation in the Reformed Confessional Context

From where do Reformed confessional theologians derive their grounds for the classical view of accommodation? These must arise from Scripture, since we cannot see into the eternal mind of God to discern why he accommodated his revelation in each specific case. For example, we do not know why God accommodated his people's stubbornness in the Old Testament regarding divorce but not regarding other matters such as usury or pictorial representations of God. In many instances God was relentlessly demanding, for example, in the second and tenth commandments. He could as easily have insisted on no divorce, except for cases of adultery. Therefore we must stand by the rule *Scriptura sui intrepres*. We have only what we have been given in Scripture, no more and no less. This rule also grows out of the confession that Scripture's ultimate author is the divine Holy Spirit, whose perfect knowledge assures the doctrinal unity of all Scripture.

Within the norm that Scripture interprets itself, I summarize the foregoing observations by offering the following selected hermeneutical guidelines for our use of the accommodation construct. I am not pretending that these are exhaustive, nor that they are superior to other sets of

---

75. Augustine, *Teaching Christianity*, 2.9.14; Augustine, *The Augustine Catechism*, 9.32.

hermeneutical rules, but I do think that their guidance will help us continue to use the accommodation construct without falling into the higher critical errors.

1. The obvious and literal meaning is correct unless otherwise specified by the author or unless the text uses obviously figurative language.
2. Less clear texts are to be interpreted in light of more clear texts.
3. Explicit denials govern implicit affirmations and vice versa. Absolute statements must be understood absolutely unless otherwise specified.
4. Context determines meaning; first, immediate context, then wider context, finally all of Scripture. This context may include progress in the history of revelation.

More specifically relating the rules to accommodation, I continue with the following:

5. God never uses language to deceive us about himself.[76] In fact, although God uses accommodated means, he establishes true communion with himself by these means.
6. Exegetical appeals to accommodation by Reformed theologians would benefit from establishing whether each instance is of ontological or soteriological accommodation, and being aware of its continuity or discontinuity with past uses of accommodation, to avoid undermining the very revelation it seeks to explicate.
7. Accommodation as a genus always concerns spiritual matters, specifically: God's nature and perfections, expressions of his will and activities, and God's relation to humanity.
8. Ontological accommodation always concerns the relation of the infinite to the finite.
9. The direction of interpretation should begin with faith in Scripture, not with science or contemporary culture, nor should human reason function as the measure of what's believable.
10. Scripture's authority extends to all matters on which it teaches.
11. It is valuable to distinguish accommodation from culturally specific commands (cultural adaptation), which are but applications of principles.
12. It is likewise valuable to distinguish accommodation from the use of phenomenological language.

---

76. Zachman, "Calvin as Analogical Theologian," 170–71.

13. Regarding the types, signs, and symbols by which the Old Testament is related to the New Testament, one must hold to the express statements of Scripture rather than inventing one's own types, signs, and symbols. One must also ground the reference in the genuine sense of Scripture and use these signs and symbols with moderation. Finally, the appeal to types, signs, and symbols must have salvific purpose.[77]

Conclusion

Have Reformed exegetes always followed these rules? One should hardly expect so. But if exegetes and theologians in this tradition would ground their appeals to accommodation in a more explicit understanding of accommodation and seek to follow the above rules, they could more consistently pay tribute to Scripture as the sole source of our knowledge of God.[78] Scripture is self-attesting, and accommodation should not be shaped like a wax nose, nor should it make Scripture into a wax nose.

If the arguments of this essay are correct, then we also have an answer for Pannenberg's observation about the onward march of the accommodation theory. We can say that it did happen that way, but that the appeals to accommodation made by the higher critics could not claim the illustrious history of the accommodation construct. The more recent appeals of evangelical feminists and the critique of open theists should also be opposed by confessional Reformed theologians.

Bibliography

Aquinas, Thomas. *Summa Theologica*. Blackfriars ed. London, 1920–1942.
Augustine, Aurelius. *The Augustine Catechism: The Enchiridion on Faith, Hope, and Love*. Translated by Bruce Harbert. New York: New City Press, 1999.
———. *The Confessions*. Translated by Maria Boulding. New York: New City Press, 2001.
———. *Teaching Christianity*. Translated by Edmund Hill. New York: New City Press, 1996.
Balserak, Jon. "'The Accommodating act par excellence?': An inquiry into the incarnation and Calvin's understanding of accommodation." *Scottish Journal of Theology* 55.4 (2002) 408–23.

---

77. Zachman, "Calvin as Analogical Theologian," 176, 181.

78. I take general revelation to reveal nothing about God that cannot be known better by special revelation. See Gootjes, *Teaching and Preaching the Word*, 3–21; Gootjes, "General Revelation and Science," 94–107.

―――. *Divinity Compromised: A Study of Divine Accommodation in The Thought of John Calvin*. Dordtrecht: Springer, 2006.

―――. "The God of Love and Weakness: Calvin's Understanding of God's Accommodating Relationship with His People." *Westminster Theological Journal* 62 (2000) 177–95.

Bartensen, Jack. "The Validity of Human Language: A Vehicle for Divine Truth." *Grace Theological Journal* 9.1 (Spring 1988) 21–44.

Battles, Ford Lewis. "God was Accommodating Himself to Human Capacity." *Interpretation* 31.1 (1977) 19–38.

Benin, Stephen D. *The Footprints of God: Divine Accommodation in Jewish and Christian Thought*. Albany, NY: State University of New York Press, 1993.

―――. "Mere Stories and Ordinary Words." *Jewish Social Studies* 6.1 (Fall 1999) 83–97.

Calvin, John. *Commentary on the Psalms*. Translated by James Anderson. Grand Rapids, MI: Baker, 1984.

―――. *Institutes of the Christian Religion*. Translated by Ford Lewis Battles. Edited by John T. McNeill. Philadelphia: Westminster Press, 1960.

―――. *Selected Works of John Calvin: Tracts and Letters*. Translated and edited by Henry Beveridge. Grand Rapids, MI: Baker, 1983.

Caneday, A. B. "Putting God at Risk: A Critique of John Sanders's View Of Providence." *Trinity Journal* 20.2 (Fall 1999) 131–163.

Clanton, Jann A. *In Whose Image? God and Gender*. New York: The Crossroad Publishing Company, 1990.

Cooper, John W. *A Cause for Division? Women in Office and the Unity of the Church*. Grand Rapids, MI: CRC Publications, 1991.

―――. *Our Father in Heaven: Christian Faith and Inclusive Language for God*. Grand Rapids, MI: Baker, 1998.

De Jong, Jacobus. *Accommodatio Dei: A Theme in K. Schilder's Theology of Revelation*. Kampen: Dissertatie-Uitg. Mondiss, 1990.

De Moor, Leonard. "The Problem of Revelation in Eighteenth-Century Germany: With Particular Reference to Lessing." *The Evangelical Quarterly* [three part series], 39.2 (Apr–June, 1967) 66–74; 39.3 (July–Sept, 1967) 139–151; 39.4 (Oct–Dec, 1967) 205–215.

Dowey Jr., Edward A. *The Knowledge of God in Calvin's Theology*. Grand Rapids, MI: Eerdmans, 1994.

Dreyfus, François. "La condescendance divine (*synkatabasis*) comme principe herméneutique de l'Ancien Testament dans la tradition juive et dans la tradition chrétienne." In *Congress Volume Salamanca 1983*, edited by J. A. Emerton, 96–107. Leiden: Brill, 1985.

Frei, Hans W. *The Eclipse of Biblical Narrative: A Study in Eighteenth and Nineteenth Century Hermeneutics*. New Haven: Yale University Press, 1974.

Gamble, Richard. "Calvin as Theologian and Exegete: Is There Anything New?" *Calvin Theological Journal* 23.2 (Nov 1988) 178–194.

Gangel, Kenneth O. "Biblical Feminism and Church Leadership." *Bibliotheca Sacra* 140.557 (Jan 1983) 55–63.

Gootjes, Nicolaas H. "General Revelation and Science: Reflections on a Remark in Report 28." *Calvin Theological Journal* 30 (1995) 94–107.

―――. *Teaching and Preaching the Word: Studies in Dogmatics and Homiletics*. Winnipeg, MB: Premier, 2010.

Haas, Guenther. *The Concept of Equity in Calvin's Ethics*. Waterloo, ON: Wilfred Laurier University Press, 1997.

———. "Patriarchy As An Evil That God Tolerated: Analysis And Implications For The Authority Of Scripture." *Journal of the Evangelical Theological Society* 38.3 (Sept 1995) 321–336.

Helm, Paul. *John Calvin's Ideas*. Oxford: Oxford University Press, 2004.

———. *The Providence of God*. Downers Grove, IL: InterVarsity Press, 1994.

Huijgen, Arnold. *Divine Accommodation in John Calvin's Theology*. Göttingen: Vandenhoek & Ruprecht, 2011.

Klauber, Martin I. "Francis Turretin on Biblical Accommodation: Loyal Calvinist or Reformed Scholastic?" *Westminster Theological Journal* 55 (1993) 73–86.

Klauber, Martin I., and Glenn S. Sunshine. "Jean-Alphonse Turrettini on Biblical Accommodation: Calvinist or Socinian?" *Calvin Theological Journal* 25.1 (1990) 7–27.

Lee, Hoon J. "Accommodation—Orthodox, Socinian, and Contemporary." *Westminster Theological Journal* 75.2 (2013) 335–48.

Lindner, Helgo. "Johann Georg Hamann on Bible and Revelation." *Evangelical Review of Theology* 2.1 (April 1978) 113–123.

Muller, Richard A. "Accomodatio." In *Dictionary of Latin and Greek Theological Terms*. Grand Rapids, MI: Baker, 1985.

———. "Divine Covenants, Absolute and Conditional: John Cameron and the Early Orthodox Development of Reformed Covenant Theology." *Mid-America Journal of Theology* 17 (2006) 11–56.

———. *Post-Reformation Reformed Dogmatics: The Rise and Development of Reformed Orthodoxy, ca. 1520 to ca. 1725*. Four vols, 2nd ed. Grand Rapids, MI: Baker, 2003.

Otto, Randall E. Review of *In Whose Image? God and Gender*, by Jann A. Clanton. New York: Crossroad, 1990; and of *Matriarchs, Goddesses, and Images of God: A Critique of a Feminist Theology*, by Susanne Heine, translated by John Bowden. Minneapolis, MN: Augsburg, 1989. In *Westminster Theological Journal* 54.1 (Spring 1992) 202–4.

Pannenberg, Wolfhart. *Systematic Theology*. Translated by Geoffrey W. Bromiley. Grand Rapids, MI: Eerdmans, 1988.

Polman, A. D. R. *The Word of God According to St. Augustine*. Translated by A. J. Pomerans. Grand Rapids, MI: Eerdmans, 1961.

Porter, H. C. "The Nose of Wax: Scripture and the Spirit from Erasmus to Milton." *Transactions of the Royal Historical Society*, 5th ser., vol. 14 (1964) 155–74.

Rogers, Jack, and Donald McKim. *The Authority and Interpretation of the Bible: An Historical Approach*. San Francisco, CA: Harper and Row, 1979.

Rogers, Mark. "Charles Hodge and the Doctrine of Accommodation." *Trinity Journal* 31 (2010) 225–42.

Sanders, John E. *The God Who Risks*. Downers Grove, IL: Intervarsity Press, 1998.

Schaff, Philip, ed. *The Creeds of Christendom, With a History and Critical Notes*, 3 vols. Grand Rapids, MI: Baker, 1993.

Scholder, Klaus. *The Birth of Modern Critical Theology: Origins and Problems of Biblical Criticism in the Seventeenth Century*. Translated by John Bowden. London: SCM Press, 1990.

Selderhuis, Herman J. *Calvin's Theology of the Psalms*. Grand Rapids, MI: Baker, 2007.

Spinoza, Benedict de. *A Treatise Partly Theological and Partly Political* . . . . London: n. publ., 1689.

Te Velde, Rudi. *Aquinas on God: The 'Divine Science' of the* Summa Theologiae. Aldershot: Ashgate, 2006.

Van der Kooi, Cornelis. "Within Proper Limits: Basic Features of John Calvin's Theological Epistemology." *Calvin Theological Journal* 29 (1994) 364–387.

Van Wijk-Bos, Johanna W. H. *Reformed and Feminist: A Challenge to the Church.* Louisville, KY: Westminster John Knox Press, 1991.

Willis, E. David. "Rhetoric and Responsibility in Calvin's Theology." In *The Context of Contemporary Theology: Essays in Honor of Paul Lehmann,* edited by Alexander J. McKelway and E. David Willis, 43–63. Atlanta: John Knox Press, 1974.

Wolterstorff, Nicholas. *Divine Discourse: Philosophical Reflections on the Claim that God Speaks.* Cambridge: Cambridge University Press, 1993.

Woodbridge, John D. "Biblical Authority: Towards an Evaluation of the Rogers and McKim Proposal." *Trinity Journal* 1.2 (Fall 1980) 165–236.

Woodbridge, John D. "Recent Interpretations of Biblical Authority: Part 1: A Neoorthodox Historiography under Siege." *Bibliotheca Sacra* 142.565 (Jan 1985) 3–15.

———. "Recent Interpretations of Biblical Authority: Part 2: The Rogers and McKim Proposal in the Balance." *Bibliotheca Sacra* 142.566 (Apr-June 1985) 99–113.

———. "Recent Interpretations of Biblical Authority: Part 3: Does the Bible Teach Science?" In *Bibliotheca Sacra* 142.567 (July 1985) 195–208.

———. "Recent Interpretations of Biblical Authority: Part 4: Is Biblical Inerrancy a Fundamentalist Doctrine?" *Bibliotheca Sacra* 142.568 (Oct 1985) 292–305.

Wright, David F. "Accommodation and Barbarity in John Calvin's Old Testament Commentaries." In *Understanding Prophets and Poets: Essays in Honour of George Wishart Anderson,* edited by E. Graeme Auld, 413–27. JSOT supplement 152. Sheffield: Sheffield Academic Press, 1993.

Zachman, Randall C. "Calvin as Analogical Theologian." *Scottish Journal of Theology* 51.2 (1998) 162–87.

Subject Index

accommodation, accommodated revelation, xix, 72–73, 77, 213, 227–48
  definition of, 230
  ontological accommodation, 231–36
  soteriological accommodation, 231–36
  sub-species of accommodation, 233–36
  truly reveals God, 230, 236–38, 247
  guidelines for use, 247
apologetics, 38, 210, 213
archaeology, role of, 91–92, 118
archetype and ectype, 213, 231, 237,
Augustine, Aurelius, 68, 183, 188, 230–31, 246,
authority of Scripture, 24, 138–39

Barth, Karl, 34–38, 81
Benin, Stephen D., 230
Bavinck, Herman, 21, 81
Belgic Confession
  Article 2, 9–12
Bonhoeffer, Dietrich, 62–64, 73

Calvin, John, 11
Carson, Donald A., 25–26, 52n40, 147n23,
Cartesianism, René Descartes, 188, 191, 198, 208, 209, 213, 241
Chandieu, Antoine de la Roche, xviii, 188, 190,
Childs, Brevard, 38–40
clarity of Scripture, 81, 245

condescension, divine. See accommodation.
context. See hermeneutics, context, role of.
Contrario, 171, 179, 183
Copernicus, Copernican revolution, 6, 238
creation
  days of creation, 13–14, 19–20, 21
  ordinances, 148–51
critical, pre-critical, post-critical, higher critics, higher criticism, xv, xvi, xviii, 24–27, 29, 33–36, 42–45, 49–53, 84, 87, 90, 93, 95, 100–101, 105–6, 127, 135–36, 139, 227, 238, 240–42, 247, 248
critical realism, 209–13
culture, 152–53

de Brès, Guido, 11
DeJong, Jack, 72n16, 77n5, 227n5 227n7, 230n30, 231n24, 237n46, 239n50,
Diehl, David, 4–9
divorce, 150, 172, 173, 176, 177, 178, 232, 246
dogma
  catholicity of, 69–71
  hermeneutics of, 64–73
  metaphor in, 72–73, 76–78, 80–81

Enlightenment, 24, 30, 86, 93, 96, 101, 108, 119, 188, 190, 196, 208, 209, 240

Subject Index

ethics, xvii, xx, 149, 162, 171–83, 187–93

feminists, feminism, feminine, 78, 179, 227–28, 244n71, 243, 246, 248
foundationalism, 171–93, 195–99, 208–13
Frei, Hans, 28, 240, 295

Gabler, Johann P., 30
Galilei, Galileo, 227, 239–42
Gootjes, Nicolaas, 8n26, 248n78
Groen van Prinsterer, Guillaume, 69

hermeneutics
　archaeology, role of.
　　See archaeology.
　Bonhoeffer, D., 62–64
　church, role of, 119, 224
　clearer texts govern, 12, 14, 245, 247
　context, role of, 101–2, 217–24, 246
　culture, role of, 120, 152–53
　faith, role of, 100
　foundationalism.
　　See foundationalism.
　genre, 88–91, 102–3
　grammatical-historical, 25–26
　historical-critical.
　　See historical-critical.
　human authors, role of, 223
　Holy Spirit, role of, 221–24
　narrative, 97–99
　participation in Christ, 199–204
　plain sense, 95–96, 247
　post-critical, 33
　postmodernism, 173, 187, 209–13, 215–16
　pre-critical. See pre-critical.
　presuppositions, role of, 101
　proposed guidelines, 247–48
　reader-response criticism, 25, 119, 215
　redemptive-historical, 152, 164–65, 175, 187
　Reformed.
　　See Reformed hermeneutics.
　rhetorical criticism, 137–38

triangle of biblical historical narrative, 119–20
historical-critical, 30–33, 37–41, 48–53, 57–61, 86, 104, 107, 121
Holwerda, Benne, 175
homosexuality, 171, 173, 176, 178, 180, 182, 183, 192

immutability of God, 245

Kepler, Johannes, 227, 229–40
Kuyper, Abraham, 139, 209

Lessing, Gotthold Ephraim, 241
Lindbeck, George, 40–43
Lundbom, Jack, 137

metaphor, 72–73, 76–78, 80–81, 183
modern, modern era, modernism 25–27, 30–33, 37, 48, 99–100, 105, 108, 119, 136n19, 172–74, 187–88, 195–97, 209–11, 213
Mullenberg, James, 137

open theism, open theists, 228, 244–45

participation in Christ, 199–204
phenomenological language, 238, 240,
pillarization, 198
postmodern, postmodernism, xiv, xviii, 25, 40, 43n34, 51, 52n41, 95, 101, 106, 119–20, 173, 183, 187–89, 192–93, 209–11, 215–16, 221, 224
pre-critical, 27
pre-modern 25, 78
principles, xix, 56–57, 99n54, 148–49, 152, 163, 164n22, 172n6, 183, 189–90, 196, 229, 239, 241, 243–44, 247

Reformed hermeneutics, 44–53, 57–59, 60–61, 67–69, 117–18, 138–39, 159–60, 171–93, 195–213
revelation
　general, 2–15, 18
　history of, 57–59, 60
　special, 2, 18–19

Report of deputies male/female in the church, 142, 149, 152, 155
rhetorical criticism, 137–38
Ricoeur, Paul, 204
Rogers, Jack B. & McKim, Donald K., 172n6, 238n49, 239n50, 242n55
rule of faith, 26, 28, 37, 47, 51–52

salvation-historical narrative, 178, 191–92
Schilder, Klaas, 69, 72n16, 77n5, 81, 175n14, 237n46
Scholder, Klaus, 239, 241–42
science, 17–18, 22
Scripture
    accommodation. *See* Accommodation.
    and archaeology. *See* Archaeology.
    and creation, 148–51, 161–62, 169
    and culture, 120, 152–53
    and ethics, 171–91
    authority. *See* authority of Scripture.
    Clarity. *See* clarity of Scripture.
    context, 217–24, 246
    God's use of, 181–83, 193
    genre, 88–91, 102–3
    historical narrative, 119–20
    inspiration, 24
    message, 105
    metaphor. *See* metaphor.
    plain sense, 95–96, 247
    prophetic character, 103
    sola scriptura, 118, 120, 202, 216
    structure of Jeremiah, 127–40

truth. *See* truth, truth claim.
    unity, 105
Semler, Johann, 240
Socinus, Faustus, 227, 240
Spinoza, Baruch, 240, 241,
spiritual formation, 202–3
Sunday observance, 177

Ten Commandments, commandments, xviii, 130–31, 133–35, 172, 175, 188, 191, 246
theodicy, 19, 22
truth, truth claim, truth value, universal truth, rational truth, xvi, xix, 3, 9, 30, 41, 52n41, 78, 83–108, 116–25, 168, 173, 196, 198, 199–203, 208–13, 230, 236, 239, 242
Turretin, Jean-Alphonse, 241

Van Hoozer, Kevin J., 34n18, 164n23&24, 174n13, 199n13, 203n18, 209n2
Van Til, Cornelius, 209–10
veil, veiled, 144–46, 155, 168
von Harnack, Adolf, 64–67

Winter, Bruce, 143–45, 155–56
Wittich, Christoph, 240
Wolterstorff, Nicholas, 164n22, 172n7, 197n6, 204n21, 228n11,
woman, women, new woman, 142–53, 155–65, 168–70, 242–44

Scripture Index

Old Testament

Genesis
1–2	13–14, 19–20, 21, 58
1–11	241
6:6	227
11:5	227, 245
18:21	245

Exodus
11:2	188
20	129–35
32:14	227, 245

Numbers
23:19	227, 245

Joshua
10:12–13	238–40

1 Samuel
8–13	90
15:29	245
15:35	227
17	89

1 Kings
8:27	245
12:34—13:34	120–25
13:32	116
17–22	89

2 Kings
1–13	89
20:10–11	90

Job
12:7–9	7

Psalms
19:1	5
33:1	245
33:13	245
139:7	227, 245

Proverbs
15:3	245

Isaiah
66:1	245

Jeremiah
1–52	127–41
23:24	227, 245
36	128
51	128

Hosea
14	222

Jonah

3:10	245

Malachi

3:6	227, 245

New Testament

Matthew

5:33-37	177
10:29-30	227
19:4-9	177
19:8	232

Acts

2:16	235
2:34	235
15	163

Romans

9:16	245

1 Corinthians

2:9-10	208
7:12-16	176
11	143-47
11:8-10	244
14	146-47
14:34-35	146-47
14:36	244, 245

Galatians

3:28	244, 246

Ephesians

2:20	189
6:3	135

1 Timothy

2	147-51, 156-58, 169
2:13-14	244, 245
3:15	168, 189

Hebrews

3:5-6	235
6:17	235
10:1-4	233

James

1:17	227, 245

www.ingramcontent.com/pod-product-compliance
Lightning Source LLC
Chambersburg PA
CBHW071244230426
43668CB00011B/1574